THE COSMOPOLITAN IDEAL IN THE AGE OF REVOLUTION AND REACTION, 1776–1832

The Enlightenment World:
Political and Intellectual History of the
Long Eighteenth Century

Series Editors: *Michael T. Davis*
Series Co-Editors: *Jack Fruchtman, Jr*
                        Iain McCalman
                        Paul Pickering

Titles in this Series

Harlequin Empire: Race, Ethnicity and the Drama of the Popular Enlightenment
David Worrall

Forthcoming Titles

Writing the Empire: Robert Southey and Romantic Colonialism
Carol Bolton

Adam Ferguson: History, Progress and Human Nature
Eugene Heath and Vincenzo Merolle

The Evolution of Sympathy in the Long Eighteenth Century
Jonathan Lamb

Adam Ferguson: Philosophy, Politics and Society
Eugene Heath and Vincenzo Merolle

The Scottish People and the French Revolution
Bob Harris

THE COSMOPOLITAN IDEAL IN THE AGE OF REVOLUTION AND REACTION, 1776–1832

BY

Michael Scrivener

Routledge
Taylor & Francis Group
LONDON AND NEW YORK

First published 2007 by Pickering & Chatto (Publishers) Limited

Published 2016 by Routledge
2 Park Square, Milton Park, Abingdon, Oxfordshire OX14 4RN
711 Third Avenue, New York, NY 10017, USA

First issued in paperback 2015

Routledge is an imprint of the Taylor & Francis Group, an informa business

BRITISH LIBRARY CATALOGUING IN PUBLICATION DATA

Scrivener, Michael Henry, 1948–
The cosmopolitan ideal in the age of revolution and reaction, 1776–1832
   1. Cosmopolitanism – Europe – History – 18th century 2. Cosmopolitanism
   – Europe – History – 19th century 3. Internationalism – Europe – History
   – 18th century 4. Internationalism – Europe – History – 19th century 5.
   Enlightenment 6. Romanticism 7. Europe – Intellectual life – 18th century 8.
   Europe – Intellectual life – 19th century
   I. Title 306'.094'09033

ISBN-13: 978-1-138-66517-0 (pbk)
ISBN-13: 978-1-8519-6833-6 (hbk)
Typeset by P&C

CONTENTS

To my sisters Patty Ludlam, Kathy Scrivener and Susan Scrivener –
with love and admiration.

ACKNOWLEDGMENTS

I want to thank Michael T. Davis, the editor of the series, *The Enlightenment World: Political and Intellectual History of the Long Eighteenth Century*. Dr. Davis has been helpful and generous. Wayne State University assisted the writing of the book with grants and time for research. I am grateful for the following: a Humanities Center grant to study Habermas (2005), the Board of Governors Distinguished Faculty Award (2003) and the sabbatical leave (2004) to study Jewish representations and conduct research in the British Library. I want to thank Professor Walter Edwards of the Humanities Center and Professor Richard Grusin, Chair of the English Department, for valuing research during a time of budgetary constraints.

My intellectual debts are too numerous to mention. First, at conferences and lectures I have been able to present my work which has received valuable criticism: NASSR conferences (2002–6), the Wayne State 'Brown Bag' lecture series (2005) and Humanities Conference (2005), the International Conference on Jews, Empire and Race, at University of Southampton (2005), and Temple University English Department (2003). The NASSR conference on Romantic Cosmopolitanism (2004) was especially inspiring and useful. Teaching the graduate seminars on romantic-era women and the Godwin-Shelley circle I have learned much from my students. I want to thank the following colleagues and scholars: Robert Aguirre, Charles Baxter, Arthur Efron, Elizabeth Fay, Frank Felsenstein, Marilyn Gaull, Willi Goetschel, Herb Granger, R. Cole Heinowitz, Jacques Khalip, Donna Landry, Jake Lassner, Phyllis Lassner, Kathryne Lindberg, Arthur Marotti, Irving Massey, Fred Moten, Victoria Myers, Steven Newman, Jan Plug, Ross Pudaloff, Arthur Ripstein, Jasmine Solomonescu, Sheila Spector, Judith Thompson, Renata Wasserman, Karen Weisman and Susan Wells.

I have used all or part of the following essays and am reprinting them with permission:

'Habermas, Romanticism, and Literary Theory', *Literature Compass*, 1 RO 127 (2004), pp. 1–18.

'Trials in Romantic-Era Writing: Modernity, Guilt, and the Scene of Justice', *The Wordsworth Circle*, 35:3 (2004), pp. 128–33.

'British-Jewish Writing of the Romantic Era and the Problem of Modernity: The Example of David Levi', in Sheila A. Spector (ed.), *British Romanticism and the Jews. History, Culture, Literature* (New York: Palgrave Macmillan, 2002), pp. 159–77.

'Following the Muse: Inspiration, Prophecy, and Deference in the Poetry of Emma Lyon (1788-1870), Anglo-Jewish Poet', in Sheila A. Spector (ed.), *The Jews and British Romanticism: Politics, Religion, Culture* (New York: Palgrave Macmillan, 2005), pp. 105–26.

INTRODUCTION

A familiar narrative about the period following the American and French Revolutions is that the cosmopolitan Enlightenment gave way to a romantic nationalism that was ascendant until World War I. That nationalism and conservative romanticism gained strength after 1789 can hardly be disputed, but the cosmopolitan ideal exerted influence and developed creatively during the same period. After the end of the Cold War in 1988–9, the cosmopolitan political ideas of the Enlightenment, especially Kant's, attracted considerable interest. Other features of the Enlightenment – tolerance, secularism, internationalism and commerce des lumières (exchange of enlightened ideas) – also acquired appeal in light of recent developments like ethnic cleansing, xenophobic hatred and politicized religious fundamentalism. One could do worse than studying Enlightenment cosmopolitanism in search of a useable past for intellectual models of multiculturalism in the global village.

That cosmopolitan signifies both world citizen and worldliness suggests a dialectical relationship between political arrangements and cultural-psychological dispositions. Those in intolerant, fearful cultures are unlikely to support political initiatives for international cooperation and trans-national dialogue, whereas those who travel outside their own communities and learn about experiences different from their own do not find political cosmopolitanism immediately threatening.

This study treats cosmopolitanism in three different spheres: the political, the philosophical and the literary. Although there are versions of political cosmopolitanism other than and even opposed to that of Kant and Habermas, the book concentrates almost exclusively on the ideas for 'perpetual peace' first put forward by the philosopher from Königsberg and developed further by the most important thinker of the Frankfurt School's second generation. Even if one finds Habermas's cosmopolitan ideas flawed in whole or in part, one encounters in his writing a fully worked-out argument that is richly elaborated and rigorously developed. He not only illustrates in great detail the limitations and achievements of the Kantian legacy but opens his revision of Kant to a critical dialogue with other traditions. A more centrally positioned proponent of Enlightenment ideas would be difficult to find because since the 1960s Habermas has defended the Enlightenment against numerous adversaries. The first chapter explores the political and philosophical cosmopolitanism of Kant and Habermas.

According to Habermas, one of the important preconditions for political cosmopolitanism both then and now is an open, tolerant and intellectually fearless public sphere with trans-national currents. Only a public sphere in the special Habermasian sense of the phrase – private people coming together as a public to subject the prevailing norms to critical examination and discussion – can move society toward a deliberative democracy that achieves legitimacy through uncoerced and open discussion. In the words of Seyla Benhabib, essential 'to the deliberative model of democracy is the idea of a "public sphere" of opinion-formation, debate, deliberation, and contestation among citizens, groups, movements, and organizations in a polity'.[1] The second chapter is devoted to the theory and history of the public sphere, including the extraordinary efforts to expand the public sphere in a more democratic direction in the 1790s. Kant in Prussia and the *Analytical Review* and John Thelwall in Britain both reflected on the public sphere and acted boldly within it. The second chapter also addresses the richly layered discussion on the public sphere that followed Habermas's influential treatment of the subject in the early 1960s.

The *Analytical Review* deserves close study because it professed Enlightenment values the entire span of its existence from 1788 until 1799 when it ceased largely because of political repression. The *Analytical*'s Enlightenment was experimental, self-critical and cosmopolitan. Its founder Thomas Christie became a revolutionary activist in Paris after 1789 and its publisher Joseph Johnson took risks choosing principal reviewers like the feminist Mary Wollstonecraft and the liberal Catholic priest Alexander Geddes. Although the journal was anchored in the culture of Protestant Dissent, it was not a sectarian publication; it was rather a 'worldly' periodical, interested in and engaged with what happened everywhere. The *Analytical* is a good example of the public sphere at work. Similarly, Thelwall is a useful example because he tested the limits of the already existing public sphere by popular lecturing and writing that provoked harsh repression. Moreover he was in the unusual position of participating in both the plebeian and the bourgeois public spheres. Although I have written about Thelwall and the public sphere extensively elsewhere, especially in *Seditious Allegories*,[2] here I give an exposition of how his public-sphere ideas and actions relate to specifically cosmopolitan concepts.

The next three chapters focus on the cosmopolitan aspects of feminism, abolitionism and Jewish emancipation. Women, Africans and Jews were complexly implicated in the process by which the modern world came to define itself. Three separate kinds of binary value systems of gender, race and religion collaborated to construct the superiority of Christian, male Europeans who were entitled to empire abroad and patriarchal domination at home. The French Revolution's liberal divorce (1792) (but not the franchise and full citizenship for women), Jewish emancipation (1791) and slavery abolition (1794) mark out the areas of contestation between an emergent cosmopolitan politics and an emergent nationalistic politics.

The central figure of the third chapter, 'Women and Justice', has to be Mary Wollstonecraft, because her ideas outpaced those of other feminists like Catharine Macaulay and because she created texts of such richness and complexity that they reward close attention. I structure the chapter around two moments, the courtroom speech of Wollstonecraft's Maria at her lover's 'crim. con' trial and Wollstonecraft's satirical deconstruction of Rousseau's character Sophie from *Émile* (1762). I provide a context for understanding the extraordinary speech in *The Wrongs of Woman* (1798) in terms of how justice for women is constructed in the law and fiction of the romantic era. The critique of Sophie depends on Wollstonecraft's reading the 'paradoxical' Rousseau as conflicted because she deploys one part of his thinking against another part. Wollstonecraft finds especially useful the writing in Rousseau's educational treatise unrelated to the almost cartoonishly sexist depiction of Sophie because *Émile* has some of the strongest arguments against aristocratic injustice. Although the *Vindication of the Rights of Woman* (1792) has attracted no shortage of strong opinions, there have not been a large number of close readings of this extraordinarily rich text. By paying attention to specific passages and lines of argument I hope to convey the depth and power of Wollstonecraft's writing. Although no other woman writer's life was perhaps as cosmopolitan as hers, the chapter concentrates on the writing and its overall argument for sexual equality that is profoundly cosmopolitan.

The fourth chapter, 'Writing Against Slavery, Race and Empire', focuses on the Enlightenment's invention both of race theory, and of ways to subvert that theory through the articles in the *Analytical Review*, through Equiano's magnificent protest against slavery and racism in his *Interesting Narrative* (1788) and through Thelwall's neglected abolitionist and anti-imperialist texts, his two plays (*Incle and Yarico* (1787) and *The Incas* (1792)) and his feminist novel *The Daughter of Adoption* (1801). The Enlightenment's limitations and errors are prominent in its creation of race science and in the credibility it leant to forms of biological determinism. The triumph of race science was hardly certain in the romantic era because the science itself was so incoherent and strong voices condemned it from the start. As one of the most liberal periodicals, the *Analytical* discloses an interesting range of views on race and empire. While the *Analytical* articles and Thelwall texts have received little attention up to this point, the same cannot be said about Equiano's *Interesting Narrative*, which is a secure part of the new literary canon. I delineate what I consider to be a rhetorical reading of this slave narrative. The principal goal of Equiano's rhetoric is to persuade the British political culture to abolish the slave trade – and then slavery. At the same time the text produces astonishingly forceful moments of irony that go beyond the immediate rhetorical occasion. Few writers could have the cosmopolitan credentials of Equiano, world traveller and transatlantic citizen, but the text itself develops a cosmopolitan argument against racism and for hybridized national identity – an argument pertinent to multiculturalism. Although never produced on stage (mostly for political rather than aesthetic reasons), Thelwall's two plays present versions of British identity that are militantly cosmopolitan, as the heroes take up arms with native Americans against Europeans. Thelwall's novel, which integrates a strongly feminist concentration with a critique of aristocratic culture, racism and slavery, offers a sympathetic representation of the St. Domingo slave rebellion (1791–1803) – the historical moment that conditions attitudes on race and slavery throughout the romantic era. It undercuts systematically the most popular history of the slave rebellion, the one written by the Jamaican planter Bryan Edwards.

Chapter 5, entitled 'Jewish Questions', starts by examining two influential plays by Gotthold Ephraim Lessing that promoted Jewish toleration and emancipation – *Die Juden* (The Jews) (1749) and *Nathan der Weise* (Nathan the Wise) (1779) – and then positions two Anglo-Jewish voices – David Levi and Emma Lyon – beside a philo-Semitic Anglo-Irish voice – Maria Edgeworth. Levi the pugnacious theological controversialist is interesting less for the particularities of his rebuttals of Christian biblical interpretation than for his role in 'Englishing' Judaism and his unapologetic defences of Judaism to Christians utterly unused to such impertinence. Lyon's poetry is readable as an artful and measured performance of deference towards, and in defiance of, the codes of gender and religion. She too contributes significantly to the project of multicultural, hybridized national identity. Already marked by a mixed national identity, the Anglo-Irish Edgeworth repents her numerous offences against Jews in her fiction by constructing the first anti-anti-Semitic novel that deconstructs some of the key myths supporting anti-Jewish prejudice. Because *Harrington* (1816) has received lively and thorough interpretations recently, I concentrate on a limited but important aspect of the novel, its scepticism about naming, which challenged racial prejudice in a fundamental way. Jews were treated not just as religiously different but as racially different as well.

In the conclusion, 'Postnational Cosmopolitanism?', I present a brief discussion of the Shelley circle's cosmopolitanism centred mostly on readings of two travel narratives by Wollstonecraft and the Shelleys, and commentary on two Mary Shelley texts, *Mathilda* (1820) and *Valperga* (1823). Finally, Habermas's recent essay on the Kantian project and the divided West appropriately returns our attention to the political and philosophical issues with which we began.

Although the book covers intensively both well-known and neglected cosmopolitan writers whose importance my work tries to illustrate, it does not attempt or claim exhaustive treatment of the topic. The study opens up a field of inquiry for others to explore further; I am only too aware of the many interesting lines of research I had to forego because of practical constraints. The particular emphases of Habermas, Kant, the public sphere, women, race, slavery, empire and Jews are neither arbitrary nor wholly constitutive of the cosmopolitan field. One can do only so much. Areas I wish I could have explored include economic theory, war, Orientalism, the theatre, more periodicals and more German, French and American writers. The cosmopolitan aspects of Byron, the Shelleys and their circle I only begin to sketch out in the conclusion. If the book sparks interest and further research in a critical but ignored area of literary and intellectual history, it will have been useful.

1 COSMOPOLITANISM THEN AND NOW

'... the highest purpose of nature, a universal *cosmopolitan existence*, will at last be realised as the matrix within which all the original capacities of the human race may develop'. Immanuel Kant (1784)[1]

'The contemporary world situation can be understood at best as a transitional stage between international and cosmopolitan law. But many indications seem to point instead to a regression to nationalism'. Jürgen Habermas (1996)[2]

Cosmopolitan Narratives

The competing accounts of eighteenth-century cosmopolitanism dispute in effect the meaning of the Enlightenment, and one's understanding of the Enlightenment leads sooner or later to an account of modernity and – ever since Lyotard – postmodernity as well. Referring to the significance for the French of the Enlightenment and the Revolution, Darrin McMahon observes that they 'continue to serve as benchmarks by which men and women gauge their allegiances and identity in the present'.[3] Studies of the Enlightenment are necessarily entangled in the pressures and commitments of the moment in which they are written. Ernst Cassirer's and Peter Gay's descriptions of the Enlightenment, as astute as they are, reflect their understanding of how Enlightenment counters political irrationalism, most especially a Nazism that threatened them both as German Jews.[4] Isaiah Berlin's very different story about the Enlightenment and Counter-Enlightenment (a historical category he invented) was shaped by his perception of totalitarianism, not simply Nazism – so that the Counter-Enlightenment offers a durable set of ideas to oppose the coercion and violence of modernity, something neither Cassirer nor Gay countenanced.[5] The influential *Dialectic of Enlightenment* (1947) by Theodor Adorno and Max Horkheimer, written in exile during the darkest days of World War Two, finds the Enlightenment complicit with domination and makes positive use of a Counter-Enlightenment figure like Nietzsche, whom the Nazis also found congenial.[6] The Frankfurt School philosophers, however, never became committed Nietzscheans like the poststructuralists. In the words of Jürgen Habermas, for Adorno 'there is no cure for the wounds of Enlightenment other than the radicalized Enlightenment itself'.[7] Habermas himself is writing from the position as a defender of Enlightenment against right and left versions of anti-rationalism.

Before examining the conflicting narratives about cosmopolitanism and modernity, I want to focus closely on an important study that seems to be unmarked by philosophical politics, Thomas J. Schlereth's *The Cosmopolitan Ideal in Enlightenment Thought* (1977).[8] Writing before the postmodernism controversy, apparently untouched by a personal encounter with a murderous political regime of the Right or Left, unconnected with the anguished history of Western Marxism, Schlereth portrays sympathetically but not messianically an eighteenth-century cosmopolitanism centred in Voltaire, Franklin and Hume that flourishes until the French Revolution and nationalism force its decline and eventual marginalization. The nineteenth century belongs to a revival of religion and romantic, democratic nationalism. Schlereth points to several surviving forms of cosmopolitanism – Karl Marx, the working-class socialist movement, the anti-slavery movement, August Comte and Positivism – but the nineteenth century finds cosmopolitanism too aristocratic and rationalistic, with not enough emotional appeal for a democratic age.[9] A brief summary of Schlereth's five chapters will provide a sketch of the cosmopolitanism to which I will be making reference throughout the book.

Well-travelled, a prolific correspondent and a broad reader, the cosmopolitan *philosophe* and *Aufklärer* (enlightener) wrote for a European and transatlantic republic of letters, not an exclusively national readership. By means of a public sphere – salons, coffee houses, Reviews, scientific and literary societies – ideas circulated and networks of publications and friendships were established. Animating the cosmopolitan discourse was the Kantian motto for enlightenment: 'dare to know (sapere aude)', or, as Diderot expressed the ideal in the *Encyclopédie*, 'All things must be examined, debated, investigated, without exception and without regard for personal interest'.[10] Goethe's concept of *Weltliteratur* (world literature) was as typical as the Orientalist and travel writing that expanded and decentred perception away from parochial, local and national topoi. The experimental method of the natural sciences – from Bacon and Newton – engaged empirical reality without preconceptions (at least in theory), and created new notions of time and space, as the origins of the earth were debated and even proto-evolutionary ideas were entertained. The practitioners of literature and science assumed that an inquisitive humanity was trying to know itself and nature. Schelereth points to several contradictions of the dominant universalism – the elitism that undermined the humanitarianism, the Eurocentrism that permitted a race hierarchy with the 'Caucasians' on top – but these were the exceptions to the rule of cosmopolitan 'brotherhood' (there is little discussion of 'sisterhood').[11]

Wary of systematic and rationalistic constructions of knowledge, the eighteenth-century thinkers gravitated toward the essay, the sketch and the dialogue rather than the treatise because these 'tentative' genres fit most closely with sceptical attitudes about the difficulty of knowing the world and the self. Strenuous efforts to know the 'other' produced Orientalist writing that idealized places like Persia and China in order to criticize the failings of Europe, but they were conducted under the assumption of a single humanity. Schlereth's fourth chapter highlights religious syncretism, another universalist theme in his study, as the *philosophes* eclectically pieced together a 'natural' religion consisting of the various strands of the world's different faiths. In addition to syncretism the cosmopolitans were committed to religious toleration, an essential component in their overall worldview, as it promoted social harmony and nonviolently negotiated, conflicting allegiances. This worldview was not without its contradictions, and as Schlereth points out, a surprisingly large group of cosmopolitans, including Diderot, Holbach, Hume, Franklin, Price, Paine and most notoriously Voltaire, were extraordinarily harsh, even bigoted in their attitudes to Judaism and Jews. It is surprising because this too is the age of philo-Semitic toleration, when Moses Mendelssohn was accepted as an *Aufklärer*, when Gotthold E. Lessing's tolerationist plays were well received and when Christian von Dohm's proposal for the emancipation of German Jewry was brought forward. If the *philosophes* were divided about Jews, they were practically unanimous about opposing slavery – although even here one finds appallingly racist statements about Africans by luminaries like Kant and Jefferson.[12]

Schlereth's final chapter links the cosmopolitan ideal of peace among nation-states with the new economic doctrine of free trade and laissez-faire. Counter to mercantilist theory, free trade imagined 'the entire world as the natural economic unit'.[13] Economic liberalism was the favoured strategy to undermine the root causes of warfare, with which the era was exceedingly familiar: from 1688 to 1802 there were six major international conflicts with enormous casualties and destruction. That Kant's famous proposal for 'perpetual peace' was one of many plans offered at the time indicates how much war threatened the stability of the political order.

If Schlereth's study were ideological, it would be liberal and internationalist, with the eighteenth-century toleration, secularism and humanitarianism he writes about existing at a dialectical distance from the xenophobia, racism, religious zeal and isolationism that represented significant if not dominant aspects of American political culture in the 1970s. Published during the bicentennial, when the political identity of the nation was often discussed, his book presents a 'Founding Father', Benjamin Franklin, whose intellectual and political project was not easily recuperable within conservative assumptions. Schlereth, then, undermines the simplistic narrative about American identity by illustrating the Enlightenment and broadly internationalist origins of the American idea.

Thirty years after Schlereth's study, Enlightenment cosmopolitanism makes an even starker contrast with American political culture, which now has an aggressively unilateralist foreign policy and a politically influential, religiously fundamentalist minority. When Schlereth wrote and published his book, liberalism was still the dominant (if embattled) political ideology; the journey back to eighteenth-century cosmopolitanism would have been a salutary exercise in refreshing the vision of toleration and moderate scepticism upon which liberalism rested. American liberalism now, however, has long been in a state of crisis, as the decline of the social-democratic welfare state and the rise of neoliberal free trade policies have all but destroyed the consensus upon which it enjoyed its popular support.[14] The emphases in my own study of cosmopolitanism reflect the post-liberal global conditions under which we live: racism, anti-Semitism, xenophobia, religious intolerance, genocidal wars, terrorism and human rights violations. The more extreme versions of the religious revival, international in scope, challenge the very basis of the Enlightenment project and seek to undo modernity. This project is of interest precisely because the cosmopolitan project is so dialectically antithetical to dominant aspects of our present world.

To bring out the antithetical nature of cosmopolitanism I want to focus on Kant's political writing as it has been interpreted and revised by Habermas, and challenged by what Isaiah Berlin called the Counter-Enlightenment and its criticism of Kant. The debate between Kantian liberals like Habermas and communitarians like Berlin discloses important features of the cosmopolitan ideal and its evolution from the eighteenth century.

From Kant to Habermas

In the two hundred or so years from Kant's essays on cosmopolitanism to Habermas's extensive writings on the European Union and what he calls the 'postnational constellation', Kant's faith that history was on the side of cosmopolitanism has been rendered absurd (by several centuries of extraordinarily violent nationalism, including two world wars), but also paradoxically prescient (by the subsequent creation by nation states of cosmopolitan structures like the United Nations). However imperfect and often tragicomically inadequate, the United Nations has survived over half a century, occasionally doing more good than harm, and there are other transnational institutions that approximate the spirit if not the letter of Kant's practical proposals for avoiding war: the International Criminal Court, the Kyoto Accords, the European Union and international human rights organizations. If one takes the long view, it is difficult to escape the perception that because of objective historical forces – ecological and pandemic crises, economic globalization, weapons of mass destruction and the universalization of human rights – societies are moving, as Kant thought they would, toward cosmopolitan formations and away from narrowly conceived national interests. Kant died before the full romantic development of democratic and autocratic nationalism; the kind of war-making against which he, Rousseau, Saint-Pierre and Swift protested was the limited warfare conducted by monarchs to gain land and wealth, as well as expand empire. The Enlightenment writers were hardly naïve: the religious wars of the sixteenth and seventeenth centuries were almost as brutal and irrational as the twentieth-century wars, and the great novel by Johann Jacob Christoffel von Grimmelshausen (1621–76), *Simplicius Simplicissimus* (1668), expresses vividly the Thirty Years' War's traumatic absurdity, much as Bertolt Brecht was to do in his *Mother Courage* (1939). Nevertheless even the *philosophes* could not have anticipated the full barbarity of two world wars.

If this barbarism provided incentive after 1945 for cosmopolitan institutions, it was also symptomatic of an unstable if not diseased political unconscious capable of producing ever more monstrous surprises. As Habermas notes in the epigraph to this chapter, our contemporary moment is two-sided, with one aspect turned back to bloody, discredited and obsolete nationalisms that do not seem ready to expire. If I were to explore intensively the contemporary moment in all its irrationality, I would be working with texts like Freud's *Civilization and Its Discontents* (1929) and the neglected masterpiece of political analysis, Rudolf Rocker's *Nationalism and Culture* (1937), but I am limiting myself to the cosmopolitan ideal and for that I must turn to Habermas, the modern Kantian who has done the most to rehabilitate cosmopolitanism. First I will summarize briefly Kant's cosmopolitanism, then examine how Habermas develops the cosmopolitan ideal.

Kant's Cosmopolitanism

If Kant's ethics can still speak to us fairly directly without the need for much historical contextualization, his teleology, anthropology and theory of history are another matter entirely and have come in for some justified criticism, especially his various affirmations of racial hierarchy. Although the cosmopolitan argument is fundamentally a moral argument, it is also attached to the more dubious aspects of Kant's thinking. It is important, however, not to dismiss what strikes us as especially dated because Kant is worth paying close attention to, even when he seems to be going in directions we would prefer he did not.

In the earliest cosmopolitan essay, 'Idea for a Universal History with a Cosmopolitan Purpose'(1784), Kant objectifies individuals in two ways, treating them as a 'species' and viewing them over time, real and counterfactual. He objectifies humanity in order to discover a purpose to history, a design, a teleological pattern ('Naturabsicht, bestimmten Plane der Natur'). An important Enlightenment genre was the examination of theodicy, justifying the ways of God to man, so that Kant's taking up these questions in this manner, however intellectually arrogant it might strike us now, was then ordinary philosophical inquiry. Using 'nature' instead of 'God' as the directing force in history, Kant asks if history has natural laws similar to the ones described by Kepler and Newton. The important word here is 'discover' ('entdecken'), as Kant does not want to impose his own limited conceptions on history. If a teleological theory of nature works for the natural sciences, Kant assumes such a theory has to be used for history too; otherwise history would be 'an aimless, random process' ('zwecklos spielende Natur').[15] The third proposition of the essay claims that 'Nature gave man reason, and freedom of will based upon reason', so that man would then 'produce everything out himself'.[16] The next step in the argument is to show how adversity and conflict bring out the developmental qualities of humanity over time; apparent disorder is really hidden purpose, hardly a unique idea, as the concept of 'concordia discors' (harmonious discord) was an Enlightenment topos. Competition and even war over time discipline the species towards acceptance of law and control of selfish instinct. As Kant notoriously affirms that 'man is *an animal who needs a master*' ('der Mensch ist ein Their, da ... einer Herrn nöthig hat'),[17] one can see the Hobbesian aspect of Kant's theory that disturbed Herder, who found it both 'facile and noxious'.[18] Several things need unpacking here: the idea of animality and the apparently authoritarian idea of mastery. Although Kant was a Rousseau enthusiast, he was also the product of a Pietistic upbringing that emphasized strict moral discipline and harshly critical introspection. By animality Kant means an instinctual life without thought, the kind of existence he sometimes attributes to the lowest 'races' of humanity. After Darwin, Freud and ecology, we cannot accept Kant's simplistic and dangerous concept of animality, but a modern translation might look like this: acting with moral responsibility in relation to other people requires the internalization of norms that have the authority to subordinate and control merely selfish desires. Whether these norms are understood as coming from a feminist 'ethic of care' or Habermasian stages of moral development does not matter.[19] Or one could use the narrative of the Freudian ego exerting control over desire. Kant's animality is the pre-social that requires the work of civilized rationality. Kant's master is internalized in order to effect independence and the exercise of free will. What bothered Herder about these ideas is Kant's insistence that only law attached to a coercive state could produce a moral civilization, whereas he was developing an alternative model of the organic nation for which a coercive state would be intrusive, mechanical and foreign, as well as unnecessary.[20] The Kant–Herder dispute is an early version of what we now call the dispute between liberalism and communitarianism.

The hidden purpose of wars, Kant argued, as bloody and barbaric as they were, was to develop necessary aspects of human nature until the species would be compelled to find cosmopolitan law as the most suitable form of international relations if civilization were to develop its moral capacities more fully. War was a step forward from 'purposeless savagery' ('der zwecklos Zustande der Wilden') as the competition between states forced societies to develop, but in order for the 'highest purpose of nature' to be realized, 'a universal cosmopolitan existence' was necessary; then and only then 'all the original capacities of the human race may develop'.[21] Kant is aware of the outrageous nature of his argument, of writing history according to a rational cosmopolitan idea; as he says, 'it would seem that only a *novel* could result from such premises'.[22] It is one thing to desire a nonviolent cosmopolitan order to replace the warfare of states; it is another thing to claim that nature is compelling the species to accept such an order. The necessity of a cosmopolitan order will be argued also by Habermas, as we will soon see in the next section, but the irony of Kant's essay has to be noted: humanity is being compelled toward freedom.

Habermas pushes Kant's cosmopolitanism in directions that are Kantian: for example, towards world government, a position Kant actually took in 1793 only to moderate it later.[23] There are two other ways of reading Kant's cosmopolitanism that I have found useful. Theodor Adorno, writing on Kant in general and not just the political work, offers the idea that we read Kant's philosophy as a 'force field' and in terms of a specific Kantian 'block'. To read philosophy as a force field, one sees that 'the abstract concepts that come into conflict with one another and constantly modify one another really stand in for actual living forces'.[24] The Kantian block is the conflict in his thinking between 'system, unity and reason' on the one hand and 'consciousness of the heterogeneous' on the other hand.[25] Karl-Otto Apel's reading of 'Perpetual Peace' is a good example of dealing with the Kantian block, as Apel reads Kant with Kant, in this instance reconstructing the cosmopolitanism with a greater emphasis on freedom and lesser emphasis on teleological factors of history. Apel points to the third antinomy of the *Critique of Pure Reason* (1781), the antinomy between the world of causal necessity and the world of moral freedom. The aporetic force of the third antinomy is weakened by the recent scientific breakthroughs in the area of chaos theory and microphysics that force us to modify the idea of an invariably nomological nature; in fact, nature's laws are more variable than was conceived within the Newtonian paradigm. Thus Kant's ideas on moral freedom can develop more fully without fear of contradicting the natural laws. The third antinomy asserts that if freedom were determined by law, freedom would be the same as nature.[26] We understand 'merely nature' now to be more unpredictable. For Apel the weakened antinomy permits a fuller engagement with the freedom of practical reason, so that it is possible to develop a transcendental pragmatic reason that is not metaphysical but based instead on the a priori conditions of the communicative community to which Kant actually belonged; Apel teases out the unlimited nature of this communicative community for the sake of moral reason.[27] Apel's reading of 'Perpetual Peace' illustrates the way Kant's teleology blocks the full development of the ideas on freedom. There are essentially two kinds of philosophical reconstructions, in one of which there is an hermeneutical obligation to make judicious use of what Habermas called the 'undeserved hindsight' of historical distance and to read Kant with Kant. What Adorno calls the 'block' is not a flaw in Kant's thinking but a contradiction forced upon him by reality and the limiting constraints of his own historical moment in relation to the rigour and courage of his thinking. The other kind of philosophical reconstruction is critique, where the obligation is to a truth that needs revealing as it has been obscured in a philosophical text. After I discuss briefly the central cosmopolitan essay, 'Perpetual Peace', I will examine this other way of reading Kant's cosmopolitanism, particularly the numerous critiques of Kant's complicity with racism.

If the 'Idea for a Universal History' was a forceful argument presented boldly as an essay in the Enlightenment journal, *Berlinische Monatsschrift*, 'Perpetual Peace' is formally more complex. It was published as a single essay, four months after the Treaty of Basel (April 1795) concluded a phase of the war between the first Coalition and Revolutionary France, so that it has an occasional and topical quality lacking in the freely speculative earlier essay. The title, 'Perpetual Peace. A Philosophical Sketch' ('Zum ewigen Frieden. Ein philosophischer Entwurf'), signals a playful ambiguity with 'perpetual peace' also suggesting the eternity of death and with 'sketch' an experimental quality that the essay in fact delivers in its multi-layered structure. The first section presents six succinct preliminary 'articles' for a treaty of perpetual peace in the form of mostly single-sentence declarations that are then explained briefly. The second section has three definitive articles to which are added several long footnotes and two lengthy supplements; then there is a two-part appendix. The essay's form performs a version of the endlessness of nonviolent dialogue that is the heart of Kant's argument. The essay's first paragraph frames the subsequent parts in terms of tone, for there is an ironically stated opposition between 'heads of state' ('Staatsoberhäupter'), 'worldly-wise statesmen' ('weltkundige Staatsmann') and 'philosophers', theorists, 'mere' academics.[28] Kant mocks and protests his powerlessness in acknowledging the censorship regime under which he is writing by declaring his own essay on practical politics to be safe in relation to the state. But is it safe because no one cares what theorists say about politics, or do the ideas themselves present no threat to the regime?

Three of the first six preliminary articles of perpetual peace are unexceptional – corresponding mostly to norms of international relations at that time – but numbers three and four, which prohibit standing armies and national war-debt financing, two common practices at the time, and number two, which forbids the acquisition of one state by another, are pointedly critical of then-existing international norms. These three articles are deceptively simple but they undermine the very ability of the state to make war.

The second section moves on from the clever beginning to explore ways of going beyond the mere negation of war-making, and establishing the political structures for a positive peace. The three definitive articles are , firstly, that every state must have a republican constitution, secondly, that the right of nations ('Völkerrecht') should be based on a federation of free states, and finally, that cosmopolitan right ('Weltbürgerrecht') should be limited to conditions of universal hospitality ('Bedingungen der allgemeinen Hospitalität').[29] Kant here is going far beyond the norms of international relations, working in an area somewhere between utopian speculation and revolutionary manifesto, especially as the most important of the very few republics at the time was France. By politicizing the concept of world citizen in the way that he does, far beyond the mildly critical political stance in, for example, Oliver Goldsmith's *Citizen of the World* (1762), Kant turns the mostly aristocratic set of practices and styles into something imaginable as social reality. Kant redeems here some of the most radical currents of world-citizenship that circulated briefly in the French Revolution until they were violently repressed – Thomas Paine, Anacharsis Clootz, Condorcet and le Cercle Social. The Kantian redemption is not, however, a revolutionary gesture that anticipates defeat but one that presents itself as practical and modest. It is, of course, the third article on hospitality that has attracted attention from Habermas and Derrida.[30]

It would be a mistake to read 'Perpetual Peace' as a uniformly radical essay because for each step Kant makes left, he steps at least two paces to the right. I want to look at the conflicting moves in the essay by way of the Adornian 'force field' and 'Kantian block'. Two steps to the right would be the tortured explanation of the first definitive article mandating republican constitutional governments in a cosmopolitan order. Kant undermines the ordinary sense of republican as the opposite of monarchical by strenuously affirming that democracy, being despotic, is the opposite of republic, the essential features of which are separation of powers and representative government. He suggests that a constitutional monarchy could be republican. Kant here is contending with the Prussian censorship and working through his ambivalence about the French Revolution. If he were to state what seems to be the inevitable position, that only a democratic republic with separation of powers, rule of law and universal suffrage is wholly consistent with cosmopolitan law, he would be challenging his own biases on who was qualified to be a fully functioning citizen, as well as provoking the censor. Logic compels him to identify republic as a *sine qua non* of cosmopolitan order, but the Kantian block asserts itself in the discussion of republic.

With the second definitive article mandating a federation of free states, we see Kant taking a few steps to his left as he expresses some of his best satire on war. He analogizes 'savages' who cling to their 'lawless freedom' with the 'savage nations' of modern Europeans who prefer the freedom of war and conquest to the constraints of cosmopolitan law and moral right. Even savage cannibalism, he argues, has more dignity than the wars conducted by Europeans, who exploit their captives to make even more extensive war. The modern nations have to 'renounce their savage and lawless freedom ('wilde {gesetzlose} Freiheit'), adapt themselves to public coercive laws', and join a universal cosmopolitan structure.[31] Kant's concept of animality works here not just against natives of America and Africa but also against the Europeans, whose superiority is undermined.

The third definitive article on hospitality continues the Swiftian satire on war by contrasting two ways of treating the stranger. Although the right of the stranger ('das Recht eines Fremdlings') is negative, not to be treated with hostility ('nicht feindselig behandelt zu warden'), it is nevertheless a right – 'Besuchsrecht' – not just moral but legal.[32] Kant does not trust the good nature alone of citizens, who must be coerced by enforceable law to follow the dictates of reason. The citizen does not have to love the stranger, as some biblical texts command (Leviticus 19:33–4; Deuteronomy 10:18–19); rather, Kant sets up a structure within which the native and stranger may enjoy 'peaceful mutual relations'. The moral right of the stranger comes from people being born on a planet with limited resources; the earth is not infinite but being born gives one a claim to the 'communal possession of the earth's surface' ('gemeinschaftlichen Besitzes der Oberfläche der Erde').[33] The negative form of the right – not oppressing the stranger – is recurrently stated in the Hebrew Bible (Exodus 22:21, 23:9; Jeremiah 7:5–7) as Kant knew well, but the fact that the argument is made on the basis of communal possession of the earth's surface makes it rest rather on the authority of reason than revelation. The right of hospitality is both a precondition for cosmopolitan order and an effect of having such an order (as the prohibition against abusing the stranger weakens the social motivations of warmaking), but an effective outright prohibition is impossible to imagine unless underwritten by coercive cosmopolitan law. The third article is hedged with less equivocation than the other two because of the biblical support, because of the abstract nature of the right (its universality makes it not an especially Prussian issue), and because of the easy pathway from the stranger's right to an established line of Enlightenment discourse on the mistreatment of non-European natives. Two eloquent paragraphs protest against the 'inhospitable conduct' of the European states toward the natives of America, Africa, the East and West Indies, where 'the native inhabitants were counted as nothing' ('die Einwohner rechneten sie für nichts').[34] The worst oppression Kant identifies is in the Sugar Islands, the site of 'the cruellest and most calculated slavery' ('der allergrausamsten und ausgedachtesten Sklaverei').[35] The exploiters of the slave trade and sugar plantations then 'make endless ado about their piety' ('Frömmigkeit') and wish to be considered 'chosen believers' ('Auserwählte').[36] The Europeans want a clear conscience and a sense of cultural superiority that Kant will not grant them. I will return to the third definitive article when I am discussing Kant and race, but for now it is sufficient to note that here Kant's universalism means what it seems to mean, signifying everyone, without exception: for according to cosmopolitan right, 'a violation of rights' ('Rechtsverletzung') in *one* part of the world is felt *everywhere*.[37] The word 'Verletzung' suggests not only the abstract violation of law, but also 'injury'; just as in English we say sometimes a victim is 'violated', meaning her or his physical being has been attacked.

Following one of the most politically straightforward sections in the whole essay come four other sections, two supplements and a two-part appendix. The two supplements provide supporting arguments for cosmopolitanism, the first of which is the teleological argument and the second of which is a defence of the public sphere, in particular the right of philosophical discussion. Kant rephrases much of the material in the earlier essay, 'Idea for a Universal History', giving many examples of the cunning of history and nature in advancing and benefiting humanity, and in moving it toward world peace. However little such arguments work for us now, it is appropriate to acknowledge that Kant wanted to emphasize that his cosmopolitanism was not just wishful thinking and utopian dreaming, and that there were objective forces compelling society to move in the directions he was pointing. He saves the most commonly cited example for last: commerce, as an important social force against war and for peace. Another function of the teleological argument is that Kant is not requiring humanity to become more moral than it is now; a cosmopolitan order does not require 'angels', just ordinary human beings who will be forced to obey the cosmopolitan law.[38] The teleological argument is logically treacherous, as it raises difficulties with freedom of the will, and in terms of perspective, it seems to invite a privileged viewpoint that cannot be justified. Kant is certainly up to the logical challenge, but at one point he discriminates between nature and providence because limited reason cannot understand the purpose of God. Only someone with the 'wings of Icarus' could presume to see what Providence was actually doing.[39] Kant, of course, is taking a position that is very close to the Icarian presumption he is also ruling out of bounds. The figurative language registers some the uneasiness the teleological argument provokes.

The second supplement is yet another round in Kant's battle with censorship, as he defends the freedom of philosophers to criticize political power as the 'secret' article to insure perpetual peace. Philosophers without political power will keep the state honest – the state that prefers secrecy to publicity and openness. This is a familiar Kantian argument to which I will return in the next chapter on the public sphere. The two-part appendix works out some of the ambiguities of morality and politics – how they differ, and where they share an orientation – and provides critical analyses of both the utilitarian argument and the supposed right of rebellion. This interesting material, which many others have commented upon, reflects again Kant's ambivalence toward the French Revolution and indicates that he felt that it was most urgent to criticize the utilitarians – that is, the French materialists. His liberalism puts him close to, but not in the same camp as, the outright revolutionaries and radicals.

One line of criticism of Kant has to be considered – namely, the recent discussion of Kant and race. Kant's anything-but-marginal writings on race, many of them deplorably racist, were largely ignored until the 1980s, when they began to attract serious attention from German and English-language scholars. The harshest reading of these makes Kant the inventor of scientific racism, a pioneer racialist whose concepts of reason and cosmopolitan order locate non-Europeans, especially native Americans and black Africans, 'beyond the realm of reason and thus beyond the possibility of rational redemption'.[40] Scholars of the origins and development of scientific racism can hardly ignore the role Kant played and I have read no serious rebuttal of that. However, how precisely the race writings relate to Kant's universalism expressed in other texts like 'Perpetual Peace' is by no means completely settled. Robert Bernasconi insists that racial ideas are deeply within Kant's overall project, especially his teleology, and that these racist ideas are present in texts as late and as fully worked out as *The Critique of Judgment* (1790).[41] The Habermasian philosopher Thomas McCarthy, who is equally as harsh on Kant, wonders how non-whites, to whom Kant attributes so many human deficits, could possibly have the cosmopolitan destiny of those with reason.[42] Robert Louden, whose *Kant's Impure Ethics* (2000) disclosed the full extent of Kant's dubious 'anthropology', points to 'an unresolved tension ... between the core message of universality in [Kant's] ethics and his frequent assertions that many different groups of people (who when taken together constitute a large majority of the human race) are in a pre-moral state of development'.[43] While recording and contextualizing Kant's denigrating comments on women, Africans and native Americans, Louden concludes that 'Kant's theory is fortunately stronger than his prejudices, and it is the theory on which philosophers should focus. We should not hide or suppress the prejudices, but neither should we overvalue them or try to inflate them into something they are not.' Even after archiving Kant's racist and sexist statements, Louden vindicates Kant's universalism: 'Kant is logically committed to the belief that the entire human species must eventually share in the destiny of the species: moral perfection'.[44]

The controversy, which has not yet achieved the notoriety of the Heidegger or de Man controversies over their complicity with Nazism, raises issues of interpretive ethics. To read Kant with Kant in terms of his own 'blocks' and the social 'force field' is how I understand Louden is reading Kant; to read Kant by means of ideology critique is how I understand what Bernasconi and McCarthy are doing. There are ethical risks in either approach; with the former, the danger is apology and evasion of truth, and with the latter the hazard is a prosecutorial zeal that evades the truth just as certainly. In one respect there is no controversy at all: everyone deplores Kant's racist and sexist statements where they exist; everyone agrees that if Kant used a universalist rhetoric to describe the cosmopolitan order, what is universal includes everyone, and that if he did in fact exclude any group, he did so in violation of his own theory. How harshly we judge the person our historical imagination reconstructs as 'Kant' is perhaps an interesting question (for the record, I would be lenient with the sinner, unforgiving with the sin), but there is something else I find in some of the ideological criticism of Kant – namely, a way to discredit the cosmopolitan ideal and its universalism as masks behind which stands masculine Eurocentrism. Kantian liberalism is 'really' racist and sexist. In my discussion at the end of this chapter on radical criticism of liberal cosmopolitanism I will return to this subject.

Habermas and the Cosmopolitan Ideal

Jürgen Habermas, who has written extensively on globalization and imperial power, has been one of the strongest European voices in favour of what he has called, after Kant, a 'cosmopolitan social order', and since the American invasion and occupation of Iraq in 2003, has been a perceptive critic of the Bush administration. I want to describe some of the prominent features of Habermas's cosmopolitanism, its assumptions, origins, logic and overall implications, and locate it in relation to several other cosmopolitan arguments.

The conceptual point of departure for the cosmopolitan ideal, the notion of world citizenship, is of course the thought of Immanuel Kant, two of whose most pertinent essays, the 1784 'Idea for a Universal History with a Cosmopolitan Purpose', and the 1795 'Perpetual Peace', I have already discussed. Kant was hardly the first to argue in favour of a cosmopolitan order of nations – Abbé Saint-Pierre and Rousseau came earlier – and the Enlightenment itself was cosmopolitan in style and content, as philosophers themselves and their ideas regularly crossed national boundaries. Habermas treats Kant's cosmopolitanism both historically and by means of immanent critique. As Habermas phrases it, historical distance grants the contemporary writer an 'undeserved hindsight' that permits him to see the historically premature and utopian nature of Kant's proposal for a cosmopolitan federation of nation states that would renounce war but retain their sovereignty.[45] The limited war practised at that time was a means by which nation states advanced their interests and settled disputes, a political strategy that would not be forsaken by the European powers until it had ceased to fulfil its function. Kant's cosmopolitan ideas gained currency after the catastrophe of World War I, the first unlimited war whose consequences threatened to destroy Europe itself, with almost sixteen million casualties, half of them civilian. The League of Nations may have failed to prevent an even worse catastrophe, but the carnage of World War II in turn inspired the nation states to make an even stronger international federation in the form of the United Nations. According to Habermas, Kant correctly saw the necessity of a cosmopolitan world order but did not go far enough. A world federation, he argues, can function effectively only if nation states transfer substantial portions of their sovereignty to cosmopolitan institutions. Because Habermas can point to cosmopolitan institutions that already exist, his call for a reformed, stronger, more representative United Nations is not wholly unrealistic.

Habermas's Kantian emphasis on cosmopolitan law makes his approach to globalization distinctive. Nation states alone have ineffectively addressed the urgent problems of ecological crisis, disease epidemics, human rights violations, severe inequality, weapons of mass destruction and the harsh disruptions of the world's civil societies by the actions of a globalized market economy. His cosmopolitanism challenges the neoliberal faith in global markets to distribute wealth equitably enough to abolish poverty. As the multinational corporation has replaced the nation state as the centre of economic power, Habermas contends, the 'locus of control has shifted from space to time', as masters of speed replace the rulers of territory.[46] The deterritorialization of economic power weakens the nation state but does not necessarily strengthen cosmopolitan democracy because, as he writes, political power can be democratized but money cannot.[47] Globalization for neoliberals is a uniformly happy phenomenon if market forces are allowed to operate freely and if the reactionary forces of nationalism and protectionism do not disrupt the innate rationality of the market. For Habermas, however, globalization is both destructive and creative, with opportunities for moving both toward greater instability and intensified inequalities and toward more interdependent cosmopolitan democracy. Although Habermas and the neoliberals both favour the expansion and strengthening of the European Union, Habermas also proposes to place 'global economic networks under political control' and to counter the multinational capital's power with cosmopolitan solidarity sustained by a global public sphere.[48]

Several essential features of Habermas's political critique distinguish his approach to neoliberalism from other criticisms from the left. His Kantian universalism, his defence of rationality and his concept of deliberative democracy have been challenged by some communitarian, poststructuralist and postcolonial critics. I will take up each one of these aspects of his thinking and briefly sketch the terms of the debate.

Habermas's universalism, unlike Kant's, is postmetaphysical, and derives from the implications of ordinary linguistic communication: 'Reaching understanding is the inherent telos of human speech'.[49] Habermas's linguistic turn away from subject- and consciousness-centred philosophy permits him to install intersubjectivity at the heart of his intellectual project. The archetypal communicative event – coming to an agreement with another person about something in the world – leads ultimately to a carefully worked out theory of ethics. A corollary of the intersubjective grounding of his ethics in language is his conception of the Absolute, which he names as 'the unconditional right of each creature not to be overlooked, to be acknowledged for what it is'.[50] His discourse ethics distinguishes between controversies that are universalizable and those that apply only to particular ethical communities. Issues like human rights that are universalizable are placed within a realm of unlimited discourse, where something like an ideal speech situation prevails: anyone can bring up any issue of concern; speakers are equal and not under any internal or external coercion; all those who might be affected by the issue have a right to speak; the operating authority is the best argument not status. The ideal speech situation is of course counter-factual, a regulative ideal rather than something that could in fact be fully instituted, but the authority of argumentation, not natural law, divine inspiration or coercive rhetoric, nevertheless governs the logic of Habermas's ethics. He has held firm to the universal nature of human rights, insisting that the objection of Eurocentrism is spurious because it was only accidental – not teleological – that modernity happened first in Europe where human rights were initially formulated in political form; modernity has now become global.[51] He also has found spurious the claim that there are non-Western alternatives to human rights; traditional norms rather have to adjust to the effects of capitalistic modernization and cannot blame human rights for the weakening of tradition because it is modernization and not human rights that has undermined tradition.[52] Habermas differs with his fellow Kantian liberal John Rawls on the issue of tolerating or criticizing non-liberal regimes. Rawls labels as ethnocentric the criticism of politically legitimate fundamentalist regimes that are not expansionist and respect basic human rights; a Habermasian like Thomas McCarthy insists upon a single standard for 'political theory' that should 'unabashedly support liberal-democratic-egalitarian principles of international justice and the sorts of global arrangements they favour'.[53] Similarly, Habermas argues unequivocally for secularization and religious toleration, claiming that 'one's own religious truths must be brought into conformity with publicly recognized secular knowledge and defended before other religious truth claims in the same universe of discourse'. Religion should become 'reflexive' and 'open to reasonable disagreement with other belief systems' and find rules of mutual coexistence.[54] Habermas is not anti-religious but he finds fundamentalist religion incompatible with cosmopolitan democracy, a central premise of which is a human fallibility some forms of religious dogmatism cannot tolerate.

Habermas's defence of rationality is postmetaphysical but unyielding nevertheless: 'As the custodian of reason, philosophy conceives modernity as a child of the Enlightenment'.[55] He defends philosophy's truth-claims, but on intersubjective and discursive not metaphysical grounds. His position can be misunderstood, for the discursive part of it seems relativistic, but the other part, the cognitivist, seems to assume objective truths. Habermas objects, for example, to Richard Rorty's approach that turns philosophy into rhetorical and aesthetic effects, wholly abdicating the role of defending rationality and reason's truth-claims.[56] Habermas's theory of modernity makes the Weberian assumption that reason itself is differentiated along at least three different axes: the natural sciences, the legal–ethical realm and the world of the arts and subjective expression. The three areas of rationality have an autonomy that is conditioned by both interdisciplinary dialogue and understanding, as well as by mediations between these specialist knowledges and the common understanding of the lifeworld.[57] Discursive rationality is achieved when 'criticisable validity claims can be defended with good reasons'.[58] The Habermasian philosopher positions himself or herself as a 'placeholder' for the lifeworld threatened by the 'objectivating' practices of the expert cultures and, by her mediation, defends the lifeworld from the colonizing power of money and the bureaucratic state.[59] Habermas's rationality, which entails making validity claims along the familiar three-world axes of cognition, ethics, and expressiveness, vehemently resists the historicist contextualism he identifies with much current philosophy – systems theory, neopragmatism and poststructuralism. One area of disagreement is the 'epistemic authority' of community, which is decisive for the neopragmatist, neo-Aristotlean and hermeneutical thinkers, but not for Habermas who recognizes only the authority of the best argument.[60]

Habermas's argument for deliberative democracy follows from his commitment to universalism and rationality. His democratic model is communicative but balances the civic republican emphasis on public discourse with a liberal protection of human rights, especially of minorities or as he names them after Kant with a biblical accent, 'strangers', for whom, he insists, a theory of justice is primarily needed.[61] Instead of the liberal model of competing interests or the communitarian model of group rights, the Kantian model envisions increasing the rationality of democratic will formation by relying on discourse. According to Habermas, 'Anything valid should also be capable of public justification. Valid statements deserve the acceptance of everyone for the same reasons.'[62] Deliberative democracy entails pragmatic and uncoerced compromises as part of the inclusive public discussions from which political legitimacy and social solidarity derive.[63] Social cohesion comes from communicative action, the political culture, and a constitutional patriotism ('Verfassungspatriotismus') rather than ethnic loyalty and common ancestry.[64] In order to move away from nationalism, cosmopolitan solidarity is essential, and a recent example of such solidarity was the European protest against the American-British invasion of Iraq in 2003 when hundreds of thousands demonstrated. Derrida and Habermas's joint declaration against Bush's foreign policy (31 May 2003), published simultaneously in German and French newspapers, declared their common commitment to an intellectual tradition threatened by both violent antimodernism and American unilateralism.[65] Since then Habermas has expressed bitter disappointment at the failure of the European Union's constitution to win approval. Nevertheless, trends toward cosmopolitanism are real and not simply wishful thinking. In a recent lecture Habermas defended cosmopolitan legality to enforce universal human rights as an alternative to the neoconservative model of using imperial power unilaterally to impose democracy. Moral and political norms can be universalized only through a cosmopolitan legality; the self-proclaimed norms of a unilateralist superpower will never achieve legitimacy. We are already world citizens, he claims, and there is already a global civil society and a global public sphere, but these realities do not receive adequate theorization.[66] Even though human rights are moral, they remain weak if they depend wholly on the good will of people rather than on enforceable laws. Like Kant, Habermas trusts the reliability of coercive law to the good intentions of fallible people. A legal code has the advantage of being public, amendable and discursive, as opposed to a morality that depends only on the conscience.[67]

Habermas is sceptical and critical of anti-globalization efforts that justify national or social-group 'self-determination'. Although the right to national self-determination is in the UN Charter, which Habermas supports, he insists that 'national' not be understood in terms of an ethnic nation, although his interpretation might be forced. Nevertheless, not passing the test of rationality are 'populist movements ... that blindly defend the frozen traditions of a lifeworld endangered by capitalist modernization'; these 'fundamentalist movements' are 'antidemocratic'.[68] The assumed right of self-determination undermines universal human rights, multicultural tolerance and the cosmopolitan dispersal of political sovereignty.[69] Whether the national self-determination argument comes from the Nazi apologist Carl Schmitt or from apologists for contemporary violent antimodernists, Habermas describes its effects as authoritarian, dogmatic and reactionary because when the former subalterns 'after bloody purification rituals' become the dominant powers, they will still have to deal with the problems of legitimation, minority rights and adjusting the political process to globalization.[70] Even Charles Taylor's communitarian argument must respond to this kind of criticism because, if Quebec did indeed secede from Canada, it would still have to accommodate somehow the non-French speakers in its midst, and this accommodation, if it were just and not oppressive, would have to draw upon liberal and cosmopolitan ideas.[71]

Habermas's cosmopolitanism is more compatible with that of Kwame Anthony Appiah, whose recent book, *Cosmopolitanism: Ethics in a World of Strangers* (2006), has practical – but not theoretical – similarities to Habermas's ideas. Appiah celebrates the multicultural tolerance and cosmopolitan interdependency of the Ghana where he grew up and to which he occasionally returns. He finds exemplary the 'cosmopolitan contamination' of Ghana, its shameless mixing of cultural practices and its studious avoidance of cultural purity. He takes a strongly anti-nationalist stand on the proprietorship of antiquities, insisting that they belong to all of humanity, not a nation state that did not even exist when the antiquities were created, and pointing out that '[m]uch of the greatest art is flamboyantly international; much ignores nationality altogether'.[72] Like Habermas, Appiah sees as an urgent cosmopolitan responsibility the task to abolish the most egregious forms of poverty. Appiah has spoken strongly against what he has called 'tightly scripted identities', an argument endorsed by Habermas whose conception of human rights includes the right to dissent from one's birth community. Appiah, however, has serious theoretical differences with Habermas. First, Appiah's argument for cosmopolitanism is largely anecdotal, based on charming narratives and reminiscences illustrating multicultural tolerance in Ghana. There is not, by the way, a single narrative illustrating the multicultural tolerance of his British relatives, an absence that begs for comment. Appiah trusts intuitive knowledge and the rationality of what Habermas would call the lifeworld, the *Lebenswelt*. As Appiah says, 'We can live together without agreeing on what the values are that make it good to live together'.[73] A Habermasian might reply, yes, we can, but when we have a disagreement, as we inevitably will, then we will have to discuss norms and values and it would be good to have unconstrained dialogue at that time; moreover, in the absence of institutional structures permitting free discussion, how do we know that everyone is in fact getting along with everyone else and the current social practices? For Appiah, conversation is primarily a means of getting to know each other, not an occasion for persuasion and debate, and his model of social change is similarly intuitive, as people over time get used to strange things and come to see things differently without rationalistic discussion.[74] Appiah has a Humean distrust of reason and a Rousseauvian trust in intuition, but his narrative of social change omits rational moments. After President Truman integrated the armed forces in 1948, one could characterize the situation in Appiah's terms, as people 'got used' to an integrated military and they now 'saw things differently'. Nevertheless, the context for Truman's decision was many years of prior protest and argument. Moreover, even without producing complex arguments, ordinary citizens had to give reasons to each other for the new policy and had to respond to objections to the policy, and these reasons and responses were part of a process of argumentation. That the new policy was so successful suggests that the informal argumentation that actually went on provided better reasons for the policy than were given against it. In contrast we might compare the aftermath of the American abortion case in the Supreme Court, Roe versus Wade (1973): the government introduced new social policy but in this case a large minority never accepted it, never got used to it and never saw things in a different way.

A final example of Appiah's approach differing from Habermas's is Appiah's aversion to world government, which he sees as likely to be 'unresponsive to local needs' and a threat to social heterogeneity.[75] The Habermasian reply is to ask what is the alternative to cosmopolitan structures? The nation state on its own is less likely to deal with the problems that Appiah cares about than a cosmopolitan legal order based on protecting human rights. Appiah's proposals to increase aid to developing countries, and to review tariff policies in the developed countries, are much more likely to be instituted if they were the policies of a cosmopolitan entity able to punish any developed country that did not do its fair share.

The Counter-Enlightenment, Now and Then

Appiah's dispute with Kantian cosmopolitanism is serious but it is finally more of a family quarrel than a fundamental questioning of the Enlightenment project and cosmopolitan politics. Now I will turn to those who reject major premises of the Enlightenment itself and contest Kantian versions of the cosmopolitan ideal. On the more conservative political side are those who reject Kantian cosmopolitanism as an unrealistic alternative to competitive nationalisms too powerfully rooted historically and ideologically to be displaced by something as abstract as international solidarity. The 'Realism' school of international relations does not believe in the efficacy of the Kantian argument and looks to pragmatic adjustments and the 'balance of power' to enhance national interests. Michael Mandelbaum, influential international affairs scholar, defends America's imperial role as necessary and beneficial for maintaining liberal values.[76] Another view is taken by the neoliberals who see in globalization a process that will lead ultimately to a condition of peace and commercial prosperity. However interesting these arguments are, what is most distinctive about Kant and Habermas's cosmopolitanism and most relevant to my concerns shows up more vividly in contrast with the thinking of the radical left. I will start by examining the contemporary anti-rationalists and then turn to the Counter-Enlightenment of the eighteenth and nineteenth century.

From the radical left the argument against Kantian cosmopolitanism is that liberal constitutionalism is fatally tied to Eurocentrism and American power, and that the only way to break the 'hegemony' of Brussels and Washington is to 'marginalize' Europe and find other traditions from which to construct a theory of the revolutionary 'multitude'. So argued the writers in the postcolonial journal *Public Culture*, which recently devoted an issue to the topic of cosmopolitanism (2000). Sheldon Pollock, defending first-millennium Sanskrit civilization as an alternative to European cosmopolitanism, praises attractive features of the south-Asian empire at the expense of philosophical Stoicism in the Roman Empire, but the comparison is so impressionistic and unsystematic that it does not contrast two sets of norms.[77] The extent to which the contemporary discourse of human rights is Eurocentric or truly universal is controversial, but the essays in a recent anthology on women's rights in Africa written by African women argue for sensitivity in applying norms to particular communities. Although they invite dialogue between African traditions and European human rights, the overall emphasis is on intervening to empower women to change traditions that oppress them; all the essays assume that women should have sexual equality, even though such an assumption runs counter to African traditions. While the anthology's writers object to the arrogant imposition of Western norms as a form of neo-imperialism, they articulate a human rights discourse that can transform African traditions effectively to improve the lives of African women. Because there is no essay that argues for some kind of wholly non-Western human rights discourse upon which women can draw, one infers that the Kantian-Habermasian concept of universality remains unchallenged here and that *Public Culture*'s desire to 'marginalize' Europe would be frustrated in this instance.[78] In the most theoretically oriented essay in the *Public Culture* issue, Walter Mignolo argues explicitly against a Kantian-Habermasian approach, recommending instead a radical rethinking of a Western human rights discourse which merely reproduces colonial domination, but the essays in the African feminists' anthology suggest that the human rights discourse is more politically useful than Mignolo imagines.[79]

Mignolo's essay presses hard on the alleged parallels between colonialism and cosmopolitanism, including the human rights discourse. The most well known argument against 'liberal' cosmopolitanism now is that pursued by Michael Hardt and Antonio Negri, who oppose the cosmopolitanism associated with Kant and Habermas and propose instead their own form of world citizenship, depending on three maxims: universal citizenship where people live, absolute right of free movement and the right of reappropriation of the means of production.[80] Kantian liberalism can accept the first and second maxims (the second is actually not remote from Kant's right of hospitality), but the third is impossible as a basic premise of liberal cosmopolitanism, impossible to accept as a 'right' rather than something extensively debated, and impossible to translate quickly into politically workable actions within ordinary legal and political procedures.

Acting in favour of economic justice is of course fully within the parameters of Rawlsian justice as fairness or Habermasian discourse ethics (as an effect of extensive and long-term public sphere activity), but taking over the means of production, if it means anything at all, revives the Leninist idea of proletarian dictatorship. The neo-Leninism is not the only thing that makes the radical cosmopolitanism of Hardt and Negri incompatible with a more liberal version of world citizenship. In both *Empire* (2000) and their subsequent book, *Multitude: War and Democracy in the Age of Empire* (2004), they omit any description of legitimate legality, as they assume the battle between 'empire' and 'multitude' settles the legitimation problem; the only distinction that matters is the violence that sustains 'global order' and the violence that threatens it.[81] In an interview, Hardt identifies the most illustrative example of the 'rule of law' in relation to 'sovereignty' as the Nazi death camps; for a Kantian it would be just the opposite, the camps providing the most telling illustration of a lack of rule of law and the rule of dictatorship instead of democracy.[82] As long as 'empire' is sovereign, any kind of resistance to it by the 'multitude' is beyond ethics, a topic about which Hardt and Negri have nothing to say. Moreover, there are no intermediary steps sketched out to move society to their stated communist goal, nothing similar to what Habermas does with the European Union and the International Criminal Court. Hardt and Negri dismiss Habermas's intermediary steps as incapable of countering the power of the United States;[83] they reject Habermas's ideas on the public sphere and discourse ethics as 'completely utopian and unrealizable' because the power of capitalism to control and contaminate the mass media prevents any kind of genuine democratic public speech.[84] In the absence of such 'reformist' steps, Hardt and Negri rely on the myth of revolution, which they reproduce in both *Empire* and *Multitude*, revising somewhat the Leninist formula by emphasizing 'heterogeneity', but rejecting firmly parliamentary democracy as insufficiently representative.[85] Ernesto Laclau, questioning the plausibility of Hardt and Negri's political approach, finds their concept of the 'multitude' a 'purely fanciful construction'; without any form of political mediation and articulation, he judges, Hardt and Negri construct a politics of pure opposition that lacks philosophical substance.[86] Also questioning the adequacy of a purely negative political project, Slavoj Žižek asks what exactly the 'multitude' would *do* in power?[87] A Habermasian would also ask how the 'multitude' would settle disputes, exercise power, treat minorities, deal with violations of human rights and so on. Would the entire liberal project have to be reinvented or would the 'multitude' maintain an instantaneous consensus that has never happened in history before?

The idea of direct democracy, famously if equivocally affirmed in Rousseau's *Social Contract* (1762), recurrently proposed and occasionally attempted by the revolutionary left from the 1790s onwards, is actually at the heart of Habermas's idealization of the public sphere and communicative action. Although Habermas criticizes parliamentary democracy and mass media communications for their failures, he does not reject them outright, and seeks to reform them; moreover, he separates politics and ethics, the former permitting pragmatic compromises and the latter allowing more rigorous norms of reciprocity. Kantian liberalism places direct democracy as an ideal to be aimed for but never fully achieved, tinkering instead with the clumsy representative machinery that actually does exist and occasionally works. Kant's fear of revolution, based largely on the single example of the French Revolution (and, to a much smaller degree, the English revolution of the seventeenth century), is either lucidly prescient or ideologically over-determined, depending on one's own politics – for we now have a wealth of historical evidence on how revolutions have been conducted and how they ultimately turned out. Hardt and Negri are imperturbable before this historical evidence, none of which shakes their faith in revolution. Habermas, by contrast, allergic to political irrationalism of any kind from right or left, finds in deliberative democracy and in the formalism of Kantian ethics fences to protect vulnerable political rationality. That their disagreement is fundamental is suggested by their contrasting views on the ideas of Carl Schmitt. Hardt and Negri accept Schmitt's critique of parliamentary democracy, including his idea that 'some unitary political subject – such as a party, a people, or nation' must exercise sovereignty.[88] The peculiar symbiosis of 'empire' and 'multitude', both unitary, both escaping clear definition, reflects Schmitt's ideas of sovereignty, expressed in one of Schmitt's famous statements: 'Sovereign is he who decides on the exception'.[89] For Kantian liberalism the law itself is sovereign, not the state, but Schmitt argues consistently for just the opposite, the priority of the state over law, citing the Hobbesian maxim that 'autoritas, non veritas facit legem' (authority not truth makes law).[90] Schmitt aligns his thought with counterrevolutionary ideas from Maistre, Bonald and Donoso Cortés.[91] Although Hardt and Negri do not perpetuate Schmitt's ideas of ethnonationalism, they do continue a version of his political romanticism, relying on spontaneity instead of legal procedures, practicing a form of antimodernistic hostility to legal and bureaucratic logic and substituting the sovereignty of the rebellious 'multitude' for the sovereignty of the Schmittian dictator.

For Schmitt romanticism is an ambiguous concept, meaning both a form of innovative aesthetic creativity and a tradition of Counter-Enlightenment thought, an important part of which is the counterrevolutionary political tradition with which he identifies. Romanticism created both the French Revolution and the counterrevolutionary philosophy of nationalism. According to Schmitt, Joseph de Maistre realized that a religiously based nationalism was the only adequate alternative to the revolutionary community, the cosmopolitan brotherhood of man symbolized dramatically in the National Convention's decree of

19 November 1792 offering military assistance to 'all peoples who want their liberty'.[92] Not people as such – not the autonomous ego of Rousseauvian romanticism, not the popular sovereignty of republican liberalism – but history itself was in control; the mysterious *Volksgeist* (spirit of the people) providentially produced the nation and guided historical development, as aristocracy and religion reinforced a sense of continuity.[93] Schmitt takes the counterrevolutionary tradition that developed in France, Germany and Britain,[94] and makes it his own, insisting that dictatorship over an ethnically homogenous nation is not necessarily anti-democratic and that it is the only effective way to avoid the ill effects of a bourgeois parliamentary democracy.[95] What Schmitt calls 'parliamentarism' is a child of the Enlightenment, as the liberal public sphere with its ideal of openness and transparency combated 'superstition, fanaticism, and ambitious intrigue'.[96] Schmitt gets from Georges Sorel the irrationalist alternative to 'intellectualist' parliamentarism, namely, the vitalistic 'life instinct' of violent political struggle.[97] Just as Schmitt sees the commonality of Bolshevism and Fascism in their shared contempt for liberalism, Hardt and Negri find in Schmitt a congenial figure for their political genealogy.[98]

Habermas, however, as he defines and explains his version of Kantian cosmopolitanism, finds it necessary to dispute the ideas of Carl Schmitt. The Habermasian constitutional state acquires its legitimacy through protection of civil and human rights, through rule of law, through publicly accessible and correctible procedures open to inspection and through self-correction by means of the public sphere and judicial review. Law, not the state, is sovereign. Instead of ethnic homogeneity, a common political culture generates *Verfassungspatriotismus* – a constitutional patriotism. Legitimacy derives from 'the *intersubjectivistic* understanding of procedural popular sovereignty'.[99] Schmitt, like Hardt and Negri, objects to international interventions justified by the discourse of human rights, but Habermas sees such interventions as hopeful cosmopolitan moves toward the juridification of human rights. For neither Schmitt on the right, nor Hardt and Negri on the left, does 'the cosmopolitan transformation of the state of nature among states into a legal order' have any appeal, as it smacks of liberal proceduralism and bureaucratic legalism, hypocritically concealing the 'real' sovereign.[100]

Hardt and Negri are not wholly within the Counter-Enlightenment, as they make use of the materialist and Spinozan currents of the Enlightenment. Although they leave much to the hypothetical spontaneity of the 'multitude', they do not reject reason itself. Carl Schmitt is not simply anti-liberal, as are Hardt and Negri, but also strongly opposed to the Enlightenment itself. Although some scholars like Ellen Kennedy have located Schmitt close to the Frankfurt School, Martin Jay has persuasively refuted this attempt to make Schmitt more politically respectable.[101] Schmitt's commitment to ethnonationalism and the priority of political force over the rule of law reflects his opposition to reason as it was understood by the Enlightenment.

In part because of Isaiah Berlin's writing on the Counter-Enlightenment, and in part because of anti-rationalistic expressions by poststructuralists, the whole question of being within, outside or after the Enlightenment has been raised and has, in fact, some relevance to the issue of cosmopolitanism. I will look first at Berlin's writing then examine briefly the question of the Enlightenment in poststructuralist thinking.

Berlin's extensive work on the Counter-Enlightenment does not always clearly distinguish between anti-rationalistic ideas and a philosophical movement identifiable as the Counter-Enlightenment; nor does he always clearly explain how the Counter-Enlightenment relates to the specifically political movement of counterrevolutionary thinking and the specifically aesthetic movement of romanticism. In Berlin's *Three Critics of the Enlightenment* (2000), only Hamaan seems wholly within the Counter-Enlightenment, as a kind of German William Blake who defended imagination, intuition and religious faith against the main currents of Enlightenment thinking.[102] While yoking together Blake and Hamaan for the Counter-Enlightenment makes sense up to a point, Berlin has no comments on their differences that are at least as important, especially Blake's alignment with the political left and democratic rebellion in contrast to Hamaan's ultra-conservatism. The extremism of Hamaan's antirationalism gives Berlin pause, as Hamaan's affinity with Maistre and nationalistic anti-Semitism is too apparent to ignore.[103] The mystical Hamaan influenced Herder, Jacobi and the early German romantics (*Fruhromantiker*) but, according to Berlin, the anti-rationalist tradition of which Hamaan is the founder has done more harm than good, although he nevertheless finds much to like about the 'magus of the North'.[104] Berlin's harsh view of the mechanistic, materialistic and deterministic currents of the Enlightenment makes him interested in a Counter-Enlightenment, but his ultimate historical narrative is more complicated and equivocal. Vico is clearly an opponent of Cartesian rationalism and his thinking is probably the most thoroughly worked-out alternative to mainstream Enlightenment thought, but Vico wrote well before the French, Scottish and English Enlightenments and well before the *Aufklärung* matured. Moreover, the second wave of Enlightenment thinkers like Kant also opposed Cartesian rationalism, and Viconian providential history is not unlike Kant's teleological history. Because Vico was not part of any 'movement', it is hard to place him within the Counter-Enlightenment. If Herder is the leader of the Counter-Enlightenment, a not implausible move, then his inconvenient cosmopolitanism cannot be ignored; indeed, Herder is often a better cosmopolitan than Kant, especially on the issue of sympathetically understanding non-European cultures.[105] Heinrich Heine's favourite writer was the exemplary *Aufklärer* Lessing, but his second favourite writer was Herder.[106] Indeed, Herder is one of the cosmopolitan writers that Heine names specifically as one of the 'great minds' ('unsere großen Geister') 'which all educated Germans have always believed in' ('gehuldigt haben' – 'paid homage to' would be more literal).[107] It is of course undeniable that Herder disputed many of Kant's ideas, that Herder influenced the *Fruhromantiker* and that Herder is properly associated with a kind of nationalism, but attaching him to something as coherent as the Counter-Enlightenment simplifies the history of ideas. Herder certainly was a critic of important Enlightenment currents, but so were Kant, Hume and Rousseau.

Is the Counter-Enlightenment a useless concept? Not at all. It is most usefully deployed dialectically, as Berlin usually deploys it, so that one can see, for example, the specifically Prussian opposition to the French Enlightenment fostered by the 'benevolent despot' Frederick the Great, or the German opposition to French ideas after the invasion of Napoleon's armies. Romanticism was a critical response to the main currents of Enlightenment thinking but it retained as well important Enlightenment assumptions. The one movement of thought that achieved the most antithetical position in relation to the Enlightenment was the counterrevolutionary tradition, especially the French tradition that embraced monarchy and the Catholic Church, but this movement would have been merely reactionary without the newer elements from nationalism and romanticism, more dialectical constructs in relation to Enlightenment. The Counter-Enlightenment and romanticism acquired authority after the defeat of Napoleon. As Berlin explains, 'The failure of the French Revolution to bring about the greater portion of its declared ends marks the end of the French Enlightenment as a movement and a system'.[108] Enlightened thinking within the project of enlightenment continued but the Enlightenment as such ceased.

If Berlin's search for the intellectual roots of Marxist-Leninism led him circuitously to develop the history of the Counter-Enlightenment, it was the specifically French intellectual culture during the Cold War that produced some of the strongest poststructuralist repudiations of the Enlightenment. As the dust has settled, so to speak, it turns out that Foucault actually gestured toward a reconciliation of sorts with the Enlightenment in his final essays before his death; moreover, Derrida in the final phase of his work, turned to ethics, politics and religion, hardly fitting well within the Counter-Enlightenment. Lyotard, who popularized postmodernity as the anti-Habermasian scepticism toward metanarratives associated with the Enlightenment, wrote recurrently on the *Aufklärer* who also is Habermas's most significant influence, Immanuel Kant. Just how *counter*-Enlightenment can Lyotard be? Like thinkers before them, the poststructuralists were critical of and revised currents of Enlightenment thought, but without finally dismantling the project of enlightenment; they did not ultimately begin Western thought anew. Their writing, at its best, responded

sensitively to the rich singularity of particulars in danger of losing their unique-
ness to abstraction, a worthy project in the mainstream of Western philosophical
writing. However one might view the different styles of art and literature in our
present moment, the aesthetic categories of 'modern' and 'postmodern' do not
undermine the strength of Habermas's Weberian depiction of modernity as
destroying the metaphysical and religious myths by which individuals used to
form their identities and sense of social belonging.[109] Although there are powerful reactionary movements, some of them dangerously violent, that are trying
to reverse the effects of modernity and reinstall myths that cannot be defended
rationally, there are few genuine antimodernists of which I am aware at the level
of serious philosophical writing. The Enlightenment will be carried forward in
cosmopolitan directions or it will be thwarted violently by reactionary antimodernism.

2 EXPANDING THE PUBLIC SPHERE

When the classical public sphere – *die Öffentlichkeit* –grew in the latter part of the eighteenth century, expanding rapidly in the 1790s, the intellectual culture was cosmopolitan in both Paris and London. The public sphere, defined by Jürgen Habermas as 'the private people, [who] come together to form a public ... [to] compel public authority to legitimate itself before public opinion',[1] has historical, theoretical and literary significance. Almost fifty years after Habermas's pioneering study, there are still questions about the public sphere, its origins, development and usefulness as a critical category. This chapter will clarify some of the historical and theoretical issues connected with the emergence and development of the public sphere, especially as it relates to cosmopolitanism. The most theoretically rigorous deliberations on the public sphere at the very time it was assuming its distinctiveness were by Immanuel Kant, whose most perceptive insights were further deepened much later by Habermas. After the theoretical and historical sections on the public sphere, this chapter turns to two specific examples from the romantic era to illustrate the public sphere both in its expansive mode, and in a crisis brought on by political repression and the contradictions of social class: John Thelwall, the most important public lecturer of the democratic movement of the 1790s, and the *Analytical Review* (1788–99), perhaps the purest example of Enlightenment cosmopolitanism in the 1790s. The public sphere in Habermas's account consists of literary and political spheres that mediate between private individuals and the state. The literary sphere includes much that is political and the political sphere is permeated with literary meanings, so that the distinction between the two is not absolute but still conceptually useful. Thelwall, one of the few figures who acted in both the bourgeois and plebeian public spheres, was both a popular lecturer and an ambitious poet. Although the *Analytical Review* was unquestionably a bourgeois periodical, competing for readers with the *Monthly Review* and the *Critical Review*, it usually had a respectful attitude toward products of the plebeian public sphere and it was victimized ultimately by the same forces of reaction and repression that destroyed the London Corresponding Society and other institutions of popular radicalism.

Narrating the Public Sphere

In a special issue of *Criticism* (2004) entitled 'When Is a Public Sphere?', Michael McKeon argues that the public sphere is 'virtual', an 'imagined collectivity' like the market, so there is no need to correct Habermas with reminders about inequality and oppositional 'counterpublics'. Rather, the public sphere re-conceives the imagination as a 'powerful and productive sort of human solidarity'.[2] Although the essays in this special issue make a strong case for dating the public sphere's emergence from the seventeenth century, if not earlier, McKeon focuses on what one might call the transhistorical essence of the public sphere, something that gets lost discussing the institutional minutiae and subtleties, however important they also are. When the focus is on how the subject imagines intersubjectively, it does not matter so much when and where exactly the public sphere emerged, whether it was in Habermas's London coffeehouses and Parisian salons, in early print culture's cosmopolitan verse translations, or in seventeenth-century letter-writing; regardless, the remarkable thing is a new form of discourse.[3] The institutional and material forms that the public sphere assumes require description and analysis but McKeon's shift to the imagination is salutary, for it suggests a connection between the public sphere and the cosmopolitan ideal. The imagination does something difficult, extraordinary and unnatural when it takes up Kant's Enlightenment slogan of knowing boldly and thinking against the familiar patterns set by customary authorities. Whether listening to a Thelwall lecture in a crowded hall in the Beaufort Buildings or reading a feminist novel by Mary Hays, the imagination works through material that resists immediate consumption and that entails conflict and ambiguity as well as liberation and joy. The lecture hall auditor and the novel reader both bond with an imagined community oriented toward justice.

Many have disputed the normative nature of the public sphere. Hegel argued in *The Philosophy of Right* (1821) that the conflicted civil society of which the public sphere was a central part required the ethical rationality that only a state power could generate, while Marx famously saw the public sphere as a reflection of power constituted elsewhere: as Marx wrote in *The Eighteenth Brumaire of Louis Bonaparte* (1852), 'When you play the fiddle at the top of the state, what else is to be expected but that those down below dance?'[4] Rousseau's *Social Contract* depicts a 'general will' ('volunté général') that is 'a consensus of hearts rather than arguments', for Rousseau sees the agonistic debating public as rhetorical and theatrical rather than a process that leads to truth.[5] The numerous contemporary objections to the Habermasian public sphere come from a long tradition in romantic political thinking. It is necessary to return to Kant who first theorized the public sphere in such a controversial way.

Kant seems to have been the first thinker to conceptualize the public sphere as a politically fundamental institution with an inner logic that was powerfully anti-authoritarian. Kant's very conception of reason and rationality makes the public sphere necessary. Kant's reason is not monological and requires social structures to ensure its ability to function properly. Reason is most healthy when it is permitted free play – 'freien Vernünfteleien'[6] – that is, constrained internally by the labour and difficulty reason exacts and externally by powerful authorities who try to control public discourse to suit their own interests. The self-exertion ('Selbstbemühung') reason demands is not at all natural, for 'people want to be led ... duped' ('Das Volk will geleitet ... betrogen sein'), as people like to follow their 'inclinations' ('Neigungen').[7] The intellectuals most interested in exercising rationality as freely as possible are the historians and philosophers, who comprise what Kant calls the 'lower faculty' and who are in perpetual conflict with the 'higher faculty' whose reason serves church and state. Kant assumes that the conflict between the state and the philosophers is inevitable in the context of popular Enlightenment ('Volksaufklärung'), which is the 'public instruction of the people in its duties and rights vis à vis the state' ('öffentliche Belehrung des Volks von seinen Pflichten und Rechten in Ansehung des Staats').[8] To make sure that popular Enlightenment thrives, the 'lower faculty' has to be granted complete freedom of inquiry and expression. Kant makes the case for intellectual freedom less offensive to the authorities when he insists that scholars are addressing one another and not the indifferent public[9] but the very fact of popular Enlightenment and the concept of progress clearly point to communication (however mediated) between the philosophers and *das Volk*. Indeed, in *The Metaphysics of Morals* (1797) Kant argues that philosophy should be popular, clear to everyone, even though formal metaphysics requires a precision that makes clarity difficult.[10] In a letter to Christian Garve (7 August 1783) he discusses popularizing the first Critique: 'every philosophical work must be susceptible of popularity; if not, it probably conceals nonsense beneath a fog of seeming sophistication'.[11]

The *Critique of Judgment* has a remarkable meditation (section 40) on the connection between individuals and cosmopolitan community. The immediate point of departure is Kant's assertion that the judgments of taste are not idiosyncratic but are 'universally communicable', even 'without any mediation by concepts'.[12] It does not seem immediately apparent that subjective responses to beauty are the same for everyone, so Kant tries to explain the logic of his argument. The first step is to establish that taste is not a sensation but something like 'common sense' – *sensus communis* – that is, common understanding. Common understanding, a universal capacity, makes judgments by means of taking account 'of everyone else's way of presenting [something], in order *as it were* to compare our own judgment with human reason in general and thus escape the illusion that arises from the ease of mistaking subjective and private conditions for objective ones'.[13] By putting ourselves 'in the position of everyone else', we overcome the merely idiosyncratic and adopt a universal standpoint, transferring ourselves to the 'standpoint of others'.[14] What I am renaming as the cosmopolitan imagination is only one of three principles of common understanding – the other two being thinking for oneself and thinking consistently.[15] Kant's common sense is a normative category, for each of the three principles has its antithesis: passively letting others think for one, narrowly confining one's thoughts within the merely subjective conditions of judgment and irresponsibly thinking without consistency. Nevertheless, a prominent feature of Kant's *sensus communis* is that it is common, ordinary, not learned ('gelehrt'). The project of popular Enlightenment is not unrealistic and utopian if common understanding has in place already the principles by which 'superstition' and 'prejudice' can be overturned.[16] The next step in Kant's argument is to claim that taste has an even stronger title to the category of *sensus communis* than common understanding.[17] The imagination is described as interacting with understanding to produce a judgment of taste that presents itself in communication 'not as a thought but as the inner feeling of a purposive state of mind'.[18] If common understanding is shared intellectual knowledge, then even more shareable would be aesthetic knowledge that lacks concepts.

I am less interested in the persuasiveness of Kant's *Critique* than I am in the seemingly en passant argument for the cosmopolitan imagination and popular enlightenment. Characteristically Kant insists that reason be both independent and intersubjective. 'For Kant', according to Susan Meld Shell, 'the most important "public" is the cosmopolitan republic of the mind'.[19] The universalizing effect of the cosmopolitan imagination is also the effect of the categorical imperative – to act as though the deed were to become a universal law of nature[20] – something that Onora O'Neill finds informing all of Kant's philosophy, not just the ethics.[21] Connecting with community is something performed not simply within the imagination but in actuality, for, as Hannah Arendt remarks, for Kant philosophical truth has to be communicated to be tested in public discourse; the testing is an indispensable and ordinary part of serious thinking.[22] In more than a few texts Kant paid attention to practical ways that the public could act philosophically. Robert Louden challenges Hegel's claim that Kant's ethics were empty formalism by showing the ways Kant paid attention to pragmatic applications of ideas, including education of children who, according to the philosopher, 'must rejoice at the highest good in the world even if it is not to the advantage of their fatherland or to their own gain'.[23] Cosmopolitan morality needs supportive institutions and citizens of the world require practical training as well.[24] Kant illustrates with egalitarian associations another way that the public sphere promotes the cosmopolitan ideal. The example is independent Protestant congregations where equality prevails and such an institution 'contains within itself something great, expanding the narrow, selfish, and unsociable cast of mind among men ... toward the idea of a cosmopolitan *moral community*'.[25]

For Kant, then, the public sphere is where philosophy defends itself and challenges superstition and prejudice, where the free press forces the state to explain and justify its actions, where common understanding and the aesthetic *sensus communis* undertake popular enlightenment. The public sphere as he conceives it, a site of liberal discourse, is threatened from two different directions, the repressive state and violent revolution. After Frederick II's death in 1786 the aggressively Counter-Enlightenment regime of his successor Frederick William II threatened 'unpleasant measures' ('unangenehmer Verfügungen') against Kant if he persisted in publishing texts like *Religion Within the Limits of Reason Alone* (1793).[26] After the death of the Prussian monarch in 1797 Kant published *Conflict of the Faculties*, which discloses the exchange of letters between Justice Minister Wöllner and Kant over the publication of the 1793 religious treatise from which the Prussian censors had actually withheld permission. Kant circumvented the censorship laws by getting his text approved by the Jena philosophy faculty; Wöllner retaliated by 'forbidding any professor to lecture on Kant's philosophy of religion'.[27] Publishing both Wöllner's threatening letter and Kant's extensive defence of his treatise is Kant's way of combating state repression: exposing secrets, making transparent the operations of power and openly defending one's exercise of reason.

The degree to which Kant's own thinking was afflicted by self-censorship is difficult to gauge, for if we assume his deference to already existing authority in state and church is a symptom, then we must also take note of his open questioning of both. A perceptive article by Peter Nicholson on Kant and revolution observes the important inconsistencies in Kant's views, but surprisingly does not imagine the unconscious effects of a censorship that could have been internalized.[28] In the 1790s the opponents of the Enlightenment, led by Friedrich von Gentz, translator of Burke's *Reflections on the Revolution in France* (1790, trans. 1793), recognized Kant as their enemy and openly attacked him. The unusual defence of the French Revolution in *Conflict of the Faculties* (1798) seems to be a defiant gesture against the German Burkeans like Gentz, Rehberg and Möser.[29] As Kant seems to stumble upon an explanation of the cosmopolitan imagination in section 40 of the third *Critique*, so the comments on the French Revolution in *Conflict of the Faculties* seem to be digressive. Kant had always been strongly invested in the idea of progress, reacting sharply against Mendelssohn's insistence in *Jerusalem* (1783) that only individuals but not societies progress morally, and he brings up the issue of progress again, offering another kind of argument in its favour.[30] Because humans, being mortal, cannot take a providential perspective ('der Standpunkt der Vorsehung'), they depend on experience alone to infer the existence of progress, and the experience Kant chooses is the disinterested enthusiasm and sympathy by the Germans for the French Revolution.[31] There can be only one explanation for these 'spectators', having no personal stake in the revolution, being able to identify so closely with a revolution from which they will gain nothing: 'a moral predisposition (Anlage) of the human race'.[32] To protect himself Kant inserts a long footnote that reassures the Prussian authorities that he does not favour a revolution in his own country, but even to express as much approval for the French Revolution as he did in 1798 was politically risky.

Kant's ideas on the public sphere were hardly without some problematic aspects. According to James Schmidt, Kant's peculiar definition of public and private in the *Conflict of the Faculties* conceded more than was absolutely necessary to the state and church when he sanctioned the supine obedience of the 'higher faculty' and ministers of the state church, merely echoing Prussian state policy.[33] His deferential moves to the state seem to violate his theory of 'right', notes Ciaran Cronin.[34] Equally problematic, as Schmidt points out, is Kant's conception of the public as being exclusively a world of readers, a 'Leserwelt'.[35] Although Kant's public entails discussion and debate, he rarely pays attention to anything other than a literary sphere. Salons, discussion groups, debating clubs and other sites of political speech he seems to distrust as a location for bad rhetoric. In the third *Critique* he expresses his preference for poetry over rhetoric in a romantically extreme way that is difficult to reconcile with his statements about the public sphere.[36] If the literary sphere is central for Kant, he fails to offer practical manoeuvres to counter state censorship and repression, so that enlightenment seems to depend wholly on the despot's will.[37] Kant has no answer to a Frederick William II with good health and a long life.

I place these problematic aspects in two categories: one being the effects of historical constraints exerting pressures on not just Kant but everyone in his society at that time, and the other being the difficulties of drawing out and applying practically the 'radical implications of his ideal political principles'.[38] It is hardly news that Kant frequently is inconsistent and unable to carry through the most radical inferences of his ethical and political ideas. Kant's core ideas on the public sphere were developed more consistently and coherently by Habermas, thus illustrating just how radical those original ideas were.

Habermas and the Public Sphere[39]

The reception in the Anglophonic world of Habermas's *Structural Transformation of the Public Sphere* has been coloured by the lateness of its translation into English (1989), twenty-seven years after it was first published in German (1962).[40] In romantic studies, for example, the Habermasian public sphere first received attention at a panel in the 1993 MLA convention, and then the next year as the focus of a special issue of *Studies in Romanticism*. The place of *Structural Transformation* in Habermas's development and the role that the public sphere as a concept plays in his mature thought are hardly ever considered by romanticists who make use of the public sphere idea and who criticize Habermas for the alleged inadequacies of his approach. A work that served as his *Habilitationsschrift* at Marburg University (his earlier dissertation was on the romantic philosopher Schelling), and a product of the late fifties in its historical research, *Structural Transformation* was responding to the Frankfurt School's theory of modernization, especially the work of Theodor Adorno, for whom Habermas was a teaching assistant. Habermas finds most 'classical' the earliest stages of the bourgeois public sphere rather than the more mature developments. The eighteenth-century coffeehouses and salons, the literary sphere of the novel- and magazine-reading public and the emergence of a public opinion that had to be reckoned with for the first time by those who governed nation states represent for Habermas an imperfect historical anticipation of a radically democratic discourse-community open to all participants whose discussion would be without constraints. In *Structural Transformation*'s account of the public sphere, the great promise of radical democratic participation was closed down by strategies and techniques of manipulation that engineered, coerced and manufactured public opinion. Operating within an explicitly Marxist paradigm, Habermas portrays the transformation of the eighteenth-century public sphere into twentieth-century public relations, advertising and mass-media deception of the public as the work of first monopoly and then advanced capitalism.

Habermas's gloomy trajectory of the public sphere resembles the narratives of modernization by the Frankfurt School under the influence of Max Weber's depiction of modernity as an 'iron cage' without freedom or meaning, after the 'disenchantment' of traditional religion and metaphysical worldviews. Habermas is responding not just to Weber's 'iron cage' but to Lukács's 'reification' and Adorno and Horkheimer's 'dialectic of Enlightenment'. Lukács turns Marx's 'commodity fetishism' idea into a narrative about estranged labour whereby workers become commodified things in a world they produce but perceive as alien (*History and Class Consciousness* (1920)). Adorno and Horkheimer withdraw entirely Lukács's hope in a revolutionary proletariat, and radicalize the degradation of capitalist society by locating in rationality itself the deadening power of reification In controlling nature, reason deforms human nature, so that ineluctably every advance of enlightened emancipation from the terror of nature is also an intensification of reason's power to dominate human nature. Reason in its emancipatory aspect is in eclipse, as modern reason has been reduced to instrumental reason – mind used solely as a means to control and dominate nature and people (*Dialectic of Enlightenment* (1944)). Whatever hope the mature Frankfurt School allowed was contained exclusively in a philosophical engagement with avant-garde art. For the masses of people there was mass deception delivered by the culture industry.

In this context one can see *Structural Transformation* as Habermas's early attempt to work his way out of the aporias he inherited from his precursors. The key move in *Structural Transformation* is away from the dialectics of production and toward the relations of labour and social interaction. If the public sphere – private people gathered to reflect on and discuss critically matters of public interest – has such a powerful effect, then it presents a historically material force for democratic reform that can wage battles against the dehumanizing forces described so chillingly by Weber, Lukács and Adorno. The classical bourgeois public sphere operates both historically as a moment of early modernization and conceptually as an anticipation of what a truly emancipatory public sphere would look like. Habermas's philosophical career after 1962 has been in the direction of a 'linguistic turn' toward discursive rationality and away from the productivist and philosophy-of-history perspective he inherited from Western Marxism. In his mature thought the public sphere is the extraordinarily important site where the *Lebenswelt* defends itself from the incursions of 'system' – the economy, government and bureaucracy.

Because of the peculiar timing of English translations of Habermas's work, his overall reception, including his reception by romantic studies, has been subject to misperceptions, minor and major. *New German Critique* published Habermas's 1964 encyclopaedia article on the public sphere in 1974 and, five years later, Günther Lottes's study, published only in German, *Politische Aufklärung und plebejisches Publikum* (*Political Enlightenment and the Plebeian Public*), demonstrated with rich historical detail that Habermas's characterization of the plebeian public sphere as a mere variant of the bourgeois public sphere was empirically mistaken. Building upon the work of E. P. Thompson, Lottes used the London Corresponding Society and the Jacobin intelligentsia – especially John Thelwall – to demonstrate that the plebeian public sphere, although modelled after the bourgeois sphere, is much more than a mere variant and innovatively develops the public sphere.[41] Habermas accepted fully Lottes's criticism in his 'Further Reflections on the Public Sphere' – published in English in 1992 – and notes approvingly as well E. P. Thompson's and Bakhtin's work on the plebeian public sphere.[42] Unfortunately Habermas's extensive comments on the public sphere in 1992 are infrequently cited by scholars who instead criticize Habermas's original treatment of the concept. His ideas on the public sphere, generated so many years ago, had to be expanded and revised with further empirical research and theoretical refinement – a task Habermas himself has contributed to – but to ignore his own revisionist activity is to sow confusion unnecessarily.

After Lottes's study of the plebeian public sphere, the next important moment in *Structural Transformation*'s reception was Peter Hohendahl's *The Institution of Criticism* (1982), an application of the public-sphere ideas to the example of German literature and culture, as well as a description of Habermas's reception in Germany; his study covered the romantic period without, unfortunately, much effect on English-language romantic studies. Hohendahl's study seems to have provoked Terry Eagleton's brief book, *The Function of Criticism* (1984), an important text in popularizing Habermas's concept of the public sphere. Eagleton's sketchy comments on romantic-era writing influenced later romanticist discussions of the public sphere, especially the emphasis on 'counter-public spheres', a concept originated by Oskar Negt and Alexander Kluge in their 1972 New Left critique of Habermas, *Public Sphere and Experience*. Nancy Fraser's influential essay of 1985, 'What's Critical about Critical Theory? The Case of Habermas and Gender' initiated the important feminist criticism of the public sphere concept, and was followed by Joan Landes's *Women and the Public Sphere in the Age of the French Revolution* (1988), the feminist critiques offered at the 1989 conference on Habermas's *Public Sphere* and Mary P. Ryan's *Women in Public* (1990). Habermas agreed with much of the feminist criticism in his 'Further Reflections' and in his comments at the end of the 1989 conference, where he described the bourgeois public sphere as 'patriarchal' and acknowledged that the exclusion of women from the political public sphere had a 'structuring significance' he had neglected earlier;[43] he addresses gender explicitly in later works like *Between Facts and Norms* (1996). The feminist discussion of Habermas's public sphere continues in the 1995 volume edited by Johanna Meehan, *Feminists Read Habermas*. One of the essays, 'Critical Social Theory and Feminist Critiques' by Jean L. Cohen, while not wholly uncritical of Habermas, takes issue with some of his feminist critics, especially Nancy Fraser, whose best known treatment of Habermas has been reprinted a number of times (in her own *Unruly Practices* (1989), in Bruce Robbins's collection *The Phantom Public Sphere* (1993) and in *Feminists Read Habermas* itself). Cohen's argument cannot be summarized briefly but it is notable that very few who write about Habermas and the public sphere in romantic studies seem to even know about Cohen's essay or about the other feminist work that is sympathetic to Habermas, like that of Seyla Benhabib and Susan Wells.[44] To summarize, then, Habermas ultimately corrects two of the most criticized areas in the 1962 study, the plebeian sphere and the treatment of gender, but these corrections infrequently register with those who comment on the public sphere.

A curious chapter in the reception of Habermas's *Public Sphere* is the translation into English of Oskar Negt and Alexander Kluge's *Public Sphere and Experience* in 1993, with a long introduction by Miriam Hansen. This 1972 reaction to Habermas came out of the milieu of the militant New Left, introduced the concept of the counter-public sphere – *Gegenöffentlichkeit* – and was widely discussed in North American New Left circles. As Peter Hohendahl explains,

Habermas never directly replied in print to Negt and Kluge because by '1974 it was clear that the cultural revolution of the New Left had failed'.[45] Of the German critics of *Structural Transformation*, Habermas felt compelled to answer the critique of Niklas Luhmann, the systems theorist.[46] Moreover, Kluge, a friend of Habermas's, turned against his own earlier ideas on the public sphere and accepted Habermas's.[47] *Public Sphere and Experience* is relevant for contemporary media theory in relation to concepts of the counter-hegemonic but it is not helpful now for reading Habermas's 1962 text on the eighteenth and nineteenth century; nevertheless, the concept of the counter-public sphere has been taken up by some recent scholars who want to stress the heterogeneity of the public sphere. Many critics of Habermas fail to distinguish between the historically variable public sphere, which has multiple centres of activity and various degrees of rationality, and the presuppositions, logic and structure of communication itself. The latter implies norms of consensus, universal access and unrestricted discussion – norms the historical public sphere never fully actualizes.

The Negt-Kluge concept of the counter-public sphere gets so much play in the 1994 *Studies in Romanticism* special issue that Orrin Wang comments that the essays are less interested in Habermas's study than in his critics and *their* concepts. Two of Wang's criticisms hold up well after a dozen years: first, that the preference for the heterogeneity promised in the term counter-public sphere applies more to contemporary cultural politics than the romantic era, when radicals strongly emphasized unity and consensus; and second, that the historical recovery of so many women writers of the romantic era complicates the issue of women's supposed exclusion from the literary public sphere.[48] Regardless of the counter-public sphere issue, the 1994 essays suggest fruitful areas of research that will be developed in greater detail over the next decade. Edited by Jon Klancher, whose 1987 study *The Making of the English Reading Audiences, 1790–1832* parallels aspects of Habermas's work, the special issue indicated where public-sphere research would be most productive, especially in recovering women and popular radical writers. The very emphasis on publicness, coming as it did near the end of New Historicism's strongest influence, marked the paradigm shift away from the symbolic centrality of the romantic lyric. A great deal of work in the decade after 1994 took up the issue of the public sphere: Kevin Gilmartin on popular radicalism (1996); Anne Janowitz on the communitarian lyric (1998); Paul Magnuson on public romanticism (1998); Jeffrey Cox on the social network of the Cockney School (1998); Paul Keen (1999), Andrew McCann (1999) and myself (2001) on the cultural politics of the 1790s; Anne Mellor on the 'mothers' – political theorists – of the nation (2000); Jon Mee and Saree Makdisi on religious enthusiasm (2003); Kevin Binfield on the Luddites (2004); and several collections of essays, one devoted wholly to women and the Enlightenment public sphere (2001) and another to romantic sociability (2002).[49] By now public-sphere research in romantic studies is well established.

Because so much has been written on the romantic-era public sphere, I want to evaluate some of those achievements and return the discussion eventually back to Habermas.

The issue of multiple public spheres versus a single sphere has pertinence for romantic-era writing in distinguishing between the bourgeois public sphere and the plebeian public sphere, which needs much more research, not as a fully autonomous counterpublic defining itself wholly against the bourgeois sphere, but as a sphere connected with but different from the bourgeois sphere. The research of Anne Mellor and others has demonstrated emphatically that women writers, as novelists, poets, political theorists and playwrights, were anything but marginal. It does not make much sense to speak of a female counterpublic when women participated extensively in the literary public sphere. The only sphere that approximates a counter-public sphere is the plebeian sphere, whose ambiguous status requires precise, nuanced attention that can only be distracted by the Negt-Kluge focus.

An area that also needs more careful examination is the tension between the literary and the political public sphere, discussed in the sixth and seventh chapters of Habermas's *Structural Transformation*; women were prominent in the former and marginalized in the latter, although the historical research on women's public lives, far from complete, may make it necessary to make adjustments in the received view that the male-dominated political sphere of coffeehouse culture before 1750 was replaced by the female-centred literary sphere after 1750. At this point, the revisionists have forced us to take a more nuanced outlook. For example, a recent essay insists that 'the Enlightenment public sphere was in fact constituted and defined by women as well as men'.[50] Habermas's information on coffeehouse culture derived from sources that idealized this culture, leaving out women's participation. However, the most recent research suggests that even including some women's participation, historians find the coffeehouse culture predominantly masculine.[51] The extent and nature of women's participation in the plebeian public sphere are also controversial. Although many historians claim that women played a minor role in radical artisan culture, the historian Anna Clark insists that 'women, too, shaped plebeian culture through their own formal institutions and informal networks'.[52] There were female friendly societies, several women unions and women enjoyed a public life outside their small crowded dwellings.[53] Disagreeing strongly with E. P. Thompson, Clark complicates our sense of the past by affirming that sectarian religion, including Methodism, provided women with cultural satisfactions that radical politics did not.[54] The work of Jon Mee and others in the area of popular religion lends support to Clark's interpretation, as it now appears that religion has been neglected.

Anne Mellor has also concluded that for middle-class women writers religion was a more meaningful cultural resource than for many of the well-known men writers who actively opposed religion. Romantic-era religion constituted important parts of the public life for men and women, both middle-class and plebeian. Women unquestionably participated in the political public sphere – in the anti-slavery and other reformist movements, at political lectures and even, like Georgiana, the Duchess of Devonshire, in elections– but this participation hardly proves that sexual inequality was irrelevant.

As empirical research has greatly complicated our sense of both the classical and later public spheres, several questions suggest themselves. Firstly, with so much diverse public activity constituting the public sphere, does it make sense to label this multiplicity as 'the' public sphere? Secondly, in the romantic era specifically, was publicity cohesively integrated as 'a' public or were there rather multiple publics that did not necessarily share a focus? These questions require a methodological and a theoretical answer. Methodologically, empirical research has to probe the specificity and inner-logic of each manifestation of publicness, without forcing historical description into any preconceived configuration. Also, however, the dialogical and dialectical nature of public discourse necessitates linking each public expression with those it contests and aligns with, as no public discourse exists wholly unto itself. Theoretically, the unity of a public sphere posits a discursive site within which diverse meanings circulate, interact and modify one another in relation to a private sphere, on the one hand, and the state, on the other. Just as multiplicity is taken for granted in the private sphere, it is theoretically coherent if also abstract to use the singular for the public. On the other hand, recent public-sphere research, in order to stress the contested nature of the public sphere, has described multiple public spheres, not a single one, as singleness suggests a monolithic quality that is not empirically evident. This approach is also theoretically coherent in its consistent focus on the conflict along various axes of gender, class, religion and so on. The level at which cohesiveness exists in the diverse romantic-era public sphere is abstract, as the public sphere is positioned between the private sphere and the state, and semiotic, consisting of a common idiom for discussing important cultural issues: constitution, nation (what constituted Englishness and Britishness), liberty, corruption, sensibility, ambition, domestic virtues, rights, slavery and so on. Jane Austen, the Tory daughter of an Anglican clergyman, deployed 'sense and sensibility' in ways comprehensible to artisan Painites, middle-class rational Dissenters and liberal Whig magnates. They all shared a common discourse and participated, if asymmetrically, in the same public sphere. If the public sphere expanded in the revolutionary decade, then political repression, as Paul Keen observes, diminishes 'the scope and authority of the republic of letters'.[55]

The asymmetrical participation in the public sphere suggests the importance of the ways in which the public sphere was policed and regulated, one of the most well researched public-sphere topics. Government tried to stop or at least moderate the influence of the print culture that followed the cessation of pre-publication censorship in 1695, and with mixed results it used strategically chosen repression (libel and sedition prosecutions, 'gagging' acts, legislation against political associations and lecturing), bribery of editors and publishers, underwriting loyalist publications, prohibitive taxation on publications ('taxes on knowledge', as the protestors phrased it) and hostility to public education and other efforts to increase literacy. According to William St Clair, the literary public sphere was in fact effectively policed after 1695 by self-censorship, selective prosecution of libel, the intellectual property laws and authoritarian control over access to writing. The great increase in readers came only during the brief copyright window, 1774–1808, when cheap reprints became widely available.[56] Cultural assumptions concerning who could and could not participate in public were powerful but also fiercely contested, as artisans proudly and defiantly –and ironically – assumed the identity of a 'swinish multitude' in their own publications and women like Wollstonecraft and Hays refused to accept the restrictions on gender. Religious expression deemed 'enthusiastic' was culturally suspect but managed nevertheless to affirm meanings in the public sphere where prophecy, millennialism and apocalyptic expectations were taken seriously enough to provoke argument. Although there were attempts to keep the public sphere tidy with social, gender and religious restrictions, the public sphere's inner logic encouraged a wide range of discourses and permitted fundamental challenges to the restrictive rules that rested not on persuasive argument but merely customary privilege.

The conceptual complexity of the public sphere can be suggested by pointing to the *Monthly Magazine*, founded in 1796, which shared many similarities with the *Analytical Review* that I will discuss later. The *Monthly Magazine* complicates the ordinary distinctions between the literary and political spheres and fails to conform wholly to the pattern of male dominance that characterizes if not defines the Enlightenment periodical. The fact that the *Monthly Magazine*'s readership itself also wrote for the magazine made its readers-writers a kind of political association, even though the magazine for prudent reasons avoided explicit politics. Middle-class religious Dissenters dominated the journal, which was edited by John Aikin with assistance from his daughter Lucy and his sister Anna Barbauld. The three feminist Marys wrote for it – Wollstonecraft, Hays and Robinson – as did Coleridge, Godwin and Thelwall. If the journal is a 'portable coffeehouse',[57] and if the coffeehouse is part of the political public sphere, then a journal like the *Monthly Magazine* is perhaps a hybrid entity, in this case with extensive participation by women in an institution ordinarily dominated by men. During its first fifteen years, the *Monthly Magazine* helped sustain middle-class liberalism at a time when explicitly political activism was dangerous.

The public sphere with numerous institutional manifestations is where different kinds of legitimation claims get tested, challenged, rejected and redeemed. Although in the most repressive times it was not possible to question directly the actions and policies of state and church, it was both possible and ordinary to interrogate other kinds of authority in order to sustain the project of rational political inquiry. Controversies in the *Monthly Magazine* over chemistry, biblical and classical philology, political history and theology implicitly assumed that the strongest argument would prevail, not the longest purse, the most influence at court, the most powerful connections or the most impressive title. Although the government stoked the fires of Francophobic nationalism, the *Monthly* calmly examined the writing of French authors and promoted the translation of German texts, another cosmopolitan gesture. The international scope of the magazine tended to undermine a narrowly nationalistic orientation that prevailed in the 1790s and Napoleonic period. The literary public sphere, especially with journals like the *Monthly Magazine*, permitted a politics of culture that was sophisticated, self-confident and ultimately effective, if we judge effectiveness in terms of a social group getting many of the things it wanted: abolition of slavery, religious toleration and complete civil rights for religious minorities, greater economic liberalism, more sexual equality, parliamentary and educational reform, and in general the authority of scientific rationalism over 'superstition' and 'custom'.

The logic of the public sphere usually favoured and sometimes threatened cosmopolitanism, mostly for reasons of social class. Liberal cosmopolitanism substitutes trade and economic development for the incentive of war, but the 'moral economy' of customary norms for wages and prices appealed primarily to the labouring classes, whose participation in the public sphere was both inevitable and morally urgent. On issues like the Corn Laws the middle class and working class collaborated, but the divide between the classes on trade unions, factory legislation, poor laws and other social issues was a chasm rarely bridged. Whereas liberal dogma insisted upon the long view when unemployment, food shortages and depression were the consequence of market forces, the working class that actually suffered found more attractive populist appeals to protectionism or xenophobic nationalism. Working-class socialism was more cosmopolitan than middle-class liberalism, however, especially during revolutionary periods when class solidarity provided models for action and promised genuine results. Prior to 1832 the discussion of economic policy and philosophy was serious, fundamental, diverse and broadly speculative. Thomas Spence, Godwin, Charles Hall, Paine, Owen and Thelwall, as well as the Ricardian socialists (William Thompson, Thomas Hodgskin), reflected on the economy in ways that gave weight to both rationalistic science and the moral economy. The most fearless investigations into political economy bring Jacobin thinking to the brink of modernity with anticipations by Paine and Thelwall of social democracy, by Spence and Hall of socialism, by Godwin of anarchism and communism. Ideologically, according to Gregory Claeys, two tendencies emerged from the utopianism of the 1790s. One 'led from a new democratic form of commercial republicanism towards the more welfare-oriented forms of liberal democracy', while the 'second, scouted by Godwin and Spence, pointed towards socialist proposals for a complete community of goods in order to abolish vice and poverty, and to efforts to eliminate political conflict altogether'.[58] After 1832 popular economic theory became more predictable and rigid, exemplified by the dogmatic proponent of laissez faire, Harriet Martineau, an intellectually talented woman who came out of the same Unitarian milieu from which earlier had come the *Analytical Review* and the *Monthly Magazine*. Martineau's influential *Illustrations of Political Economy* (1832) pointed the way for the utilitarian tradition coming out of the Enlightenment and providing ideological guidance for middle-class liberalism.

To return to Habermas, it is fitting to observe that the public sphere is both an empirical reality, always imperfect, always failing to live up to its ideals and a politically normative necessity within the modern world. Moreover, there is no substitute for the public sphere that, in its various manifestations, permits society to talk to itself, to interrogate its policies and values, to defend and revise its practices, to describe how the impersonal forces of 'system' – the bureaucratic state and the market-driven economy – affect experience. Just as the public sphere is always constrained by pressures from the state and other sources of coercion, the public sphere is periodically renewed by insurgent and novel discourses and social movements. Theoretical attempts to dismiss the public sphere in its classical period and even now as worthlessly 'phantom', incapable of generating adequate criticism of an unjust society, are subject to performative contradiction and are weakened by the absence of any alternative model of social self-correction. Modern political societies with extremely weak public spheres lacking the liberal freedoms of press, assembly and speech must rely on authoritarian elites who have proven to be less reliably 'benevolent' than the eighteenth-century despots like Prussia's Frederick, whose bellicose policies were the background for Kant's writing on 'perpetual peace' and a cosmopolitan order. Kant was wrong in thinking that a good republic could be something other than completely democratic but he was right in thinking that only republics would move toward a cosmopolitan constitution.

One of the most important ideas in Habermas's work is the differentiation of reason (science, ethics, art), something that comes ultimately from Kant, although also by way of Max Weber. In the 'Idea for a Universal History with a Cosmopolitan Purpose' there is a strong anticipation of Habermas's emphasis on the structure of rationality that will insist upon a cosmopolitan social order, even though individuals, nations and even historical generations resist its logic. Habermas's work, early and late, has strongly defended rationality in its intersubjective aspect as it inheres in the act of argumentation and of communication. At some point the human species will understand that the cosmopolitan order is superior to competitive nationalism. Kant's faith in the rational structure of human understanding and the eventual enlightenment of human societies is reminiscent not just of Habermas's ideal speech situation but of Shelley's *Prometheus Unbound* (1820), where a similar moment of recognition that is neither arbitrary nor wilful is determined by the structure of reality, so that in Shelley's poem the process of emancipation is also a process of recollection. Kant has the hope that 'after many revolutions, with all their transforming effects, the highest purpose of nature, a universal cosmopolitan existence, will at last be realised as the matrix within which all the original capacities of the human race may develop'.[59] For Kant and Habermas it is only by means of the public sphere that cosmopolitan structures can be built.

John Thelwall and the Public Sphere

'... Socrates was found, as usual, in the places of public resort – in the workshops of the artists, and among the labourers in the manufactories, uttering seditious allegories, and condemning the desolating tyranny of the Oligarchy'. John Thelwall, *The Rights of Nature*, Letter 1 (1796)[60]

As I show in my earlier book, *Seditious Allegories*, Thelwall, like Kant, made use of and reflected upon the public sphere that was problematic because of the political repression that victimized him throughout his career. Although there was disagreement over the quality of Thelwall's poetry – Wordsworth praised it, Hazlitt belittled it – there was none about his skill as a public speaker and peerless radical[61] orator in the 1790s, and he was the inevitable choice for delivering the eulogy for his friend and fellow treason trial defendant, Thomas Hardy, before at least 20,000 mourners at Bunhill Fields in 1832. The most dangerous threat to his political lecturing before the treason trials came from John Reeves, the leader of the so-called Crown and Anchor Society, a loyalist association that assisted government prosecutions of reformers. Reeves, who tried unsuccessfully to get the grand jury to indict Thelwall, attempted as well to get a press gang to capture him for the navy, from which Thelwall was saved by the actions of Joseph Ritson the antiquarian.[62] His political lecturing was the reason Thelwall was the third treason trial defendant after his friend Thomas Hardy and his mentor Horne Tooke. As he said in a speech he wanted to deliver at his treason trial but delivered after his acquittal:

When they crushed the societies for political debate, I was the only individual who openly resisted that arbitrary measure. I was the only individual who for two years [1792–3] openly struggled for the restoration of that free discussion so essential to the preservation of liberty, but so dangerous to a corrupt and vicious Administration; and when I found it impossible to communicate my own resolution to the minds of others, I stepped forward to supply the deficiency to the utmost of my power, and to revive, in another shape, that investigation which others had so timidly abandoned. This is the reason they seek my destruction [for treason] – this is the crime I have committed.[63]

Acquitted of treason in December 1794 after seven months in the Tower and Newgate Prison, Thelwall resumed his successful political lectures in 1795 at the Beaufort Buildings until the Two Acts – designed especially to suppress his lectures – forced him to lecture on Roman history rather than current events, although the auditors on his provincial lecture tour had little difficulty discerning the political allegory. Barely observing the letter and defying the spirit of the Gagging Acts of 1795, Thelwall in 1796–7 lectured on classical history in East Anglia where loyalists, sailors and soldiers disturbed his speeches and attempted to kidnap him and impress him into the navy. Thelwall's own skill in self-defence as well as the timely intervention of friends prevented him from harm or worse. Although the Pitt government did not order Thelwall's elimination, it certainly did nothing to discourage local authorities from acting boldly to rid the nation of an 'acquitted felon'.[64] After political lecturing became physically impossible in 1797, Thelwall re-entered public life in the early years of the new century as a speech therapist and elocutionary expert, correcting speech impediments and training people in the art of public speaking. When the movement for parliamentary reform revived after Waterloo, Thelwall took over the *Champion* newspaper, turning it from 1818 into a vehicle advocating radical reform – universal manhood suffrage – until the threat of a libel prosecution in 1822 forced him yet again to retreat from activism. This retreat, only temporary, was followed in 1825 by a period as the last liberal editor of the *Monthly Magazine*, and then, in 1826, by his assumption of the proprietorship and editorship of the *Panoramic Miscellany*. When he died in Bath in his sixty-ninth year he was in the middle of yet another lecture tour, concluding his life as he had lived it, in the public world.[65]

Political repression and the cultural reaction against so-called Jacobinism were the conditions under which Thelwall had to lecture and write. Thelwall and others in the London Corresponding Society courageously circumvented the repression, turning their criminal trials into political trials, the transcripts of which became artful and comic anti-government propaganda. Allegory became the preferred literary form to exploit ambiguity for legal and aesthetic purposes. During Daniel Isaac Eaton's trial for publishing Thelwall's satire in *The Politics for the People* on a beheaded regal gamecock, the defence attorney reminded the jury of the difference between symbolic and real action, abstract and actual references to political figures.[66] The repressive atmosphere made even apolitical texts seem sinister, the playful gothic romance *The Monk* (1796) being read at the time as far more blasphemous and anti-religious than the novel merited, largely because readers associated the anti-religious themes with the French Revolution.

The political repression exploited a great fear: of popular violence that would come from the subversive education of the populace. Continuing the Enlightenment tradition of democratizing culture, a major reformist project was making texts accessible to a wide audience that, ordinarily, because of their limited opportunities for learning, would never have had the chance to read them. Taking advantage of what William St Clair has called the copyright window of 1774–1808, radicals made popularly available inexpensive periodicals and pamphlets that reprinted extracts from authors whose copyright had expired. Excerpts from older and contemporary authors were featured in Thomas Spence's *Pig's Meat* (1793–6) and Daniel Isaac Eaton's *Politics for the People* (1793–5), both of which became digests of Jacobin writing. The main goal of the London Corresponding Society from 1792 to 1798, according to Michael T. Davis, was educating people in their political rights by producing 'democratic literature': over eighty pamphlets and broadsides, in addition to two periodicals, *The Politician* (1794–5) and *The Moral and Political Magazine* (1796–7).[67] Thelwall himself popularized classical and republican writing in his essays and lectures. His edition of Walter Moyle's *An Essay Upon the Constitution of the Roman Government* (1698) is a radical translation of that seventeenth-century treatise, as he re-titled it *Democracy Vindicated* (1796), translated the Latin into English and explained the historical references in long notes.[68] St Clair points out that after 1774 a flood of anthologies and abridgements carried out the process by which a 'shared memory' of canonical literature was created.[69] What the political radicals did at the time was part of an overall cultural popularization made possible by the relaxation of the intellectual property laws. Thelwall ironically asks why government ministers permitted inexpensive publications, for they spread enlightenment: 'why did you not make it high treason to propose to publish histories in cheap editions, like these [Hume's histories]? Such books, though written by *high-flown* Aristocrats themselves, are strong advocates for reformation'.[70] Thelwall does not have the Foucauldian fear that popularized texts would subject the readers to repressive disciplinary structures; rather, he has faith that the readers will make good use of the new information to which they now have access. Like Kant, Thelwall assumes the existence of a *sensus communis*. Godwin feared popularization because he considered that orderly enlightenment required the non-violent transmission of knowledge only through a gradual process of education; accordingly he suspected popularization as well as political associations and public meetings as leading to intellectually shallow political consciousness that was not securely rational. The London Corresponding Society itself was an object of contention between Godwin and Thelwall because, whereas for the latter the plebeian public sphere was a source of hopeful education and enlightenment, a normative process of democratic culture, but for Godwin it was dangerously uncontrolled and open to demagoguery.[71] If they disagreed about the plebeian public sphere and popular oratory, they both had a naive faith in print culture: 'It is easier to sweep the whole human race from the surface of the earth than to stop the torrent of information and political improvement, when the art of printing has attained its present height'.[72] Although Thelwall wrote that statement, Godwin could have authored it just as well.

In the 1790s, and then in the Waterloo-Peterloo period, democratic insurgence struggled against a repression that eventually prevailed. The effects of repression, which were felt everywhere not just among the politically active, were strenuously resisted by activists in the London Corresponding Society. According to an overly optimistic Thelwall, Burke's *Reflections on the Revolution in France* 'made more democrats, among the thinking part of mankind, than all the works written in answer to it'.[73] Burke's *Reflections*, however, also confirmed the anti-democratic views of many in the leisure and professional classes, turning them decisively against not just the French Revolution but the Enlightenment that was assumed to have been the Revolution's foundation. At a popular level Hannah More's government-sponsored propaganda, the *Cheap Repository Tracts*, were distributed in tens of thousands of copies between 1795 and 1798 to the labouring classes.[74] That More's propaganda had no ideological effect on its readers would be surprising and doubtful because one has to acknowledge the extent to which the loyalists also made skilful use of the literary market for their own reactionary purposes. Although some readers must have resisted the intended meaning of Burke and More, many more evidently were persuaded by the effective rhetoric wielded by two highly competent writers.

Thelwall believed that the public sphere inherently strengthened enlightenment and reform: 'nothing can be fatal to truth but silence (or commotion). Do but write or speak, no matter how absurd the principles you set out upon, and it [truth] must triumph'.[75] The *Analytical Review*, remarking on a provincial literary society, shared Thelwall's enthusiasm for the growth of the public sphere: 'Societies instituted for the purpose of a free communication of ideas, whether in conversation or writing, may be ranked among the most useful means of improving knowledge. It is to be regarded as a favourable indication of the progress of science and letters in the present age.'[76] The London Corresponding Society's *Moral and Political Magazine* (1797) remarked enthusiastically on the forty-one reading societies for 'labouring people' in western Scotland.[77] Thelwall considered the British reformist culture superior to the French because the French salons were too polished and the British literary circles were more 'bold, resolute, bristling and disputatious' with 'thronged and promiscuous audiences' in the 'theatre and halls of assembly'.[78] Unlike Wordsworth and Coleridge, he was optimistic about the new urban, industrial culture in Britain, for he saw humanity as naturally communicative: 'whatever presses men together, therefore, though it may generate some vices, is favourable to the diffusion of knowledge'. Viewing the modern city as a new polis like ancient Athens, Thelwall remarks that 'every large workshop and manufactory is a sort of political society, which no act of parliament can silence'.[79] Over the course of time, despite repression's ephemeral victories, the urban culture will become more democratic and enlightened because of the irresistible power of rationality and the public sphere.[80]

Unlike the enlightening process conceived by Godwin and Kant, who preferred an exclusively literary and polite exchange of views, Thelwall conceived of enlightenment as an agonistic process of public discussion, debate and face-to-face argument:

> unless you uphold that every man has a right to his opinion, you cannot be a friend to genuine liberty and justice; you are hostile to human intellect: for though you think you are right, the man in direct opposition thinks he is right also, and if you want no other judgment than your own opinion to justify coercion, universal massacre must ensue, society must be unhinged, chaos return, and 'darkness be the burier of the dead'.[81]

The quotation from the Earl of Northumberland's speech in *2 Henry IV* (I.i.160) ironically criticizes feudal constraints on democratic expression – constraints that Burke so hyperbolically defended. The premise of mutual toleration – for any kind of opinions, including religious (and anti-religious)[82] – leads to an affirmation of a cosmopolitan order like Kant's. As Thelwall explains in one of his political lectures, we derive pleasure from rational inquiry and public discussion because we sympathetically connect with our fellow creatures, regardless of differences in physical appearance, nationality, language, religion or party. Pursuing knowledge, 'man feels and enjoys the noble superiority of his nature – his faculties expand, his heart dilates, his sense acquires a keener sensibility – he looks abroad on the universe, and every part of it expands and brightens; while a crowd of pleasures rush upon his imagination, to which the eye of Ignorance is for ever closed'. The intellectual inquirer experiences an affective bond with others that Thelwall describes in the idiom of enthusiasm and sensibility. 'He looks in the face of his fellow creature; and he sees indeed a brother – or a part rather of his own existence; another self – He contemplates in every individual the faculties of sufferance and enjoyment, and feels one nerve of sympathy, connecting him with the whole intellectual universe.'[83] Thelwall conceives political virtue not as nationalistic but cosmopolitan, oriented toward promoting 'happiness of mankind' and the welfare of 'Fellow Citizens of the world' and not 'Citizens of a town or district'.[84]

What starts with rational inquiry ends with cosmopolitan enthusiasm, as Thelwall mixes philosophical rationalism with the emotional style of plebeian forms of political and religious dissent. The very word 'enthusiasm' in the 1790s evoked unrespectable radicalism, as Jon Mee has explained.[85] Although a secularist, Thelwall uses a religious-like language to describe the workings of the cosmopolitan imagination:

> could we persuade mankind to consider the universe, as in reality it is, one continuous system of animated being, could we persuade the individual to think himself only a part, a portion of that great, and, as far as we can perceive, immortal existence, think how those energies would be prolonged, and reflect what must be the beneficent consequences! ... Let any individual who has once felt this enthusiastic ardour consider what he has attained by its means, and it is impossible that he should conclude that ardour and enthusiasm are fruitless.[86]

Solidarity with people leads to an emotional identification with nature, a move that invites comparison with Wordsworth's title for the eighth book of the 1805 *Prelude*: 'Love of Nature Leading to Love of Mankind'. For Thelwall it is the other way around, love of mankind leading to love of nature; Thelwall has no option of solitary fulfilment within nature, an option which Wordsworth has to work hard to get out of.

From 1793 until 1815 the political reality of Britain was nationalistic war, loyalist propaganda, organized burnings of Thomas Paine's effigy, invasion scares and of course political repression. An opportune time for promoting cosmopolitanism it was not, but Thelwall and others associated with the London Corresponding Society and similar organizations routinely countered nationalism and war. Thelwall mocks nationalistic historians as 'romance writers' of fiction, inculcating hatred for the French and other foreigners and inspiring excessive devotion to everything English. Ancestor worship is another aspect of nationalism that does not hold up to critical scrutiny, as Thelwall shows that nationalism is structurally identical for every nation, with absurd exaggerations of one's own virtues and absurd exaggerations of everyone else's shortcomings. The childishness of nationalism he heavily stresses, as cosmopolitan sympathy is more appropriate from grown ups. He mockingly reduces nationalism to its most bellicose essence: 'remembering the cut-throat virtues of my ancestors, I must be sure to carry on the same trade of cutting throats in my time also'.[87] If nationalism is one way of remembering, radical commemoration is another, cosmopolitan way. The celebrations at the Crown and Anchor Tavern commemorating the treason trial acquittals began fortuitously on Guy Fawkes Day, 5 November 1795 and continued for a half-century until 1842. These important rituals by which the radical culture reproduced its values constitute the counter-history to nationalistic history. In addition to commemorative dinners, memorials were a way of creating an alternative history to the official one embodied in Westminster Abbey and state-sponsored statues. Monuments honouring the reformists and victims of repression in the 1790s were constructed only later in the nineteenth century – the Edinburgh's Scottish Political Martyrs Monument for the LCS leaders transported to Botany Bay (Margarot, Muir, Gerrald, Palmer and Skirving) in the 1840s, and the two Kensal Green memorials, the Robert Owen Memorial in 1879 and the Reformers' Memorial in 1885. These physical sites of remembrance sustain a dissident political culture. For, as Iain McCalman remarks, 'to be without a memorial is often to be lost to history'.[88] A similar kind of counter-history that clarifies the radical political culture is the selective idealization of ancestors – republicans like Algernon Sidney, after whom Thelwall named his son, and rebels like Wat Tyler, whose story in Southey's version was a staple of nineteenth-century radical education. Indeed, the nineteenth-century radical canon itself – Paine, Volney, Voltaire, Holbach, Byron, Shelley, Owen – illustrates effectively the cosmopolitan quality of the political culture.

Because of Lord Eldon's ruling (1817) that seditious publications like Southey's *Wat Tyler* did not have copyright protection, radical pirate publishers rushed to make cheap editions of the poet laureate's embarrassingly subversive text and over time published other texts lacking copyright protection: Shelley's poetry, especially *Queen Mab* (1813) and the popular songs; Byron's poetry, especially *Don Juan* (1819–24) and *The Vision of Judgment* (1822); Volney's *Ruins of Empire* (1791; trans, 1795), one of the favourite pieces of reading for Mary Shelley's monster; Godwin's *Political Justice* (1793); Lawrence's *Lectures on Anatomy* (1823); Elihu Palmer's *Principles of Nature* (1801); Robert Owen's *New View of Society* (1814) and of course Paine's *Rights of Man* (1791–2).[89] This canon, both predictable in some ways and strangely arbitrary in others (where are Thelwall, Cobbett and Wollstonecraft?), is religiously sceptical, anti-authoritarian, not systematically socialistic but fiercely opposed to class privilege and concentrations of wealth and power, fundamentally reflecting the radical and cosmopolitan Enlightenment. Most of the texts come out of the French Revolution in one way or another, perpetuating long into the nineteenth century the largely artisanal radicalism of the late eighteenth. As Michael T. Davis, citing Francis Place, has remarked on the London Corresponding Society, it did not succeed in realizing its political goals but it had a cultural influence in promoting reading and education among artisans.[90] The extraordinary popularity of *Don Juan* – 'read by more people in its first twenty years than any previous work of English literature'[91] – is remarkable evidence that the radical readers could enjoy a poem – a poem! – that made serious demands on them, especially in terms of irony, digression and narrative complexity. There is no better text to illustrate a cosmopolitan imagination: an Italian poetic form (ottava rima), a Spanish hero/ antihero, a narrative that takes place in numerous European locales, ending up in England. The poem's dizzying ironies anticipate the boldest moves of deconstruction, relegating nationalism to an impossibly simplistic ideology without compelling authority.

In the 1790s the 'principle of universal manhood suffrage raised the spectre of mob rule and frightened most men of property', according to H. T. Dickinson.[92] The enlightened eighteenth century prior to the 1790s was also socially conservative, even if middle-class Dissenters and unpropertied plebeians could become reader-writers of the British Enlightenment. When the leisure and professional classes largely abandoned the Enlightenment in 1790s, Jacobins like Thelwall deepened the Enlightenment with greater egalitarianism. Loyalist nationalism replaced the cosmopolitan, international, encyclopaedic Enlightenment that had been a cultural consensus for the learned classes.[93] Similarly, it was during the 1790s that philosophical thought itself became suspect as unreliable and perhaps French; the new consensus was an anti-intellectual nationalism.[94] The rise of nationalism, localism and particularism, and the concomitant decline of internationalism and rationalist rigour took place violently and coercively in an atmosphere of panic, not reasoned discussion.

The great cultural fear that provided the legitimating structure of feeling for massive political repression was of popular violence fuelled by radical education. Perhaps the Pitt repression was excessive – even Tories like Southey and Coleridge thought so – but many others like Walter Scott believed that the repression was necessary to suppress a truly revolutionary threat. Most modern historians dismiss the idea of a revolutionary danger but there is a difference between retrospective and lived history. Looking back on the period from a scholarly distance, J. R. Dinwiddy concludes that a revolution in the 1790s would have been possible only if three things happened to coincide: a French invasion, an Irish rebellion and severe economic distress.[95] For the people in the leisure and professional classes living at the time, however, the most fearful aspect of democratic reformism, exaggerated or not, was the social radicalism of a growing public sphere. The stunning popularity of Paine's *Rights of Man*, coupled with the huge increase in cheap publications after 1774, restructured literacy and provoked an intensive campaign of counter-propaganda by loyalist forces. The unprecedented sales of parts one and two – easily in the tens of thousands within two years – illustrated that the literary market for democratic literature was far greater than anyone at the time had imagined.[96] Either Paine tapped into an already existing audience that was merely waiting for the right text or Paine's essay created this audience.

The 1790s pattern of democratic insurgence and reactionary panic repeated itself in the Waterloo-Peterloo period. Repression was effective in the short run but it failed to stem the growth of the plebeian public sphere which was able to sustain an entire political counterculture by the 1830s. Thelwall is an example of someone who spoke and wrote to two antagonistic audiences divided by class. His ability to mediate between the two, at least during the 1790s, suggests a historical plausibility to Habermas's idealized public sphere, able to suspend the power of class to exercise reason in open dialogue.

The *Analytical Review* as Cosmopolitan Text

The paradigmatic shift in what a quarterly Review should accomplish is evident in the 1802 *Edinburgh Review*. Whereas the older Reviews (the *Monthly*, the *Critical* and the *Analytical*) aimed for encyclopaedic inclusiveness of published material and valued impartial description of books over critical commentary, the *Edinburgh* – to be followed by the *Quarterly Review* in 1809 – published far fewer, longer reviews that avoided quotations and analytical descriptions. The new emphasis, whether the in Whiggish *Edinburgh* or the Tory *Quarterly*, was authoritative opinion; the reader of the new Reviews was not the Enlightenment reader-writer of the *Monthly Magazine* but instead a consumer of fashionable maxims. The new reader was not so much interested in actually reading any of the books reviewed; rather, the intention was to learn enough to play an opinionated role and to appropriate the Review's pretension to omniscience. While the older Review was 'an objective chronicle of cultural progress', according to Derek Roper,[97] the new Review practised the making and unmaking of signs unanchored to the world of things; it was the mind itself with which the new, romantic Review was concerned. In the words of Jon Klancher, 'The middle-class audience achieves its sense of cultural power by continually dismantling and reconstituting signs, but not without a recurring anxiety about its own acts'. A 'fear of saturation, repetition, and fragmentation' haunts the semiotic struggle of the middle-class readers and critics.[98]

By exploring further the distinctive features of the Enlightenment intellectual journals that Roper perceptively describes, and by expanding upon some of Klancher's insights into the characteristic qualities of the romantic Reviews, it will be possible to identify the *Analytical Review* in its historical context. The contrast between Enlightenment inclusiveness and romantic omniscience derives from something Roper mentions and William St Clair describes in great detail: namely, the impossibility of achieving inclusiveness when the sheer number of publications became too large. As the quantity of publications to be reviewed increased fourfold from mid-century to 1800,[99] Reviews faced a daunting task to turn all those texts into useable knowledge that followed coherent disciplinary categories.[100] One finds some desperation in William Enfield's suggestion to the editor of the *Monthly Review*: 'It would be better to give a *single line* to

many articles, or even as formerly the bare titles, than to omit them entirely'.[101]
The Review performs the function of a chronicle, a historical record of the
congregated intellect of Europe. Omitting mention of a book, however trivial,
does violence to the chronicle-function of the Review. A single line, even just
a title, is retrievable by some future scholar who could find something of value
in what at the time did not seem important. Even after the number of publications exceeded the ability of the Reviews to cover them, periodicals such as the
Monthly Magazine did indeed record without comment whatever was published
that particular month, well into the nineteenth century. The intellectual Review,
including the *Monthly Magazine*, was marked by both time and timelessness, as
the most current issue was destined to become part of a bound volume, which
would become part of a continuous and open-ended sequence of volumes, to
be kept and not destroyed as newspapers were. The Reviews did indeed include
sections of 'news' that were meant to be historical records. The *Annual Register*, devoted largely to representing current history, was another Enlightenment
cultural product, founded in 1758 by Edmund Burke; the *Annual Register* was
meant to be saved and consulted as a chronicle of the times. Its status as impartial
chronicle, however, was challenged by the *New Annual Register* in 1780, which
disputed the political orientation of the precursor journal. The *Analytical* took
the *Annual Register* of 1791 to task for numerous errors: the *Annual Register*,
it asserted, violated the norm of inclusiveness by neglecting important political events, barely treating the Birmingham riots and the history of France and
Poland; its historical narrative paid too much attention to motives rather than
deeds; it represented the Burke/Fox debates in a slanted way; it lapsed stylistically into 'low colloquial expressions not consistent with the dignity of history';
it harmed the public interest through the lateness of its publication; and even its
poetry selection was marred by political bias.[102] The *Analytical*'s criticisms here
were not simply the routine partisan retaliations, for the journal not only promoted the ideal of impartiality but practised this ideal when it was inconvenient.
During the most heated months of the pamphlet war on Burke's *Reflections on the
Revolution in France* and his other inflammatory writings and speeches against
the French Revolution and religious Dissenters, the *Analytical Review* praised
Burke's *Letter to Sir Hercules Langrishe* (1792) because of Burke's overall position on religious toleration and the Irish poor.[103] This is a good example of the
Analytical's exercising the cosmopolitan imagination: suspected to be Catholic,
certainly Irish, Burke had notoriously vilified both the French Revolution itself
and one of rational Dissent's intellectual heroes, Richard Price, and prejudice
against him was strong among the English Protestant Dissenters who wrote and
read the journal.

The goal of maintaining an annual historical record of political, military, dip-
lomatic and legal proceedings, which began in the Enlightenment, continues up

to the present in a variety of annual registers – almanacs, encyclopaedia appendices and so on. The chronicle of intellectual progress through published writing that the Enlightenment Reviews attempted, however, has no contemporary analogue. Following the differentiation of reason into the natural sciences, law and ethics, and the arts – all of which have become increasingly specialized and complex – there is no literary form that can contain an evaluative overview of the mind's development. Although each individual discipline has its own methods of chronicling and registering its domain of knowledge, the Enlightenment dream of comprehensive knowledge was actually rather short-lived, for it seems to have become insupportable by 1802. One has to ask this question: if it was becoming apparent for both practical and theoretical reasons that comprehensiveness and encyclopaedic breadth were futile goals for an intellectual Review, why then did the *Analytical*, initiated and written by rational Dissenters, political progressives, the most highly educated and culturally advanced people in London, emphatically reaffirm comprehensiveness and impartial 'analysis' – that is, the objective description of a text's parts? The intellectual avant-garde, not reactionaries, wrote for the *Analytical*, even though a fundamental dimension of their overall project was unsound.

One answer is that the avant-garde was actually cognizant of the project's vulnerability and reaffirmed the old model of knowledge in an attempt to strengthen what they perceived as weakening. When the *Analytical* changed its format in a small way in January 1797, almost a decade after its founding, it introduced a 'Retrospect of the Active World' that anticipates the opinionated essays of the *Edinburgh* and the 'lead article' of romantic journalism. These retrospective essays, not tied to a single publication, described broad trends in a particular field, from the anthropological study of religion one month and the history of technology another, with no apparent logical sequencing, in addition to supplying some current information on international political news. It is not so much that these essays seem hastily composed, which they do, but that their purpose seems uncertain. They stand out as different from the other review-essays and declare their importance accordingly but they are also searching for a coherent identity. The essay for August 1797 describes agricultural improvements in great detail and then reflects on the process of progress itself. Citing Dugald Stewart and Condorcet as authorities, the author describes how the new knowledge of a single mind influences a few, who then educate the learned class, until eventually the new knowledge is diffused through the society as common sense. The essay then moves on to a current political event whose importance he assumes is self-evident, the peace negotiations between France and Britain. The current diplomacy leads then to a reflection on the recent writing on 'perpetual peace', as the author evidently was familiar with Kant's essay.[104] The *Analytical* essay, which is typical of the retrospective pieces, links different realms of knowledge, in this case science and philosophy, then politics and philosophy, connecting the concretely historical with the abstractly theoretical. The essay struggles with arbitrariness, for there is no compelling reason to be discussing agricultural improvements in the first place and the topic of the peace negotiations is just one of many that are current. The philosophical threads of the essay are the most interesting but the least developed. Neither the agricultural improvements nor the peace negotiations can explain themselves; they both require some kind of illuminating context that philosophical discourse provides but the essay restrains what could give it more coherence and unity. The *Analytical's* principal difficulty is reconciling two different tendencies, its commitment to encyclopaedic breadth, which sacrifices unity for the sake of inclusiveness, and its commitment to rationality itself, which demands coherence.

The *Analytical* inherited its contradictory agenda from the great Whig and Tory Reviews that had been publishing since mid-century. Both the *Monthly Review* and the *Critical Review* reflected the European Enlightenment's cosmopolitanism, despite the rivalry and traditional animosity between Britain and France. The *Analytical* is remarkable for maintaining its cosmopolitanism in the 1790s when nationalism was reshaping British culture. The journal's founder and editor, Thomas Christie, spent more time in Paris than in London after the French Revolution began, forcing the already busy Joseph Johnson to assume editorial duties.[105] Both before and after the declaration of war in January 1793 the *Analytical* not only followed the events in France with careful attention and sympathy (and sometimes enthusiasm) but also explored in depth the theoretical complexities of the revolution – not just the Burke controversy (which it covered thoroughly), but the entire pamphlet war of ideas. The philosophical and religious leader of the journal, if one had to identify such a presence, would have to be Joseph Priestley, all of whose publications were prominently reviewed and discussed. The Birmingham riots of July 1791, which drove Priestley out of the city, were intensively studied as late as the June 1793 issue and were still a topic in December 1795.[106] Priestley's immigration to the United States in 1794, closely reported in the *Analytical*, hardly added to the nationalistic perspective of the journal, as Mary Wollstonecraft, who lived in revolutionary Paris for several years, remained the prominent literary reviewer and Alexander Geddes, a liberal Catholic priest from Scotland, the principal religious reviewer.

The journal's cosmopolitanism derived partially from the cosmopolitan personnel that wrote for it but mostly from the *Analytical's* intellectual commitments. Every issue devoted an entire section to 'Literary Intelligence of Europe', which discussed the most current scientific, philosophical and poetic publications and debates in France and Germany, as well as other European countries. Foreign books, if deemed important enough, were routinely reviewed in the main section of the journal, which as a matter of course reviewed books for their ideas not national origins. Thomas Christie's preface for the *Analytical* identifies the 'true idea of a Literary Journal' as giving 'the history of the republic of letters'.[107] This republic, it hardly needs explaining, is international and without political partisanship. When the *British Critic* announced its existence in 1793, it declared it would follow the norms for Enlightenment Reviews except that it promised not to oppose 'the favourite opinions of our countrymen'.[108] Such a promise, not surprising from an Anglican, Tory periodical, for the sake of nationalism violated the Enlightenment commitment to truth and reason. In the *Analytical's* entire preface there is no mention of England and Britain but Christie recognizes that a conflict is inevitable between the intellectual elite – 'the learned and thinking few' – and the public readership, and that the journal must compromise not its ideal of impartiality but its ideal of pure analytical description. The public at large requires more of the reviewer's critical opinions than are needed by the 'learned few', who could be served adequately by using appropriate conceptual categories to provide accurate descriptive accounts of a text's most salient features.[109] The *British Critic* would leave the prejudices of its readers unchallenged but the *Analytical* promised only to spare its readers some intellectual labour they might not be able to perform.

The *Analytical* conceives its readers to be independent fellow citizens in the international republic of letters who were capable of thinking for themselves. The difference between the intellectual elite and the public at large being not essential, the reviews are largely descriptive (according to Derek Roper, three-quarters of each review is devoted to summary and quotation, only one quarter to critical opinion).[110] Its readers are also imagined as capable of being engaged by any topic within the encyclopaedia of knowledge. The lead article of every issue receives emphasis simply for being the first but also for being almost always the longest review. A survey of lead articles for the first eight issues reveals an unpredictable diversity of subject matter: biblical textual criticism, Gibbon's *Decline and Fall*, scientific reports on electricity, an anthropological description the Pelew Islands in the Pacific, the Scottish philosopher Thomas Reid on epistemology, a biography of the explorer Captain Cook, a new edition of the Greek poet Anacreon and a ornithological report from a scientific society. The only pattern is the apparent absence of pattern, with the exception perhaps of contemporary imaginative literature, which only once receives a lead review in eleven years: the prominent dramatist Richard Cumberland's religious epic, *Calvary* (June 1792). Other than that rather unusual exception, the closest to English literature that a lead review gets is Boswell's *Life of Johnson*, which heads the July 1791 issue, and Malone's edition of Shakespeare (August 1791). Lead reviews of translated literature were possible if it was not contemporary, for example the translation of a Sanskrit epic (August 1790).

Behind that apparent absence of pattern, however, is actually a strong interest in the objective world. The *Analytical* loves to study the world outside the individual self: natural phenomena like electricity and birds, places and people that are unfamiliar, histories of people who have done extraordinary things. The literature which is of most interest – Cumberland's epic excepted – is high canonical (the Bible, classical literature), that which presents philological difficulties for which scientific procedures are useful. Returning to Jon Klancher's point that the romantic readers and reviewers assumed a process of making and unmaking signs, unanchored by a world of things, one notices that the *Analytical* readers and reviewers assumed that there was a truth anchored in or at least mediated by things. The world of things fascinated them, whereas the romantics were more interested, according to Klancher, in the arbitrary, subjective constructions of things by mind and language. The late-Enlightenment worldview, however, was far from naïve, as attested by Humean scepticism and Kant's argument against being able to know the thing-in-itself. The *Analytical* reviewer experienced the anxiety of modernity in specific ways that took the project of Enlightenment for granted. One anxiety was that coercion threatened to overwhelm Enlightenment, especially in the form of modern warfare. 'All war, but especially such a war as the present [March 1798], which unites all the arts of refinement with the most savage ferocity, disheartens, and mocks the labours of the humane philosopher, who aims to exalt the excellence of our nature, by exercising our powers and regulating our passions; and to make us happy by making us wise and good.' Scientific progress has made war more destructive, while war itself has stimulated further scientific, technological and commercial advances. The same war that is deadly to humane philosophy seems to be the motor of a paradoxical advancement unrelated to justice. The most moving and effective of the monthly 'Retrospect' essays, this meditation on war and modernity fears the irrelevance of moral norms in a world governed by deadly force, not the force of the most persuasive argument.[111] Another major anxiety is coping with the surprise of the new during a period of accelerated change. An article on the scientific classification of insects remarks that in modern entomology the 'divisions and subdivisions are crumbling every hour into dust amid the shock of discovery and new arrangement'.[112] Knowledge that depends on empirical investigation, the Baconian project of Enlightenment that defines the orientation of the *Analytical*, has an open-endedness that requires frequent revision and adjustment, if not sometimes complete rethinking.[113] The rhetoric of 'shock' registers the unease with an uncertainty that is structural, not just accidental and occasional. The world of things to which the Enlightenment journal is dedicated also generates anxieties that will sooner or later make especially appealing the romantic excursions into subjectivity.

Although there were moments of doubt and unease, the *Analytical* engaged the external world with fervent attention, keen to acquire and assimilate new knowledge. Enthusiasm for the foreign runs throughout all the volumes of the *Analytical*. In addition to the Sanskrit epic mentioned already, there were reviews of books on Turkish literature (February 1789) and the Turkish empire (July 1798); the aborigines of Australia (May 1789); Dahomey (July 1789), southern Africa (August 1789), northern Africa (May 1790), the African interior (May 1797); the interior of America (August 1789), Jamaica (February 1791), the history of the West Indies (August 1793), Jamaican maroons (March 1797), St Domingo (June 1797) and Grenada (December 1796); the history of 'Hindustan' (November 1789), the Hindus (April 1791), travel in India (May 1793), William Jones's 'Asiatic researches' (March 1794) and Hindu literature (October 1794); Gibraltar (January 1792); antiquities of Ireland (May 1792); travel in Arabia (January 1793); anthropological studies of ancient religion (March 1796), Islam (October 1797) and a cross-cultural anthropological study of morals (May 1799). There was a range of views on the non-English and non-European by the books' authors and the *Analytical* reviewers themselves, from liberal and racist imperialists to republican opponents of empire who harshly repudiated racism in both its crude popular form and emergent scientific form (see Chapter 4). The *Analytical* also paid considerable attention to Jewish issues, the situation of Jewry in Europe and the prospects for emancipation (see Chapter 5). The main schools of thought on locating the non-European in a historical framework, articulated in a review of 1793, were the religious and the secular, as the former assumed God instructed humanity in the proper moral code at various points in history and the latter assumed that humanity without divine assistance taught itself over time. The religious perspective implicitly justified imperial conquest of peoples uninstructed in divinely sanctioned ideas.[114] Most but not all the *Analytical* reviewers opposed the conquest of foreign people.

The *Analytical* attended also to the discussion of cosmopolitan theory. A review of Anacharsis Cloots's *La République Universelle, ou Addresse aux Tyrannicides* (1792) (The Universal Republic or Address to the Tyrannicides), which follows the model of impartial descriptive analysis by withholding any critical commentary, provides substantial quotations and clear summary. The Prussian nobleman who had renounced his privileges and joined the French Revolution argued in the 210-page book for a universal republic and the abolition of national distinctions, or, at the very least, a single European republic. Rejecting Saint-Pierre's concept of a congress of sovereigns, Cloots 'wishes that all the barriers might be thrown open, and all the fences levelled, which by separating have hitherto been so fatal to the interests of the human family'. Favouring 'one immense city' and its liberal culture instead of the provincial, narrow culture of scattered small towns, he wants a republic of the world to overcome mankind's petty differences and to replace war with productive association. His cosmopolitan order requires a single language for all, and instead of an artificial language, it is the French language that he proposes as the unifying tongue. 'A society never makes war upon itself, and the human race will live in peace the moment that it forms only one nation'.[115] That this book, available only in French, should get a 1,500-word review almost entirely in the author's own words and ideas illustrates how open the *Analytical* was to radical ideas like Cloots's. The reviewer had to have gone out of his way to obtain a text so removed from the mainstream. The review attends to the ideas and not the exotic personality of Cloots because the *Analytical* wanted these *ideas* to be taken seriously.

Cloots, who was beheaded in early 1794 by the Jacobins, was not the only proponent of cosmopolitan political ideas. The *Analytical* played a role in the English reception of Kant, especially in the 'Literary Intelligence' section that recorded reviews of Kantian writings in German academic journals. The reviews of Nitsch's and Willich's critical summaries of the Kantian philosophy were not favourable and did not emphasize the political ideas, but the review of the translation of 'Perpetual Peace' provided a brief summary, which was supplemented later by a short comment on Kant's *Rechtslehre* (Theory of Right) well before it got translated into English. This made note of Kant's republicanism and his looking forward to 'the future establishment of one universal republic, when the differences of nations may be settled by a permanent congress, and perpetual peace reign over the earth'.[116] Although Kant's ideas on a cosmopolitan political order were fairly well circulated among liberal readers, as both the *Monthly Magazine* and the *Monthly Review* published Thomas Beddoes's lucid summaries,[117] the *Analytical* also gave a review to an enthusiastic pamphlet by a Kantian proponent of radical Enlightenment. J. A. O'Keefe's *Essay on the Progress of Human Understanding* (1795), which included a summary of Kant's philosophy, strongly praised the enlightened religion that was developing in Germany and France, as there was no greater obstacle to political progress than religious delusion.[118] At a time of war and loyalist propaganda, the *Analytical* deliberately offers its readers an aggressively cosmopolitan essay by an unknown author.

If the *Analytical*'s cosmopolitanism was compromised to some extent by its occasional acceptance of colonialism, racism and empire, its fierce opposition to the war with France and the repression of domestic democratic radicals earned the journal both notoriety and attention from the government, which moved against the editor/publisher Joseph Johnson in 1798. Why the government decided to target Johnson and the *Analytical Review* is not wholly clear, but Helen Braithwaite's account is persuasive. She suggests that the *Anti-Jacobin Review* identified Johnson and the *Analytical*, especially the politically engaged 'Retrospect' sections of 1798, as centres of anti-Pitt activity. The government used Gilbert Wakefield's pamphlet, *A Reply to Some Parts of the Bishop of*

Landaff's Address (1798), sold but not published by Johnson, as a pretext to go after Johnson and the publisher J. S. Jordan. The fact that the actual printer of Wakefield's pamphlet served no jail time at all confirms the suspicion that the attorney general wanted to intimidate Johnson, who served nine months in jail. Marilyn Butler's conclusion seems sound: by prosecuting the classical scholar Wakefield and Johnson, the government, feeling vulnerable and at a disadvantage in its war with France, was taking steps to protect itself.[119] It is also possible that the intention was to send a message to those within the bourgeois public sphere that publications sympathetic to the cause of revolution in France and radical reform in England would no longer be tolerated. That message had been delivered earlier to the plebeian public sphere, which was why Thelwall in 1798 was in Wales looking for a farm. That the government's message was received too by middle-class reformers seems apparent, for the *Analytical* closed down in 1799 and Johnson avoided publishing political titles from that time onward – a stunning reversal of fortune as Johnson had previously brought out more liberal publications than any other publishing firm.[120] Moreover, even before the *Analytical* folded, propaganda targeted at middle-class patrons of libraries had made it disreputable to subscribe to the journal. A library in Sheffield, for example, decided in 1798 to replace the *Analytical* with the *Anti-Jacobin Review*.[121] The plebeian public sphere by 1797 had been systematically dismantled by trials and legislation; the Wakefield prosecutions completed the suppression of liberal and radical political culture.

The *Analytical*, long before it became a victim of repression, paid minute attention to the repression itself and to the arguments for and against. As mentioned earlier, the journal followed everything related to the Birmingham riots of July 1791 because Priestley and the Dissenters in general were targets of the loyalist mob. The May 1792 Royal Proclamation against Seditious Writings and Publications culminated an early movement of repression that had begun at least a year earlier. The *Analytical*'s review of Paine's *Rights of Man*, part two, which was published in a popular format and was distributed by the political societies, was unapologetically and boldly positive, as the reviewer carefully laid out the argument using a generous quantity of quotations, concluding that the style, though 'popular', was not 'vulgar', and that Paine was 'no common man; this is the poor man's friend'.[122] The *Analytical*'s review of Paine's *Letter Addressed to the Addressers* (1792) is not nearly as affirmative, as the reviewer distinguishes accurately between Paine's call for a convention to replace parliament and the petitionary approach to parliamentary reform taken by the Society for Constitutional Information. Even this review, however, impartially explains Paine's ideas, which at this point seem revolutionary rather than reformist.[123] The review of Paine's trial withholds reformist criticism of the convention strategy and defends Paine along with the freedom of the press and freedom of expression.[124] During the especially repressive year of 1794 reviews condemned not just the treason trials but the trial of John Frost, Thomas Walker and the other Manchester defendants.[125] The *Analytical* reviewers strongly attack Paine for his anti-religious book, *The Age of Reason* (1793), but never entertain the idea that such arguments should be kept from the public. Indeed, the *Analytical* praises a pamphlet by Anna Barbauld who extols deist publications for provoking strong Christian responses, thus illustrating the strength of a freely debating public.[126] An interesting moment is when John Reeves, one of the architects of the repression, published an overly zealous pamphlet that the House of Commons found libellous. Even in this case the *Analytical* reviewer rejects prosecutions for opinion, however odious.[127] When the journal discusses the repression of John Thelwall's provincial lectures, it disapproves of the government, but so laconically as to imply that nothing can be done about this injustice.[128] The *Analytical* exercises its moral outrage, however, when Thomas Erskine, the most famous lawyer to defend reformers and the right of free speech, became the *prosecuting* attorney in the case of Thomas Williams for selling Paine's *Age of Reason*. Erskine's betrayal was unforgivable.[129]

Subsequent chapters of my study treat the *Analytical* as an example of Enlightenment cosmopolitanism only moderately compromised by inconsistencies and equivocations. The journal's position in the bourgeois public sphere, upholding the ideals of the Enlightenment, had radical implications in the 1790s. Providing a platform for dissident intellectuals like Alexander Geddes and Mary Wollstonecraft, whose writing the next chapter examines, the *Analytical* was the journal of advanced Enlightenment thinking on the Higher Criticism of the Bible and sexual inequality. Its cosmopolitanism was rigorous, even transmitting to English-language readers Kant's political ideas on 'perpetual peace' and cosmopolitan order. The courageous Joseph Johnson had no answer to the kind of repression the government was willing to mete out. Like Gilbert Wakefield, he assumed he would not find himself being treated as badly as the plebeian radicals had been. Although the *Analytical* consistently took a principled stand against, and vigorously disapproved of, all acts of repression and violations of free speech when most of the victims were plebeian radicals, it never carried its conflict with the government beyond polite forms of protest. The effect of the *Analytical*'s demise was catastrophic for a particular kind of Enlightenment approach to reform and culture. While Wakefield, whose health was ruined by his two years in jail, died shortly after his release, middle-class reformism itself continued. With the end of the *Analytical*, however, came the final moment of its heroic age, and in the future it took a more cautious, more pragmatic and class-conscious approach. The *Westminster Review* in 1824 revived important aspects of the *Analytical* but the utilitarian journal sustained the Enlightenment project on a much narrower intellectual foundation. Another way the radical Enlightenment survived in a different form was the romantic imagination, which retained universality but gave up the unbounded enquiry of Enlightenment for the 'spiritual capital' and private pleasure of individualistic experience.[130]

3 WOMEN AND JUSTICE

The feminists who came after the Bluestockings carried the argument for gender justice to a higher level conceptually and a lower level socially. The Bluestockings, according to Sylvia Myers, had taken the feminist project forward in two important ways: by developing an awareness of injustice and a sense of 'sisterhood'.[1] One of the important cultural battles was earning respect and acceptance for the woman of learning, a battle Elizabeth Carter won as the woman scholar became at mid-century a source of national pride and an illustration of British and Protestant superiority.[2] Coming from the middle class, not the social elite, Mary Wollstonecraft, Mary Hays, Helen Maria Williams and Mary Robinson used the inspiration of the French Revolution to move feminism into ideological and conceptual areas previously neglected. It is not just that the feminists of the 1790s lived their own lives as cosmopolitan intellectuals who exercised far more freedom in their sexual lives than was the norm at the time, but that they proposed radical changes in women's political, educational, economic and familial status. This late Enlightenment feminism (continued later by the Shelley circle and then the Owenite socialists)[3] – radical not moderate, religiously modernist and even secular, cosmopolitan rather than nationalistic, broadly political rather than narrowly focused, more expansively utopian than pragmatic – is in many respects more similar to the feminism of the 1970s than to the Victorian feminism which followed it chronologically. The harsh reaction against this Enlightenment feminism, vividly illustrated by the poignant omission of Wollstonecraft in Mary Hays's six-volume collection of biographies of famous women,[4] is an important story but it is not the focus of this chapter. I want instead to show how Enlightenment feminism emerged, and of what elements it consisted, by concentrating largely on Wollstonecraft, the most representative figure.

It has been conventional to label the feminism I am describing as 'liberal' or 'equality' feminism, separate from 'radical' and 'socialist' feminism, but Virginia Sapiro finds that the distinctiveness of Wollstonecraft's ideas cannot be represented by means of the stereotyped 'liberal' category.[5] There is no meaningful way in which Wollstonecraft's ideas can be contained within the dismissive conceptual category of 'bourgeois liberal individualism' and to approach her work in this way is to miss the powerful originality of her writing. Although Wollstonecraft's life has attracted more attention than it probably needs, *A Vindication of the Rights of Woman* (1792), recognized as a major work in political and cultural history, has received surprisingly few close and thorough readings. Primarily it is Wollstonecraft's writing and ideas that concern me here.

This chapter has two sections, the first of which highlights women on trial and the scene of justice, with the central text being *The Wrongs of Woman* (1798), Wollstonecraft's unfinished novel. The law, an obvious site for feminist argument, provided also a set of richly meaningful metaphors and symbols for novelists. Where and how justice gets determined are controversial questions in terms of both law and public opinion. The second section, 'Justice for Sophie', examines how Wollstonecraft contested the conventional gender economy described by Rousseau in *Émile* (1762), one of the Enlightenment's most influential texts, innovative in so many areas but not in the area of the sexes.

Women on Trial and the Scene of Justice[6]

Culturally central, spectacular trials – the trial and execution of Louis XVI and his family (1792–3), the sedition and treason trials of the London Corresponding Society defendants (1793–4), the Reign of Terror (1793–4), William Hone's blasphemy trials (1817), the Cato Street Conspiracy trial and execution (1820), Queen Caroline's trial in the House of Lords and the court of public opinion (1820) – affected literary texts both directly and indirectly. Representations of actual trials in popular prints, trial transcripts and parodies eroded the power and prestige of the crown and aristocracy who tried to control through repression the public discourse on matters of state and class privilege. Even before the royal scandal of the Queen Caroline Affair, the published divorce trials of the social elite were embarrassingly popular and exposed the aristocracy to morally compromising ridicule. Concurrent with the publication of actual trials was the struggle against what was called the Bloody Code, the legal system punctuated by over two hundred capital crimes (most of which were crimes against property). This anti-aristocratic reform effort culminated in the 1830s and 1840s with a sharp reduction of capital crimes, in part because of an effort to rationalize the legal system according to a logic sketched out by Jeremy Bentham in his *An Introduction to the Principles of Morals and Legislation* (1789). Not all opposition to the Bloody Code and class domination of the law was by Enlightenment philosophers, however. Artisan radicals such as the republican Richard Carlile and the anti-slavery lecturer Robert Wedderburn also changed the legal institutions by their principled resistance.[7] The arguments they – and others – deployed against legal oppression were often constitutionalist and traditional rather than philosophically utilitarian, as the historian James Epstein has illustrated.[8] Some literary texts (*Caleb Williams* (1794), *Frankenstein* (1818)) with fictional trials complicated the utilitarian rationalization of the law by insisting on the particularity of crime, the complexity of which rendered impossible quantifiable norms for punishment. Such texts challenged the Bloody Code from the left, but other texts with fictional trials questioned the law and modernity from another angle, with providential narratives that affirmed divine justice. There were, then, three distinct conceptions of how law worked in the early nineteenth century: a paternalistic law sanctioned by divine right within a strictly hierarchical society; a law reformed on a utilitarian basis compatible with the pursuit of self-interest within a market society; and an ethically radical critique of law. The first conception has been described vividly in Michel Foucault's *Discipline and Punish* (1977), especially in the dramatic opening scene of the drawing and quartering of Damiens the regicide.[9] The second, the Bentham-Mill project of legal reform, has been described in Elie Halevy's study of the philosophical radicals.[10] The third, the ethical critique of law, exists in many forms, having acquired a self-consciously disciplinary focus in recent work by Levinas, Derrida and Habermas, and those influenced by them.[11]

Modernity is a concept by which the competing legal models can be understood. As developed in Jürgen Habermas's work, modernity is a historical project with a long prehistory that articulated many of its goals in the Enlightenment: the differentiation of reason, the demythologization of traditional worldviews, the disenchantment of magical thought and overall the replacement of authoritarian bases of human interaction with rational purposive action and communicative action.[12] Traditional law, based on religious, natural and customary law, could not dispense with interpretation, but the hermeneutics were grounded in authority that could not be questioned: divine revelation and divinity expressed through nature and customs whose origins were not recoverable. Post-traditional law justifies its authority only by defending its validity claims in public discourse. Early nineteenth-century institutional law resisted modernity by affirming the timelessly divine order overseen by God's representatives within the state and church. Legal, political, religious and moral spheres were intertwined, as was evident at the public scene of a hanging: the sovereign could intervene with mercy at any point before the actual execution; the criminal was expected to confess and ratify the correctness of the punishment; the community as a whole witnessed and legitimated the exercise of divinely sanctioned law. William Blackstone's strained efforts to reconcile natural and common law in his *Commentaries on the Laws of England* (1765–9) reflect the imperative to tie law ultimately to theology, even within a project that appears committed to Enlightenment rationality. The utilitarian model separates what is joined together in the traditional paradigm: the legal is autonomous, developed according to its own immanent logic, distinct from the other forms of differentiated reason within the project of modernity. (The scientific and aesthetic are the other two forms of reason, according to Habermas's Weberian account.) Bentham's wholly secular treatment of law assumes the priority of the greatest good for the greatest number, a market society of self-interested economic agents and a democratic state emancipated from feudal paternalism. The radical ethical critique of law moves between two different emphases, the populist and anarchistic. The populist logic defines justice in terms of tradition to support democratic empowerment, while the anarchistic treats crime as a moment of semiotic excess that eludes rational codification but not reason itself. While the populist critique is ambivalent about modernity and sceptical about the rationalization of the law, the anarchistic critique assumes the decentring power of modernity.

The changing nature of the jury in the early nineteenth century illuminates aspects of both the populist and anarchist critiques of law. If the role of the jury was restricted to deciding only the facts of the case, leaving to the state the interpretation of the law, then the government's task in a libel case was simply to prove that a criminal publication had indeed been issued by a particular individual. It was not until the 1792 Fox Libel Law that juries were permitted to decide not simply the fact of publication but whether or not the published material was indeed blasphemous or seditious. A rarely exercised power that juries possessed historically was actually making law – going beyond the facts as such and nullifying what they deemed to be unjust laws. The numerous courtroom scenes in literary texts reflect the popularity of criminal representations, from ballads at public executions to the seven volumes of *Trials for Adultery; or, The History of Divorces* (1781). Thomas Erskine's trial speeches were collected and edited by the radical publisher, James Ridgway, into four volumes, and were reprinted many times, from the first edition in 1810 to the last edition listed in the British Library, 1870. During this time the role of the jury was redefined, contested and idealized, as the jury – 'the glory of the English law', according to Blackstone[13] – became an institution that had democratic legitimacy. The Fox Libel Law that allowed juries rather than the presiding judge to determine what was libellous was part of the struggle for a more democratic judicial system, but the jury in fact was then a socially exclusive institution that kept out three-quarters of the adult population due to the property qualification, all women and almost all labourers and servants. This elitism was made worse by special juries for genteel defendants and by the social deference to gentry who served as jury foremen. Nevertheless, because juries were also comprised of farmers, tradesmen and artisans and because there was a tradition going back to the medieval period of jury resistance to the authority of the bench, juries were available for citizen action.[14] They were notoriously unreliable in seditious libel cases and had famously acquitted treason trial defendants in 1794 – Hardy, Tooke and Thelwall – and numerous reformers in 1817, including William Hone. From John Lilburne's trials in 1649 to

Thomas Erskine's acquittal for Lord George Gordon in 1781 and to the judicial
battles in the 'War of the Unstamped' in the 1830s, for two hundred years juries
were challenging the limits and defining the nature of civil liberties like freedom
of the press and freedom of speech. When defendants could not appeal to the
existing laws or rely on the discretion of the bench, they addressed the jury, the
one legal body that was persuadable. The jury was a site where social agency in
the name of justice could and occasionally did produce unexpected verdicts.

Writers conceive of readers as jurors and jurors as legislators. The reader
as juror is a trope one finds in Shelley's *Defence of Poetry* (1821) – 'the jury ...
impannelled by Time' that judges poetry.[15] Modern critic Martha Nussbaum's
formulation of the 'judicious reader', modelled after the institutional history of
the criminal trial and Adam Smith's 'judicious spectator', is a recent revision of
romantic-era assumptions about the imagination and its social responsibility.[16]
Both the jury and the reader were objects of hope for those promoting progressive
political change through public opinion; law and literature share an ethical discourse that develops in the public sphere. William Godwin, who ascribed social
progress to print culture's development, conceived of the jury in *Enquiry Concerning Political Justice* (1793) as the last legitimate institution of the state before
its dissolution into a rational anarchy.[17] A fragment of Percy Shelley's prose finds
current jury trials inadequate but imagines a reformed alternative where, if only
'men were accustomed to reason, and to hear the arguments of others, upon each
particular case' without the obfuscating distractions of so-called common sense,
the common law and judicial precedents, the opinion of the public would not be
'fenced about and frozen over'.[18] Shelley affirms the law-making function of the
jury to construct the outlines of his utopian anarchy, but idealizing the jury was
not restricted to poets. At the funeral service in 1832 for Thomas Hardy, treason
trial defendant and founder of the London Corresponding Society, John Thelwall before a crowd of over 20,000 honoured both the court official who blocked
the government's attempt in 1794 to pack the jury and the twelve jurors who
actually acquitted Hardy; the jurors's names were engraved in gold on a purple
tablet.[19] His eulogy praised both ancient democratic legal procedures and the
courage of the jurors to resist manipulation by the government.

While Godwin, Shelley and Thelwall criticized institutionalized law from the
left, Scott, from the right, expressed his ambivalence about modern law by means
of providential narratives that diminish the importance of juries. Providential
narratives resist modernity by defending the pre-modern myth of divine justice.
Scott's novels, *The Heart of Midlothian* (1818) and *Ivanhoe* (1819), both take
providential turns at crucial moments. The providential narrative, a dominant
structure in English fiction from *Robinson Crusoe* (1719) to *Jane Eyre* (1848), is
not simply a story with a happy ending, or a story shaped by poetic justice, but
a narrative in which God or one of God's agents intervenes decisively to affect

the plot. The metaphysical implications of the providential narrative are that without divine oversight the hero or heroine would not succeed; merely human justice is not sufficient. (However, providential narratives need not entail a providential worldview, and secularized versions of the providential shape George Eliot's work, as demonstrated by Thomas Vargish.) [20]

There is a version of divine justice in *The Heart of Midlothian* where the Porteous Mob acts in the name of an authority higher than the government that pardoned Porteous and where legal procedures require the intervention of paternalistic aristocrats and royals, suggesting that only God and God's agents can maintain order. When Jeanie Deans pleads for her sister, sentenced to death for infanticide, the Duke of Argyle and then Queen Caroline respond favourably to Jeanie's eloquent appeal, but Jeanie at no point challenges the authority of the Hanover line or the aristocracy. In *Ivanhoe* it is God who provides the justice, and here, a duke and a queen. *The Heart of Midlothian*, which redundantly affirms the paternalistic structure of justice, judges harshly the various representatives of insurgent democracy – the Porteous Mob and the mob that kills Madge Wildfire – but the novel is hardly uncritical of the legal killing of Andrew Wilson and Meg Murdockson, as Bruce Beiderwell shows us. [21] Jeanie's speech is a symbolic action that is both democratic and apolitical, an expression of sincerity that seems beyond politics. But it is not really beyond politics, as Jeanie will not disclose the identity of George Staunton for reasons of Scottish nationalism – and as it is impossible to forget that the Duke of Argyle stage-manages the behaviour of Jeanie Deans, even attending to the way she is dressed, so that her speech is also a performance. [22] One has to recognize what the speech is not: it is not an appeal to the reader to overturn unjust institutions, as is the radical speech of Maria Venables in Wollstonecraft's *Wrongs of Woman*, a text I will discuss later. Moreover, the awkward conclusion of the novel, the paternalistic utopia overseen by the Duke of Argyle, suggests social contradictions that are more threatening than Scott's fiction is able to reconcile in what Beiderwell aptly calls a 'morally pragmatic compromise'. [23] Jeanie's successful appeal is not really a resolution so much as another deferral and containment of the effects of inequality and domination. Scott's providential novel makes concessions to the spirit of modernity: although God intervenes, human affairs are so complicated that there is no simple way to rectify the numerous problems.

The encounter between the innocent Jeanie and the compassionate duke and queen in volume 3, chapter 12 intensifies and resolves themes Scott develops through the whole novel. The novel's portrait of eighteenth-century Britain is thoroughly Burkean and resonantly allegorical in its contrast between good and bad forms of aristocratic cosmopolitanism. Queen Caroline's political acumen at court, her befriending of Lady Suffolk in order to control her husband's mistress more effectively, her British acculturation to compensate for her husband's

Germanic orientation and her poised performance with the Duke and Jeanie all illustrate a sophisticated aristocratic worldliness that offends a narrowly moralistic Puritanism, certainly, but that redeems itself ultimately. Silences and speech define the two styles of communicating. An icon of Scottish nationalism, the plaid-dressed Jeanie appears more naïve than she actually is, as she withholds from the queen information she has about the riot, but her two insulting comments – against the queen's treatment of her son and against Lady Suffolk's adultery – are completely unintended; Jeanie did not try to wound the two 'Leddies'. The Duke and the Queen have a complicated relationship stemming from the political necessity of their cooperation; they need each other, even if each dislikes important things about the other. Jeanie could never imitate the ironic, self-conscious style of their conversation. However appealing Jeanie's innocence and integrity, there is no question where the allegiance of the novel's narrator rests. Only a sophisticated, ancient culture could produce someone as wise, moderate, benevolent and politically effective as the Duke of Argyle. George Staunton, Effie's lover, represents the bad cosmopolitanism of the rogue aristocrat who colludes with criminals and rioters. Whereas the Duke of Argyle represents a timeless aristocratic family, Staunton is the son of a Creole mother who spoiled him in the West Indies where he frequented the company of 'negro slaves'.[24] The novel approves the German/English mixing of the Hanover dynasty but not the Scottish/African mixing. While the novel frowns on Staunton's adopting the ways of the unrespectable classes, it smiles approvingly at the stylized, deferential, respectful relations between upper and lower classes. Scott's overall strategy, valorizing the mixing of Scottish and English while retaining a measure of Scottish nationalism, co-opts and redefines cosmopolitanism as moderate nationalism.

If in *The Heart of Midlothian* the Duke of Argyle acts as an agent of God, highly refined by aristocratic culture, God himself seems to act in *Ivanhoe* when he dispatches Bois-Guilbert during the trial by battle with a sick and almost defenceless Ivanhoe to decide the fate of Rebecca (chapter 43). Bois-Gilbert (a completely irreligious materialist in pursuit of only his own self-interest, and a symbol and spokesman for modernity) dies, according to the narrator, 'a victim to the violence of his own contending passions': namely, his passion for Rebecca and his pride as a warrior.[25] Scott inserts the psychological conflict into a providential narrative accepted by all the characters, including Bois-Guilbert who, after Rebecca rejects yet another of his offers to become his lover, tells her: "'Thou and I are but the blind instruments of some irresistible fatality, that carries us along, like goodly vessels driving before the storm, which are dashed against each other, and so perish'".[26] If God had not intervened with the providential aneurysm, Bois-Guilbert would have killed Ivanhoe and Rebecca would have been consumed in flames. Scott is uncomfortable enough with the providential narrative to offer a psychological explanation for Bois-Guilbert's death, but *Ivanhoe* is so heavily invested in conservative ideology that Scott restrains his urbanity rather than his paternalism. The first paragraph of chapter 43 expresses great anxiety about the public scene of justice, the large gathering of people who evoke for Scott the dangerous 'meeting of radical reformers'. The novel stages a pre-modern scene of justice but the very public nature of the trial makes Scott a judicial reformer despite and because of his commitments to a stable, hierarchical society. A public hanging is as bad as a radical meeting because the democratic crowd is not as docile as he imagines the pre-modern crowd to have been. Scott's ambivalent moves in favour of legal rationalization are motivated by fear of radical democracy.

Both Godwin and the Shelleys produced narratives with trials to tell stories about justice that would resonate with a large audience, but these stories are an antithetical response to the providential worldview; in these fictions God has been withdrawn from the issues of justice. In *Caleb Williams* (1794), one of the most influential texts of romantic-era literature, inequality and domination are prominent in several trial scenes that illustrate Godwin's distrust of rhetoric and preference for spontaneous speech, and that reveal anarchistic assumptions about the law and jurisprudence that run counter to the Benthamite rationalization of law. An important difference between these two Enlightenment philosophers is that Godwin placed his faith in open-ended enquiry, which would lead ultimately to social cohesiveness, while Bentham was committed to the 'artificial' (not 'natural') identity of interests' achieved by enlightened legislation.[27] In the fictional trials examined here, where a trial yields truth, the institutional consequences and implications are equivocal, and where trials produce neither truth nor justice, they are instruments of deception and class oppression. The first trial that promotes truth is accidentally related to Caleb Williams's quest to discover Falkland's guilt, of which he is intuitively aware long before he has any evidence. Falkland presides as Justice of the Peace in a case regarding a quarrel between two peasants that roughly resembles the quarrel between Tyrrel and Falkland that resulted in the former's murder, and the reactions of Falkland himself as judge provide Caleb with what he interprets as the definitive proof of his master's guilt. The trial scene in chapter 5, volume 2 reveals the guilt of Falkland in a *Hamlet*-like manner, but in actuality all that is disclosed is Falkland's emotional involvement in the case, not any specific culpability. The trial of the peasant, then, is a metaphor by which Caleb achieves certainty of Falkland's guilt. The so-called evidence could not pass muster by the rules of evidence, but the empiricism governing the rules of evidence and informing the rational reform of law is foreign to Caleb's intuitive method of reading Falkland's face, body, tone and overall emotional presentation. The description of Caleb's state of mind after making the discovery of his master's guilt is one of lyrical transport, after he conceals himself in a biblical-like garden:

> My mind was full almost to bursting. I no sooner conceived myself sufficiently removed from all observation, than my thoughts forced their way spontaneously to my tongue, and I exclaimed in a fit of uncontrollable enthusiasm: 'This is the murderer!' ... I felt as if my animal system had undergone a total revolution. My blood boiled within me. I was conscious to a kind of rapture for which I could not account... I seemed to enjoy the most soul-ravishing calm. I cannot better express the then state of my mind, than by saying, I was never so perfectly alive as at that moment'.[28]

Having eaten from the tree of knowledge, Caleb is intoxicated with power as he feels he is no longer socially inferior. Acting out the script of the French revolutionary drama, Caleb the servant symbolically topples his master because he has seen through the aristocratic appearance to the human reality. The mystique of aristocratic power no longer enchants Caleb, who has destroyed the pleasing illusions that Burke praised in his *Reflections on the Revolution in France*. His master is simply another human being. Mythologically, the garden scene after the trial stages a fall from an innocence that was never anything but coerced ignorance. Caleb's exhilaration is the joy of the emancipated subaltern who suddenly has a broad realm of choice.

Caleb's freedom, however, brings him mostly grief, as Falkland torments and pursues him as a prisoner in jail, an escaped prisoner and a legally 'free' citizen who is slandered by public opinion. Although Caleb himself has penetrated the illusions of aristocratic power, he has not been able to persuade others that Falkland is a liar and murderer. Caleb hopes that a public trial will finally clear his own name and establish the guilt of his master, but Caleb's empathetic response to Falkland's suffering, which has turned him into a ghost more dead than alive, undoes all his righteous indignation. 'Shall I trample upon a man thus dreadfully reduced?'[29] The novel's final trial scene stages an act of anti-rhetoric as Caleb disavows his prosecution of Falkland even as he performs it, thus exemplifying Godwin's call in *Political Justice* to reject oratory for private conversation, as Victoria Myers has recently pointed out.[30] By revealing his emotional anguish and his ambivalence, Caleb performs what seems like an artless speech, free of rhetorical strategy and self-interest, thereby winning the conviction he seeks, only to find himself at the end nearly as guilt-stricken as Falkland. Proportionality of punishment, one of the legal reform movement's most important goals, seems irrelevant in this novel because Falkland lives only three days after his public confession; moreover, he has punished himself for many years with an excruciating torture that is written on his body. The world created by the novel is not one in which Bentham's techniques of legal calculus have much pertinence.

One aspect of Godwin's critique of law more compatible with Bentham's democratic reforms is the role aristocratic power plays in the triumph of falsehood over truth in the numerous trial scenes. The artfulness of Falkland's oratory in deceiving the court about his murder of Tyrrel has a parallel in Percy Shelley's *Cenci* (1819), where Beatrice's eloquence intimidates the hired assassin Marzio to change his testimony. Falkland's failure to testify truthfully at the trial of the Hawkins family, which is falsely accused of murdering Tyrrel, is repeated in *Frankenstein* where Victor fails to testify at the trial of Justine Moritz. When Victor finally tells a magistrate the whole story, it is too late to be of use to anyone, the creature having already committed his murders, thus illustrating the ineffectiveness of judicial institutions to effect justice.

In these two texts, it is not just the guilty who experience guilt, but also the innocent, as illustrated by the false confession of the hapless Justine Moritz. As Peter Brooks has illustrated recently, it is not difficult for determined police to coerce false confessions out of defendants because people all the time have a high level of guilt, whether or not they have committed any actual crimes.[31] The culture produces – or rather overproduces – guilt, which is a psychological disposition authoritarian political systems, as well as profit-seeking corporations, have exploited with efficiency. The guilt of Caleb Williams, like that of Coleridge's ancient mariner, is finally irrational because it is bottomless. A Kafkaesque judgment for which there is no appeal has been pronounced on Caleb and the mariner: both are guilty of symbolic aggression against a sacred order that punishes curiosity and ingratitude, ordinary dispositions of mind within a lifeworld structured by modernity. Similarly, Victor Frankenstein's aggression against nature is a cautionary tale of modernity, as his violence is returned in the form of the creature's retaliatory acts, in what is only an apparently providential turn in the narrative. Walton and Frankenstein, avatars of modernity, do not feel as guilty as the creature who has killed the very beings whose acceptance he yearns for and can never have. *Frankenstein* is in some sense an extended trial, with Walton justifying the deaths of his sailors because of his ambition, with Frankenstein defending his murderous dissections of nature and with the creature pleading his innocence as a murderer. Although Frankenstein and Walton should feel guiltier than they do, the creature's promise of suicide at the novel's end seems to be the appropriate form of self-administered justice, thus elevating him ethically far above his monstrous identity and far above his human tormentor and double, Victor. As the creature achieves ethical self-understanding, he assumes the allegorical role of social victim and indeterminate Other many readers have found him to be. Such an ingenious turn in the fiction suggests a theme of modernity healing the wounds created by itself – and not a reactionary return to a premodern nature.

Percy Shelley's *Cenci* is a bitterly ironic treatment of divine justice and modernity: if there is providence, it operates sadistically to torment the innocent and reward the wicked. Count Cenci prays for and gets the deaths of his inconvenient sons; the Pope finally acts against the Count, but only after Beatrice has been raped and has had her rapist murdered. These two details, as has often been noted, are pure inventions, lacking in Shelley's factual sources. Shelley satirically parodies providence to emphasize God's absence or, more scandalously, his sadism – justifying James Rieger's argument that *Cenci* seems to be upholding a Gnostic worldview within which the entire material world is controlled by an evil being.[32] Shelley's corrosive mockery is not content with Gnosticism, however; his play which (as Stuart Curran identified) insists in existentialist fashion that we are alone, rather portrays as wishful nostalgia the yearning for divine justice.[33]

One achievement of the play is to make the reader feel that Beatrice is both guilty and innocent. Percy Shelley, upon first hearing about the Peterloo Massacre, wrote back to Charles Ollier using the words he had made Beatrice Cenci say after she had been raped by her father: 'Something must be done ... What yet I know not' (*Cenci*, III.i.87–8).[34] For Beatrice, that 'something' turns out to be patricide, a deed defensible to stop the on-going violence of a rapist, but one that proves problematic when the papal authorities finally act against the Count shortly after he has been murdered. This particular twist of the plot, another deviation from his historical sources, does not justify the Pope – far from it – but is used by Shelley to show the capriciousness of political power. Nonviolent passivity in this case would have had the same result in removing the Count, but such passivity as a principled position guarantees no such happy results; it only guarantees an absence of violence by the victim of injustice. Like Caleb, after whom she is modelled, Beatrice fails to persuade the public to act against her oppressor. The Pope and the nobles could have chosen to prevent an injustice the play shows is structural and institutional, not just personal, but, for self-interested reasons, they do not. Beatrice's failure to be an ethical paragon is not meant to distract the reader from the more urgent truth, that injustice permeates the institutions of church, state and family. Beatrice's 'guilt' weighs little in comparison with the forces arrayed against her. 'I / Have met with much injustice in this world; / No difference has been made by God or man' (V.iv.80–2). At the very end of the play as Beatrice is about to be executed, the irony of the last lines – 'Well, 'tis very well' – could not be more dramatic, as just the opposite is the case.

Whereas aggression in the fictions of Godwin, Mary and Percy Shelley is balanced by guilt, the representations of the royal and aristocratic sexual adventures in divorce trial narratives are gleefully aggressive; the only guilt is the conventional one of the adulterer having misgivings upon discovery. A. Moore's *The Annals of Gallantry; or, The Conjugal Monitor* (1814), a collection of adultery trials from the eighteenth and nineteenth centuries in three volumes with well-executed coloured prints (some by George Cruikshank) is an example of openly anti-aristocratic writing that expresses moral outrage at the misbehaviour of the upper classes, while at the same time hypocritically inviting pornographic enjoyment. One obvious purpose of such texts is to torment the aristocratic men and women who are humiliated by the publicity of their sexual deeds, thereby detracting from the legitimacy of aristocratic rule. A full-page print of the Duke of Cumberland who was sued by Lord Grosvenor in 1771 accompanies the longest section devoted to a single case – at over one-hundred-and-seventy pages. The forty-year case still has interest because of the royal lineage of the Duke, his similarities with the Prince Regent and perhaps the notorious case of the new Duke of Cumberland, suspected of murder and other crimes in 1810. The actual prose contained in these three volumes is taken mostly from court transcripts, but each chapter reads like a story or novella because the attorneys deploy novelistic techniques to portray the characters of their clients. The actual evidence in the depositions and testimony is so fragmentary that the attorneys' summaries are essential for narrating the acts of adultery. Embedded in the sensationalistic material of the first volume is also the editor's eloquent and well reasoned argument in favour of liberal divorce, made on grounds somewhat similar to those argued by Mary Wollstonecraft.[35]

Wollstonecraft's fictional trial is, among other things, an argument in favour of liberal divorce laws. A key moment in the *Wrongs of Woman* dramatizes Wollstonecraft's challenge to judicial institutions and public opinion. In the climactic court scene where Maria's lover, Darnford, is on trial for adultery, Maria herself cannot deliver the speech she has written because in trials addressing what was known as 'criminal communication' or 'crim. con.' the wife had no autonomous legal standing; moreover, the plaintiff and defendant both spoke through their attorneys. Undermining sentimental conventions, Wollstonecraft has Maria rather than Darnford conduct the defence, but the wife in a case like this would not have been permitted her own, separate attorney who could speak in court. Numerous critics have commented on the eloquence of Maria's courageous speech in court, on the ownership she takes of her sexuality – she admits to having sex with Darnford but denies she was 'seduced' – and her moral decisions, but several other things are important as well. Firstly, compared with the speeches of Caleb Williams, Jeanie Deans and Beatrice Cenci, Maria's speech is certainly a piece of rhetoric from start to finish. Not trying to perform an innocent spontaneity with purely emotional appeal, Wollstonecraft makes a conscious effort to avoid representing Maria as a sentimental victim whose only attractive feature is her suffering. Secondly, the speech's first paragraph announces the speaker's intention to link her individual case to women in general using a politically charged rhetoric. Thirdly, although Maria declares the dissolution of her marriage to Venables, she avoids a radically individualist stance by insisting that 'I wish my country to approve of my conduct' and appealing directly to the jury to make law, not just determine fact. 'I appeal to the justice and humanity of the jury –a body of men, whose private judgment must be allowed to modify laws, that must be unjust, because definite rules can never apply to indefinite circumstances.'[36] Although the speech might seem imprudent, individualistic and scornful of institutional constraints, Maria crafts her words to evoke the cause of jury nullification, a politically contentious legal tradition from the time of Lilburne onward. While the novel does not represent the jury's decision, what Maria is asking for is not just a refusal to levy damages against Venables, which would be symbolically important, but an unprecedented granting of a real divorce with permission to remarry – something that was not institutionally possible. Indeed, the very few times women sought divorce in the House of Lords in the eighteenth and nineteenth centuries, they were refused. Maria wants to persuade the jury to act boldly, but she is going to live her life uncompromisingly and avoid playing the role of sentimental victim who needs male protection or readerly pity.

One of the greatest pieces of literary criticism Wollstonecraft ever wrote was her letter to Godwin's friend George Dyson, whose reading of *Wrongs of Woman* appeared outrageously misguided to the author. I will quote from the letter at length.

> ... I am vexed and surprised at your not thinking the situation of Maria sufficiently important, and can only account for this want of – shall I say it? delicacy of feeling by recollecting that you are a man – For my part I cannot suppose any situation more distressing than for a woman of sensibility with an improving mind to be bound, to such a man as I have described, for life – obliged to renounce all the humanising affections, and to avoid cultivating her taste lest her perception of grace, and refinement of sentiment should sharpen to agony the anguish of disappointment. Love, in which the imagination mingles its bewitching colouring must be fostered by delicacy – I should despise, or rather call her an ordinary woman, who could endure such a husband as I have sketched – yet you do not seem to be disgusted with him!!![37]

Those three exclamation points indicate a frustration with even finding an adequate way to tell Dyson where and how he is wrong. Indeed, Dyson's misreading is a repetition of the wrong Maria suffers. At the heart of Wollstonecraft's anger is her shock that Dyson does not see Maria as a victim of injustice. The novel portrays Venables as limiting his odious behavior to technically legal deeds, except for adultery, which was a commonplace behaviour within the hypocritical double standard; significantly, he does not strike her physically, confining his abuse to her sensibility. (The injustice experienced by the working-class Jemima is another story, entailing significant physical oppression.) To say the least Maria and Venables are deeply incompatible. As Maria begins to develop intellectually and aesthetically, attending plays, conversing with intelligent people and expanding her horizons within a modern urban culture, she comes to loathe her boorish husband. Rather than choosing to stoically or masochistically endure a dreadful marriage, rather than staying married and finding a lover (an option the 'liberal' Venables offers her),[38] Maria on her own divorces Venables after he crosses a particular line – trying to sell her sexual services. Certainly egregious, the attempted prostitution is also the proverbial last straw, not necessarily different from his previous offences against her sensibility and autonomy. If the jurors/readers grant Maria the right to divorce Venables, then they concur with Maria that her own act of divorcing her husband was morally justified. She divorces Venables in front of both him and a witness, the man who wanted to purchase her body: "'I call on you, Sir, to witness", and I lifted my hands and eyes to heaven, "that, as solemnly as I took his name, I now abjure it", I pulled off my ring, and put it on the table; "and that I mean immediately to quit his house, never to enter it more. I will provide for myself and child. I leave him as free as I am determined to be myself – he shall be answerable for no debts of mine"'.[39] Her action is not conditional on subsequent legal ratification. Rather, she boldly divorces him in an ad hoc ceremony with quasi-legal trappings. The appeal to the jury to make law and grant her a divorce is also redundant; she herself has already divorced Venables.

The cosmopolitan meaning of Maria's self-authorized divorce is that she is claiming a violation of her human rights and not of British law, which leaves her without any recourse. She acts on her intuition that the injustice she has suffered simply as a human being, not a citizen of Britain, is intolerable and requires her to leave her husband. About two months before Wollstonecraft arrived in Paris, the revolutionary government of France instituted an extremely liberal divorce law on 20 September 1792. The Napoleonic Code modified the law to make it more restrictive and the Bourbon restoration in 1816 made divorce as difficult as it was in the ancien régime; divorce restrictions were relaxed again only in 1884.[40] That liberal divorce existed in France, however briefly, nevertheless illustrated that fundamental changes in the family were not simply utopian speculation but a matter of political will. Maria's appeal to the jury's power of law-making is more compelling when situated with the concurrent changes in France. That Wollstonecraft does not propose divorce reform in her *Vindication of the Rights of Woman* might be attributed to the text's emphasis on the 'revolution in female manners'[41] and her plans for a second volume that would address legal issues. There is no question however that Godwin questions the rationality of the marriage law – 'the worst of all laws' – in his *Political Justice*, where he imagines that 'the spirit of democracy' will soon lead to 'the abolition of surnames'.[42] Godwin's critique of marriage is on four grounds: cohabitation itself limits the usefulness of both people; marriage monopolizes a woman who becomes a possession; marriage's permanency violates both human nature and the ideal of free association; and marriage violates the freedom of choice, a basic human right. Godwin, who characteristically slights the sexuality of marriage and emphasizes more the 'conversation' and 'friendship' that men and women could have without the marriage laws, imagines a serial monogamy within a community that cares for all its children.[43] This anarcho-communist solution to the marriage problem is not all that different from what occurs in *Wrongs of Woman*, as in one conceived ending of the novel Wollstonecraft imagines Maria's daughter being taken care of by Jemima and a Maria who had just attempted suicide; neither Venables nor Darnford plays any role in the child's upbringing. The 'community' in this case is a small one but it points to the dissolution of the father-centred family and its replacement by an ethical association of people acting for the public good not just their own welfare. 'I will live for my child', Maria says, who represents not a single mother lacking a husband but rather a woman whose choices have pointed the way toward a new society.[44] Whereas Godwin is vague about how children will be tended in the new society, Wollstonecraft makes the issue central – not just here in the novel but in her writing on women's education.

Justice for Sophie

The fifth book of Rousseau's *Émile* (1762) is so outrageously arbitrary in its treatment of gender that it is surprising it took as long as it did for someone – notably Wollstonecraft in 1792 – to criticize the illogical arguments with the harshness and thoroughness one finds in *Vindication of the Rights of Woman*. Although Catharine Macaulay disputes it in her *Letters on Education* (1790), the rebuttal, which is not a central feature of the overall book, is largely contained within the twenty-second letter of the first part. Wollstonecraft's review of Macaulay's text in the *Analytical* highlights the irrationality of Rousseau's assumption that the human mind is sexed in precisely the ways to normalize the most stereotypical 'feminine' behaviour. Citing Macaulay's assertion that there is no 'characteristic difference' in the sexes, no sexed innate ideas, Wollstonecraft ridicules the notion that because girls' 'system of nerves is depraved', girls have to be educated in ways to 'complement' and please the other sex.[45] Although Wollstonecraft's *Vindication of the Rights of Woman* has been often described as derivative from Macaulay's *Letters on Education*, the *Vindication* far more rigorously subverts the ideas of Rousseau and other masculine authorities than the earlier text. Gender injustice, which is only one of several themes in Macaulay's book, is the *Vindication*'s only focus.

Wollstonecraft is the first to illustrate the disgraceful inconsistency in the thinking of Europe's most famous anti-aristocratic writer. Rousseau's construction of the ideal mate for his male pupil, Émile, reproduces most of the negative stereotypes in the misogynistic repertoire. Man's active strength requires the woman's passive weakness, and woman, whose 'strength' consists of her 'charms', must be trained to 'make herself pleasing in his eyes and not provoke him to anger'.[46] Drawing upon ancient misogynistic myths, Rousseau insists that woman's 'boundless passions' ('désirs illimités') can be restrained only by 'modesty' ('pudeur').[47] Women have no right to complain about unequal treatment because the male 'is only a male now and again', according to Rousseau, but 'the female is always a female'.[48] Although women's character is feminine by nature, Rousseau insists that girls get strict training in 'docility', for a woman has to learn to 'submit to injustice and to suffer wrongs inflicted on her by her husband without complaint'.[49] The obvious contradiction that Rousseau does not recognize is that if women were docile and obedient according to nature and instinct, then there would be no need to teach and instruct girls in their 'natural' behaviour. To compensate the female sex for its subordination to the male sex, nature has given women beauty and cunning.[50]

Just as we have seen Kant's appalling failure to be philosophically logical in his statements on race (and gender), so Rousseau's similar breakdown is not entirely surprising, as in both cases their respective moments of blindness – Eurocentrism and sexism – seem traceable to their being European men. Because neither could see beyond the categories provided by their European and masculine identity, both fell short in precisely the area of my concern in this study, the cosmopolitan imagination. Rousseau, as a great pioneer of anti-aristocratic thought, earned the praise and careful attention of feminists like Macaulay and Wollstonecraft who made frequent use of his ideas and methods. Rousseau's principal move in *Émile*, perhaps the most influential book Kant ever read,[51] is cosmopolitan: by moving from language to nature, from cultural idealizations to the body with its feelings and intuition, from theological dogma to inner light, from custom to experience, from maxims to experiments, from timeless truths to temporal development, Rousseau's philosophy subjects European politics and religion to a radical rethinking, rejecting the old and starting over again. Centuries of aristocratic culture, much to the annoyance of writers like Edmund Burke, were toppled over by drawing out the full implications of individual experience.

The most explosive section of *Émile*, the story of the Savoyard vicar, challenges European Christianity not by means of theological subtleties but by exploring what happens to one particular priest who trusts the validity of his own experience. Becoming a priest to escape poverty, he finds he cannot conform to the celibacy rule. After a long period of anguished doubt and spiritual crisis brought on by his body's rebellion against the Church's law, he affirms a new faith by following his 'inner light': 'I see God everywhere in his works; I feel him within myself; I behold him within myself; I behold him all around me.'[52] What made this romantic deism influentially distinctive was not its conventional affirmation of an immaterial soul and a future state of reward and punishment but its intuitive morality: 'at the bottom of our hearts' ('ames') there is 'an innate principle of justice and virtue'.[53] Replacing the sacred text of the Bible with the 'one book which is open to every one – the book of nature',[54] Rousseau carries out the next step of Christian development from modernist premises. The amorphous concept of nature, accessible either externally by means of sense experience or internally by means of intuitive feeling, provides an essential metaphysical category for insurgent democracy to contest a well-established aristocracy and monarchy. No one lacked experience with nature, a much greater leveller than Bible-reading, always vulnerable to the inevitable hierarchies of interpretation. The much cited lessons of *Émile* against binding infants in swaddling clothes and in favour of biological mothers breast-feeding infants acquire allegorical resonance in Rousseau's overall philosophy of democracy. 'Civilised man is born and dies a slave. The infant is bound up in swaddling clothes, the corpse is nailed down in his coffin. All his life long man is imprisoned by our institutions.'[55] Infants deserve the organic connection with their real mother, no substitute allowed. Rousseau's distrust of language is one form of his anti-aristocratic ideology, as he assumes that what Lacan calls the symbolic order is fully dominated by aristocratic injustice. Pointing to pre- and non-linguistic experiences as forming the first and most authentic language – intonation of sounds, facial expressions, gestures and bodily movements – Rousseau anxiously recommends that the child's first words be taught as clearly attached to objects.[56] Ideology uses a corrupted language in which signifiers are not attached securely to signifieds. 'Once you teach people to say what they do not understand, it is easy enough to get them to say anything you like.'[57]

As unswaddled infants crawl and exercise their growing bodies, learning from experience, they develop without the benefit of language and without the burden of original sin. If there is no original sin, there is no need for the divine expiation of Christ. In fact, there is a powerful image of the crucifixion in *Émile* but it is not what the Romans inflicted on the preacher from Galilee. The crucified figure is the swaddled infant hung on a hook attached to the wall, a common eighteenth-century practice considered a safe method to keep babies out of harm's way.[58] Instead of the conventional child's transition from swaddled confinement to cultural brainwashing, the child of *Émile* passes from a richly meaningful childhood to an adulthood informed by moral agency. A new epoch in philosophy commences when Rousseau says of childhood that it 'has its own ways of seeing, thinking, and feeling' ('L'enfance a des manières de voir, de penser, de sentir qui lui sont propres').[59] Not only does childhood have its own logic but adult rationality and morality cannot and should not try to impose upon this logic. Because morality is a creation of reason and the child does not act according to the dictates of reason, the child does not know right from wrong as these categories are understood by adults. Accordingly, punishing the child for moral reasons is both pointless and ineffective.[60] Rousseau wants to give the developing child a sanctuary for as long as possible from civilized culture, its rationality and moral precepts, because that culture is so powerful and difficult to resist. The vein of individualism and self-reliance that runs through *Émile* – for example, making Defoe's *Robinson Crusoe* (1719) Émile's first book – sustains what Rousseau considers a fragile self in relation to the overwhelming power of 'society'. The various prohibitions against rote learning are designed to preserve a structure of learning that depends wholly on the experimental method of testing ideas by observable experience. If historical narratives are the primary way a society passes on its myths and representations to subsequent generations, the discipline of history is especially inflected with ideological significance. Not surprisingly Rousseau considers teaching history to children a 'ridiculous error'.[61] His distrust of cultural knowledge is so great that he wants his pupil to learn a useful trade, work with his hands and mix manual with intellectual labour. 'He must work like a peasant and think like a philosopher.'[62]

The three fundamental maxims of education that Rousseau identifies are all aspects of the cosmopolitan imagination and can be summarized in the following commandment: acquire solidarity with other people by means of imaginative sympathy with their suffering.[63] The fundamental quality of human self-love cannot and should not be effaced, but to be fully human requires pity, putting ourselves in the place of others. A sense of solidarity with other people will develop according to nature, not religious instruction. On precisely this point one can see how Rousseau's cosmopolitan ideal conflicts with the pressures of ordinary experience, as he is forced to make contradictory statements: he both rejects religious instruction as abstract, authoritarian, arbitrary and foreign to the radical empiricism *Émile* has been promoting insistently and contends that the child be indoctrinated into the religion of the father.[64] That it matters not at all which religion the child has to adopt indicates the merely pragmatic nature of the religious instruction. Some kind of Christianity, however inadequate, is at least partially true, so until the philosophical creed of romantic deism attracts more adherents, it apparently does not harm the child too much to accept the father's religion (girls are supposed to accept the religion of their mothers and then later husbands).[65] The philosophical attitude of the text assumes toleration, religious relativism and cosmopolitan understanding but the practical advice goes in the opposite direction.

Wollstonecraft liked to characterize the contradictory aspects of Rousseau as 'paradoxical', a good way to register her recognition of the inconsistencies and to acknowledge the value of his original ideas.[66] The conception of Rousseau that appears in her writing is multidimensional, as Wollstonecraft recognizes his strengths and flaws existing in a unique configuration, like a 'sublime mountain'.[67] She mobilizes the strengths of Rousseau's anti-aristocratic writing in the *Vindication of the Rights of Men*, while she acerbically deconstructs the weaknesses of Rousseau's ideas on gender in the *Vindication of the Rights of Woman*, but even in the latter text she uses Rousseau's stronger ideas against the weaker.

A dialectic of weakness and strength informs both *Vindications*. In the *Rights of Men*, Wollstonecraft's rebuttal of Burke's *Reflections on the Revolution in France*, she satirically contrasts Burke's defence of the 'weak' Marie Antoinette, threatened by the revolutionary crowd, with his moral indifference to mass poverty, in particular the poor women who marched on Versailles against whom Burke directs his chivalrous outrage. The chivalrous Burke who protects the weak out of a sense of feudal obligation is the same Burke who attacked the mentally ill George III during the Regency crisis and who targeted the elderly Richard Price for 'unmanly' political and religious slander.[68] Seeming to defend the weak, Wollstonecraft's Burke actually is a bully who enjoys exercising power over the weak. In the *Rights of Woman* Wollstonecraft satirically exploits the one apparent advantage man seems to have over woman, physical strength, to illustrate the irrationality of male superiority. If women are weaker physically, they are still human and not animals governed by instinct alone, and whatever virtue of which men are capable, that is the exact same virtue toward which women aspire. Women's relative physical weakness does not make them a separate species and does not constitute feminine virtue. Insofar as women's weakness is accentuated and eroticized, Wollstonecraft detects culturally constructed hypocrisy by women who do not own their sexual desires honestly and 'voluptuous reveries' by men.[69] A fundamental premise of her argument in both Vindications is that relative weakness in terms of social class and gender does not provide a moral justification for the domination of the stronger party.

The dispute between Burke and Price, which predates the French Revolution controversy, centres on the moral nature of political power. Although Burke and Price were more or less on the same side during the American Revolution, their respective positions were distinctive, as Burke favoured a compromise with the Americans, whom he liked to call 'the American English',[70] and as Price found the conflict animated by abstract political concepts with universal relevance. The pragmatically nationalistic Burke, who stressed the 'organic' connections between Britain and America, objected to the cosmopolitan Price whose support for the Americans was always critical, calling attention to the undesirable practices of religious tests and racial slavery, and always connected with broader philosophical ideas.[71] It is not surprising that Price's outspokenly cosmopolitan *Discourse on the Love of Our Country* (1789) provoked Burke whose political centre of gravity was remote from Price's. One of Wollstonecraft's important teachers, Price places 'Universal Benevolence' above mere love of country,[72] a love that 'does not imply any conviction of the superior value of it to other countries'.[73] Moreover, a primary duty is to enlighten one's own country, not idealize its traditions,[74] for it is a common error to 'overvalue' what belongs to us.[75]

Mere partiality to one's own 'tribe' is just love of 'domination', 'conquest', 'glory', expanding territory and enslaving others.[76] By loving a country, one loves not the particular land but the political community and its legal traditions that are still developing and subject to change.[77] The importance of Price in Wollstonecraft's intellectual development has been long recognized but I am emphasizing especially the cosmopolitan dimensions of Price's thought that she was able to make her own. The first *Vindication* is as extraordinary as it is partially because of the emotionally powerful position in which Wollstonecraft found herself: she was defending a father-figure against what she perceived as injustice by a powerful politician.

Although, like the second *Vindication*, the *Rights of Men* was written quickly in a rush of inspiration – 'the effusions of the moment'[78] – without the benefit of much planning or revision, the text is tightly unified around three categories: virtue, beauty and property. Wollstonecraft deconstructs Burke's defence of tradition by showing that his chivalrous idealization of beauty in the person of Marie Antoinette is a realization of the aesthetic concepts in Burke's earlier essay on the sublime and beautiful. Poverty, which is not beautiful, does not attract Burke's imaginative sympathy, which instead finds sustenance in the most refined productions of aristocratic society.[79] Employing a materialist critique, Wollstonecraft points to the foundation of Burke's ideology of beauty – aristocratic property and its various institutional supports, namely primogeniture, the game laws, enclosures and inherited titles. Burke's aesthetic values legitimate his political ideas, which support the economic system of the aristocracy. Price, with whom Burke vehemently disagrees, represents another approach entirely, the beauty of virtue on behalf of the poor and middle class – improving social conditions, reflecting on and correcting one's own actions, carrying out the intellectual labour of scientific and moral development. The pivotal concept is the gendered notion of beauty that Wollstonecraft connects with slavery in a strongly satirical passage. The 'fair ladies' exercise their powers of sensibility, reading novels and cultivating an artificial weakness to make themselves more attractive, more beautiful according to Burke's aesthetic theory, while their slaves, 'the captive negroes', are tortured.[80] The material wealth that sustains the beauty of the privileged women is created by the labour of the suffering slaves – a suffering the very escapist nature of the culture guarantees they will not understand. Ethics, politics and aesthetics meld and reinforce one another, as Wollstonecraft here and throughout her work anticipates the feminist idea of the 'situated body' as a means of social critique.[81] *Rights of Men* works out a dialectic of wealthy women's bodies, artificially made weak in order to heighten their erotic value, which depend on the labour of enslaved black bodies, male and female.

Wollstonecraft, who uses the classical rhetorical categories of ethos, logos and pathos in relation to virtue, beauty and property, confutes *Reflections on the*

Revolution in France by attacking Burke's moral credibility, the rational basis of his argument and the rightness of his appeals to the emotions. She undermines Burke's ethical standing by emphasizing his dependence on the aristocracy (the £1,500 per annum pension)[82] whose interests he can never betray. She construes his hostility to political innovation as symptomatic also of his religious authoritarianism, his crypto-Catholicism figured as blind obedience to establishments in the 'Jewish' killing of Jesus. If Burke, the supporter of tradition, had been a Jew at the time of Jesus, Wollstonecraft suggests, he would have applauded the crucifixion.[83] Such is the 'bad' Burke who emerged after the 'good' Burke no longer could sustain his Ciceronian greatness.[84] Price, dedicated to cosmopolitan virtue, plays the role of the British, Protestant ethical hero in her critique of Burke. It is disconcerting to see the cosmopolitan Wollstonecraft positioning topoi from anti-Semitic, anti-Catholic and anti-Irish myths but she uses these dubious weapons, all of them standard in English Dissenting reform politics, to strengthen her argument against what she considers a narrow British nationalism and in favour of a more tolerant, peaceful democracy. Rousseau was not the only progressive writer with 'paradoxes'.

Her rebuttal of Burke's logos depends not just on deconstructing the aesthetic categories of the beautiful and the sublime but also on tracing the consistency of Burke's thinking to his idolatrous worship of aristocratic property. While he worships the 'demon' of property, Wollstonecraft describes a God of cosmopolitan universality that makes property a social not a private good.[85] Her conception of God in this essay is a God of justice who oversees a providential world with a system of divine rewards and punishments according to moral criteria.[86] A belief in God's distributive justice, if not in this world immediately, then eventually in the historical or post-mortal future, was a common belief in the late eighteenth century, especially among Rational Dissenters like Priestley and Price.[87] The Rational Dissenters insisted that history was animated by providential justice; otherwise, there was nothing to distinguish their own theological conception of post-mortal justice from that of William Paley and conventional Anglicans who were anxious for the poor to believe in life after death as a means of controlling their anger at injustice and inequality in this world. Wollstonecraft waxes indignant when Burke writes apparently cynically about the religious faith in immortality by people living in poverty. She finds Burke's theological politics 'contemptible hard-hearted sophistry' because the material conditions of the poor 'in this world' can be made better 'without depriving them of the consolation which you gratuitously grant them in the next'.[88] Her proposals for breaking up large estates and making uncultivated waste land available to the poor complements her protests against the game laws and enclosure acts.[89] The idol of aristocratic property worshipped by Burke signifies injustice, suffering for the poor and a violation of the highest moral ideals.

Wollstonecraft challenges Burke's strategy to bolster his defence of the aristocracy with emotionally provocative scenes of violence by appealing to a higher concept of the sublime – divine justice – and by offering counter-scenes of violence to the poor (capital punishment for deer-killing and impressment of workers).[90] According to Wollstonecraft, Burke's 'respect for rank has swallowed up the common feelings of humanity'.[91] The most striking appeal to the emotions in *Rights of Men* is the already discussed contrast between the women of leisure and the tortured slaves whose labour supports an economy of 'luxury'. That gender plays an important role in the first *Vindication* is not surprising but it invites comment before we examine the second *Vindication* in detail.

As Moira Ferguson points out, Wollstonecraft was perhaps the first feminist thinker to link the rights of European women to enslaved women, some of whom had rebelled recently in St Domingo (see Chapter 4). Ferguson, who perceptively shows how important slavery and slave trade abolition were in Wollstonecraft's writing – counting over eighty references to slavery in the second *Vindication* – criticizes Wollstonecraft for several political inadequacies. One way to start focusing on the second *Vindication* is to work through some of the feminist objections to the text. The first objection is that Wollstonecraft lacks 'emotional solidarity' with women, especially white women, and the second is that Wollstonecraft never conceives of collective action by women, only actions by individuals. Both shortcomings can be attributed to her limitations as a liberal feminist in thrall to bourgeois individualism.[92] Ferguson's criticism would not warrant much attention if she were one of only a few to make such observations, but in truth feminist criticism of Wollstonecraft has been harsh and extensive.

Ferguson and other feminist critics are repelled by the severity of Wollstonecraft's criticism of women and girls in the second *Vindication*. It is not difficult to find many examples of a harsh tone but I will limit myself to one characteristic example. The final chapter focuses on 'feminine weakness of character', an important specimen being the sentimentality illustrated by the 'women who are amused by the reveries of the stupid novelists'. 'Stupid' is strong, rather unforgiving phrasing, but the point is that the novelists know little about reality and cover up their ignorance with 'meretricious scenes' written in 'sentimental jargon'.[93] As most of these novelists are women, Wollstonecraft seems to be blaming the victim. Numerous reviews of novels and romances in the *Analytical Review* illustrate the numerous ways Wollstonecraft could say that a piece of fiction was worthless. Unless the novel was written by a skilled novelist like Charlotte Smith or Mary Robinson or Elizabeth Inchbald, Wollstonecraft unleashed her critical expletives. In the *Analytical* reviews and in the passage just quoted, Wollstonecraft only seems to blame the victim. Although the moral language implies ethical choice and responsibility, the full argument provides layers of analysis that are passionately engaged; she ultimately assigns the blame for 'weakness' to the system of sexual injustice, not women themselves. An argumentative passage, coming twelve paragraphs after the 'stupid novelists' sentence, is remarkably forceful: 'Ignorant women, forced to be chaste to preserve their reputation, allow their imagination to revel in the unnatural and meretricious scenes sketched by the novel writers ... whilst men carry the same vitiated taste into life, and fly for amusement to the wanton, from the unsophisticated charms of virtue, and the grave respectability of sense'.[94] The word 'ignorant' seems judgmental but describes a process the *Vindication* redundantly pictures: women receive educations that keep them ignorant; they are prohibited from using their reason; they are made weak and dependent in countless ways. The bluntness of 'ignorant' is typical of Wollstonecraft's satirical wit. To paraphrase the first half of the sentence: poorly educated and deliberately manipulated women are coerced into sexual abstinence not from free choice but by the massive propaganda about women's reputation backed up by inexorably punitive consequences for sexual misbehaviour; to compensate for the pleasure lost in the sexual repression these same women enjoy imaginary pleasures while reading novels that depict desire that is distorted and exaggerated. The second half of the sentence reads: meanwhile, the men who benefit from this system of repression and control are free to pursue their sexual desires with the women without 'reputation' and to spurn intelligent, sensible, morally responsible women. Ultimately she is not blaming the victim because she unpacks the sexual subtext and compensatory fantasy of novel-reading. In terms of blame, the hypocritical men receive far more of it than the women, but the *Vindication* actually locates the majority of the blame in the sexual system itself. Ferguson and others are responding to something real in Wollstonecraft's text but they are not taking sufficient notice of the other elements in the argument.

The most consistent form of emotional solidarity with women is the satire itself against the sexual system, especially the heavy use of irony and sarcasm. I will again limit myself to a single example, but dozens could be found. In the third chapter Wollstonecraft is developing aspects of female dependence, one of which is the woman's deference to men when it comes to religion. A 'Sophie' trained under the Rousseauvian system would never 'presume' to think for herself about religion, as she is 'a dependent creature' who 'piously' believes whatever 'wiser heads' have chosen for her. Her faith is depicted thus: 'not to doubt is her point of perfection'. Finally: 'She therefore pays her tythe of mint and cummin – and thanks her God that she is not as other women are. These are the blessed effects of a good education! These are the virtues of man's help-mate!'[95] The sarcasm, which runs throughout the *Vindication*, is emotionally direct and aggressive, mobilizing the anger of women readers in particular. Although Wollstonecraft addresses Talleyrand in the preface and seems to be addressing male readers, the *Vindication* frequently invites the female reader to take special pleasures in the ironic subversion of masculine authority. The paragraph's main irony is that woman's socially constructed religious piety betrays the very religious ideology of Christianity embodied in the New Testament. She does what she is told but the Gospel makes more demands of a Christian. The phrase 'tythe of mint and cummin' alludes to Matthew 23, where Jesus illustrates the superficial adherence to religious law the New Testament associates with the Pharisees. The allusion also works as a domestic symbol of woman's intellect subordinated and reduced to the materialism of the house. The phrase 'not as other women are' alludes to Luke 18, where the Pharisee is quoted as congratulating himself on being more pious than others, only to have his self-congratulation undermined by Jesus's insistence that obedience to the Jewish law is not the kind of piety he is advocating. 'Sophie', then, who accepts her religious faith as it is handed to her, believes she is the best of Christians, but Wollstonecraft's main point is that she is not, even by the criteria of Christianity itself. The implication is that making women so dependent and weak violates Christianity, even though religion is one of the authorities cited to support woman's subordinate position.

This brief satirical paragraph I have been examining is typical of the satire throughout the *Vindication*: richly meaningful, complex, witty, allusive, multi-levelled, passionate and aggressive. The pleasure of reading such a text, which is considerable, would be available to women readers who could enjoy the many reversals of conventional values and the upheaval of the domestic virtues. What seemed to be most moral – not thinking, accepting blindly what men told women – is shown actually to be a betrayal of morality and religion. Irony and sarcasm are rhetorical means of building and drawing upon the common assumptions of community. The woman reader who 'gets' the irony joins a community of understanding that strengthens her perception of gender injustice. A stronger bond of emotional solidarity with other women is hard to imagine. Similarly, the numerous harsh criticisms of bad novels and romances in the *Analytical Review* illustrate how seriously Wollstonecraft takes the novel as a genre and how high she sets standards for literary works. Some women readers, also dismayed by the emotionally manipulative fictions, could have taken satisfaction from the fact that the reviewer was not condescending and was upholding rigorous intellectual principles. The emotional solidarity of intelligent women is also something real.

Ferguson's second point is that Wollstonecraft imagines only individual but never collective actions against injustice. That Wollstonecraft neglected to establish a feminist political organization is certainly true, but to consider it a culpable omission on her part would be astonishingly ahistorical and anachronistic. Wollstonecraft's argument is completely social. She calls for a 'revolution' in female manners, a radically reconstructed educational system, universal suffrage, greater job opportunities for women to permit them economic independence (freeing them from the necessity of marriage and prostitution), legally mandatory support for children of unmarried women and equality under the law. In the first *Vindication* she called for the aristocratic estates to be broken up into small farms and for uncultivated land to be made available to the poor, as well as urging the abolition of primogeniture and slavery. *Wrongs of Woman* calls for not just divorce but for juries to make law, a bold political proposal. Wollstonecraft's political thinking is also profoundly dialectical, as she understands that a revolution in female manners cannot take place without revolutionizing the rest of society and forcing a revaluation of masculinity.

Revolution in Female Manners

'It is time to effect a revolution in female manners – time to restore to them their lost dignity – and make them, as a part of the human species, labour by reforming themselves to reform the world'.[96]

Wollstonecraft boldly frames the second *Vindication* in the public letter to Talleyrand by calling attention to the revolution's political exclusion of women and by demanding that women receive either political equality or a coherent, rational justification for the exclusion. Wollstonecraft as a British woman had no political standing in France on two grounds, but she claims the subject position of citizen of the world and a member of the republic of letters. Her 'affection for the whole human race' and commitment to republican 'virtue' provide the cosmopolitan grounds from which she addresses an influential revolutionary politician. She urges that the revolutionary men correct the 'flaw' in the new French constitution; otherwise 'you *force* all women, by denying them civil and political rights, to remain immured in their families groping in the dark'.[97] Enlightenment norms that Talleyrand and Wollstonecraft share do not permit self-identified rational political actors to make important decisions without explaining them and providing public reasons that can be challenged. She cleverly cites a sentence from a report on education authored by Talleyrand and others that confesses it is 'impossible to explain' why women should be disqualified from citizenship. If the revolutionaries are treating women arbitrarily rather than rationally, then they are 'immuring' women in the Bastille of the unreconstructed family, the rhetoric calling to mind one of the most emotionally evocative revolutionary symbols of the ancien régime.

Another compelling aspect of the prefatory letter is the immediacy with which it dramatizes the moral responsibility of the revolutionary reconstruction of the educational system, removed by the Convention from the church. Talleyrand and the other revolutionaries – all men – can remake the system in such a way to accord justice to women, or they can remake the system to repeat the injustice to women; the choice is theirs. The focus on moral and political agency works in two ways, to pressure the French revolutionaries and to inspire British readers who recognize the constructedness of social institutions. Wollstonecraft's proposals for educational reform are not utopian but practical, measured plans that could be instituted right away.

It is worth noting that the prefatory letter confidently addresses Talleyrand as though Wollstonecraft expected him to read the letter and take it seriously. (John Thelwall's various public letters to Edmund Burke assume just the opposite.) Translated into French almost immediately, the *Vindication* had currency in Paris because there were numerous Britons actively supporting and even participating in the revolution, including Thomas Christie, who founded the *Analytical Review*, Wollstonecraft's primary source of income at the time. There was a brief moment during the revolution but before the declaration of war between Britain and France in January 1793 when the cosmopolitan 'commerce des lumières' (exchange of ideas among the enlightened) was both normative and extensive.[98] As a new constitutional monarchy France could be seen as imitating the example of Britain, long idealized by the French Enlightenment as the counter of French absolutism, but after France becomes a republic and executes the King, British cosmopolitanism comes to be depicted as seditious if not treasonous. The cosmopolitan context, central to the origins of the *Vindication*, rarely gets even acknowledged in the later commentaries on the text.

A problem with linking Wollstonecraft's writing on education, especially the *Vindication of the Rights of Woman*, closely with other women reformers like Sarah Trimmer and Hannah More is that one thereby diminishes the importance of the cosmopolitan meaning of Wollstonecraft's overall project. More, whom Anne Mellor has called 'the most influential woman living in England in Wollstonecraft's day',[99] was as a Christian moralist certainly an architect of cultural changes that helped create central Victorian structures, such as the special role for women as moral advocates, the shaping of public policy by domestic values and the definition of 'female virtue' in terms of 'rational intelligence, modesty and chastity'.[100] In addition to Mellor, Mitzi Myers and Harriet Guest have made similar comparisons between Wollstonecraft and More.[101] The effect of these comparisons, which I hope to counter, is to make Wollstonecraft less strikingly original and to elevate the importance of More. Although More and Wollstonecraft both sought to reform a corrupted femininity, they did so in such different ways that their commonality could not be more superficial. It would be analogous to saying Karl Marx and Henry Ford both promoted the modernization of industrial capitalism.

The revolution in female manners that Wollstonecraft announces is dialectical in that women's reforming themselves reforms the world. 'The two sexes mutually corrupt and improve each other.'[102] The second *Vindication* imagines women exercising their rationality and their bodies in ways that would necessarily subvert masculinity. The various institutional reforms from the political franchise to state-run coeducational schools would have to accompany the revolution in manners, as Wollstonecraft does not conceive of the personal and political as utterly discrete entities that would permit personal transformation preceding legally instituted changes. The corrupted femininity that she targets for reform is a social creation and only a new social construction can replace it.

One of the most effective techniques in the *Vindication of the Rights of Woman* is the forceful deconstruction of misogynistic cultural creations, especially at the very heart of British religious and literary culture. Susan Wolfson captures the style and meaning of this deconstructive labour in her essay, 'Mary Wollstonecraft and the Poets', where Wollstonecraft is portrayed as 'reading society as a text'.[103] Wolfson pointedly contrasts Wollstonecraft's anti-authoritarian, romantically 'Satanic' way of reading Milton's *Paradise Lost* with the 'conduct-book' conformism of Hannah More.[104] She also appreciates the importance of Wollstonecraft's discussion of 'Moses's beautiful, poetical cosmogony, and the account of the fall of man'.[105] Wollstonecraft, by seeing the Bible as poetry rather than infallible dogma, reads the central religious text of the culture more like William Blake than Hannah More. Just how radical Wollstonecraft's theological politics were can be gauged by comparing her comments on 'Moses's poetical story'[106] with the comments of Mary Hays who criticizes the Adam and Eve story only in minor ways: even if the first human couple was punished, subsequent generations were not similarly damned.[107] Hays does not contest the historicity of Adam and Eve, whom Wollstonecraft reads as poetic fictions. Hays, it will be recalled, was on the far left of the religious spectrum, a liberal Unitarian, but she does not challenge the authority of the Bible as Wollstonecraft does.

Another way the second *Vindication* articulates its vision of the revolution in female manners is satire, as I already briefly discussed. Two drawn-out comparisons between women and soldiers and women and rich people are both witty and designed to subvert misogynistic culture fundamentally. Hyper-masculine symbols of national strength and valour, the military soldiers who, like women, 'practice the minor virtues', are rewarded for unthinking obedience, attention to their appearance, a penchant for dancing, 'crowded rooms, adventures, and ridicule'. Like women they are taught to 'please'. How exactly soldiers are superior to women 'it is difficult to discover'.[108] Similarly, the women who resemble the wealthy élite 'are not to be contradicted in company, are not allowed to exert any manual strength; and from them the negative virtues only are expected' – none, of course, connected with intellectual effort.[109] Wollstonecraft aims her satire at two iconic representatives of the social order, soldiers and the rich, producing the irony that the qualities deemed undesirable in women are the same that are tolerated if not praised in the socially privileged. (Mary Robinson actually challenges the premise that women are physically weaker and incapable of being soldiers.)[110]

The theme of the 'degradation' of women gets a whole chapter – the fourth – and receives emphasis throughout the *Vindication of the Rights of Woman*. Women's reduction to animal-like status is wittily captured in a phrase Wollstonecraft uses numerous times: the 'spaniel-like affection' of women and girls.[111] A quotation from *Paradise Lost* develops the degradation motif with great effectiveness. She quotes from the eighth book where Adam speaks to Raphael about the way that sexual desire for Eve, to whom he feels superior in every way, enchants him – making her seem powerful, as if in her presence and only in her presence 'All higher knowledge ... falls / Degraded' (VIII.548–54).[112] Eve's physical beauty alone is enough to provoke a degradation of Adam's spiritual idealizations, so that his attraction to her body is the principal cause of his 'fall'. Wollstonecraft astutely locates the source for women's degradation in man's inability to reconcile his intellectual aspirations with his sexual desires.

The final two examples of Wollstonecraft's satire probably influenced other women writers. When the *Vindication of the Rights of Woman* mocks the cultural assumptions of Clarissa's rape in Samuel Richardson's novel (1747–9), namely that a raped woman loses her 'honour' and 'virtue' even though she is blameless,[113] it exposes the absurd sexual fetish of female virginity. Mary Hays's *The Victim of Prejudice* (1799) illustrates the destructiveness of the fetish in two generations of women, the novel's intradiegetic narrator Mary, who is raped by a wealthy landowner Sir Peter Osborne, and Mary's mother whose single 'lapse' into sexual activity condemns her forever afterwards to a life outside of respectability. Even though the raped Mary could not be more blameless, she is looked upon as no different than a 'whore'.[114] The *Vindication* points to the common hypocrisy of the double standard: while women can do nothing to regain 'respectability' after any kind of illicit sexual encounter, men lose no moral status whatsoever by their sexual adventures, even when they morally contaminate the women with whom they have sex.[115] An irony Wollstonecraft frequently exploits is the double bind that the culture puts on women – their bodies are dangerously attractive but their minds should not be cultivated lest they too become dangerous – leading her to wryly quote from John Gregory's *Father's Legacy to His Daughters* (1774): 'But if you happen to have any learning, keep it a profound secret'.[116] In *Northanger Abbey* (1818) Jane Austen's narrator comments just as ironically: 'A woman especially, if she have the misfortune of knowing any thing, should conceal it as well as she can'.[117]

The highly contested word 'virtue' is at the focal point of Wollstonecraft's philosophical project, appropriating the word from both misogynistic fetishism and the republican tradition. She develops an almost Freudian triadic schema of passion, reason and virtue which presupposes liberty and equality for the exercise of reason and the educating of virtue. Liberty, 'the mother of virtue',[118] permits passion and reason to work their way toward resolution in experience that educates the virtuous life. The very opposite of liberty is the condition of coerced weakness and dependence under which women are forced to live. The psychological preconditions of moral agency are 'solitude' and 'reflection' that 'give to wishes the force of passions' and 'enable the imagination to enlarge the object'.[119] Countering the premises of the moral-sense school of philosophy and the assumptions of sensibility, Wollstonecraft affirms the deliberate and willed nature of virtue that comes out of reason not 'impulse'. Countering also the utilitarian school, she adopts an ethics whereby 'virtue must be loved as in itself sublime' and 'not for the advantages it procures'.[120]

Wollstonecraft understands the project of virtue in terms of the situated body. Women's oppression is through their bodies: the unnatural and exaggerated weakness of the female body, the ornamentation of the body to attract men, the body's utilitarian investment in attracting a husband, the virginity fetish, the modesty complex and the beauty system. 'Taught from their infancy that beauty is woman's sceptre, the mind shapes itself to the body, and roaming round its gilt cage, only seeks to adorn its prison.'[121] The alienation of the body from the woman's identity is from the thoroughly instrumental functioning of the body to acquire things it cannot obtain in any other way. Because the sexualization of the body is so much a part of how women's dependence and weakness are constructed, the *Vindication* has numerous statements against investing too much in sexual love – enough statements to make some critics like Cora Kaplan call them out-rightly anti-sexual.[122] The final position on sexuality, however, is not repressive; Wollstonecraft has no objections to the 'artless impulse of nature', criticizing instead 'the sexual desire of conquest when the heart is out of the question'.[123] The *Vindication* has numerous affirmations of the female body. A typical example is the passage citing Dr Gregory's advice to his daughters that they should inhibit expression of whatever enjoyment they might have from dancing, as such expressions would not be ladylike. Wollstonecraft counters with unqualified praise for the body in dance, arguing that it should be allowed 'innocent vivacity' and 'the natural frankness of youth'. To give the young woman instructions to curb her pleasure out of fear of how it might be construed by men is the truly 'indecent' manoeuvre.[124] Similarly, the *Vindication* applies *Émile*'s condemnation of confining the body with swaddling clothes and its encouragement of free physical movement to girls, who, it is proposed, should be raised with the same physical freedom as boys.[125] Wollstonecraft puts extraordinary emphasis on the necessity for girls to have strong, healthy bodies that enjoy play and exercise, for them to be permitted to be as 'wild' as boys, and for them to be allowed to 'frolic' without inhibition. The fundamental structure upon which the edifice of female weakness and dependence is built starts with the training of a girl's body to avoid vigorous and strenuous exercise for fear of being masculine and unattractive. Wollstonecraft's insistence that the reformed state schools be coeducational throughout all levels also depends on the insight that the sexes have to be given the same opportunities, intellectual and physical, if the revolution in female manners is to be successful in dismantling the full structure of woman's oppression.

Conclusion

The inability of the male French revolutionaries to provide good reasons for excluding women from citizenship suggests the limits of Enlightenment cosmopolitanism, in that they were unable to carry through logically where reason actually led, but were rational enough to know that what they were doing was indefensible. Wollstonecraft's feminism subverts the rigid gender system that creates exaggeratedly dominant masculinity and equally exaggerated submissive femininity; such a system fuels political violence in the form of xenophobic nationalism and war that preys on weak scapegoats. It is impossible to conceive of a cosmopolitan political culture that does not make sexual equality an indispensable principle as a central part of its ideology because the violence of the hierarchical exclusions based on gender always becomes expressed in other violent forms as well. Wollstonecraft's achievements were a quantum leap beyond what had been written previously and her writing made that of others possible – the final work of Mary Robinson and the best work of Mary Hays.

4 WRITING AGAINST SLAVERY, RACE AND EMPIRE

Introduction

The Enlightenment, which provided compelling arguments against slavery, also developed the theory of scientific racism that justified the expansion of empire, especially the conquest of Asians, Africans and native Americans. Slavery, race and empire were conceptual and political opportunities for developing cosmopolitan departures from current ideas and practices, departures that are evident in the pages of the *Analytical Review*, Equiano's *Interesting Narrative* (1788), two plays by John Thelwall (*Incle and Yarico* (1787) and *The Incas* (1792)) and his remarkable novel, *The Daughter of Adoption* (1801). These texts do not comprehensively cover the topics of slavery, race and empire nor does the chapter attempt any such coverage. My justification for the chapter is that these texts have not been examined in terms of cosmopolitan ideas and that none but Equiano's *Interesting Narrative* has received much critical attention of any kind. If the chapter advances the discussion of cosmopolitanism in relation to these not inconsiderable topics, the chapter will have earned its existence.

That slavery became a major political point of contention in the eighteenth century – and not before then – provokes David Brion Davis, prominent historian of slavery, to remark that the new development was 'momentous' in terms of the evolution of morality.[1] Discussing slavery in terms of morality is in itself contentious because economic explanations of slavery and its abolition seem to have more currency now as scholars are rightly sceptical of anything appearing to be self-servingly 'idealistic'. Eric Williams and Walter Rodney, for example, look askance at the moral explanations for slavery's abolition, attributing the dismantling of slavery to its being unprofitable in relation to the more efficient free labour of the Industrial Revolution – whose 'take-off' was funded by the proceeds from slavery – and the exploitation of colonies.[2] Robert William Fogle and Stanley L. Engerman argue on the other side of the economic analysis, claiming that slavery in the American South was in fact enormously profitable well into the nineteenth century.[3] Davis does not claim that economic motives were irrelevant to either slavery's flourishing or demise but he considers the moral dimension substantial enough to warrant serious deliberation.[4]

'By the 1750s', according to Davis, 'the classical justifications for slavery, already discredited by Montesquieu and Hutcheson, were being demolished by the arguments of Rousseau, Diderot, and other philosophes'.[5] Quakers, who began repudiating slavery as early as 1657, initiated the first political challenge to the slave trade in the 1770s.[6] By 1788 the Society for Effecting the Abolition of the Slave Trade was actively organizing on multiple fronts and twenty years later the slave trade was indeed abolished. For political reform of a major institution involving colossal amounts of money, capital, land and wealth, not to mention the thousands of enslaved Africans transported every year to the West Indies and North America, twenty years is actually short, especially when compared to the length of time other important political changes took place, such as the reforms of the franchise in Britain: the universal manhood suffrage advocated by the London Corresponding Society in 1792 was not even fully achieved in the 1884 Reform Act, and Mary Wollstonecraft, hardly the first woman to put forward the idea of woman's franchise, proposed a reform that was not enacted until 1918. Although it had been accepted as a necessary institution for centuries almost everywhere in the world, slavery becoming morally unacceptable in the eighteenth century – obviously long overdue – is an achievement not to be slighted.

An alliance of Enlightenment rationalists and liberal Christians was able to win the battle of public opinion soundly enough to force parliament to end the slave trade in 1807 – aided by the French restoration of slavery in 1802 , which made abolition patriotic and Christian rather than French and Jacobin as it was in the 1790s.[7] Abolishing slavery in the empire altogether was a much more difficult task, given the political strength of the West Indian planters and merchants that was not broken until after the 1832 Reform Act.[8] The stark contrast between the abolitionists and the defenders of slavery is apparent in their discourse: the abolitionists launch arguments founded on biblical texts, the domestic affections, liberal rights theory and various shades of moral theory, while the apologists for slavery cede the moral argument entirely to their opponents and shield slavery as a 'necessary evil' justified by practicality, the rights of colonial governments to self-determination and finally property rights.[9] The pro-slavery arguments were so weak that abolition might have come sooner if it had not been for the slave rebellion in St Domingo in 1791 and the formation of the Haitian republic of former slaves in 1804. The 'spectre of Haiti' made rapid progress toward abolition less likely.[10]

Peter J. Kitson suggests racism as the primary reason why chattel slavery of Africans did not become a moral issue any sooner for Europeans, who viewed their neighbours to the south as inferior beings in need of Christianity and civilization.[11] Racial attitudes are socially constructed by multiple pressures and lines of influence, as Winthrop D. Jordan's research discloses in his study of how slavery in America became exclusively racial over time.[12] While powerful social forces deepened and naturalized racist assumptions through colonial legislation and propaganda, the triumph of racism did not go unchallenged. The religious assumption that everyone was a child of God subverted the logic of racial hierarchy, which was also undermined by humanitarian beliefs in social unity. The icon of the abolitionist movement from 1787 was the image of an African kneeling in chains asking the question, 'Am I not a man and a brother?' If the answer was affirmative, then slavery became insupportable. Although racism was a fundamental prop for slavery, abolitionists also upheld racist assumptions, for they routinely urged enslaved Africans to acquire Christianity and civilization to become more fully human, just as supporters of Jewish emancipation demanded that Jews change themselves to become more like Christian Europeans. Being an abolitionist did not necessarily entail a conviction that whites and blacks were equal. Opposing prejudice against Africans was a major cultural project to promote the overall goal of abolishing slavery. As long as the battle against prejudice was conducted within a moral and religious framework, certain traditional lines of argument had validity, but the transition to race science and biological determinism made the older ways of thinking completely obsolete. The motto, 'Am I not a man and a brother?' works well for either a religious or a secular orientation but within the conceptual framework of scientific race theory, one of the most unfortunate products of Enlightenment rationalism, the answer to those questions was not necessarily affirmative. The tension between science and morality is an inevitable dimension of modernity and cannot be wished away. Liberal Christians used slavery, as David Brion Davis suggests, as an issue upon which to develop moral clarity that would transcend the troubling complexities of relativism and religious scepticism.[13] When France restored slavery, the British abolitionists contrasted the morally corrupt regime informed by the Enlightenment rationalists and sceptics with the morally superior Christians on the other side of the English Channel. Secular abolitionists, like most of those in the London Corresponding Society, while allowing Wilberforce and other religiously motivated actors to take the lead, worked toward a cosmopolitan, democratic order in their own political work.[14] It is not surprising to learn that abolition served ideological purposes unrelated to the welfare of enslaved Africans. While not the most daunting threat to the abolitionist efforts in the early nineteenth century, scientific race theory later in the century displaced the moral and religious discourse about human differences with dire consequences for European Jewry. This chapter pays attention to the early forms of race science before it became culturally hegemonic.

When the final volumes of Edward Gibbon's *History of the Decline and Fall of the Roman Empire* were published in 1788, it is doubtful that a more intriguing text could have been delivered to a Britain in the early middle stages of developing a world empire. William Pitt the Elder, having led Britain in one of its greatest military victories over France in the Seven Years' War (1756–63), left an imperial legacy that troubled some but earned the strong approval of many. Imperialism was popular in Britain across all social strata.[15] Nevertheless, having just 'lost' their colony in North America, Britons reflected on the morality of their imperial ambitions during the lengthy (1787–95) impeachment trial of Warren Hastings, governor general of India (1773–86). Burke's dogged pursuit of Hastings, ultimately ineffective as his target was acquitted, raised questions about empire similar to those raised by Gibbon. A minority of republican idealists thought it was better to lose empire and cultivate a more nationally self-sufficient 'virtue' than to increase empire by imposing British will on the world for more wealth and power. The example of Rome was notoriously sobering, as 'luxury' from imperial wealth and power led to moral corruption and political decay. Gibbon's provocative treatment of Christianity brought protests from almost all quarters, including the *Analytical Review* (whose reviewer complained of Gibbon's 'indecent and puerile sarcasms' directed against Christianity)[16] but empire itself had a relativizing effect on national culture. The eighteenth century was the great moment for the intellectual fascination with the non-European Other, from Montesquieu's *Les lettres persanes* (1721; translated as *Persian Letters* 1751) to Lady Montagu's *Turkish Embassy Letters* (1763) and Sir William Jones's translations of Sanskrit poems at the end of the century. The cosmopolitan effects of empire derive from the necessity of acknowledging and adjusting to the reality of people who are emphatically different. The violence that empire inflicted upon an already existing, organically intricate community with ancient traditions troubled some but the intoxicating prospect of adding to national wealth and power while spreading Christianity and civilization was hard to resist. Empire's intimate connection with slavery and race in the West Indies – especially, Jamaica, which became, after the St Domingo rebellions, the largest sugar producer in the world – was a moral and political conundrum only partially solved by slave trade and finally slavery abolition. Opposing slavery, to be sure, did not guarantee a position opposing empire. Indeed, the most zealous colonizers of Africa were abolitionists.[17] Slavery, race and empire were intertwined in complicated ways that require careful attention.

The *Analytical Review* on Race, Empire, Slavery and Translation

The relevance of early race science and biological determinism to late-Enlightenment and romantic-era literary representations becomes apparent in the very title of a nineteenth-century American text: *How to Read Character. A New Illustrated Hand-Book of Phrenology and Physiognomy* (1872).[18] Phrenology, physiognomy and race science, all of which developed in the eighteenth century, make epistemological claims for understanding mental phenomena – moral, intellectual and emotional – by being able to decipher external, physical signs. How to read character is also the literary project of realistic fiction as well as the broadly philosophical project of autobiography. Just at the historical point when racial slavery was losing its moral legitimacy and European Jewry was experiencing the dissolution of some of the religiously based forms of oppression, a new kind of secular and scientific racialism was emerging.

The ambivalence of the Enlightenment toward race can be seen in the intellectual project of one of the architects of race science, Johann Friedrich Blumenbach, 'the most influential writer of the period on the subject of human difference', according to Peter J. Kitson.[19] One of Coleridge's teachers at Göttingen, Blumenbach was compelled by the power of the evidence, as he describes it, to abandon the four-race model of Linnaeus, which was largely based on geography and the four humours, for a hierarchical five-race model. The primeval, central and original race from which the other four are degenerations is the Caucasian, a term he himself coined, as he concluded that the beautiful Georgians who lived near Mount Caucasus were the earliest human beings.[20] Rather than hiding the aesthetic and indeed erotic basis of his theory, he presented it unselfconsciously to a European scientific community that largely accepted the thesis of Caucasian superiority and priority. Blumenbach the scientist sometimes sounds just like an ordinary bigot as when he claims that he could always tell a Jew by his eyes because they 'breathe of the East'. By 1806, however, he was alarmed enough by the outright racism of much race theory to devote a long chapter – the thirteenth – arguing strenuously for the humanity, intelligence and attractiveness of black Africans, as he insisted that they were as fully human as Caucasians.[21] He did not, however, retract any part of the five-race theory, nor did he withdraw his opinion on the superiority of the Caucasians; indeed, he still refers to dark skin as 'disagreeable'.[22] Like many other European opponents of slavery, Blumenbach assumed the Caucasians were better but he was offended when supporters of slavery used race science to justify an inhumane institution. The abolitionist Blumenbach was not a racist in the ordinary sense of that term but he was unselfconsciously Eurocentric, as Stephen Jay Gould has pointed out.[23] By following what were considered at the time normative scientific procedures, Blumenbach offered the most gripping alternative to Linnaeus's much looser theory of human types. The example of Blumenbach, political liberal and empirical scientist, demonstrates both the arrogance of Enlightenment reason and the unavoidable historicity of all knowledge. Blumenbach's example also teaches yet another Enlightenment lesson, according to Gould, namely the power of social forces over ideas, regardless of individual intentions.[24]

The utterly capricious origin of the word Caucasian might have discredited the entire project of race science and its underlying paradigm of biological determinism, but such was not the case. The craniometry of Pieter Camper (1722–89) established mathematically exact facial angles to determine races that proved once again that Caucasians were both the most beautiful and the most intelligent race.[25] The *Analytical Review* thought so highly of Camper that it used its lead article for July 1796 to discuss *The Works of the Late Prof. Camper*. One looks in vain for critical and sceptical remarks on Camper's treatise describing where the various peoples of the world fit into the racial hierarchy.[26] The *Analytical*, which tried being as current and up to date as possible, had no compelling reason to review the book, for it was published several years earlier. A plausible inference is that the overall outlook of the *Analytical* was receptive to some forms of biological determinism as long as its racism was not strident. Physiognomy and phrenology, although frequently ridiculed and disputed, had considerable popularity and influence, as commonplace generalizations and stereotypes about people were able to pass as scientific data. Even the *Analytical Review* circle was largely favourable to the greatest popularizer of physiognomy, Johann Caspar Lavater (1741–1801), friend of the painter Henry Fuseli (who in turn was a friend of publisher Joseph Johnson).[27] Lavater's physiognomy study, translated by Godwin's best friend Thomas Holcroft, who would become in 1794 one of Thelwall's fellow treason trial defendants, was enormously popular and became a kind of coffee-table book with finely executed illustrations.[28] Wollstonecraft herself was working on a translation of Lavater's book until her publisher Joseph Johnson became aware of the Holcroft edition. The *Analytical* article on the Lavater translation complains about the reduction of material from the German edition but offers no critical remarks whatsoever about the scientific credibility of Lavater's inferring psychological and moral characteristics from the way faces look.[29] The craniometry of the later Victorian era secured its respectability as a valid science declaiming on comparative brain weights, and the bizarre criminology of Cesare Lombroso (1835–1909), with its reading of criminal and degenerate faces, was taken with the utmost seriousness. These more destructive forms of biological determinism merely repeat at a more sinister level the slightly more benign pseudo-sciences of the eighteenth and early nineteenth centuries. Richard T. Gray's recent study of physiognomy from Lavater to the Nazi race scientists Guenther and Clauss makes a strong case for a tradition of pseudo-scientific writing with deadly consequences. What might have started as innocent parlour games with reading silhouettes and physiognomies concluded with earnest applications of biological determinism in pursuit of eugenics which, as Stephen Jay Gould observes, became fully discredited only after World War II and the defeat of the Nazis.[30]

The Enlightenment produced such morally and politically baneful ideas because of Eurocentrism and a philosophical orientation toward psychological determinism that came out of empiricism. A characteristic statement in the *Analytical Review* is pertinent here: 'The dispositions of men are more formed by the external circumstances of their situation, than moralists in general are disposed to allow'.[31] Locke could be said to have ushered in modernity when he established that ideas were not timeless and innate but came from sense experience within temporality. Biological determinism as a form of empiricist logic assumes that the mind does not generate its own creations but is instead created by forces over which the mind has no control. Hegel, who in the *Phenomenology* (1807) challenged Lavater's physiognomy by reversing the priority from physical being to deeds performed by the subject, articulated what would be the obvious objection to all forms of physical determinism: people created themselves to some extent and were not wholly formed by inherited and environmental structures.[32] The Lavater example is especially interesting because the Protestant pastor who badgered Moses Mendelssohn to convert to Christianity was anything but a scientific materialist. Lavater, who paradoxically upholds intuition as an instrument of cognition to infer moral qualities from bodily configurations, banishes something that makes him anxious, namely, the contingency of meaning and the uncertainties of knowing the world reliably.[33] Whether he purchases the metaphysical certainty in Protestant Christianity or the crackpot notions of physiognomy, Lavater expels the doubt of modernity, the legacy of Descartes and Locke.

Science promises certainty and verifiable knowledge, and for several centuries biological determinism seemed to deliver on these promises. The ideal of objectivity, however, also entails self-correcting procedures that only occasionally were applied to the error of Eurocentrism. The anthology of Enlightenment statements on race put together by Emanuel Chukwudi Eze reveals a degree of philosophical blindness that is truly disturbing, especially the prevalence of aesthetic judgments operating in lieu of scientific investigation of evidence. Blumenbach was not the only scientific observer who discovered that the European Caucasians were the most attractive race and that the ugliest race happened to be the same people who were enslaved by the Europeans. Georges Cuvier, for example, the most influential naturalist in France in the early nineteenth century, finds Blumenbach right on target about the beautiful residents of Georgia near the Caucasian mountains, but finds that Africans look like monkeys.[34] Linnaeus, Buffon, Hume, Beattie, Jefferson, Kant and Hegel all make similarly foolish comments. One cannot infer from this appalling irrationality that the Enlightenment was always and everywhere racist or that a necessary aspect of the Enlightenment was racism. The long march from eighteenth-century physiognomy and craniometry to Nazi science was by no means inevitable because at each step of the way counter-arguments and rebuttals were directed at biological determinism and its racist applications.

A journal more strongly committed to Enlightenment ideals than the *Analytical Review* would be difficult to find; it almost always opposed racism, even though it affirmed certain kinds of biological determinism and it did not recognize the dangerous tendencies in Lavater's and Camper's ideas. The cosmopolitan affirmation of humanity itself is more typical than the ethnological division of people into races. Commenting on Lavater's *Aphorisms* (1788), for example, the *Analytical* reviewer offers embarrassingly naïve (and undeserved) praise for the philosophical acumen of the Swiss author: 'perhaps it is necessary to love the human race, and to be one of its ornaments, before the virtues and vices which adorn and debase it can be discerned and unfolded'.[35]

The *Analytical* also strongly *opposed* certain manifestations of biological determinism – theories of human origins that assumed differences were innate and unchangeable. Wollstonecraft, for example, praised Samuel Stanhope Smith for countering Lord Kames's polygenist view. (The monogenesis theory assumed a single origin for humanity and usually attributed differences of complexion and body structure to climate). Kames, 'an important literary figure of the Scottish Enlightenment', published 'one of the rare, but significant statements of the full-fledged polygenist argument for considering different human peoples as separate species of one *genus*'.[36] Smith, an American Presbyterian minister, 'put forward the classic environmentalist argument that physical variety among humankind was due to natural and social causes', but this unremarkably Enlightenment position also depended on 'a literalist understanding of scripture', particularly the 'Mosaical account'[37] of human development from Eden to the Flood.[38] It is a dilemma for a religious modernist like Wollstonecraft who for political reasons favours the Presbyterian writer to the more scientific Kames, but she has more in common intellectually with the Scottish philosopher. Biblical literalism was not Smith's only deviation from the rigours of scientific rationalism; he also claimed that whiteness had moral causes: 'the more civilised a people the fairer they became'.[39] Despite his significant weaknesses, Smith receives Wollstonecraft's praise because what matters most from a cosmopolitan perspective is unity of the human race. 'The untutored savage and the cultivated sage are to be found to be men of like passions with ourselves'.[40] She recognized that the polygenist hypothesis, regardless of how sophisticated its argument, was toxic to the Enlightenment commitments to social solidarity and the unity of the human race.

Bringing the love of the human race down to specifics, Wollstonecraft comments on a piece of North African travel literature, observing that, although there seem to be differences between whites and blacks, these differences are not disadvantageous to blacks. 'We do not here perceive any reality in the supposed inferiority of the black race to the white, but often the contrary.'[41] In another review of a book on Africa, Vaillant's *New Travels into the Interior Parts of Africa* (1796), she contrasts the cruel European planters with the 'well meaning, affectionate' natives. The heartless conduct of the invading Europeans proves 'how unfit half-civilised men are to be entrusted with unlimited power'. Wollstonecraft reads the book as an eyewitness account of African society that rebuts the claims of African inferiority by the 'degeneracy' school of race theorists. With 'domestic virtues and moral sensibility' the 'hottentots', far from 'disgusting' and dirty, compare favourably with the whites who have become 'rapacious' from the spirit of 'commerce', which has expelled 'humanity' from their 'bosoms'. Nonviolent until the Europeans invaded, the bushmen who attack the whites do so only because they have been brutalized.[42]

Wollstonecraft overcomes Eurocentrism sufficiently to make harsh moral judgments of the Europeans:

> These worthless profligates wished to enjoy the fruits of the land without the trouble of tilling it. Educated, besides, with all the prejudices of the whites, they imagined that men of a different colour were born only to be their slaves. They accordingly subjected them to bondage, condemned them to the most laborious services with harsh and severe treatment. The houzouanas, incensed at such arbitrary tyrannical conduct, refused any longer to work for them, and retired to the defiles of their mountains. The planters took up arms and pursued them; they massacred them without pity, and seized on their cattle and their country. Those who escaped their atrocities betook themselves to flight, and removed to the land which they now occupy; but, on quitting their former possessions, they swore in their own name and that of their posterity, to exterminate these European monsters, to be revenged against whom they had so many incitements. And thus, if tradition be true, was a peaceful and industrious nation rendered warlike, vindictive, and ferocious.[43]

The sarcasm typical of Wollstonecraft's style is in full display here, where she depicts the Europeans as cruel thieves and murderers who delude themselves into thinking their immorality is somehow justified by their white skin. The Africans, on the other hand, are not sentimental victims but historical actors in a violent tragedy, displaying moral agency. Wollstonecraft's shaping of the narrative constructs the bare outlines of what will become her daughter Mary's conceptual formula of the victim/victimizer for *Frankenstein*: once peaceful but now vindictive and ferocious because of unspeakable mistreatment.

The abolitionists publicized the horrors of slavery in order to exert moral pressure to end the slave trade and slavery itself. Not atypically the *Analytical* uses the many horrors depicted in Captain Stedman's *Narrative of a Five Years Expedition* and graphically illustrated by William Blake's prints to reassert the argument for slavery's complete abolition.[44] The *Analytical* was outraged by the treatment of the Jamaican maroons, a free and independent people by 1738. After the maroons rebelled against mistreatment in July 1795, influenced by the St Domingo rebellion nearby, the conflict degenerated into a brutal hunt for the demonized maroons – accused of cannibalism – at £20 a head, £100 for the leaders. In its account of the violence, the *Analytical* sides openly with the maroons, whose victimization is a 'stain' on the moral reputation of Britain.[45] Although the *Analytical* publicized as part of the abolitionist campaign atrocities inflicted upon Africans and slaves, it also pondered the difficulty people have to 'feel for distant misery' when there is ample misery right at home.[46] Another difficulty for the abolitionists was that when evidence of injustice by the Africans themselves against other Africans could not be dismissed as simply racist fiction, then it strengthened the arguments of slavery's apologists that the Africans could not govern themselves properly. The reports of Africans being horribly mistreated in the kingdom of Dahomy complicated the abolitionists' task.[47]

The *Analytical*'s treatment of the Turkish Empire, India and empire in general parallels its treatment of racism and slavery to a large extent, but there are differences. With the Turks it was their religion that was the greatest sign of difference. Not lacking were negative views of the Turks, 'bigoted, barbarous, and brutal people', according to one reviewer,[48] and in another review they are represented primarily as oppressors of the Greeks, practising a 'haughty' ethnic purity and disdaining to mix with Christians.[49] The Turks were not without their defenders in the pages of the *Analytical*, however, where, for example, a harshly critical review of *Considérations sur la Guerre actuelle des Turcs* (1788) challenged Volney's hostility to the Turks.[50] On an issue that Turks were traditionally demonized, the treatment of women, an *Analytical* reviewer vindicates the Turkish situation for women.[51] The journal was far more interested in India, its culture and religion, for the obvious reason that Britain was deeply involved there as a colonial power. Rather than accept the oppression of the poor as inevitable, the *Analytical* asks: 'Is it possible to read this last story [about the oppressed Indian peasantry] without an earnest wish, that the spirit of *political reformation* which has appeared in Europe may spread, till its healing influence reaches every wretched sufferer under despotic power upon the face of the earth?'[52] Schooled in the lessons of postcolonial scepticism, one notices that the reviewer, applying his or her Enlightenment universalism, proposes a Western solution to an Asian problem, arguably a form of liberal imperialism, certainly one of the *Analytical*'s intellectual approaches.

Related to the limits of Enlightenment tolerance for difference is the whole issue of translation, a literary enterprise in which the publisher Joseph Johnson was heavily invested and a philosophical issue with political implications.[53] Discussing Cowper's translation of Homer, the *Analytical* reviewer notes two kinds of translation, one of which hybridizes the original and the translator's language to create something unique and another that defers completely to the original.[54] Although it may seem that both kinds of translation acknowledge the value of the foreign tongue, the former is actually more open to the otherness of the different language as it allows the two languages to interact and risk transformation. The latter, by mechanically attaching literal meanings to each word and sentence, guards the translator's language from discovering new things in an interaction with the other language. The reviewer's concept of the hybridized translation is strikingly similar to the view of translation taken by Walter Benjamin. In Benjamin's justly famous essay on translation there is no nostalgia for the lost original, nor is there the romantic conviction that language's singular organic particularity can suffer translation only in terms of violence and loss. Literary works, he argues, 'undergo a complete transformation over the centuries',[55] but literary works, despite their cultural specificity, possess what he calls 'translatability'.[56] Languages in fact are 'interrelated' and are not 'strangers to one another'. The intervention of translation brings out something new that was potentially meaningful.[57] As Gadamer phrases it, 'every translation is at the same time an interpretation'.[58] Benjamin speaks of a 'pure language' disclosed by translation, bringing to the surface things that would not exist except for the interaction of the two languages.[59] Between the poles of 'fidelity' and 'license', the Benjaminian translator is encouraged to exercise freedom and creativity, as the language of translation should 'let itself go, so that it gives voice to the *intentio* of the original not as reproduction but as harmony, as a supplement to the language in which it expresses itself as its own kind of *intentio*'.[60] The kind of *intentio* to which Benjamin here refers is not subjectivistic but something objective, immanent, inherent, potential, even teleological.

Anticipations of the Benjaminian conception of translation materialize in a reviewer's attention to a new version of Livy's *History of Rome*. First, the reviewer praises translation of Greek and Latin literature for making available to readers who otherwise would have no opportunity of reading this kind of literature: 'the valuable stores of ancient literature should, as much as possible, be rendered accessible to readers, who have not enjoyed the benefit of a classical education'. Second, translation, far from being a mechanical transcription from one language to another, entails enough learning and creativity to deserve the prestige of a literary art. 'The office of translator has been too much depreciated'. Third, every age needs its own translations, as historical moments have their own specificity that requires a new experience of the classical text.[61] Translation, a democratizing process requiring artistry, provokes the reviewer to recognize the hermeneutical situatedness and temporality of all writing.

Wollstonecraft brings out the explicit political issues of translation in her review of Sir William Jones's rendering of the Sanskrit poem *Sacontalá*. Confronted with something so unfamiliar, we initially fall back on what we already know, she asserts. 'With respect to manners, we are all, more or less, under the dominion of prejudice, and so local are our senses, and even our judgment, that for a short time every thing strange appears absurd.' Similes in the translation should be 'universally poetic', a concept that prefigures Benjaminian 'pure language'. In her extensive and detailed summary of the poem's plot, she discusses the poem on its own terms, allowing the foreign text its otherness before it gets appropriated by the British reader.[62] That translation works against 'prejudice' is Wollstonecraft's insight into the political meaning of the entire literary enterprise.

The *Analytical Review*, then, as a late Enlightenment intellectual journal, demonstrated insightful understanding of many but not all issues connected with slavery, race and empire, and formulated thoughtful reflections on the enterprise of translation, the linguistic experience of the nationally and historically different Other. The journal did not adhere to a party line on political issues, so it is not surprising to see a range of views expressed on the Ottoman Empire and empire in general, but the *Analytical* consistently defends Africans from the prejudicial evaluations of race science and slavery's defenders. Paying heed to the logic and traditions of both moral-religious discourse and scientific discourse, the *Analytical* cannot avoid a clash of values, but moments of outright contradiction are infrequent, mostly from avoidance rather than intellectual resolution.

Equiano's *Interesting Narrative*

Although it is surprising Wollstonecraft did not praise Equiano's *Interesting Narrative* more forthrightly than she did, her review is strikingly positive compared with a review that appears in close proximity to hers in the same issue of the *Analytical*. The review of Captain Tench's *Narrative of the Expedition to Botany-Bay* (1789) portrays the non-European indigenous inhabitants as aliens, physically repulsive, ugly, naked cave-dwellers who are closer to animals than civilized people.[63] Neither Tench nor the reviewer makes any effort to overcome Eurocentric bias and to exert the cosmopolitan imagination in order to find some common ground with the aborigines of Australia. Wollstonecraft's review. of the *Interesting Narrative* by contrast gives long extracts from the initial chapter describing Essaka and the customs of his people and accentuates the humanity and moral subjectivity of Africans rather than atrocities committed by Europeans against Africans. Wollstonecraft does not ignore but only briefly takes note of the many disturbing 'anecdotes' of mistreatment that make the reader's 'blood turn its course', which is a shrewd move for an abolitionist because the real issue is slavery itself, its indefensible immorality, not how well or poorly the whites treat their slaves. According to the understated comments of the review, the very existence of the *Interesting Narrative* disproves the absurd claims that Africans are not fully human and that their subhuman status makes them suitable for enslavement. Wollstonecraft finds the *Interesting Narrative* to be a flawed piece of literature that is overly long, not structured well for dramatic effect, stylistically inconsistent and tediously preoccupied with his religious conversion, but she also judges that the author's evident talent places him 'on a par with the general mass of men, who fill the subordinate stations in a more civilized society than that which he was thrown into at his birth'.[64] The *Interesting Narrative*, as I will argue, is a far more inventive literary performance than the review credits it, but Wollstonecraft's defence of the text does not depend on its literary merit. Just because Equiano is not a literary genius he and his people are not inferior to Europeans; rather, Equiano and his people are like 'us', no better and no worse. As a way to present a strong abolitionist case Wollstonecraft's line of thinking is effective but as literary criticism it falls short.

The question of the *Interesting Narrative*'s authenticity, which was raised in Equiano's day, has continued to preoccupy readers. Wollstonecraft both accepts the text as Equiano's and hints that some parts might not have been written by him, pointing out 'contradiction' in the *Narrative*: 'many childish stories and puerile remarks, do not agree with some more solid reflections, which occur in the first pages. In the style also we observed a striking contrast: a few well written periods do not smoothly unite with the general tenor of the language.'[65] Even so Wollstonecraft's is mild criticism, suggesting that perhaps someone else wrote – rewrote? – the first chapter and a small number of sentences elsewhere in the text. The *Monthly Review* found that it was 'not improbable' that 'some English writer has assisted [Equiano] in the compilement, or at least, the correction of his book; for it is sufficiently well-written'.[66] As Henry Louis Gates, Jr has illustrated so vividly, race and literacy in the eighteenth century were so closely entwined that many whites assumed Africans were incapable of reading and writing, which were not simply technologies of communication but the most important signs of being fully human. Gates called attention to the Talking Book trope in slave narratives that recorded the abject relation of the illiterate to the powerful, fetishized object of print culture.[67] Srinivas Aravamudan has carried this analysis in a new direction by ascribing to literacy itself the means by which the nationalistic and colonial projects were carried forward and legitimated while at the same time marginalizing the masses of illiterate and barely literate victims of empire. In his reading of the *Interesting Narrative*, Equiano largely buys into the hegemonic literacy, an interpretation I do not find persuasive.[68] If Equiano wrote the *Interesting Narrative*, or most of it, or even a small part of it (given the racist assumptions of African sub-humanity that Gates discloses), a major justification for slavery was removed.

Another way in which the *Interesting Narrative* was subjected to the question of authenticity was the challenge to Equiano's status as an African. Letters in the *Oracle* and the *Star* in April 1792 claimed, on what evidence we do not know, that Equiano was not born in Africa but rather the West Indian island of Santa Cruz (or St Croix as it is now known).[69] Equiano and his friends interpreted the letters as attempts by supporters of slavery to undermine the successful book tour in Britain.[70] As reconstructed in a recent article by John Bugg, Equiano's book tour, at least until the political repression of the reform movement in 1794, succeeded in selling copies of books and spreading the abolitionist message throughout major cities in England, Scotland and Ireland. Making use of the radical network of abolitionists and members of the London Corresponding Society, Equiano appealed to readers as political actors engaged in changing unjust institutions and practices.[71] When in London revising the first edition of the *Interesting Narrative*, Equiano stayed with Thomas Hardy, founder of the London Corresponding Society.[72] If it had been believed that Equiano was really born in the West Indies and not Africa, then his first two chapters would have been rendered wholly fictional and Equiano's overall credibility would have been shattered. He remarks that the accusations in the *Oracle* immediately depressed sales of his book.[73] One of the most powerful parts of the *Interesting Narrative*, the eyewitness account of the Middle Passage, would have become the invention of a proven liar. If the *Interesting Narrative* had power, it depended on its being a truthful report on events that were otherwise hidden from public view for being too shameful and disturbing. Ultimately the attempt to discredit Equiano did not succeed in undermining the popularity of the *Interesting Narrative*, which went into numerous editions and at least three translations, continuing to be purchased, read and cited well into the 1820s.[74]

Vincent Carretta played the role of reluctant messenger of bad news when he reported his research discoveries that Equiano's baptism document listed his place of birth as Carolina, not Africa. Moreover, a ship on which Equiano is known to have sailed lists a 'Gustavus' from South Carolina. There was no 'smoking gun' that proved definitively that Equiano the African was in fact Gustavus Vassa the South Carolinian, but Carretta indicated that the evidence pointed in that direction.[75] One response to Carretta's discoveries was to argue that Equiano's misrepresentations about his birthplace did not matter because, as Ross Pudaloff writes, regardless of 'biographical fact, the contesting evidence of birth and life ought to remind the reader that she or he is reading a book, not gazing at a life as it was'.[76] Eighteenth-century literature delighted in playing games with the reader about the authenticity and truthfulness of narratives, *Robinson Crusoe* (1719) and *Gulliver's Travels* (1726) being good examples. Defoe and

Swift play with readers' desire for dependable truthfulness in exotic narratives that are related to philosophical truth – religious and moral – in ways remote from factuality. *Don Quixote* (1605, 1615), arguably the first modern novel, engages the issue of false and true representations in dizzyingly complex ways that explore the literariness of fictional narratives. The postmodern indifference to clear distinctions between authentic and fabricated has origins that go back to early modernity. Paul Youngquist takes the postmodern approach to Equiano's uncertain place of birth by treating him as 'DJ Vassa', a hip-hop artist with multiple identities who 'samples' already-written texts to produce desired effects. As a member of the cosmopolitan transatlantic proletariat, Equiano has a typically dispersed identity.[77]

Youngquist, agnostic on whether Equiano was from Africa or South Carolina, relocates authenticity to his imperialistic subjection that accounts for his fluid identity, a theme developed too by Susan Marren.[78] In Ross Pudaloff's reading Equiano acquires the position of a subject with agency at the point he is able read and write 'the language of the dominant culture', which he can then interpret.[79] According to Pudaloff, Mr King agrees to carry out the promise of freeing Equiano for the agreed sum of money that Equiano has earned, not for economic reasons as such but only because as a businessman in the public eye he guards his reputation, his 'credibility' and how he is perceived by other people. It is finally 'Mr. King's conformity to the cultural values of a market economy' that results in Equiano's manumission. The public space where market transactions come to pass, then, is not a site of dehumanization for Equiano but just the opposite.[80] Pudaloff's Equiano, hardly the proletarian described by Youngquist and others, acquires his authentic self, if one can call it that in this context, in the impersonal market where he obtains his freedom and independence and where he is able to sell his book. Houston Baker aptly phrases Equiano's manumission as the 'ironic transformation of property by property into humanity'.[81] The truth or fictionality of Equiano's African origins does not finally matter in an analysis like Pudaloff's, for if the public space of market relations is the authenticating site, then the decisive thing is whether Equiano can 'sell' his reading audience on his origins. He certainly did so with the first generation of readers.

For a rhetorical approach to Equiano's *Interesting Narrative* that emphasizes the text's usefulness in promoting slavery abolition, the authenticity of the account matters only to the extent that the text loses its effectiveness politically if it is proved fictional. Long after Equiano's death (1797), slave trade abolition (1807) and abolition of slavery in the empire (1833), serious questions have been raised about his reliability as a narrator. These questions, if compellingly raised at the time he published, would have been devastating for Equiano, especially when one looks at his text with the traditional rhetorical focuses of ethos, logos and pathos. If he loses persuasiveness as an ethical agent appealing to an audience, it does not matter how expertly he has shaped the rational arguments and how movingly he has constructed scenes to win readers' sympathy. Both John Bugg and Paul Monod, who have read Carretta's research with careful scepticism, have concluded that it would have been unlikely (but of course not impossible) for Equiano to have claimed an African birth if he had not in fact been born in Africa. Bugg sees the baptismal certificate as thin evidence, for the designated Carolina birthplace could have been a careless clerk's error or a way to ward off seekers of runaway slaves, as African-born slaves were less likely to have been manumitted. The other documentary evidence, the muster roll of the *Racehorse*, is equivocal because the full name Gustavus Vassa does not appear, and Gustavus Weston and Gustavus Feston were actual names of soldiers. Counter-evidence is also weighty: Equiano referred to his African origins a decade before the *Interesting Narrative* in a letter to the Bishop of London; in a 1785 letter to the Quakers he used the phrase 'we Africans'.[82] Monod also questions the baptismal certificate because the parish clerk would have asked the adult sponsors where the young slave boy was born and their answer of 'Carolina' cannot be taken as decisive. If Equiano saved this certificate to prove residence in order to obtain poor relief at some point, he also might have used it on ship as well to prove his identity; the 'South Carolina', then, could have been passed on in that way. Monod doubts that Equiano would lie about his big details like his birthplace because the *Interesting Narrative* is so careful about small details. Most importantly, knowing that slavery apologists would attack his book, Equiano would not have risked public exposure by making lies that would not have been difficult to detect. Monod concludes that 'Equiano was ambitious but not reckless'.[83]

If the *Interesting Narrative* was written in order to promote the cause of slavery abolition – and not just to make Equiano enough money to get married and have a family (as Pudaloff reminds us, Equiano was a shrewd businessman)[84] – then it seems reasonable to assume with Bugg and Monod that he would not have made his ethical status so vulnerable to challenge. Although few readers have ignored the obvious truth that the *Interesting Narrative* was written and published to promote the cause of abolition, the extent to which the text coheres in terms of abolition has not been fully appreciated.

Viewed as an abolitionist text, the important parts fit together and reinforce one another: the multiple framings of the text, the first chapter's anthropological description of Essaka, the enslavement narrative that culminates in the Middle Passage, the spiritual autobiography, the *Robinson Crusoe*-like entrepreneurial story of self-emancipation, the tale of his British identity, the various moments of betrayal and the accounts of racist violence and oppression. Finally, the text's use of irony to satirize racism suggests that Equiano was a more sophisticated writer than he has been usually viewed.

The first edition of the *Interesting Narrative* has the framing device of the frontispiece which is an image of Equiano, dressed like a gentleman, holding open a Bible to Acts 4:12. The inscription underneath the image is 'Olaudah Equiano or Gustavus Vassa, the African'. The frontispiece presents the British reader with the author's difference – his physical appearance – spliced onto visible signs of British Protestant identity, the clothing (jacket, vest, shirt, cravat) and the Bible. He has two names, one African and the other British, but he also calls himself 'the African'. Britishness and Africanness are mixed together to create something new, a British citizen of African origins who is not just minimally literate but religiously literate, capable of interpreting the culture's most prestigious text, a sign according to Pudaloff of his having become a subject with agency. Equiano's eyes in the image are directed not at the reader but are at an angle, suggesting his engagement with someone or something; he is not distracted or alarmed but situated in a world where he is at ease and belongs. The facial expression is relaxed but serious, as though he were ready to start a conversation. The image, which does not communicate victimhood, counters the hegemonic meanings of 'African': slave, savage, abject sufferer and cannibal. The title page announces that the *Interesting Narrative* has been 'written by himself', the African, illustrating his 'humanity' according to cultural assumptions of the age. The title page's inscription from Isaiah 12:2, 4 complements the New Testament allusion – that 'salvation' is available only through Christ – because it too cites 'God' as 'my salvation' and adds something new, the commandment to declare God's 'doings among the people', an obvious allusion to the *Interesting Narrative* itself and its holy mission.[85]

The next framing device after the frontispiece and title page is the petitionary letter to parliament that expresses Equiano's hope of becoming an 'instrument towards the relief of his suffering countrymen' by assisting the abolition of the slave trade.[86] The self-presentation here is one of stylized deference to the political powers, as he identifies himself as 'an unlettered African' whose writing is 'wholly devoid of literary merit'. Although he seems to have gone too far in the direction of self-effacement, he is actually covering up an extraordinarily bold act of political assertiveness: he assumes that he has the political standing to petition parliament to abolish the slave trade; he is exercising his political agency by offering his government (*his* government!) a lengthy petition that is the equivalent of a committee report. Seemingly obsequious, Equiano the African uses that appearance to transform a mere autobiography into political evidence for ending one of the most lucrative commercial enterprises in Britain. His *Interesting Narrative* is claiming representative power, as Equiano mediates between 'his suffering countrymen' and parliament. The next move in the framing process is to list the names of the 311 subscribers who supported Equiano's project, among whom were royalty, clergy and well-known abolitionists. Although a subscription list is utterly conventional and unremarkable in itself, it also functions as 311 additional names on his petition and becomes evidence of Equiano's political savvy, his 'pull'. The implication of the list is that parliament should listen to what this man has to say because he has already impacted public opinion. The list and the petition illustrate that Equiano can mobilize the forces of the public sphere, while the frontispiece and title page demonstrate that he can wield effectively the powerful symbols and conventions of the culture. Over 100 abolitionist petitions had been submitted to the House of Commons already by the summer of 1788,[87] so that if Equiano wanted his to be given attention, he had to make his own stand out from the others. The ninth edition adds another layer of framing by inserting a series of letters between the title page and the subscription list to make the petitionary letter to parliament just the fourth of twelve letters.[88] The letters and two reviews are signs that Equiano and his *Interesting Narrative* have been active in the public sphere where controversial challenges to his authenticity have been rebutted and where he has accumulated significant accolades and praise. Their publication is designed to increase his influence and sell more books.

The rhetorical purpose of the first chapter, the anthropological description of Essaka, his birthplace, is to oppose the racist images of African society and to establish the humanity of Essaka's people in order to remove one of the justifications for racial slavery. The sexual modesty, cleanliness, sobriety, artistic creativity, religion and Jewish-like customs (circumcision, purity taboos) of the Essaka people confirm their humanity against the racist stereotypes of nearly animal-like Africans, and suggest similarities with the British. Arguing in favour of an environmental explanation for skin complexion and the Abrahamic origins of Africans, the chapter tries to repel the polygenist account of skin colour and to counter the biblical interpretation of African descent from Noah's son Ham. The abolitionist case had to be fought on two fronts at once, the scientific and the religious. The chapter concludes with a paragraph of sermonizing addressed to white Britons, mostly asking rhetorical questions: 'Let the polished and haughty European recollect that his ancestors were once, like the Africans, uncivilized, and even barbarous'. Were they inferior? Should they have been made slaves? An apt quotation from scripture affirming the common blood of all peoples concludes the paragraph and the chapter.[89] The white Europeans are invited to exercise their cosmopolitan imagination, to distance and abstract themselves from their immediate experience, to reflect historically on how Europeanness was developed and constructed.

Those who think the *Interesting Narrative* lacks irony need to look closely at the second chapter where Equiano first experiences the white slavers who appear to him extraordinarily repulsive in appearance, so peculiar as to be spirits rather than humans, so cruel as to be flesh-eating cannibals. 'I had never seen among any people such instances of brutal cruelty.'[90] The inhumanity of the whites is illustrated in an episode where they throw away fish they were too satiated to eat themselves rather than donating any of the leftovers to the starving Africans.[91] Equiano knows precisely where the European self-image in relation to the African Other is vulnerable to ridicule: their superior sense of moral and religious righteousness, their superior sense of being more physically attractive than other peoples, their superior sense of being diametrically opposite from flesh-eating cannibals and their humanitarian noblesse oblige to the other, poorer peoples of the world. Equiano the young boy is focalized so effectively in these passages that the British reader is forced to experience the estrangement and horror of confronting the British and Europeans as they appear to their victims. Knowing he has the reader squirming, Equiano does not relent and presses his advantage over the British readers by scolding them as 'ye nominal Christians'.[92] Quoting the golden rule back to the Christians, 'Do unto all men as you would men should do unto you', artfully removes the religious and moral basis of 'Caucasian' superiority. The vividly depicted olfactory sensations during the Middle Passage signify the stench of hypocritical morality, especially when one recalls the zealous attention to cleanliness in Essaka.

Wollstonecraft complained about the *Interesting Narrative*'s 'tiresome' exposition of Equiano's religious conversion and modern readers, including Houston Baker, have remarked on the story's loss of dramatic impact after Equiano's manumission.[93] The reader's discomfort with the narrative after Equiano buys his freedom is to some extent a resistance to the genre of spiritual autobiography, whose formal features of introspective reflection and symbolic interpretation of dreams and external signs retard narrative progress and irritate the sensibilities of those, like Wollstonecraft, at home with more modernist kinds of Christianity or like Baker, with a secular outlook. Spiritual autobiography, one of the popular eighteenth-century genres, allowed the writer to observe the minute details of everyday life for providential signs and permitted the writer to scrutinize his or her inner world through a biblically-tinged lens in order to construct (and endlessly reconstruct) a narrative of salvation. It was a genre that affirmed the supreme value of every single soul, no matter how insignificant the social status of the writer. Equiano's appropriation of the genre suggests similarities with Defoe's *Robinson Crusoe*, one of the most well-known spiritual autobiographies. That Equiano had read the novel is altogether possible, even likely, considering its popularity and different versions in chapbooks and abridged editions. By moving to spiritual autobiography Equiano employs a genre many readers from the artisan and lower middle classes would have found congenial and familiar, especially the Methodists who were prominent supporters of the abolitionist movement. I am not suggesting Equiano the historical person was insincere in accessing spiritual autobiography, but at the time he would have gained more readers than he lost, despite the aesthetic objections of some like Wollstonecraft. Equiano the writer also gains a narrative resource he can exploit for ironic effects to complicate the overall meaning of his text. Whereas the slavery-to-freedom story, enjoyably inspiring and gratifying to read, has a beginning, middle and an end, the story of a soul searching for religious answers from a silent, invisible God is repetitive and endless – actually closer to the way everyday experience is structured even for the secular. Although Equiano buys his freedom in the sixth chapter, he is frequently treated as something less than free in the subsequent chapters, where the quality of his freedom – for example, the unemployment in London that forces him to work on a ship despite the dangers for a free black – receives ironic treatment.

The eighth chapter exemplifies the *Robinson Crusoe*-like qualities of narrative that Equiano uses. Like Defoe's protagonist who has prophetic dreams, Equiano on three successive nights dreams of a shipwreck where he alone is the agent of delivering everyone to safety.[94] During the terrible storm that follows the dreams Equiano suffers a Jonah-like experience of having been chosen by God because of his sins, which he confesses and for which he repents. After the ship indeed wrecks, due to the incompetence of the captain, Equiano takes over and leads everyone to safety with the assistance of his fellow blacks and with almost no help from the whites, most of whom are too drunk to be of any use.[95] Equiano assumes the leadership role that Robinson Crusoe took on 'his' island when he manoeuvred the defeat of the mutineers and managed the colonization of the island. In his own colonizing gesture, Equiano plants a few lime and lemon trees on the island where the ship wrecked, thus demonstrating his foresight and republican virtue in providing for future castaways, but the text departs from *Robinson Crusoe* and ironizes this colonial role by emphasizing Equiano's lack of proprietorship: 'I planted several [lime, lemon and orange trees] as a token to any one that might be cast away hereafter'.[96] The tree-planting also ironizes the Jonah story, at the end of which God chastises Jonah for caring more for the plant that provided him shade than for the people of Nineveh whom he was ready to see killed. Equiano is a more morally responsible colonizer than Robinson Crusoe and displays a greater moral imagination than the prophet Jonah. Meanwhile the white captain, whose inadequate leadership almost killed everyone on board, mistakes flamingos for 'cannibals' as they step onto the island, yet another ironic allusion to *Robinson Crusoe* where the boundary between civilized and savage is cannibalism. Equiano and his fellow Africans, stereotyped culturally as cannibalistic savages inferior to whites, save with their intelligence and courage the white people's lives. Equiano not just read *Robinson Crusoe* and the Book of Jonah; he read them critically and deconstructively.[97]

Although the *Interesting Narrative* depicts the acquisition of Equiano's British identity, that identity never comes without great difficulty. Even before

Equiano's baptism and school lessons supervised by the Guerins, he sees himself as 'almost an Englishman',[98] and after baptism and some schooling he has ordinary middle-class aspirations: 'I thought now of nothing but being freed, and working for myself, and thereby getting money to enable me to get a good education', especially being able to 'read and write'.[99] The British identity is secure well before his master Pascal sells him to another man, which is represented as the most traumatic betrayal Equiano was to experience. Protesting to Captain Doran, Equiano insists that he has rights, firstly to 'all my wages and prize-money' that Pascal stole and secondly to his free status because his baptism in England gives him legal protection from being sold.[100] British identity gives him rights that he tries to exercise and social promises he attempts to redeem. Postcolonial critics who find Equiano too British and not African enough ignore the way Equiano learns about and exercises power and agency. The *Interesting Narrative* cites texts like *Paradise Lost* to de-legitimate the slavery the young Equiano seeks to escape; for example, the text uses the four lines from Milton's poem describing hell to characterize the life of enslaved people on the island of Montserrat (*Paradise Lost*, I.165–8).[101] By the late eighteenth century, *Paradise Lost*, one of the most well known poems in British culture, had almost scriptural status. The meaningful citation of the lines both satirizes the institution of slavery and demonstrates Equiano's fluency in reading and interpreting key texts of the culture. Equiano performs his Britishness by quoting Milton but this Britishness does not save him from racist violence in Savannah, Georgia.[102]

A recurrent theme is the tenuous and vulnerable situation of free blacks in the West Indies and North America. 'I had thought only slavery dreadful; but the state of a free Negro appeared to me now equally so at least, and in some respects even worse.'[103] One of the lowest points in the *Interesting Narrative* is when Equiano cannot save John Annis from being kidnapped and re-enslaved. After Annis is captured and tortured, Equiano comments that 'I often wished for death'.[104] The most ironic treatment of the 'free Negro' theme is in the eleventh chapter where Equiano, working for Dr Irving, becomes a buyer and supervisor of slaves. The nature of Equiano's freedom is ironized from several directions. First, an Indian Equiano tries to convert to Christianity asks: 'How comes it that all the white men on board who can read and write, and observe the sun, and know all things, yet swear, lie, and get drunk, only excepting yourself?'[105] The *Interesting Narrative* has few scenes as ironic as this. Equiano has become one of the white men by his literacy, Britishness, scientific knowledge and status as a free black. Equiano's difference, according to the Indian, is not the skin colour but the lack of religious hypocrisy. Equiano's investment in Christianity is far more serious than that of the Europeans because even if they swear, lie and get drunk they will still be white, feel superior to and enjoy dominating blacks and Indians; Equiano's whiteness, rather, is only performative. The second occasion for rich irony is the aftermath of Equiano's stint as a benevolent slave supervisor. After a cruel white overseer replaces Equiano all the slaves die and he himself, the free black, unprotected by the powerful white man, Dr Irving, is humiliated, threatened with violence and almost sold into slavery again. At the moment of greatest danger to Equiano the *Interesting Narrative* records 'not one white man on board ... said a word on my behalf'.[106] Here and in many other episodes Equiano scathingly exposes the reason why free blacks live such anxious lives. The reason is virulent white racism.

The *Interesting Narrative* achieves a difficult rhetorical success by appealing to a mostly white readership, whose institutions and cultural practices Equiano is shown to fully accept and perform; but those same institutions and cultural practices are bitterly ironized. Equiano artfully depicts an African who embraces wholeheartedly the Christian and British identity available to him, but who nevertheless is victimized because of racism. The institution of slavery, not just the slave trade, is incapable of being reformed and made benevolent, as Equiano's moment as kind overseer tragically illustrates. The *Interesting Narrative* is a cosmopolitan text not simply because of its geographical expansiveness and its important role in different literatures (African American, Afro-British, Black Atlantic and romantic-era British) but because in its argument against the slave trade, an international form of commerce, it brings to the surface racist myths upon which slavery and ultimately European empire rest.

Thelwall's Two Plays Against Empire, *Incle and Yarico* and *TheIncas*[107]

Cultural myths upholding slavery and empire are exposed as well in John Thelwall's plays, an operatic farce and a historical opera. *Incle and Yarico* comically treats the well-known eighteenth-century story of Inkle and Yarico, in which an English merchant betrays and sells into slavery his Indian lover, represented as a 'Noble Savage'. The play translates the intertextual narrative into a forthrightly abolitionist satire of the slave trade and wittily represents English middle-class status anxieties and crude materialism, deploying urban middle-class speech and malapropisms. By making the Indian characters speak a black African stage dialect, the play blurs the differences between African and native American slaves to highlight the common victimization of the non-Europeans. *The Incas*, a full-length drama designed as a theatrical main piece, translates the Spanish Conquest narratives into an anti-imperialistic play, justifying the native rebellions against the Spanish in South America and allegorizing the French Revolution and the English suppression of political dissent. Drawing upon and extending some of the central precepts of the Enlightenment, Thelwall undermines the justifications for European empire. The play's hero, known first as Faulkland and then as the historically evocative Sidney, fights with the Incas against the Spanish and becomes embroiled in a complicated but typically operatic love triangle. At the heart of the play is his betrayal and near execution by the Incas for whom he fought, a plot sequence evoking the contemporary revolutionary politics of Paris and London. The play expresses an encounter with the New World mediated by Enlightenment texts that in some sense Thelwall translates. Marmontel's *Les Incas* (1777) was Thelwall's chief source and other likely sources include Las Casas (*A Short Account of the Destruction of the Indies* (1552)), Abbé Raynal (*A Philosophical and Political History of the Settlements and Trade of the Europeans in the East and West Indies* (1774)),[108] Helen Maria Williams (*Peru* (1784)), and William Robertson (*The History of America* (1788)).

The fictionality of Thelwall's New World natives does not mean they are arbitrary, for his knowledge came by way of an intellectual engagement with slavery and empire. His participation in the debating clubs of 1787 during the first wave of the anti-slavery agitation resulted in his losing his Toryism and gaining an abolitionist stance. Reading these two plays as translations highlights the issue of mediation and language. Textually mediated events – the Spanish conquest of Peru, the Tupac Amaru revolt of the 1780s, the transatlantic slave trade, the abolitionist movement in England, slave rebellions, the French Revolution, the London reform movement and its loyalist opposition and government repression – all contribute to the construction of meaning in these two plays. How Thelwall turns these diverse meanings into coherent plays is roughly analogous to the task of the translator.

Applying the translation model to Thelwall's two plays, one can say that his *Incle and Yarico* translates the intertextual fable to bring out its abolitionism through two different kinds of English, the London demotic speech and the African stage dialect. Thelwall's *Incas* translates the Spanish conquest narrative to affirm the justice of native rebellion and resistance, as well as making allegorical connections with European revolution. That less radical and more overtly nationalistic treatments of Thelwall's topics became popular on the London stage – Colman's *Inkle and Yarico* (1787) and Morton's *Columbus* (1792) – indicates that the London theatre did not easily accommodate the abolitionist and anti-imperialist intentions produced by Thelwall's aggressive translation of conventional texts about the New World.

The 1787 farce, designed as a two-act afterpiece for the London theatre, revises one of the most well known eighteenth-century fables about Englishmen and slavery, the Inkle and Yarico story popularized by Richard Steele's narrative in the *Spectator* (11 (13 March 1711)). Based on the supposedly true account by Richard Ligon, Steele's tale, situated within a dialogue between a male narrator and a female interlocutor on the theme of woman's inconstancy, is presented as an anti-misogynistic counter to the Petronius story about the faithless Ephesian matron. Arietta, the female interlocutor, brings to the surface the politics of literary representation with a fable about a lion and a man. The man taunts the lion with man's superiority by pointing to a painted sign showing a man killing a lion. The lion replies: '*We Lions are none of us Painters, else we could show a hundred Men killed by Lions, for one Lion killed by a Man*'. Arietta draws out the moral as it applies to sexual politics: 'You Men are Writers, and can represent us Women as Unbecoming as you please in your Works, while we are unable to return the injury'. Arietta's story of Inkle and Yarico, hardly a morally neutral account, is intended to injure men who harm women.[109]

That Thomas Inkle, young English merchant, harms Yarico is beyond dispute. When the English ship, nearing Barbados, desperately needs supplies, it stops at an inlet where Indians attack but Inkle escapes and is then protected by Yarico, an Indian woman who hides him and provides food and shelter. During their two-month idyll of love 'they had learn'd a Language of their own' in which Inkle promises to bring Yarico to London. After an English ship brings the two of them to Barbados, Inkle views his idyll with Yarico as wasteful ('a loss of Time'), and starts to calculate ways to recoup his losses ('to weigh with himself how many Days Interest of his Mony he had lost during his stay with *Yarico*').[110] He starts back on the road to prudence by selling his lover into slavery, and when she protests that she is pregnant with his child, he happily notes she will bring a higher price. That the popularity of the Inkle and Yarico story – included for example in Wollstonecraft's *The Female Reader* (1789)[111] – coincided with West Indian slavery and the flourishing transatlantic slave trade suggests the deep cultural ambivalence about race and slavery.[112]

In Thelwall's comic treatment of the story the two-month idyll of love between Incle (as he is here called) and Yarico becomes a two-year idyll, long enough for Incle to become restless and homesick, but not long enough to lessen Yarico's devotion. A Thelwall invention is the improbable happenstance of Incle's parents and uncle, who are on a slave-trading expedition from London and who become stranded in the same area of Central America as Incle himself. Discovering his parents and uncle in the first scene of the second act, Incle is torn between his sense of obligation to Yarico who saved his life and a desire for self-advancement that would be gratified by selling into slavery both his lover and her friend, another Thelwall addition, Yahamona. Among the sailors who were on the Incles' ship is a character named Williams, who sides with the Indians against the English and who pairs up with Yahamona. The Indians, who intervene before the British kidnap Yarico and Yahamona into slavery, establish the terms by which the farce is finally resolved: at first they plan to enslave the British as agricultural labourers but after Yarico's discussion with her father, the Indian leader, the British are permitted to live among the Indians but not permitted to return to their country to 'do you wicked designs some oder time'.[113]

By the play's end a penitent Incle is back together with a disappointed Yarico, another Thelwall innovation.

A principal technique in Thelwall's farce is reversal, comically illustrated in act one, scene one when the servant Timothy finds himself with an Indian woman who desires him; because her friend Yarico has a white lover, she too wants one. Faced with the frankly sexual Yahamona, Timothy adopts the role of coy maiden, explaining himself thus: 'I supposes now she'll think nothing of me if I'm won too easy, for I thinks they say we're in the Auntoy Podes, and so every thing's reversed'.[114] According to Frank Felsenstein, Yahamona's 'predatory' sexuality comically inverts the conventional designation of the desirable woman as the 'trophy' to be won.[115] In Thelwall's play the cultural stereotypes are reversed. The civilized English are crudely materialistic, even animalistic, for Incle's uncle is named 'Turtle' suggesting a complete identity between himself and his appetite for turtle meat and the name of Incle's father, 'Traffic', evokes the phrase 'traffic in human beings' referring to the slave trade. In contrast the Indians are altruistic, self-sacrificing, noble, idealistic and generous. Countering the pathos of Yarico's betrayal by Incle is the betrayal of Timothy by Yahamona, the Indian woman who leaves him for the sailor Williams, a more affectionate lover who is also the moral centre of the play. Countering the mercenary Incle is the plain-speaking democrat Williams who articulates the play's most explicitly political ideas. The most dramatic reversal is Williams's decision to side with the triumphant Indians against the English who have lost all moral authority. When the supposedly cannibalistic American natives have the opportunity to dispose of the morally worthless English in any manner they choose, they practise the 'forgiveness' associated with Christian morality and end up granting them freedom – but not freedom to continue slave trading.[116] By having the Indian characters speak the black African stage dialect, Thelwall blurs the distinction between African and American slaves, not unlike some visual representations of Yarico with African features.[117] Thelwall deconstructs the racial binary in the play, white and coloured, through numerous reversals. The sexuality of Yarico and Yahamona derives from the Enlightenment's assumption of a free, natural sexuality enjoyed by those uncontaminated by sexually repressive Christianity and especially the commercial corruption of sexuality. Thelwall deploys the Indians' sexuality satirically against what he sees as the hypocritically puritanical middle class, something he does as well in his later novel about the slave rebellion in St Domingo, *The Daughter of Adoption*.

There are two contrasting visions of Englishness, one of which is the ruthless pursuit of self-interest, an economic liberty to compete for wealth and power without the distractions of pity and morality. When Uncle Turtle tries to persuade the reluctant Incle to put his lover on the slave market, he tells his nephew not to worry about his conscience. 'Conscience! Ha! Ha! Tom. I'll tell you this, my boy: if your conscience is not as elastic as an alderman's stomach (take my word for 't), you'll never add another plum to the one your father has accumulated'.[118] Williams's version of Englishness rejects slavery because of the golden rule – 'Split my mainmast if I don't think it bloody cruel not to do as we would wish to be done by'; moreover, he conceives of national liberty reflexively – 'What then did we only fight for own freedom that we might rob others of theirs?'[119]

If Incle is an unappealing character – he is bored with Yarico and is homesick for London after two years in a tropical paradise – his parents and uncle are even more morally repulsive. His mother, who cares only about social status, is a former servant who inherited £2,000 after the death of her bachelor master; his father, who cares only about money, did not hesitate to abandon the woman with whom he already had a relationship when someone richer came along. Each loathes the other, and they bicker constantly. The second scene of the first act satirizes commercialized sexuality in a comic song about 'boarding school misses' who are trained to attract men, who in turn purchase the girls. 'Thus completely accomplish'd, at fifteen years old, / To some rake fortune-hunter young madam is sold'.[120] The sexuality of the Indian women, although stereotypically 'free' and 'natural', acts principally to contrast the artificial construction of women's sexuality tied to commercial and status advancement. Anticipating Blake's analysis of sexuality, Thelwall shows that slavery expresses a morally degraded commercial culture fuelled by a commodified sexuality. When Incle's father and uncle urge him to sell his lover and her friend into slavery, they dismiss as unreal the authority of moral claims such as 'gratitude' and 'conscience', and legalistically dismiss any obligations he might have to his child by Yarico. Such moral concepts are fine for 'poets' and impoverished writers who live in garrets but not applicable to those who want the pleasures that money can buy in a commercial society.[121] Slavery and empire in Thelwall's play depend less on race than on greed and a corrupted sexuality.

The version of Englishness depicted in the later play, *The Incas*, strongly parallels that articulated by Williams, as the play's hero, Faulkland (who occupies a higher social position than the sailor in Thelwall's farce) also sides with the native Americans against the Europeans. The drama's setting is sixteenth-century Peru in the early years of the Spanish conquest. Faulkland is an English soldier who fights with the Spanish, and then – under a new republican name, Sidney – on the side of the Peruvian natives. After the Spanish have been defeated, Faulkland bonds with the Inca and his son, but two impediments prevent marriage between Faulkland and the Inca's daughter Myrrha. Firstly, out of gratitude and not love Faulkland is engaged to marry Elvira, the daughter of the Spanish leader to whom he was obligated. Secondly, Masseru, an envious Peruvian general who wants to marry Myrrha and who resents the prominence of a foreigner, accuses

Faulkland of blaspheming the Sun, a capital crime in Peru. The opera concludes with Faulkland's vindication, as Masseru's treachery and the collaboration of Elvira and Myrrha are finally made public. That Elvira attempted to have Faulkland killed frees him from his obligation to marry her, allowing him finally to marry the woman he loves, Myrrha.[122]

The most remarkable thing about Thelwall's translation of the Spanish conquest is that the Peruvians in his opera triumph over the Spanish completely. It is as though the Amerindian uprisings of 1780–1 in the Andes had succeeded, rather than resulting in the torture and mutilation of the rebel leaders and the slaughter of over 100,000 native Americans.[123] Thelwall presents a range of native characters, each with moral agency, from the progressive enlightener Rocca, the Inca's son, to Masseru, distrustful of the European and his ways. Myrrha, the Noble Savage, is reminiscent of Yarico; the Faulkland–Myrrha relationship parallels the one between Inkle and Yarico, for while Faulkland betrays his American lover out of 'duty' rather than greed, the betrayal is just as real. Faulkland has a prior commitment, just as Colman's Inkle does in the person of Narcissa, daughter of the Barbados governor.[124] Thelwall's Myrrha, when she learns about Faulkland's prior commitment to Elvira, blithely suggests that he marry both women, as the custom in Inca culture allows men to have more than one wife. Faulkland replies: 'Your Father's laws sanction such custom – mine forbid it'. While he justifies monogamy as benefiting both the husband and wife who get one another's 'undivided affection', she suggests a compromise that he rejects impatiently; 'you have yet no idea of the duties of us Europeans'.[125] Although Faulkland is clearly the hero of the opera, his rigidity absolutizes the moral value of monogamy while he refuses to make any equitable adjustment that would grant legitimacy to the cultural norms in her society.

The play satirizes the exemplary nature of his fidelity to 'duty' because, for one thing, his fiancée Elvira vows revenge for his having killed her brother. Elvira, even before she hears about the romance between Faulkland and Myrrah, knows that the promise to marry her was given only out of gratitude, not the love that she really wants.[126] Intent on revenge, she has no intention of marrying the murderer of her brother anyway. At one point expressing a wistful regret that she might have been happy with him, she is somewhat ambivalent in her retribution.[127] A good operatic actress could make Elvira, a complicated character, an object of real interest, and although she is European, her situation as a captive, an abandoned woman belonging to a defeated nation makes her a figure of colonial subjection. Thelwall got the name undoubtedly from Mozart's *Don Giovanni* (1787) where Elvira, a former conquest of Giovanni's, is determined to get her revenge on her seducer.

The Inca's son Rocca illustrates the themes of enlightenment and political reform, for he is the one who intervenes several times to save Faulkland's life, firstly when he and Pedrillo are shipwrecked and secondly when he is about to become a human sacrifice. According to Faulkland's servant Pedrillo (undoubtedly named after Mozart's Pedrillo, Belmonte's servant in *The Abduction from the Seraglio* (1782)), Rocca persuaded his fellow warriors to spare the Europeans because he 'discerned our merits' and supervised their gradual acculturation.[128] Defending Faulkland from the charge of blaspheming the Sun, Rocca reminds his people that the Englishman had 'instructed us successfully to oppose those tyrants to whom we had previously paid such slavish and unavailing adoration.'[129] The anti-imperialistic message passes from 'Sidney' to Rocca to the American natives. The debate between Vilacuma and Rocca pivots on the moral nature of the culture, whether God's commandment is Vilacuma's 'revenge' or Rocca's 'forgiveness'.[130] Although the play gives voice to both the traditionalist and the modernist, it ultimately vindicates the modernist who intervenes in the final scene to save the hero from execution.

The name change from Faulkland, as he is known to the Spanish, to Sidney, as he is known to the Americans, is an intriguing detail that is only partially and inconsistently realized in the manuscript of the play. Faulkland probably takes after the same seventeenth-century moderate, highly cultured royalist Viscount Falkland (1610–43) that Godwin used as the name for his aristocratic character who tormented Caleb Williams. Politically motivated names and name changes were not unknown during the period of the French Revolution. Thelwall inscribed his political ideals onto his sons, naming his eldest Algernon Sidney Thelwall (1795–1863), and his second, John Hampden Thelwall (1797–1876?), after the two famous seventeenth-century republican heroes, Algernon Sidney (1623–83) and John Hampden (1595–1643), while the new name of Baron de Clootz (1755–94), 'Anacharsis', corresponded with the renunciation of his aristocratic privileges and his advocacy of a revolutionary world federation. Faulkland becoming Sidney reflects a similar transition from being affiliated with the Spanish colonizers to leading an anti-colonial struggle with native Americans. Sidney then is a figure like Anacharsis Clootz or Tom Paine, a republican citizen of the world fighting for revolutionary ideals that transcend nationalistic ideology.

One might ask why Thelwall did not make the European revolutionary who sides with the native Americans a Spaniard, as Marmontel does in his novel *Les Incas* with the character Alonzo.[131] Faulkland/Sidney appeals to specifically English political history and republican ideals in ways that Alonzo – or some other Spanish character – does not. If Alonzo were the opera's hero, the play could not gesture as clearly as it does toward expressing solidarity with the native American rebellions against the Spanish colonists. Moreover, Faulkland/Sidney does not act on behalf of the British government, or British society or even Europe, but according to universal political ideals (compromised, it has to be admitted, by inevitable Eurocentrism). Rocca gives Faulkland an opportunity to play the aggressive colonizer role, something Faulkland consistently declines to do: he refrains from criticizing a religion in which he does not believe; he does not resist his imminent execution undertaken according to traditional Incan laws; he does not use his position as military leader to impose European ideas on the culture. Overall Faulkland/Sidney's actions as an anti-colonial organizer encourage the enlighteners like Rocca that already exist in the Incan society, but also respect the native traditions. Just how much Thelwall actually knew about the Incas is difficult to say. Married to Myrrha, in charge of the military and the closest advisor to the future Inca himself, 'Sidney' carries European values and practices into the American culture; intentionally he promotes universal principles but unintentionally he is a liberal imperialist on behalf of European culture.

Given the level of political conflict and violence in 1792, the struggle between revenge and forgiveness and the tension between duty and desire have allegorical resonance. The defenders of monarchy and aristocracy employed a rhetoric of settling scores; the Duke of Brunswick's 'manifesto' of May 1792 notably bristled with threats of violent retribution, echoing the tone assumed in Burke's *Reflections on the Revolution in France*, especially its call to defend the honour of Marie Antoinette. The English anti-Jacobin reaction by 1792 was well under way with the public burning of effigies of Paine and loyalist societies organizing the suppression of reformist political speech. Until the Reign of Terror (1793–4) the revolutionaries were not identified with revenge, and never revenge in the name of traditional values, as both Elvira and Vilacuma advocate. The quarrel between desire and duty was a clash within the logic of republicanism. The more romantic and sentimental dimensions of Enlightenment culture bolstered the legitimacy of desire, exemplified in a text like Blake's *Marriage of Heaven and Hell* (1794), while the more Stoic and Roman dimensions idealized dedication to duty, epitomized by the famous illustration of utilitarian morality in Godwin's *Political Justice*, which stated that if only one person could be saved from a deadly fire, the more socially valuable philosopher was to be chosen over one's own family members.[132] The desire versus duty opposition was played out in the writing of Rousseau who sided unpredictably with one or the other. *The Incas* seems uncertain about which one gets priority because Faulkland's fidelity to duty, perhaps endorsed by the resolution of the plot, is balanced by the clear exploitation of duty's authority in the case of the punishment for blasphemy against the sun (a locution that evokes blasphemy against the Son as well).

For Walter Benjamin, translation at its most authentic brings out things that are new but that also existed as potentiality, as something inhering within both languages, something called pure language, an 'intentio' occupying the interrelationship of the languages rather than author or translator. Thelwall's treatment of the New World in these two plays, precisely because of their intertextuality, is similar to Benjaminian translation. Arietta's complaint about the politics of representation in Steele's *Spectator* narrative, Yarico's sentimental protest to Inkle and the tragic triumph of the Spanish over the Inca civilization are translated into something new, in part because of a new social creativity in the abolitionist movement and in the French Revolution. The social forces of 1787 provide what we might call the 'translatability' by which Thelwall's *Incle and Yarico* makes universalist moral claims about opposing slavery, and by which it counters the possessive individualist national identity with an enlightened republican national identity. Similarly, *The Incas* rewrites the defeat of the Peruvian natives in both the sixteenth and eighteenth century as a current cosmopolitan victory on the strength of the world-historical events in France, which had begun to move against abolishing slavery. Thelwall's translations had the freedom sufficient to bring out the immanent and potential meanings that might otherwise have been undeveloped.

Thelwall's Feminist, Anti-Racist, Anti-Imperialist Novel

Unaccountably never reprinted, John Thelwall's *The Daughter of Adoption; A Tale of Modern Times*[133] develops new areas of the feminist novel as practiced by Mary Wollstonecraft and Mary Hays, creates out of the 'Jacobin novel' tradition of Thomas Holcroft and William Godwin a cosmopolitan version of the 'novel of purpose' informed by the New Philosophy[134] and intervenes forcefully in the debate over slave trade abolition to push the argument beyond mainstream parameters into challenging empire and – to a lesser extent – racial superiority. Thelwall's comments on the novel in the autobiographical essay introducing his 1801 volume of poems suggest that the rapidity of composition detracted from the aesthetic quality of the novel, a writerly protest one finds as well in comments by Mary Wollstonecraft, Charlotte Smith and others who were not permitted the luxury of extensive revision.[135] As a quickly written, lengthy novel that could have benefited from rigorous editing, *The Daughter of Adoption* ambitiously but effectively coheres on several levels.

The West Indies were anything but marginal in the 1790s in terms of the British economy and the military struggle against Revolutionary France. Representing reformist opinion on British policy in the sugar islands, the *Analytical Review* routinely exposed the abuse and torture of black slaves and argued for the cultivation of the islands without slave labour.[136] Retaining control of its own islands, suppressing slave rebellions and trying to steal colonies from the French was costly to the British in treasure and manpower. In St Domingo alone, from 1794 until 1797 when it withdrew, Britain expended over £4,000,000, losing thousands of soldiers mostly to tropical diseases, according to the classic account by C. L. R. James.[137] If the British – and French – had heavy losses, they hardly matched the fatalities of the St Domingo blacks, who in the ten years between 1791 and 1801 saw a third of their people die in the fighting.[138] James's history emphasizes not just the hideous level of violence but the political significance of the St Domingo Revolution, depicted by him as the first successful anti-colonial, anti-imperialistic insurrection against European powers. James persuasively argues for the importance of this revolution for modernity in general and transatlantic political history specifically. That Thelwall makes St Domingo central in his political novel suggests that even in 1801 he intuited its world-historical significance when other writers did not.

The plot of the novel puts the two main characters, Henry Montfort and Seraphina Parkinson, through their paces in a slave rebellion in St Domingo where they barely escape with their lives and in London 'society' where Henry almost loses his soul. Henry, who is represented as being torn between the influence of his planter father and his liberal mother, is possibly modelled after London Corresponding Society martyr Joseph Gerrald (1763–96) who was the rebellious son of a wealthy West Indian planter and who received a liberal education from Samuel Parr (1747–1825).[139] Seraphina seems to have been modelled after Mary Wollstonecraft.

Having already fallen in love during the slave rebellion and consummated their relationship on the trip back to London, the sixteen-year old Seraphina and twenty-one-year old Henry cannot marry until several obstacles are overcome: the wealthy Pervical Montfort threatens to disinherit his son if he marries a woman he believes to be a poor orphan and a 'Creole whore'; Seraphina will not marry Henry until he both overcomes his addiction to leisure-class pleasures in London (gambling, 'wenching' and heavy drinking) and adopts the ideals of the New Philosophy (social equality and republican virtue) he supported when they first fell in love. Meanwhile Seraphina is being aggressively courted by a young planter-smuggler, Lucius Moroon,[140] one of the wealthiest Creoles in Barbados and Henry is being aggressively pursued by Melinda Lewson at the direction of her mercenary brother. After Moroon's scheme to kill his rival Henry and kidnap Seraphina in order to rape her succeeds only partially – Henry is injured but not killed and Seraphina is kidnapped but escapes without being raped – the novel moves toward the long-expected resolution, the marriage of the two main characters, both of whom have to learn about their origins and one of whom has to undergo a moral conversion.

The origins and education of both Henry and Seraphina are central dimensions of the narrative. After much foreshadowing and a series of recognition scenes, Henry's real father turns out to be a man his presumed father killed in a duel and his real mother is revealed as his presumed mother's best friend who died in childbirth. Henry's presumptive mother Amelia, pregnant at the same time as her friend, was able to take possession of her friend's baby without arousing suspicion because her own died within a day of Henry's birth. Amelia conceals the 'adoption' from Percival out of loyalty to her beloved friend Louisa and out of contempt and disregard for her murderous husband. Seraphina's origins are similarly obscured by deception, starting with the false name used by her biological father that made him impossible to trace. Her biological mother, Anna Newcomb, a Londoner who was living in Jamaica, thought that the father of her two children was named Woodville but he was in fact Percival Montfort, sowing his oats in the West Indies. Abandoned and poor with two young children after the smallpox had ruined her beautiful appearance upon which she had based a briefly extravagant life as a courtesan, the impoverished Newcomb attempts to drown her son Lucius and gives up her daughter for adoption to a Reverend Robertson who changes her name to Seraphina (the involuntary name change undergone by Seraphina is not unlike the several involuntary name changes of Equiano). After Robertson's death Seraphina is adopted by a pastor who has resigned his church position for philosophical reasons. Parkinson and his wife Amanda provide the twice-orphaned girl with love and an extraordinary education on a remote mountain in St Domingo. The name Parkinson possesses rich historical resonance for Thelwall writing in 1800–1, for one of the Jamaican Maroon leaders in the Trelawney uprising of 1795–6 was named Leonard Parkinson, the same surname of one of his fellow leaders in the London Corresponding Society, James Parkinson (1755–1824). Leonard Parkinson during the Maroon rebellion was one of two leaders who had a £100 bounty on him, dead or alive.[141] Seraphina is brought up as a free spirit, more like Rousseau's Émile than Sophia, along the principles of Wollstonecraft and Godwin, a former reverend too. Because Henry's father flees to Jamaica after killing his friend Captain Bowbridge in a duel, the education of the young boy falls to his mother until his eleventh year when Montfort comes back to London, a rich planter. Montfort reasserts his paternal rights and teaches his son to behave as a privileged first son to a large estate. From Eton to Oxford, Henry's education is utterly conventional except for the occasional but emotionally compelling influence of his morally sensitive mother who is able to sting the conscience formed in his early years. While Seraphina experiences a conflict between 'society' and her secure republican and feminist values, Henry works through a self-division between moral values gained through his mother's influence and social practices normative within the leisure class acquired through the influence and example of his father.

The novel applies a feminist critique to women's inequality, masculine culture and slavery itself in order to make the case that women are enslaved by a system that not only enslaves blacks but also degrades white men, figuratively enslaved by false ideals. Abolishing the slave trade provides an opportunity to revolutionize society and free it not just of racial slavery but of racial, class and gender hierarchies that have had debilitating effects on men and women. Thelwall follows Mary Wollstonecraft so closely in both his forceful parallels between slavery and women's oppression and his critique of women's miseducation that *Vindication of the Rights of Woman* and *Wrongs of Woman* are the most important intertexts governing the novel's meaning. After describing how the feminist critique is worked out in the novel, I will turn in a concentrated way to how the novel deals with slavery and race.

Two intelligent women characters, Amelia and Louisa, are forced by their families to marry men they neither loved nor respected. Amelia laments long after the fact that she 'yielded to the wishes of those to whom obedience was a settled habit, and was sacrificed, without a murmur, at the shrine of prudence'.[142] Although the eighteenth-century novel from *Pamela* (1740) and *Clarissa* (1748) onwards thematizes women's marriage choice, Thelwall's treatment of the question entails a critique of woman's education and masculine culture itself. The young woman's decision to marry is constrained and predetermined by an educational process that wholly distorts the development of natural desire and of rational judgment. Nerissa, the woman to whom Amelia is revealing the secrets of her history, plays a minor but significant role in the novel by contrasting unfavourably with another 'orphan', Seraphina, and by collaborating with one of the villains, Rev. Woodhouse, in order to harm the interests of Henry Montfort, whose attentions she herself tried unsuccessfully to attract. The narrator characterizes her education using the satirical tone of the *Vindication of the Rights of Woman*:

> Nerissa was an unfortunate young lady, about eighteen years of age; of a person and mind *truly feminine*; and who had acquired all the feminine graces and accomplishments of a boarding school education. She could dance in the most fashionable style; sing the most fashionable airs; write long letters without the unfashionable aid of pronouns, prepositions, or conjunctions; work silk pictures, *vastly like copper-plate*; and make fillagree like nothing but itself. She could draw both flowers and landscapes an immense deal finer than any thing that was ever seen in nature; could run her fingers over the keys of a harpsichord with astonishing velocity, and had acquired such skill and erudition in the English, French, and Italian languages, that she could mingle them altogether in a single sentence, so as to make it equally intelligible to the native of either the respective countries.

The narrator, who also adds that she was good-natured, kind and not mean-spirited, attributes Nerissa's comically deficient abilities not to woman's innate inferiority but to her poor education.[143] Based on the Lockean assumption that the mind is shaped according to experience, the Enlightenment feminist argues that if women are educated to be intellectually incompetent and sexually attractive then most women will indeed exhibit those characteristics, but if women were educated rationally they would become rational creatures – thus

Wollstonecraft's *Vindication of the Rights of Woman*. The version of empiricism that the novel draws upon is modified by a Rousseauvian emphasis on 'nature', a powerful force to counter Calvinistic innate sinfulness and supply the mind and feelings with largely healthy and benign influences.

Another example of woman's miseducation that could have come from the pages of the *Rights of Woman* comes in the depiction of a character more polished than Nerissa, Melinda Lewson, Seraphina's 'rival' for the affections of Henry.

> She was acquainted, of course, with all the etiquette of the card-table, and the draw-ing-room; knew how to assume the easy familiarity, and display all the graces and accomplishments of her order – could outshine all her rivals in the every varying decorations of fashion; and had, more than once, enjoyed the distinguished honour of setting the mode in bonnets, plumes, and turbans; points, festoons, plaits, flow-ers, and furbelows; and all the innumerable decorations of female paraphernalia. She could moreover dance, and sing, and play upon the harp, with a degree of taste and execution not frequently to be met with among mere lady performers. In short, she was the very paragon of taste, the arbitress of elegant amusement – the blazing star of fashion! the delight, the life, the pride of the ball, the masquerade, and the ridotto.[144]

The narrator's account of Melinda treats all her accomplishments as alienated and her instrumental performances as designed to achieve some kind of compet-itive advantage over her adversaries. She lacks completely genuine enthusiasm and zeal. The 'delight' and 'amusement' are as utterly false and hollow as the prostitute's performance of sexuality.

Louisa, Amelia and Nerissa who are women from the upper social strata are not wholly unlike the women characters representing the lower social strata. The character known through most of the novel as Morton (in fact Anna Newcomb, Percival Montfort's lover, mother of both Seraphina and Moroon) takes one of the most cynical attitudes toward sex, power and money. Her history, a milder version of Jemima's in *Wrongs of Woman*, not surprisingly generates a demystified outlook on the relations between the sexes. The beauti-ful daughter of a London laundress, expecting soon a modest advancement in social status as she was about to marry a shopkeeper, she has sex with a wealthy man and assumes that if there is a pregnancy the infidelity will be obscured by her soon-to-be married condition. Unexpectedly the wedding is delayed, her pregnancy publicizes her infidelity and she loses her 'reputation'. After the death of her baby she determines to advance herself socially by means of her sexual attractiveness:

> She threw out her lures and glances at suitors of fortune and fashion, and by the dexterity with which she played her part, had soon a train of lovers at her feet, whose devotion she imagined would enable her to look rather with satisfaction than regret on the disappointment of those hopes which had been inspired by the attachment of

the young mercer; an expectation in which she had the more reason to confide, as she had command enough over herself to yield her favours only upon long and earnest solicitation, and to make the conquest a matter of importance to the vanity as well as the desires of her lovers.[145]

Her artful eroticism attracts an ambitious schemer, Staunton, whom she follows to Jamaica where he loses his fortune and her sexual attention. In the West Indies she discovers new 'artifices' practiced by 'the mulatto women' with whom she competes for the favours of the wealthy white planters,[146] one of whom is 'Woodville' – that is, Montfort. After having two children, Anna and Lucius, 'Morton' is afflicted with a double catastrophe: a smallpox infection that ruins her appearance, and abandonment by the father of her children. Years after giving up Anna for adoption, Morton seeks out her daughter, whose servant she becomes without arousing any suspicion that they are mother and child. The novel represents Morton as loving her daughter, whom she advises to marry Moroon rather than Henry simply for reasons of material self-interest. Unaware that Moroon is Seraphina's brother, Morton knows Henry's father will oppose his son marrying a poor Creole orphan and she also knows Moroon is a spectacularly rich Creole smuggler passionately attracted to her daughter. Ever the unsentimental materialist, Morton is unconcerned that Moroon has no claims to respectability as the former lover of his mulatto foster-mother who murdered the foster-father when the affair was discovered. Advising Seraphina, Morton tries to pass on to her daughter the cynical wisdom she has gained through experience:

> 'It is the privilege and prerogative of man, nay he sometimes calls it his glory, to play the fool at our bidding. Nature has given him personal force, and laws of society have given him property and power; but Heaven, to counter-balance these advantages, gave us beauty, and education gives us art, to compel him to lay his boasted superiority at our feet, and throw every thing away again for our amusement'.[147]

Morton teaches her daughter to be ruthlessly businesslike in the affairs of the heart because the only opportunity women have to exercise power is when men want something from women. 'Happy is that woman who makes the most of the power of her charms, while they last – for they are frail and perishable.'[148] After Seraphina rejects Moroon for his immorality Morton calculates that her daughter would gain more as Henry's mistress than his wife because she anticipates the hostility of Henry's father. Accordingly she deliberately fails in her expected role as chaperone in order to allow Henry and Seraphina to be carried away with sexual desire.[149]

Morton's distrust of men, the consequence of bitter experience, has Wollstonecraftian overtones in its exposure of the fraudulently moralistic oppression of women who – like Louisa and Amelia in a genteel way, and, like Morton, in a less respectable manner – are forced to use their sexuality for wealth and power. In a passage of free indirect discourse Morton declaims on the social construction of feminine 'virtue':

> With respect to female chastity, in particular, this was a bubble of bubbles – a commodity in which she would have trafficked, at any time, wholesale or retail, with as little remorse as though she had been a West-Indian by birth, and all womankind had been negroes. And she did verily believe that no rational woman (whatever rout might be made about it) did ever set one shilling value upon it, further than as it might be subservient to her more essential interests.[150]

Seeing herself as a performative West Indian, someone who has played the role of mulatto women, Morton thinks of women, blacks and slaves as commodities to be traded and exchanged. Within her perspective nothing is sacred and everything and everyone is for sale, including the culture's fetish object, women's virginity. Seraphina herself, after she loses her virginity, expresses no regrets; her disappointment and disillusionment with Henry cause her much grief but the mere facts of premarital sex and her pregnancy do not occasion remorse. She does not, as her mother did, objectify her sexuality to use it instrumentally as something apart from her. Both mother and daughter see through the illusions of the virginity fetish but the novel prefers the daughter's affirmation of her sexuality to the mother's reification of hers.

Mother and daughter also differ on 'independence', perhaps the primary Wollstonecraftian virtue. The mother considers the daughter's ideal of independence from men and the whole gender system unrealistic, and blames her daughter's reading material for the dangerous fantasies of social justice: 'You have been reading those vile poets till your brain is turned. I wish to God the attorney general would prosecute them all in a lump. For it is they (after all) that put the foolish romantic notions into people's heads'.[151] Seraphina insists that because she can work to support herself she does not need to depend on a man's wealth: 'The mind that is resolved to be independent, will always find within itself the resources of independency'.[152] Defending her rejection of Henry's marriage proposal as long as he fails to conform to moral norms she considers legitimate, she protests: 'Shall I be bought like a slave – shall I be hired like a courtesan?'[153] To avoid the need to prostitute herself she vows to reduce her material needs, another Wollstonecraftian manoeuvre with republican and Stoic overtones.[154] When Gilbert Imlay proposes to give Wollstonecraft money after he dissolves their relationship Mary declines his offer: 'I never wanted but your heart – That gone, you have nothing more to give'.[155]

In terms of the conventions of the British novel, Seraphina upsets the norms at least as much Wollstonecraft's Maria in the *Wrongs of Woman*. Firstly, Seraphina does not conceal her sexual attraction to Henry, violating one of the rules of prudence in Dr. Gregory's popular conduct book, which is mocked by the narrator and criticized extensively in *Rights of Woman*.[156] She affirms her sexuality, refusing to repress it as recommended by the conduct books and refusing to make instrumental use of it as recommended by her mother. Secondly, neither her premarital sexual experience nor her pregnancy shames her. That Clarissa takes refuge in death after the 'dishonour' of being raped suggests the extraordinary power of the culture's virginity fetish to which Seraphina is utterly indifferent. A novel Thelwall almost certainly read, Mary Hays's *The Victim of Prejudice* (1799) depicts the harsh difficulties suffered by an orphan named Mary who is socially stigmatized after being raped.[157] Even if Seraphina had been raped by Moroon, the novel makes clear that neither she nor Henry would consider the deed in any way as having morally contaminated the victim.[158] Thirdly, the poor Creole orphan establishes the terms of her marriage to which Henry and Henry's father finally agree; these terms redeem the educational programme of Amelia and the 'petticoat philosophers' (Anna Barbauld among them) once ridiculed by Amelia's husband.[159] By maintaining her integrity and refusing to make any concessions that would have violated her ethical norms, she is the unmoved mover of a series of actions that effect the moral reformation of the gambling, whoring and heavy drinking son Henry and of the slave-owning father Percival. Finally, the novel carries out under Seraphina's leadership a triumphant feminization of values based on a feminist critique of masculine culture. The novel reinforces the sexual equality of Henry and Seraphina by having each one in turn take care of the other when they are ill and helpless. The delegitimated male activities, duelling and gambling, parallel the most harshly delegitimated male activity of all, racial slavery. The very first morning Henry spends in St Domingo at the mansion of his father's business partner he wakes up in bed with a devastating hangover and 'the beautiful negress Nannane'.[160] The moral insensitivity of slavery is symptomatic, according to the novel, of the overall moral obtuseness found in normative social practices and beliefs.

This latter point requires some elaboration. The logic of the novel demands that Henry reform his behaviour to achieve the comic resolution of marriage and to avoid the tragic outcome of having Seraphina return to St Domingo. It is not essential that Henry's father also reform, but that he does indeed mend his ways constitutes a stunning victory for the forces of reform and the New Philosophy, something Thelwall – as one of the primary victims of the anti-Jacobin reaction and government campaign of political repression – certainly had to relish. Imaginary victories were better than imaginary defeats when real victories were elusive. The politicization of the formula used by Richardson in *Pamela* – virtue gets rewarded over time – was most influentially used by Thomas Holcroft in *Anna St. Ives* (1792), arguably the first 'novel of purpose' or 'Jacobin novel' and a key intertext for Thelwall's novel. The plot is fairly simple: class differences prevent Frank Henley, the steward's son, and Anna St Ives, the landowner's daughter, from marrying after they fall in love. Sir Arthur St Ives, an 'improving' landlord who is swindled by Frank's father, Abimelech Henley, favours the aristocratic Coke Clifton for his son-in-law. Frank and Anna, both advocates of rational social utility, try to reform the reactionary Clifton whom they envision as a potentially effective agent of social progress. Anna and Frank set aside their emotional ties for the sake of a more utilitarian union between Anna and Clifton, who, however, resists their reforming efforts to the point where he kidnaps and tries to rape Anna. He ultimately begins a process of moral enlightenment that starts with feelings of guilt and remorse. As the novel concludes, Frank and Anna are moving toward their marriage and Clifton is continuing his re-education.[161] The novel illustrates a maxim of the radical Enlightenment especially favoured by Holcroft, Godwin, Wollstonecraft and Hays, namely, the 'omnipotence of truth' – the mind's irresistible ('necessary') acceptance of truth when it is perceived as such. The novel affirms hope in political advancement because of the fundamentally rational nature of mind. That Clifton eventually undergoes a moral conversion and moves away from aristocratic privilege is taken as proof that rational reform of society is inevitable.

Important sections of *The Daughter of Adoption* represent the moral progress and regress of Henry Montfort as he is swayed sometimes by his mother's moral education and other times by his father's example of aristocratic privilege. In an significant episode that illustrates his moral development Henry is depicted on a lark with his fellow Etonians, drinking and stealing ducks and chickens from the local farmers. While all his mates escape undetected, Henry is apprehended and undergoes an education in class oppression as he learns that the farmer Wilson is being forced off his land by an engrossing landlord. Henry's efforts to help the farmer are morally ambiguous at best as he also tries to seduce the farmer's grateful and beautiful daughter and raises money in dishonest ways. His intentions – some of them – are good but the episode illustrates starkly the violence of class oppression even in the act of aristocratic 'benevolence'. When a labourer apprehends the poultry-stealing Henry, the Etonian protests: 'I am no thief; indeed I am not. I am a gentleman'. The pithy declaration illustrates how Henry confuses social being with social acting, so that even when he steals he is not a thief because a gentleman cannot by definition be a thief. In reply the labourer attempts to remind Henry of the unjust and bloody game laws: 'But I warrant gemman thinks they may do what they please now a days, and go scot-free with their gentility; while a poor countryman is to be hanged like a dog'.[162] The episode dramatizes Henry's struggle with his conscience that troubles him enough to provoke guilt but not quite enough to pass up an opportunity to press his advantage with the farmer's daughter, who would probably have no alternative but prostitution for a livelihood if she did have sex with him.

Henry demonstrates the greatest capacity to learn when he is exposed to slavery in St Domingo. When the slave-driver awakens the slaves in the morning by whipping them, an outraged Henry protests, but he offers no resistance to the sexual attractions of the fifteen-year-old Marian, a 'pretty mulatto' he sleeps with until he gets tired of her.[163] The scenes of cruelty to the slaves that he observes produce moral reflections: "And such", said he to himself, "are the secondary consequences of the systems of oppression! How much more horrible than the oppression itself! Thus is all sympathy exterminated by the excess of sufferance! Man ceases to feel for man, and brother for brother; and human nature is degraded below the brute!"[164] The level of abstraction he exhibits is an advance from the emotionally impulsive responses in the farmer Wilson episode, where his sympathy rarely led to moral insight and rational analysis.

A major turning point in the novel's depiction of his moral development is the episode in the mountainous wilderness of the volcanic Soufrière near the sea when Henry and Edmunds, his servant-companion, allow themselves to connect emotionally with the sublime and beautiful natural scenery. The encounter with the landscape triggers in Henry a series of reflections on time and space, his past and his present, the 'physical and moral universe' as well as 'the Chronicles of Time, and the world of Fiction'. Edmunds comments on how the beauty of nature makes one forget politics but the usually politically incurious Henry points out the ruins of Spanish mines worked by Indian slaves.[165] This is the novel's most well-known episode because of its parallel with the famous anecdote related by Coleridge when Thelwall was visiting him and Wordsworth at Nether Stowey in 1797. Edmunds's response to the landscape – 'What a scene, and what an hour, sir, ... to make one forget that treason was ever necessary in the world' – appears almost word for word in Coleridge's report of Thelwall's reaction to the beautiful landscape in Somersetshire.[166] Remarkable in the novel's episode is not nature's power to render politics irrelevant but nature's capacity to clarify political and moral truths. Henry continues his reflection on the Spanish mines thus:

> Could time tread back its steps again, Edmunds, and could you and I become Indians, possessing the souls and faculties we do, and did we meet, by design or accident; on this spot, I suspect that our minds would be occupied by other ideas than those of the picturesque and the romantic – that these rocks, these pendant forests – this deep solitude, with the foaming eddies beneath, and all those splendid luminaries above, might only embolden us, by a sense of security, to question the authority of our oppressors, and to demonstrate that against the ravages of foreign usurpation, at least, it is at all times lawful both to conspire and to act.[167]

Here is a fine example of the cosmopolitan imagination at work. Firstly, there is the strenuous effort to think outside of one's own situation and to project oneself into the historical past to take a position wholly unlike one's own ordinary role. Secondly, vivid and intense experiences of the present are relativized in terms of space and time; in contrast, the categories of the picturesque and romantic describe aesthetic moments of meaningful connection with the landscape but only in the here and now. Nature's beauties in a context of slavery would be experienced differently, perhaps as providing a moral foundation from which to contest the authority and legitimacy of the enslaving, exploiting and invading imperialists. That Henry rather than Edmunds, who is usually far more politically savvy, articulates this cosmopolitan meditation and delivers these anti-imperialistic maxims indicates just how powerful are the effects of nature on his way of thinking. As they continue their discussion Henry becomes ever more 'enthusiastic', to employ the term that would have been used then to describe an emotionally compelling experience that destroyed older structures of feeling and allowed new ones to emerge. Vowing to be no longer 'a slave to the opinions of society' and instead to follow the 'more sacred order of nature', Henry declares that Edmunds is no longer his servant but just his friend, an equal.[168] This gesture evokes the renunciation of aristocratic privilege during the French Revolution when people omitted titles and addressed one another as 'citoyen'. This philosophical excursion into nature prepares Henry for three more educational experiences that will regulate his moral compass: his meeting with the Godwinian Parkinson, his witnessing the slave rebellion and his falling in love with Seraphina.

The section of the novel that represents the slave rebellion has no comparable parallel in romantic-era literature. For many details it draws upon the account of the St Domingo rebellion in the influential *History, Civil and Commercial, of the British West Indies* (1798) by Bryan Edwards, but the moral and political analysis could not be more distant from that of the Jamaican planter.[169] Immediately prior to the novel's representation of the outbreak of the rebellion Thelwall inserts a philosophical dialogue between Edmunds and Parkinson on the moral and political wisdom of violent resistance to slavery. Rehearsing to some extent the debate between Thelwall and Godwin in 1795 over political associations and public meetings – in which Thelwall defended and Godwin criticized them[170] – Edmunds defends and justifies while Parkinson criticizes and laments slave rebellions. That slavery would be best abolished gradually and nonviolently as it has in almost every other part of the world is Parkinson's main point, while Edmunds cannot imagine the planters voluntarily giving up something from which they acquire so much benefit.[171]

The represented rebellion itself tilts ideologically in the direction of Edmunds because one of the rebels, Mozambo, displays courage and moral discrimination in saving the whites who treated blacks humanely, thus contradicting one of Parkinson's ideas that revolutionary violence is morally blind and uncontrollable. Mozambo defends the violence against the planters as political not racial. 'Me hab kill de tyrant. Him roast poor negro man no more'.[172] Explaining why he is saving the lives of the Parkinson family and their friends, Mozambo distinguishes between innocent and guilty whites:

> Me love massa. Me love madam. Me love missee. Me wish serve dem still. But me love poor negro man, whom cruel white man whip to die. Me love poor negro man, who hab no bed to lie but dirt; who groan, and sweat, and toil; eat fish dat stink like rot, and drink him tears. Dese me love, massa.[173]

Reacting to Parkinson's moral condemnation of political violence, Mozambo rejects the idea that he has been 'polluted' by killing tyrants. 'Me murder him who murder. But me not roast him. Tyrant! Debbil! Me not roast him neider. Me not scoff at him dying agony. Me not tell him laugh.'[174] That not all the rebels are observing Mozambo's moral scruples becomes apparent as the novel includes descriptions of slaughtered women and children, provoking Parkinson to call the rebels 'mere ignorant savages' and motivating Edmunds and Henry to join a group of white planters and militia who attack 'a body of negroes'.[175] After they later witness the numerous cruelties inflicted by the whites on the rebels they regret having sided temporarily with their fellow Europeans, whom they consider infected with 'canible ferocity' in their retaliation against the blacks. In a manner like the second chapter of Equiano's *Interesting Narrative*, the novel turns the charge of cannibalism against the Europeans and the whites. Edmunds 'was almost frantic. He reproached his master; he reproached himself; and began to execrate an attachment that had led him to act against his principles. He even meditated to make atonement for his error by an immediate revolt to the insurgents.'[176] The reader's sympathy with the rebellion is somewhat complicated when Mozambo is hacked to death while saving the lives of Seraphina and Morton from rebels intent on rape – a rape prevented only by the armed intervention of Henry. Even after witnessing much violence by the rebels Seraphina defends the justice of Mozambo's participation in the rebellion. 'The atrocities of revolted slaves, can never reconcile me to the tyranny that made them so atrocious.'[177]

Thelwall's novel defends the 1791 rebellion of St Domingo, but ten years later the British were worried about rebellions in Jamaica, their largest West Indian sugar colony, that had already experienced an uprising of the Trelawney Maroons in 1795–6. When the novel announces that the St Domingo rebellion began in Acul in 1795 it erroneously makes the year four years later than was the case.[178] The incorrect date could have been a printer's error but it also merges St Domingo and Jamaica, French and British slavery. The novel calls specific attention to British slavery when Edmunds exclaims to Henry after they had witnessed the French whites torturing the rebels: 'O Jamaica! Jamaica! Thou island of abominations and horrors! What [in]conceivable cruelties are there with which those who insult our national virtue by calling themselves English planters have not polluted thee!'[179] Edmunds then recalls Tacky's Revolt of 1760 and the sadistically cruel punishments of the rebels that followed, including hanging two of them alive in chains 'for nine whole days'.[180] The *Analytical Review* paid close attention to the Maroon rebellion in Jamaica, protesting the brutality of the whites and the numerous injustices to the blacks.[181] The aftermath of the most recent Maroon rebellion was notorious: the Trelawney Maroons – free blacks – were transported en masse to Nova Scotia, a region whose climate could not have been more unlike that of Jamaica. Their expulsion anticipates the ethnic cleansings of the twentieth and twenty-first centuries.[182]

Bryan Edwards, the primary source Thelwall used for many of the details of the St Domingo rebellion, did not simply describe events but also defended the white planters and blamed European abolitionists for the violence. The voice of St Valance, Montfort's business partner, articulates the central argument of Edwards's *History*, that the 'friends of the blacks' ('Amis des Noirs') assisted the rebellion in material ways. Henry's response to St Valance is to make a cosmopolitan defence of being a friend of 'the whole human race'.[183] To see the extent to which Thelwall countered his main source it is necessary to examine Edwards's account of the rebellion.

Edwards tries to undermine whatever sympathy the reader might be inclined to have toward rebellious slaves by depicting them as both the puppets of European abolitionists and subhuman beings that can be enslaved without violating ethical norms. Here is a passage from the introduction to the chronicle of the St Domingo rebellion:

> It was not the strong and irresistible impulse of human nature, groaning under oppression, that excited either of those classes [negroes and mulattoes] to plunge their daggers into the bosoms of unoffending women and helpless infants. They were driven into those excesses – reluctantly driven – by the vile machinations of men calling themselves philosophers (the proselytes and imitators in France, of the Old Jewry associates in London) whose pretences to philanthropy were as gross a mockery of human reason, as their conduct was an outrage on all the feelings of our nature, and the ties which hold society together![184]

Edmund Burke in his *Reflections on the Revolution in France* attacked Richard Price's sermon that was delivered in a chapel in the Old Jewry section of London. Burke played with the metonym of 'Old Jewry' to link Price and revolutionaries in general with negatively stereotyped Jews.[185] Edwards continues the Burkean tradition of political invective by attributing to the British reformers the power to generate converts and puppets in France – the Amis des Noirs – who in turn manage the daggers of the rebellious slaves. The moral culpability for the violence then rests with the London reformers and abolitionists who pretend to have sympathy with the suffering slaves. The propaganda of the Amis des Noirs was so effective that it manufactured undeserved hostility to the French planters who were actually kind to their slaves. At the time of the French Revolution there was strong prejudice against the French planters of the sugar islands only because of the writings of the Amis des Noirs, and not because of anything the planters did. The Amis des Noirs, modelled after the English slave trade abolition association, went beyond their British comrades by advocating outright abolition of slavery.[186]

The slavery system depended on a racial code that Edwards describes as uncompromisingly rigid:

> The privileges of a white person were not allowed to any descendant from an African, however remote the origin. The taint in the blood was incurable, and spread to the latest posterity. Hence no white, who had the smallest pretensions to characters, would ever think of marriage with a negro or mulatto woman: such a step would immediately have terminated in his disgrace and ruin.[187]

The incurable taint of blackness is something that anticipates the 'scientific' racism of the later nineteenth century that culminated with Nazi eugenics and mass slaughter of Jews. One does not have to look far to find where the late nineteenth-century antisemites found their model for racial hierarchy. Thelwall as a man of the Enlightenment would have thought the incurable taint of blackness such a bizarre idea he might not have given it enough thought to consider countering it, but his novel in a few instances demystifies the idea of blackness. Naming a white Creole 'Moroon' blurs the difference between white and black, free and enslaved. When Anna/Morton learns to imitate the sexually provocative style of the mulatto women she demystifies blackness as an essence and reveals it as constructed and performed. Finally, nobility and heroism are shown not to be 'white' when a black slave Mozambo acts with more courage and moral discernment than any of the Europeans or Creoles. In Edwards's interpretation, however, as soon as the idea of racial equality is legally declared and the notion of inferior blackness questioned the stage is set for a slave rebellion.

Through the activities and writings of 'the pestilent reformers',[188] the Amis des Noirs – Grégoire, Brissot, Lafayette and Robespierre – the idea of racial equality spread to St Domingo.[189] The great turning point was the decree of 15 May 1791 initiated by Grégoire that free blacks and mulattos be granted the full rights of citizenship from voting to holding office. Thus the 'pestilent reformers' abolished the 'taint' of blackness and undermined slavery itself.[190] Edwards sees the decree as a great injustice:

> Thus did the national assembly sweep away in a moment all the laws, usages, prejudices, and opinions concerning these people, which had existed in the French colonies from their earliest settlement, and tear up by the roots the first principle of a free constitution: – a principle founded on the clearest dictates of reasons and justice, and expressly confirmed to the inhabitants of the French West Indies by the national

decree of the 8th of March, 1790; I mean, *the sole and exclusive right of passing laws for their local and interior regulation and government.*[191]

In his analysis, all follows from the 15 May decree that undermined the 'organic' social community and its age-old traditions, just as, according to Edmund Burke, the French Revolution violated the customs and social bonds of the old regime. In Edwards's analysis the planters uphold community while the revolutionaries recklessly destroy the ancient rights and privileges of a free people – that is, the white planters.

The narrative of the actual rebellion, which broke out in Noé, Acul parish, highlights violence against innocent white people.

> Twelve or fourteen of the ringleaders, about the middle of the night, proceeded to the refinery, or sugar-house, and seized on a young man, the refiner's apprentice, dragged him to the front of the dwelling-house, and there hewed him into pieces with their cutlasses: his screams brought out the overseer, whom they instantly shot. The rebels now found their way to the apartment of the refiner, and massacred him in his bed.[192]

Deferring the issue whether Edwards's account is historically accurate, I attend instead to the rhetorical and aesthetic effects of the narrative that partake here of Gothic horror: in the middle of the night people are seized and hacked to death in their beds and in their sleep. What could be more terrifying?

Edwards's narrative, which accents the violation of the domestic sphere, focalizes a family murdered by the rebels. As in Thelwall's novel, the women and children at the start of the rebellion are sent to ships in order to escape the island, but some of the women are unable to escape.[193] 'These unfortunate women, while imploring for mercy of the savages on their knees, beheld their husband and father murdered before their faces. For themselves, they were devoted to a more horrid fate, and were carried away captives by the assassins.'[194] Edwards depicts a very similar scenario occurring in the parish of Limbé, 'the Great Ravine' where Edmunds and Henry experience their profound communion with nature and history. A 'venerable planter' with two 'beautiful' daughters, Edwards relates, was tied down by the 'ringleader' who then 'ravished' the eldest daughter before his eyes. An associate then raped the younger daughter, after which all three whites were killed. Yet another portrayal of sexual violation is even more extreme. The rebels attacked a pregnant woman, Edwards records, murdered her husband in her presence, 'ripped her up alive, and threw the infant to the hogs' before they '(how shall I relate it!) sewed up the head of the murdered husband in — !!! – Such are thy triumphs, philanthropy!'[195] In all these scenes the humiliation of the men and the sexual violation of the women present an inflammatory image of violence useful for propaganda and retribution. Burke knew what he was doing by highlighting the near rape of Marie Antoinette in his

Reflections on the Revolution in France. Thelwall in contrast modifies the racial dynamics of the novel's near rape of Seraphina by having Mozambo attempt to protect the women.[196]

Another theme in Edwards's *History* is betrayal and injustice, not to the slaves but to the planters who treated their slaves so well. All the gratitude the planters get is violent rebellion. On a plantation that was especially kind to its slaves, Edwards relates, the ingrates rebelled anyway and added insult to injury by employing an especially disturbing banner: *'their standard was the body of a white infant, which they had recently impaled on a stake!*[197] Here the gratuitous cruelty that is flaunted provides a symbol of the insurrection – a symbol of the subhuman immorality of the rebels. The logic embedded in Edwards's prose is that if especially kind white planters get this kind of treatment by the blacks, then there is no reason whatsoever to be a benevolent slave-owner; one might as well be as cruel as the worst planter because it is war between the morally benighted blacks and the civilized whites.

Edwards represents a single rebellious slave behaving humanely and it is clear that Thelwall drew upon this section for his Mozambo episode. I will reproduce the entire paragraph.

> Amidst these scenes of horror, one instance however occurs of such fidelity and attachment in a negro, as is equally unexpected and affecting. Mons. and Madame Baillon, their daughter and son-in-law, and two white servants, residing on a mountain plantation about thirty miles from Cape François, were apprised of the revolt by one of their own slaves, who was himself in the conspiracy, but promised, if possible, to save the lives of his master and his family. Having no immediate means of providing for their escape, he conducted them into an adjacent wood; after which he went and joined the revolters. The following night, he found an opportunity of bringing them provisions from the rebel camp. The second night he returned again, with a further supply of provisions; but declared that it would be out of his power to give them any further assistance. After this, they saw nothing of the negro for three days; but at the end of that time he came again; and directed the family how to make their way to a river which led to Port Margot, assuring them they would find a canoe on a part of the river which he described. They followed his directions, found the canoe, and got safely into it; but were overset by the rapidity of the current, and after a narrow escape, thought it best to return to their retreat in the mountains. The negro, anxious for their safety, again found them out, and directed them to a broader part of the river, but said it was the last effort he could make to save them. They went accordingly, but not finding the boat, gave themselves up for lost, when the faithful negro again appeared like their guardian angel. He brought with him pigeons, poultry and bread; and conducted the family, by slow marches in the night, along the banks of the river, until they were within sight of the wharf at Port Margot; when telling them they were entirely out of danger, he took his leave for ever, and went to join the rebels. The family were in the woods nineteen nights.

A footnote informs the reader that the story comes from Madame Baillon who told it to a friend of the author.[198] The parallels between this and Thelwall's novel are obvious: in both a rebel slave assists his master's family, providing food, a canoe and directions for escape. Another parallel is the detail of the canoe overturning. The differences, however, are more meaningful because in Edwards's account the nameless slave is referred to recurrently as the 'faithful negro'. Whereas Thelwall's slave Mozambo argues with his master to defend the rebellion and to criticize the cruelty of the Europeans, Edwards's slave behaves as he was trained to do – up to a point, anyway, because after all he did join the rebellion. Thelwall's Mozambo is an abolitionist who makes moral decisions and saves his master's family because he decides they are morally deserving. He plays a much more representative role accessing universal human rights as he describes his love for his people who have suffered so much under slavery.

Edwards's *History* dramatizes the victimization of the whites to such an extent that one is surprised to learn the final tally: 2,000 whites were killed and 1,200 white families lost their property but 10,000 rebel slaves were killed and hundreds more tortured to death by fire and wheel. Although he does not justify the public executions by torture Edwards has no doubt where morality resides in this conflict, and it is not with the rebellious slaves. Edwards describes the rebellion's 'cruelties unexampled in the annals of mankind; human blood poured forth in torrents; the earth blackened with ashes, and the air tainted with pestilence'.[199] Thelwall's version of events places the onus of moral responsibility squarely on the backs of the plantocracy, the Europeans and Creoles who exploited their African slaves. Whatever cruelties the rebel slaves practised altered not at all the fundamental injustice of the slavery itself. *The Daughter of Adoption* justifies the slave rebellion with utter moral clarity.

With unambiguous certainty Edwards assigns the moral blame for the violence firstly to the European reformers with their Enlightenment and revolutionary ideas about social and racial equality and secondly to the slave rebels themselves. When the planters commit indefensible actions such as torturing slaves to death Edwards stresses the aggravating circumstances – the provocative sexual violence against white women and children. That Thelwall would use ironically and critically a source like Edwards's *History* is almost predictable as Thelwall himself was one those derided 'pestilent' reformers and 'Old Jewry associates' who had to use a pseudonym 'John Beaufort' because of the anti-Jacobin reaction; the genteel novel-buying public would not likely purchase anything written by the notorious Thelwall. (Thelwall's main lecture venue in London was the Beaufort Buildings until 1796). The *Analytical Review*, which paid considerable attention to Edwards as one of the planters' most effective propagandists, also made antithetical use of his writings, turning the historical facts he would uncover against his racist defence of slavery.[200] According to the most popular history of the St Domingo rebellion in English, one that was reprinted numerous times, the planters were not to blame for the slave uprising because they treated their slaves with leniency and indulgence; rather, the unfavourable representations of the planters by British abolitionists and their French colleagues like Grégoire and the Amis des Noirs inflamed the minds of the slaves and drove them to rebel.[201] Thelwall uses Edwards's *History* to write precisely the kind of abolitionist text Edwards thought was responsible for the slave rebellion. The effects of Edwards's analysis are to excuse the planters from any responsibility for the rebellion, to deprive the slaves themselves of moral and political agency and to inflate the importance of reformist ideas and organizations. The latter effect, characteristic of the anti-Jacobin reaction from Burke onwards, provided intellectual justification for harsh political repression and censorship of the political press.

Another contemporary use of Bryan Edwards's *History* by Maria Edgeworth in her story 'The Grateful Negro' contrasts interestingly with Thelwall's novel. Drawing upon the same episode in Edwards that Thelwall exploited of the slave who spares the good master during a rebellion, Edgeworth constructs a plot that is set in Jamaica during a slave uprising. The benevolent planter named Edwards (!) argues in favour of free labour instead of enslaved, but nevertheless buys the slaves Caesar and Clara, a married couple who were to be sold off to pay a debt. During the slave rebellion Edwards's life is spared but the evil overseer Durant is killed.[202] Edgeworth also opposed slavery but her reading of Edwards's *History* is unimaginative and simplistic compared to Thelwall's.

Conclusion

Thelwall's novel is cosmopolitan for a number of reasons. Firstly, the moral centre of the fictional narrative is a Creole who spends her formative years on St Domingo raised by an Enlightenment rationalist who practices the Rousseauvian faith in nature. Parkinson remarks on her education that 'nature seemed already to have formed [her mind] to every thing that was good and excellent'.[203] Her biological parents form her character far less than her adoptive parents, her enlightened reading and her excursions in nature. As she informs Henry, she is truly a citizen of the world who would be happy to live anywhere because her inner resources can sustain her in any society.[204] Secondly, Seraphina functions within the generic conventions of the romance as a renovating agent coming from the outside – St Domingo, 'nature' – to effect a process of social transformation by converting Henry and his father to the cause of enlightened liberty and virtue. As a cosmopolitan she is ever available to be 'adopted' and integrated into new social formations that she in turn renovates. When Percival Montfort feels that he can alleviate his feeling of guilt and loss by 'adopting' Seraphina in a marriage with his son he is unaware that she is in fact his lost daughter, but according to the ethics that operate in the novel intentions are supreme. Motivated by ethical intentions rather than customary self-interest, Montfort moves in an expansive direction toward the cosmopolitan ideal; such a cosmopolitan expansion would not have been possible without Seraphina. Thirdly, the decisive turns and resolutions of the plot hinge on cosmopolitan judgments of value. Acting in some ways like Shakespeare's Portia, Seraphina, who sets the terms of the marriage, subjects Henry to a test to find out whether he willingly would give up his aristocratic and male privileges in order to live a frugal life with her. As things turn out, they will not have to live a life of poverty but, importantly, he accepts the renunciation of his traditional power ('He must imitate the example which so many of the unfortunate noblesse of France are setting before your eyes').[205] She insists as well that he earn his living honestly and not immorally through exploitation or serving aristocratic interests in a dependent patronage relationship. He has to be willing to labour for a living, the only morally uncontaminated way to get money.[206] Even when Dr. Pengarron, probably the novel's most stereotypically 'English' character, tries to impose his will on the marriage settlement by assigning his wealth to the newly married couple, Seraphina agrees only to name Henry's and her first offspring after him, while sternly reminding him that other people need his money more than they do. The principles of economic justice trump the subjective pleasures of possessive individualism. Pengarron learns his lesson finally when he is able to say 'But I suppose this is the new philosophy too; and the universe is to be *our* family!'[207]

The cosmopolitan ideal, explicitly developed through the character of Seraphina, is reinforced metaphorically by the figure of 'adoption'. Although mysterious origins have been a staple of literature at least from classical antiquity, Thelwall's particular appropriation undermines the fatalism of such traditional narratives. When the pauper turns out to be a prince or when Oedipus's wife is revealed as his mother, the recognition scene discloses a teleological process that has been at work whether the particular agents have been aware or not of its operations. Seraphina's biological parents could not be less promising for a character assigned the role of moral centre. Henry's birth parents are far more promising but do not seem to have any effect on his behaviour, which is determined instead by the war between his presumptive mother and father. When Parkinson and his wife adopt Seraphina they certainly have their selfish motives – to replace a beloved daughter who died (Thelwall himself lost his beloved daughter Maria to illness when he was living in Wales) – but they provide for her a loving home in which to grow up and nourish her moral freedom rather than restrict it. The legitimacy of adopting children as a social project undermines the mystique of aristocratic 'blood' as well as the racist constructions of blackness as a 'taint' and promotes voluntary community. Adoption then undercuts by its logic both primogeniture and slavery.

5 JEWISH QUESTIONS

Introduction

The cosmopolitan dimensions of Jews and Judaism become obvious in relation to nationalism. In France, Germany and Britain emancipation and cultural acceptance were offered conditionally: exchange a corporate Jewish identity for a French national identity (or a German, or a British) and assimilate entirely into the Christian public culture. Clermont-Tonnere, a French advocate for Jewish emancipation, could not have stated the issue more clearly: 'One must refuse everything to the Jews as a nation but one must give them everything as individuals'.[1] The whole premise of Christian von Dohm's influential argument of 1781 for emancipation required Jews to undergo a moral transformation in order to become acceptable to the German nation; only after experiencing Bildung and Kultur (education and culture) could the bearded, Asiatic, circumcised strangers with peculiar religious practices become real Germans.[2] Britain's first gesture toward emancipation resulted in a dramatic *increase* in anti-Semitic hatred as the so-called 'Jew Bill' of 1753 that eased naturalization procedures for Jewish immigrants had to be withdrawn after popular protests.[3] That Britain was the least unfriendly European country suggests the extent of the prejudice against Jews and how remote European culture was from realizing the cosmopolitan ideal. The murderous campaign against Jews in the Soviet Union between 1948 and 1953 was conducted with the circumlocution 'rootless cosmopolitans', a phrase that originated in the second half of nineteenth-century Europe. At first accused of being culturally backward 'wandering Jews' cursed and punished by God for killing Jesus and then, after emancipation, blamed for being overly sophisticated cosmopolitans too at ease with modernity, European Jews found their Christian neighbours distressingly ambivalent. British Jews were comparatively fortunate in relation to their continental cousins because in the United Kingdom a murderous anti-Semitic movement never gained strength for three reasons, according to Todd Endelman: the British ruling class was not hostile to Jewish participation in commerce, banking, trade and finance; the British anti-modernists never became powerful and British xenophobia spent itself in oppressing dark-skinned people in the empire rather than scapegoating Jews.[4]

The influential German discussion of Jewish rights attracted the attention of all Europe, including Britain and the *Analytical Review*. To establish an important context for the exploration of anti-Semitic and philo-Semitic representations it is necessary to turn to the *Aufklärung*'s pioneering writings on Jews by Gotthold Ephraim Lessing. His plays initiated a philosophical and political discussion of Jewish emancipation that the *Analytical Review*, David Levi, Emma Lyon and Maria Edgeworth all continued in their different ways.

As Britain became pressured by the political and economic logic of modernity to emancipate its Jewish population, it faced an uncomfortable dilemma between secular and religious imperatives. A purely secular accommodation with the Jews introduced a multicultural rationality hostile to the ascendant nationalism by which Britain and other nineteenth-century states were achieving social cohesion and negotiating potentially explosive class conflicts. However, political support for the important role Jews were expected to play in some Protestant versions of religious history– return to Zion, convert to Christianity and witness the Second Coming – conflicted with the agenda set by modernity and risked subjecting to derision a religion which was already destabilised by scientific rationality. The United Kingdom was not ready to detach itself entirely from its traditional faith system but it was not prepared either to act upon its ostensible eschatological beliefs. Those who tried to redeem the messianic prophecies of the Christian philosophy of history to which the established denominations paid lip service were the desperate and the poor, those unrespectable enthusiasts like Richard Brothers (1757–1824) and Joanna Southcote (1750–1814).

One sees these tensions played out in the pages of the *Analytical Review*, the religious orientation of which was Christian but liberal and modernist. Joseph Priestley is a representative figure of the journal's religious orientation. Joseph Johnson's most prolific author, Priestley was a prominent theologian of Rational Dissent and a millennialist deeply committed to the logic of biblical prophecy and the apocalyptic theory of history. Because so much of Priestley's practical politics is indistinguishable from secular liberalism it is not difficult to slight the theology which resists easy translation into twenty-first century progressive categories. A liberal modernist in the eighteenth century, Priestley advocated complete religious toleration and slavery abolition, supported the colonists against the British in the War of Independence and celebrated the French Revolution, opposed church establishments and defended freedom of thought and expression, practiced scientific research and criticised most Christians for idolatry and corrupting a pure faith. A Socinian who believed that Jesus was a prophet but not divine, Priestley denied the virgin birth of Christianity's founder but believed that most of the miracles related in the gospels were genuine. A materialist who thought the soul not essentially different from the body, he looked forward to the Second Coming, which biblical texts had already predicted; if these texts could be interpreted correctly, the date of the Messiah's arrival could be fixed.[5] Favouring Jewish emancipation and lending no support whatsoever to persecution of Jews, Priestley nevertheless campaigned vigorously for the Jews to convert to Christianity and conducted with David Levi, a Jewish scholar, a harsh polemical exchange that judged unfavourably rabbinic Judaism and Jews as a historical people. It is not surprising that the *Analytical Review* followed the Priestley-Levi debate closely. Examining Priestley's entire oeuvre one cannot say that Jews had a central position in his writing but they did play an important role in his theology, which in turn shaped the way he conceived that Jews would become fully British.

A second representative figure for the *Analytical Review* and religion was Alexander Geddes (1737–1802), a Scottish Catholic priest who ran afoul of the Church with his pioneering work in the Higher Criticism of the Bible. Never leaving the Church or the priesthood, Geddes was the main religious writer for the *Analytical*, especially the articles dealing with biblical hermeneutics.[6] As he worked mostly on the Hebrew Bible, he expressed mixed views of rabbinic Judaism and the Jewish people. From at least the time of St Augustine the Church was suspicious of millennialism, so that Geddes, who followed the Church in this instance, had little to do with eschatology, but his biblical criticism entailed numerous opportunities to declaim on Judaism. What if anything did the arcane points of textual criticism have to do with Jewish emancipation? Nothing, of course. However, insofar as this criticism reinforced or undermined the overall hostile construction of Judaism and Jews, it contributed to the cultural atmosphere within which Jews negotiated a British identity.

This chapter examines first Lessing's Jewish plays and then the ways in which the *Analytical Review* represented Jews and Judaism in relation to emancipation and religious history. As in the *Analytical*'s treatment of Africans, the issue of 'race' emerges as a contentious aspect of Enlightenment science. The chapter's third section on David Levi, the defender of Judaism against Joseph Priestley, analyses what David Ruderman has called the 'Englishing' of Judaism, specifically the ways British Jews found ways to make adjustments to English culture while at the same time retaining aspects of their tradition.[7] The fourth section continues the exploration of social identity with Emma Lyon, an Anglo-Jewish poet whose gender complicates the ways she is able to acquire Britishness through her writing. The final section of the chapter on Maria Edgeworth's anti-anti-Semitic novel *Harrington* (1816), an intriguing text for exploring the complexities of cultural and literary Jewish representations, illustrates both the achievements and limitations of the entire project of philo-Semitism in the early nineteenth century.

Lessing's Jewish Plays and the Scepticism of Naming

Lessing's Jewish plays are supposed to be about toleration of social and religious difference, didactic plays enforcing the humanitarian lessons of the Aufklärung but *Die Juden* (The Jews) (1749) is about naming and *Nathan der Weise* (Nathan the Wise) (1779) is about naming and indebtedness. However sentimental, these plays are nevertheless fascinating for the ways in which the character of the Jew is a figure for things entirely non-Jewish or at least not exclusively Jewish. Lessing's plays suggest that the agenda of toleration carried with it much more than benign treatment of the Jewish Other.

The core plot of *Die Juden* is that after the Traveller saves the lives of the Baron and his daughter from an assault by thieves, the Baron tries to reward the Traveller's noble and courageous behaviour with the hand of his daughter but the Traveller proclaims his inability to accept the generous offer because of his Jewishness. The two thieves are interchangeable: Michel Stich and Martin Krumm. Their names tell us what they do: Stich means prick, stab or trick and Krumm means crooked. The commonplace first-name plus the monosyllabic surname establishes the two near the bottom of the social hierarchy. Early in scene one Krumm tells Stich that his father and grandfather were hanged as criminals, a fate he expects for himself.[8] They prey on and define themselves against 'honest' ('ehrlich') people' who in turn define themselves against the 'thieves' ('Räuber').[9] Lessing blurs the lines between these two groups by undermining the stability of the naming process. In the first scene Stich says that hardly any of the extremely numerous thieves receive the punishment of the gallows, as if the society has decided to tolerate widespread theft while only superficially opposing it. Similarly, the way the Jewish Traveller's silver box circulates among the characters suggests a universality of stealing that undermines the rigid distinction between honest and thieving people.

By donning beards the thieves become 'Jews'. The Traveller (Reisende) points out that the thieves, despite the beards, speak ordinary German not Yiddish,[10] but the predisposition of the 'honest' people dismisses the relevance of such evidence. Jews steal and wear beards, therefore the thieves are Jews.

The Traveller's servant invents a story about his master that ironically rings true in some sense: that his master had killed an opponent in a duel, afterwards knocking down 'an impudent young fellow' who had 'insulted us' (scene 14).[11] The servant, ignorant of his master's Jewishness, inadvertently stumbles upon the condition of being Jewish: at that time and place the person who cannot kill others in gentlemanly duels and who cannot knock down others who insult him is a Jew; he is, however, someone who often must travel from place to place because of expulsions and whose travelling has allegorical resonance in terms of the anti-Semitic myth of the Wandering Jew.

The play's dramatic turning-point is when the Baron suggests marriage with his daughter as an appropriate reward for saving his party from the thieves. After the Traveller discloses his Jewish identity, the Baron is impressed by the Traveller's social graces and moral qualities and he concedes that at least this one Jew is good, that good Jews are a possibility. 'Jews would be worthy of respect if they all were like the Traveller', he remarks – but the Baron clearly thinks that the Traveller is the exception.[12] That there might be good Jews was considered at the time an extraordinary discovery – too bizarre for the prominent scholar of the biblical Higher Criticism Professor Michaelis.[13] Interestingly, the Traveller's actual name is withheld the whole play. He is 'the Jew'. Within the roles that can be performed within the world of the play there are three groups: thieves, honest people and Jews. The Jew passes for a Gentile, the Gentile thieves pass as Jews and the difference between the honest servants (Christoph and Lisette) and the actual thieves is exceedingly small.

There is an implied alliance between honest Christians like the Baron and honest Jews like the Traveller against the dishonest thieves, but the Baron's and Traveller's own servants are almost indistinguishable from the thieves. Moreover, a class alliance against the dishonest poor is undercut in several ways, firstly by the Baron's daughter's Rousseauvian innocence that calls into question social and religious distinctions altogether. Although she thinks the Traveller's Jewishness should not be an obstacle to their marriage, her very innocence depends on the highly privileged, artificial education that kept out of sight from her everything unpleasant. By contrast the earthy humour, eroticism and materialism of the lower-class characters have some appeal as well. Underlining the play's celebration of plebeian sensuality is the play's bawdy conclusion, which has Lisette and Christoph going off arm-in-arm making lewd references to Jewish circumcision. Lisette will soon find out if Christoph is 'hiding' a Jew. The contrast, especially given the generic expectations of a comedy, between the Traveller who does not get the girl and his Gentile servant's sexual success is quite brutal. Being circumcised is like being castrated in the logic of the play. The Jew's reward, if one can call it that, is not being killed.

What is really at stake with the figure of the Jew in *Die Juden* is desire. To get what they want the thieves pretend to be Jews. Christoph is going to show Lisette just how un-Jewish he is. The silver box that ostensibly belongs to the Traveller circulates among the characters like an empty signifier that acquires value and meaning only in context of struggle and conflict. The silver box is the Traveller's gentlemanly insignia, something like the beard the thieves wear to appear Jewish. The Traveller passes more convincingly as a Gentile gentleman with his silver box, an item no more 'his' than the fake beards. The silver box almost gets the Traveller ownership of the Baron's daughter. Had the Traveller more disguises and false insignias, he might have hidden his identity until the wedding night.

The agenda of tolerance carries with it the disruption of established identity-categories and the reinforcement of those same categories. The Traveller gets back his silver box but when he receives it finally it is just a mere container and nothing more. He is a Jew with a silver box ('Dose') but without the girl. His servant has power over his master now that he knows his master's name, Jew. The Baron now believes that most but not all Jews are scoundrels. The category, die Juden, is somewhat more capacious now than it was before the 'lesson' of the play, but the audience of the play could also find a current in the comedy that calls into question the stability of those social categories by which Jews are scapegoated.

Nathan der Weise is a much more ambitious play than the comedy *Die Juden*. The play is set in twelfth-century Jerusalem and centred in the household of Nathan and his adopted daughter Recha, who has just been saved from a fire by a Christian Templar, Conrade, recently pardoned by Saladin. Conrade falls in love with the beautiful Recha and befriends Nathan, but is instructed by the Christian Patriarch to kill Nathan for the inexcusable crime of converting a Christian child to a Jew. In the famous scene of the three rings, Nathan's answer to the Sultan's question of which monotheistic religion God favours the most is that, because it is impossible to tell for certain, it is best to treat each one as God's favourite. Conrade the Templar does not kill Nathan but seeks Recha's hand in marriage. In the concluding sequence of recognition and reversal scenes, it is rapidly revealed that Recha, whom everyone thinks of as Jewish, has actually been raised as a deist to respect all three monotheistic religions, that Recha is in fact Conrade the Templar's sister, that their biological mother was a German Christian, but that their father was Assad, the Sultan's brother. Once again, at the key turning-point in the plot, a major character is required to repress his sexual desire, as the Templar discovers than Recha is his sister and not the beautiful Jewess ('la belle juive') he thought she was. As in *Die Juden*, the Jewish protagonist, Nathan, a revisionary Shylock, is asexual, loving his daughter Recha, a revisionary Jessica, who turns out not to be 'his' anyway. We learn that his own large family was slaughtered by Christians.

Indebtedness drives the logic of the play, perhaps also deriving from Shakespeare's play. The Sultan has a cash-flow embarrassment that he rectifies with Nathan's gold, while Nathan makes up for the loss of his family by adopting a Christian orphan as his own daughter. The Templar is indebted to the Sultan who spares his life and Recha is indebted to the Templar for saving her from a deadly fire and so on. The condition repeated in the play is the condition of being obligated. The Christians 'owe' Nathan so he gets a Christian girl for his own. The example of Nathan reveals the violence that is structured just barely out of sight by the pattern of indebtedness. In fact, Nathan could have righted the balance by harming or even killing some Christians. Similarly, the Sultan who ordinarily might have executed the Templar spares him mostly because he reminds the Sultan of his brother. The Sultan and his sister initially believe they must coerce Nathan into giving them the needed gold. Nathan's own execution, which never is carried out, is planned by the Christian Patriarch. What one might call a cosmopolitan network of obligations and indebtedness keeps violence from destroying the pacific cross-cultural relationships that actually develop.[14]

The play suggests a pattern of symbolic exchanges as an alternative to violence. The most poignant substitution for violence is of course Nathan's Recha, whose name suggests the word *Recht* – law, justice, right. Like the Baron's daughter in *Die Juden*, she receives a Rousseauvian education that is explicitly deistic. Recha embodies the *Aufklärung* ideal by being in some sense Jewish, Christian and Muslim. Recha's education is the main point about her character and it is difficult to believe that Thelwall did not model in some way his own Seraphina after Lessing's character. Lessing emphasises the symmetry among the three monotheistic religions to undercut religious fanaticism and intolerance. Fidelity to one single religion as the absolute truth is ascribed to Christianity through the Patriarch and the Templar (before his consciousness-raising). Such zealous fidelity produces violence that is foreign to the cosmopolitan spirit of tolerance that Lessing is upholding. Edgeworth's novel *Harrington* clearly takes much from the Lessing drama, including the multicultural celebration of diversity within an overarching monotheism. In the fifth scene of the second act Nathan tells the Templar that despite their religious differences they must become friends. 'Scorn my people ('Volk') as much as you like. We both did not choose the people into which we were born. Are we wholly identical with our people? What does it mean, "people"? Are Christians and Jews more Christian and Jewish than human?'[15] Although everyone belongs by birth to a people ('Volk') and a religion, these social identities do not negate the universal identity of being human ('ein Mensch').

Nathan's raising of Recha is cosmopolitan in the sense that he is not treating her to satisfy his own emotional needs but to comply with an abstract norm of what would be best for someone in her position. He could have raised her as a Jew if Jewish survival meant more to him than anything else, but he defers his own national and religious preferences for a cosmopolitan ideal. When the Templar shifts his openly sexual desire to brotherly affection the awkwardness has already been anticipated by Nathan's deferral of his own desire for a Jewish daughter. Neither Nathan nor the Templar gets what he really wants but the pacific ideal of mutual tolerance requires the curbing of desire because everyone is in a condition of indebtedness. Both of Lessing's plays work fundamentally to undermine possessive individualism because even when one has what one wants it can be, and probably will be, taken away. The circulation of objects of desire, however, brings people together in a state of loss and indebtedness; the very instability of the economy of desire and social naming creates community. Even more than *Die Juden* Lessing's *Nathan* inculcates a scepticism about naming: the Templar's name Conrade conceals as much as it reveals; Recha's ambiguous religious identity is fundamental in that she authentically partakes of all three monotheisms. Biological origins are not irrelevant but they are not absolutely decisive; as Recha comments: 'Aber macht denn nur das Blut / Den Vater? Nur das Blut?' (But then only blood makes one the father? Only blood?)[16] The play's answer is a resounding negative because Lessing's play, like Thelwall's novel, represents 'adoption' as a central cosmopolitan action and symbol of humanity's oneness.

The *Analytical Review* and the Jews

As Christian Europe experienced its spiritual crisis precipitated by modernity, Jews became religiously and culturally meaningful in relation to the cosmopolitan ideal. Firstly, controversies over the Bible usually hinged on the nature of the 'Old Testament'. As scientific reason was applied to the Hebrew Bible, biblical hermeneutics and philology could not be contained within an academic enclave because explosive questions about the faith and identity of Christians were the inevitable consequences of scientific biblical study. In this case biblical Jews in covenant with God were used to repel the threatening ideas from modernist science, an intellectual foundation of cosmopolitanism. When present-day rather than biblical Jews acted contrary to how Christians imagined they should act, then the charge of cosmopolitanism could be levelled against them. Secondly, as history became inscribed with notions of progress, millennialist theories assigned central roles to Jews who were valued for their difference – their chosenness in the theological drama – but expected also to cancel this difference by converting. Undergoing an unprecedented transition to industrial capitalism, British society identified the Jew with demonic avarice and the destruction of tradition, as well as the very opposite, the continuity of tradition. Philo-Semitic Protestants sought to convert Jews for their assigned role in a redemptive narrative and, despite their lack of success (from 1809–59 the extremely well funded society devoted to converting Jews baptised only 367 adults [17]), the conversionists influenced British culture in favour of Jewish emancipation – even though they granted Judaism itself little legitimacy. Those parts of continental Europe that lacked such Protestant conversionists were in fact less tolerant of Jews.[18] For deists, the inconsistencies of the Hebrew Bible helped to de-legitimate Christianity, but for Christians anxious to safeguard their faith against rationalism, the

'Old Testament' was comprehended within Christian hermeneutics, either the sophisticated Higher Criticism or the more simplistic typology. British Christians and rationalists disdained actual Judaism, which was viewed as separate from the 'Old Testament', but as Endelman points out, their disdain did not amount to pressure to reform religious practices, as was the case in Germany where Jews had to prove their cultural worthiness in the details of worship to be accepted as citizens.[19] Although British Jews did not face the difficulties experienced by Jews who lived in Eastern and Central Europe, the discrimination that they did face was similar in kind if not intensity to what their continental co-religionists endured.

The *Analytical Review*, which devotes a surprisingly large number of articles to Jewish matters, focuses broadly on two issues, Jewish emancipation and biblical hermeneutics. Although the *Analytical* strongly supported emancipation, its views on biblical hermeneutics and rabbinic Judaism were sometimes strongly hostile to Jews. The two most important emphases are the conflicting perspectives of Protestant millennialism and enlightened historical criticism of the Bible represented by two very different writers, Joseph Priestley and Alexander Geddes. In contrast, it is noteworthy that the largely secularist London Corresponding Society seems to have expressed no anti-Semitism in its publications and indeed in one satire against the society, *The Decline and Fall of the London Corresponding Society* (1796), the satirist actually links it with Jews, deploying the anti-Semitic stereotypes of Jewish thieves, receivers of stolen goods and sellers of one's 'conscience' for money.[20]

A review unconnected with either emancipation or the Bible and to which I have referred in the previous chapter is the laudatory article on a translation of Pieter Camper's writings on craniometry. The *Analytical* quotes an extract from Camper on being able to identify a Jew and then the reviewer makes his own observations about detecting Jews. First the extract from Camper:

> 'There is no nation', says Mr. C. 'so distinguishable as the jews. Men, women, and children, from their births, bear the characteristic marks of their race. Mr. West, the distinguished painter, with whom I have frequently conversed upon the subject, confessing my inability to discover in what this national mark consists, places it chiefly in the crooked form of the nose. I acknowledge that this contributes much, and that it gives them a resemblance to the lascars, of whom I have seen numbers in London; and have even taken the model of a face in Paris-plaster. But there is still a somewhat unexplained. It is upon this account that the famous De Wit has so ill succeeded in the council-chamber at the Stadt-house of Amsterdam. He has exhibited in his paintings several men with beards, but they are not israelites'.[21]

Camper insists that the physical appearance of Jews is the easiest to detect but he cannot say exactly in what the Jewish essence exists. The English painter Benjamin West (1738–1820) failed to persuade him that the Jewish nose is the tell-tale body part and Camper is certain that the Dutch painter Jacob de Wit (1695–1754) did not paint authentically Jewish characters in his biblical paintings. It is remarkable that Camper seems to know what Abraham or Moses or Isaac looked like, but the fundamental assumptions operating here are that firstly there is a Jewish racial essence, that secondly this essence is readable on the Jew's body and that thirdly this essence is readily experienced but difficult to analyse. Camper goes to the painters as experts because presumably they have trained their eyes to notice racial characteristics.

The *Analytical* reviewer helpfully resolves Camper's consternation about the visible Jewish essence:

> We cannot pretend to determine whether or not, with the professor's influence and eagerness of pursuit, and during his long practice, it proved impossible to procure the skull of an Israelite for dissection. The characteristic given by the English artist is that of common and vulgar observation. A jew, *of either sex*, may be picked out of a number of people, let the nose be aquiline, flat, or turned up, and by a mark which seems to us independent of any osteologic difference from other nations, by a kind of greasy glitter on the epidermis, which remains after the most careful washing, and is not produced by perspiration.[22]

The Jewish nose, according to the reviewer, is too banal to consider seriously, especially because Jews have all kinds of noses. That slightly unpleasant epidermal shininess, however, is what Camper had missed.[23] To make some sense out of the senseless, one can see in the reviewer's idea of greasy glitter which is impervious to cleaning a version of the medieval Jewish odour that could not be concealed as well as a magically visible guiltiness for not accepting Christ, a mark of Cain. It is striking that the *Analytical* would have considered Camper as well as the reviewer worth any kind of attention at all because the logic and argument are so inadequate and violate the norms of Enlightenment rationality and the scientific method. If this review is not a mistake, which it does not seem to be, then one infers that the *Analytical* is receptive to race science in its infancy because its methods and logic appear to be within the overall project of Enlightenment scientific enquiry. If plants and animals can be classified, why not people, and if flora and fauna fall into classes and genera, why not humans? Camper and the reviewer assumed that the racial identification process had no sinister agenda.

The most bigoted article, it should be remembered, is framed as cutting-edge science and current empirical research. A more typical review from the very same issue of July 1796 explicitly advocates Jewish emancipation. Surveying a one-shilling pamphlet published by Joseph Johnson urging parliament to grant Jews, 'a much injured race', their civil rights, the *Analytical* reviewer attributes Jewish 'peculiarities' that disturb Christians to Jewish 'sufferings', a standard argument by Jewish defenders from von Dohm to Grégoire. If there are Jews whom Christians find objectionable in their public conduct, not all Jews exhibit these undesirable qualities, which are evident as well among Gentile businessmen and lawyers. The review's final paragraph rejects as did the French Convention the idea of granting Jews rights as a nation but considers Jewish schools acceptable and urges parliament to bestow full citizenship on the Jewish people.

> The author of this pamphlet, who writes with equal judgment and candour, hesitates on the expediency of giving the jews a permanent establishment as a corporate body, but is of opinion, that public schools ought to be permitted for the education of their youth, and that they should be allowed to share the common rights of citizenship. He laments, as every enlightened philanthropist must do, that the manly eloquence, and sound reasoning, of the bill for the naturalisation of the jews, brought into parliament in the year 1753, notwithstanding the justice, expediency, and policy of the measure, were not able to overpower the clamour of the populace, or combat with success the prejudice of opinion. The subject, it may be hoped, will, at no very distant period, be again brought under parliamentary discussion.[24]

The 'Jew Bill' controversy dismayed an enlightened liberal because public opinion in this instance exerted a reactionary force and made political progress seem both uncertain and capricious. The decisive importance of public opinion is acknowledged when the reviewer calls favourable attention to the recent philo-Semitic play, Richard Cumberland's *The Jew* (1794), based very loosely on Lessing's much more popular *Nathan the Wise*. The *Analytical* praised Cumberland's play as soon as it was published, applauding the drama's 'benevolent design', which was 'to rescue an injured and persecuted race of men from the general reproach which has fallen upon them' by representing a Jewish hero who was both typical and virtuous. By supplying so many extracts from the play and allowing the review to run for nine pages, as long as the longest articles, the *Analytical* was signalling its strongest support for the philo-Semitic comedy.[25] The reviewer of the 1796 pamphlet, who amplifies the earlier commendation of the play, might have considered that it was difficult enough to pressure the legislature to make rational law when public opinion was supportive; when public opinion is on the other side, as in the case of the Jews, the task of progressive reform becomes even more daunting. The pamphlet and the review are wholly political without any racializing of Jews who are represented in ways that deliberately undermine essentialism. The kind of 'rooted cosmopolitanism' that a rigorously secular acceptance of Jews into Britain might have produced is evident here.

Even before the French Revolution, the *Analytical* reflected upon Jewish emancipation. In the section of the journal reserved for articles from outside of Britain – 'Literary Intelligence of Europe' – there is a report in 1788 about an essay contest held by the Royal Society of Arts and Sciences at Metz on the question of whether there is any way to render the Jews 'more useful and more happy in France'. The reviewer describes how reforms happen in society: after a philosopher discovers a new truth there is public discussion that leads eventually to skilled orators popularizing the ideas that finally become new social practices, despite the inevitable resistance launched by traditionalists. The general public debate on Jewish integration into Europe falls into distinct camps with Rousseau, Voltaire and Michaelis on one side opposing emancipation and on the other side von Dohm and Moses Mendelssohn supporting it.[26] The reviewer curiously neglects Henri Grégoire, the priest who actually won the prize with his pro-emancipation essay.[27] Regardless of the report's errors, it is typically enlightened in looking beyond British shores for the European conversation about Jewish rights. Through the 'Literary Intelligence' section the journal kept readers informed of current philosophical publications like the correspondence between Moses Mendelssohn and his friend Lessing; the journal assumes its readers know about the Spinozist controversy about Lessing between Jacobi and Mendelssohn.[28] The *Analytical* did not slight Grégoire, despite this one omission, because his prize-winning *Essai sur la Régenération Physique, Morale, et Politique des Juifs* (Essay on the Physical, Moral and Political Renewal of the Jews) received an affirmative review, the main point of which was that Jews have been made morally problematic not by an innate Jewish essence but by social oppression that can be changed.[29] When Grégoire's essay is translated, that too is reviewed favourably.[30]

The *Analytical* unquestionably supports emancipation, full citizen rights and complete toleration of Jews but Jewish voices are rare in the *Analytical*, which typically frames the question of Jewish rights as something Christians are granting to or withholding from Jews, not something Jews themselves initiate. The *Analytical* attended to the writings of David Levi, which I will examine in the next section but the title of a reviewed book suggests the usual way the journal thought of Jews. The last of six *Letters on Intolerance* addresses the moral and legal duty to tolerate Spanish Jews and Moors, English Jews and Christian heretics.[31] Although the author and reviewer oppose strenuously all kinds of intolerance, they are exercising their moral will largely within a monological situation where the various Others are mute and interchangeable.

I want to turn now to the *Analytical*'s treatment of biblical criticism, where Jews and Judaism find a mixed reception. A good illustration of the characteristic ambivalence is the review of Geddes's translation of Judges, Samuel, Kings, Chronicles and Ruth. The reviewer infers from Geddes's introduction to his translation a critical view of biblical inspiration that the article clearly and sympathetically presents. In a footnote on the conquest of Canaan, an interpretive crux for modernist readings of the Bible, the reviewer largely concurs with deists like Paine who seized upon the immorality of God's ordering the extermination of the Canaanite populace as evidence of the shoddy ethics of the Bible. 'I confess', the reviewer states, 'my reason, and my religion, continually revolt at it: and I cannot bring myself to believe that such an order proceeded from the mouth of God; perhaps not even from the mouth of Moses. I am rather willing to suspect, that it is the fabrication of some posterior jew, to justify the cruelties of his nation'.[32] Unlike Paine whose God never speaks to people, the reviewer who does indeed believe in revealed religion struggles with the contradiction between morality and biblical text and constructs a Jewish biblical author whose immorality has three levels: he puts words in God's mouth, he covers up rather than exposes the 'cruelty' of his nation and he is complicit with whatever heinous deeds of which the Jewish people are guilty.

Geddes's perspective on the conquest and the question of biblical inspiration is more balanced than that of the reviewer whose emotional investment in so readily finding fault with Jews is disclosed in the way he refers to the biblical author as 'some posterior jew', as if the primary meaning of posterior in English speech were not the physical hindquarters. Geddes, however, carefully works out a modernist version of inspiration and sacred history. Although the Mosaic legislation is in 'some sense' inspired,[33] 'the hebrew historian, whoever he was', is 'like all other historians, [who] wrote from such human documents as they could find; popular traditions, old songs or public registers' and like other historians was subject to error, exaggeration, contradiction and inconsistencies.[34] Historians then both write history and are shaped by history, especially material, textual and ideological contingencies that have to be interpreted rather than accepted as holy writ. Geddes's critical approach to scripture is not to debunk revealed religion but to save the Bible and the biblical religions for Enlightenment and modernity:

> the Hebrew scriptures would be more generally read and studied, even by fashionable scholars; and the many good things which they contain, more fairly estimated. For what chiefly deters the sons of science and philosophy from reading the Bible, and profiting of that lecture, but the stumbling-block of absolute inspiration, which they are told is the only key to open their treasure? Were the same books presented to them as human compositions, written in a rude age, by rude and unpolished writers, in a poor uncultivated language; I am persuaded that they would soon drop many of their prejudices, discover beauties where they had expected nothing but blemishes, and become, in many cases, [instead] of scoffers, admirers. In the Hebrew scriptures, they will find a wiser legislation, a sounder theology and a purer morality, than in any other works of antiquity prior to the Christian dispensation. – They will find in the Hebrew historians a rustic simplicity, that will seldom offend; in their poets a grand though grotesque imagery that cannot displease, and a bold figurative style that often rises to the sublime; and in their prophets, properly so called, a majestic dignity peculiar to themselves.

It is not necessary to believe in the biblical 'prodigies' that can be readily understood historically as products of oriental cultural conventions.[35] Geddes's historical approach, which rescues an ethical God from the morally dubious statements attributed to him and salvages a literary masterpiece from scientific debunking, is not wholly unlike Coleridge's argument against biblical literalism and in favour of biblical interpretation in *Confessions of an Inquiring Spirit* (1840).[36] Geddes, like Coleridge, rescues the Bible from both the literalists and the rationalist scoffers. Geddes's judgment of historical Judaism is not nearly as one-sidedly harsh as that of the reviewer, for Geddes finds the biblical Jews morally adequate in their historical context. Geddes's Bible, which assumes some inspired legislation, is mostly a historical, literary document, a flawed masterpiece that rewards an enlightened approach. Geddes's articulation of historical method in reading the Bible is cosmopolitan because it requires readers to achieve distance from the text that cannot sustain an unmediated moralistic retrieval of meaning. If the Bible can be a literary marvel and ethically insightful, yet at the same time a historical document, a product of its times, imperfect and contradictory, then other literary texts regardless of their claims to truth are historically contingent. Moreover, a genuine encounter with historical otherness sustains the faculty for cultural criticism and corrective adjustment of ethical and political beliefs and practices. The inevitably relativizing effects of historical interpretation and historicized reading subvert the myths and absolute truths upon which aggressive nationalism rests. Geddes's intellectual project is especially cosmopolitan because it targets the sacred book of British culture, the most mythologically laden text in the national canon.

Turning now to the debate between David Levi and Joseph Priestley, one enters religious territory that is not wholly modernist because both disputants read scripture as inspired enough by God to sustain actual predictions of future events. As such the debate has little interest for readers fully within modernity, but if the debate is seen also as a forum where Levi can defend the community of Jews indirectly and where Priestley can work out his ideas of apocalyptic history, then the controversy acquires some appeal. Commenting on a Christian writer's invective against Levi, the *Analytical* reviewer protests against such excessive reactions to the Jewish writer, but the article is hardly offering a serious defence of Priestley's antagonist whom he labels a 'pigmy', a typical way of dismissing him taken as well by Priestley himself.[37] A serious and surprisingly even-handed review, perhaps by Geddes, of Levi's ambitious *Lingua Sacra* (1787–8), a miscellaneous compendium on the Hebrew language and rabbinic commentary, was seven pages long.[38] I suspect Geddes is the author because the reviewer characterizes the criticism of Hutchinson's theory of biblical Hebrew as irrelevant and passé, something only a scholar oriented to the most up-to-date developments as Geddes was would know. That the article finds the extensive commentary on the Book of Daniel extraneous to the Hebrew lexicon also suggests Geddes, for he had little patience with literalist, eschatological interpretations of the favourite biblical text for millennialists and those like Levi who argued with them. Levi's first reply to Priestley gets reviewed by the *Analytical*, which admires Levi's courage and supports any efforts to combat the long oppression of British Jews. The reviewer had no difficulty whatsoever reading into the technical dispute over rival interpretations of biblical passages an ethnic and national conflict.[39] The first volume of Levi's *Dissertations on the Prophecies of the Old Testament* (1793), published by Joseph Johnson, was respectfully appraised and accurately summarised.[40] Coupled with yet another review that remarked on Levi's 'learning' and 'ability',[41] the overall reception of Levi was more positive than one would have anticipated considering how central Priestley was to both the *Analytical Review* and Joseph Johnson's publishing enterprise, and factoring in as well the prejudice against Jews. The *Analytical Review* extended itself somewhat in a cosmopolitan direction in response to a writer who, as I will be discussing shortly in the next section, although for the most part theologically conservative, was theologically modernist in a few important ways.

Looking at the *Analytical*'s overall representation of Jews in relation to cosmopolitanism, one finds that there was an unacknowledged conflict between Geddes's historicism, which could make its peace with biblical and actual Jews like Levi, and Priestley's millennialism, which had little patience with either. One finds nothing like real anti-Semitism except in the discourse of race science, one of the journal's minor intellectual tastes. It supported Jewish emancipation unequivocally at a time when few in either the Jewish or Christian communities gave it much thought, but its philo-Semitism did not extend as far as opening its pages in any significant way to Jewish intellectuals like David Levi.

Modernity and David Levi[42]

The British-Jewish writing current during the romantic era illustrates how British Jews negotiated the problem of modernity, which was quite differently than the Jews in continental Europe. As explained by historians Todd Endelman, David Katz and David Ruderman, British Jews accepted and adapted to modernity while at the same time retaining a Jewish identity.[43] Whether British Jews wrote in Hebrew, like Mordecai Schnaber Levison, Abraham Tang and Jacob Hart, or in English, like David Levi, Isaac D'Israeli, Daniel Mendoza, Emma Lyon, Levy Alexander and Hyman Hurwitz, or in both, like Levison and Tang, they allowed themselves to be influenced by British and European currents of thought. Anglophone writers who addressed both Jews and Gentiles forthrightly defended the Jewish community. In numerous British Jewish texts one finds a recurrent pattern: Jewish difference makes itself fit into already existing generic conventions in much the same way that British Jews became acculturated. Against Christian conversionist pressures, these texts affirm Jewish identity with varying degrees and strategies of defiance. Although Britain had no conventional *Haskalah* (modernizing Enlightenment movement of cultural renewal and reform led by an intellectual elite) like that of the German states, it did have a modernizing Jewry nevertheless, as well as reformist writers who were critical of traditional beliefs and practices and who tried to play the role of *maskil* (scholar or enlightened man). British Jewry embraced modernity to such a high degree that there was anxiety over retention of Jewish tradition and maintenance of Jewish continuity, even if such modernism rarely took the form of Reform Judaism.

The future prime minister's father Isaac D'Israeli did indeed break with the Jewish community, but his writing, even before that crisis, was not evidently constrained by his Jewishness. His exit from the Jewish community was neither inevitable nor total, reflected by his son's provocative self-fashioning as a religious Christian and an ethnic Jew.[44] Some of the writers were theologically adventurous, like the deistic Tang, while others like Hurwitz and Joshua Van Oven were moderate reformers. David Levi, whom I will concentrate on, was a fierce defender of orthodoxy, but the style of his defence – pugnacious, idiomatically English, courageous in its choice of antagonists (members of Parliament and Anglican notables, not just Dissenters and radicals) – was so fearless that his writing does not truly resemble comparable writings from the continent. Moreover, Levi's writing illustrates a process of what David Ruderman has called the 'Englishing' of British Jewry, the adaptation of Judaism to English ideas, language and culture.[45]

This Englishing process can also be seen in many other British Jewish texts, including Daniel Mendoza's memoir in which an established, conventional aspect of British culture – boxing – becomes transformed by Jewish innovation. Mendoza's Jewishness is not prominent in his memoir but it is not repressed either. Indeed, several key parts of the narrative turn on Jewishness: as a young man before he is a professional boxer Mendoza protects with his fists the greengrocer for whom he works and who is subject to harassment solely because of her Jewishness; Mendoza has numerous fights, early and late, with anti-Semitic bullies and in virtually all representations of his fights he is known as 'the Jew' Mendoza. British boxing, because of Mendoza and other Jews, becomes Jewish and the Jews become British. Mendoza's specific contributions to boxing – defensive tactics, scientific training, reliance on balance, quickness and strategy rather than brute strength – transform the sport, thus marking a cultural hybridization. In the various prints of Mendoza at the time he is identified as Jewish but he is not caricatured as a stereotypical Jew, thus suggesting a level of cultural acceptance.[46]

Although Jews at the time did not enjoy full legal rights and were victims of snobbery, stereotyping and occasionally violent forms of prejudice, another story of the British Jews is how they retained their Jewishness while at the same time appropriating British and European culture. Accordingly, a philo-Semitic play like Cumberland's *Jew* (1794) lacks the centrality for British Jews that Lessing's two philo-Semitic plays possessed in the German states. While Lessing argued for the humanity of Jews, British Jews had gone well beyond the point where they had to defend their humanity. British Jewish writers embodied in their texts a sense of dual identity, which was not without its anxieties but it was more secure than the problematic dual identity of the *maskilim* in continental Europe. Present in Britain was a literary public sphere that permitted Jewish participation far in advance of political emancipation. The public sphere in continental Europe was not nearly as powerful, hobbled as it was by a weaker middle class and stronger absolutist governments.

To illustrate how modernity is worked out in British Jewish writing I will concentrate on David Levi, the theological controversialist. He illustrates perhaps better than anyone how a British Jew, a member of a minority community, could use the public sphere to 'English' Judaism, defend the Jewish community and effect an ambivalent hybridization of British and Jewish cultures.

The Example of David Levi (1740–99)

Of the unknown and barely known Jewish writers that David Ruderman has brought to our attention recently in his magnificent study, *Jewish Enlightenment in an English Key* (2000), David Levi stands out for a number of reasons. Firstly, unlike his friend and patron, Jacob Hart (Eliakim ben Abraham, 1756–1814), Levi wrote in English not Hebrew. Levi and Eliakim were well-acquainted, as Levi printed and sold Eliakim's books,[47] and Eliakim – a prosperous jeweller – established a philanthropic fund that supported Levi in his scholarly research on and writing of *Lingua Sacra*.[48] From Arthur Barnett's description of his work, Eliakim seems to be in several respects something like a Jewish William Blake: he defends his religion against the Enlightenment logic of scientific materialism, targeting especially one of Blake's antagonists, Newton, and also, like Blake, linking political liberty with biblical prophecy.[49] Cecil Roth characterises Eliakim thus: 'Strongly orthodox in feeling, [Eliakim's writings] are modern in conception, written in a lively and accurate Hebrew, tackle in an energetic fashion problems of the hour and show a remarkably wide knowledge of contemporary scientific literature in English and the European languages.'[50] Drawing upon the British Tory writers, Robert Greene and William Whiston in his antimodernist critique of Newton and Locke, *Milchamot Adonai* (Wars of the Lord), as well as the great rabbinical scholar, Abravanel, Eliakim attacked what he felt were the metaphysical foundations of a modernity that threatened religious faith and identity.[51] Whereas in the German states and eastern Europe, there was a sufficiently large number of literate Jews who worked in Hebrew to sustain a project like the journal *Ha'Measef* (1784–97),[52] within Britain however (until the rise of Zionism at the end of the nineteenth century), Hebrew-language literature had only a small readership – and, accordingly, few, Jewish or Gentile, were aware of Eliakim's work. By writing only in English Levi fused a Jewish and a British cultural focus and enjoyed a readership of British Jews and Gentiles

Levi courageously seized opportunities to defend the Jewish community at a time when the received wisdom was to stay out of arguments with Gentiles who were so much more numerous and more powerful. Reading the cultural situation accurately, he criticised harshly anti-Jewish writings without bringing down on the Jewish community ill treatment. In fact, Levi's combative writings raised tolerance for theological debate between Christians and Jews to a new level. A popular print of the day draws a parallel between the boxing victories of Daniel Mendoza and the debating victory of David Levi over their respective Gentile opponents. Both Mendoza and Levi were seen to have defeated Christians. Moreover, in both cases, the Jewish victory was not seen to have been counteracted by Gentile retribution.[53] Levi rebutted the anti-Jewish ideas of Anglican theologians like Henry Prideaux (1648–1724) and Anselm Bayley (d. 1794); radicals like the Unitarian Joseph Priestley (1733–1804) and the deist Thomas Paine (1737–1809); influential Christian scholars of Hebrew like Benjamin Kennicott (1718–83) and Bishop Robert Lowth (1710–87); and even members of Parliament like Nathaniel B. Halhed 1751–1830), defender of Richard Brothers (1757–1824).[54]

If one compares the debates between Moses Mendelssohn and his Christian opponents – Lavater and Jacobi – one is struck above all by the insecurity and anxiety of Mendelssohn and the pugnacious confidence of Levi. Just as German Jewry was much more vulnerable than British Jewry, so the public sphere in which Mendelssohn operated was less tolerant, permitting far less room for intellectual negotiation. Lavater, the popularizer of physiognomy, who insisted that Mendelssohn defend Judaism or convert to Christianity, forced the reluctant Mendelssohn to make a reply to the religious challenge that effectively thwarted the conversionist zeal of the Swiss cleric but cost the Jewish philosopher considerable anxiety. Mendelssohn's example was that a Jew could retain his religion and still participate in the most up-to-date discussions of philosophy, but his way of harmonizing modernity and Judaism was neither painless nor unproblematic.[55] Priestley, who invites Jews to convert to Unitarian Christianity, does not exert the coercive power wielded by Mendelssohn's opponents. In fact, only Levi decided to respond to Priestley and his response provided an extensive defence of Judaism and a critique of Priestley's theology. As a millennialist, Priestley assigns an important role to the Jews who are to be restored to Zion and whose conversion is an indispensable event in the apocalyptic drama of Jesus's second coming. The not-so-subtle subtext of Priestley's letter to the Jews, however, is that if they refuse even this most magnanimous offer they will have illustrated once again their evil propensities that God has been punishing these many centuries since they killed and denied Jesus. Even so, the enlightened Christian has no interest in harming the stubborn, wrongheaded Jews; God will mete out the appropriate correction.[56] Levi, however, is not intimidated and exploits the opportunity to cite Jewish survival as a sign of divine favour.[57]

For the Jew fully within modernity 'Jewishness forms only a portion of his total identity'. According to Michael A. Meyer 'Jewish identity becomes segmental and hence problematic' only in the second half of the eighteenth century.[58] In the eighteenth century British Jews started to act in many respects like other British people and, according to Todd Endelman, 'adopted the habits of Englishmen because they wanted to feel at home there. They quietly abandoned the ways of traditional Judaism whose practices set them apart from other men and interfered with their pursuit of pleasure and success'.[59] Yet they retained a Jewish identity, thus illustrating that modernity did not necessarily doom Jewish continuity, even if it did produce inevitable changes.

The final exemplary aspect of Levi is his effective use of the literary public sphere. An accomplished Hebraist and a religiously knowledgeable Jew but not an ordained rabbi, Levi was a largely self-taught shoemaker, hatter and finally printer who reached Jewish and Christian readers. As an artisan autodidact, Levi was a publishing author a generation before such writers in the self-taught tradition became commonplace in nineteenth-century Britain.[60] That Levi does not make his first appearance in print until he is forty-three years old indicates a long literary apprenticeship and limited opportunities not unusual for a working artisan. Shoemaking was, according to the historian Jacques Rancière, the path taken by the most intellectually ambitious artisans because the job allowed more opportunity for reading and writing than most other trades. Levi's friendship with Henry Lemoine (1756–1812), son of a Huguenot refugee, started in 1780 when they met at Lemoine's Bishopsgate bookstall, thus giving Levi an opening to the world of print culture and the literary market. With Lemoine and others Levi dined at the home of George Lackington the popular publisher who formed a lower-middle-class salon to assist him in stocking the most popular books for sale. Just as Joseph Johnson (the successful Dissenting publisher who published Levi's 1797 critique of Paine)[61] was at the centre of an intellectual hub of advanced middle-class and Dissenter thinking, hosting parties and providing literary patronage, so Lackington sponsored his own literary circle: more modest in its philosophical ambitions, more plebeian in its social style but also more aggressively popular and commercial.[62]

The importance of these literary circles in constituting, sustaining and reproducing a literary public sphere cannot be exaggerated. Writers met one another, exchanged ideas, tested arguments and formed collaborative relationships. For example, Lemoine helped Levi get various theological texts he might not have obtained otherwise. Similarly, Lemoine's Jewish contacts were indispensable when he collaborated with Levy Alexander on the sketch of Abraham Goldsmid's life.[63] These collaborative efforts, however valuable, did not prevent Lemoine from expressing an occasional anti-Semitic bias,[64] but this less than perfect cultural situation was in advance of the cultural opportunities available to Jews on the continent. Heinrich Heine and Ludwig Börne believed that they had to pay the price of baptism to participate fully in the literary public sphere of Europe. No such price was demanded in Britain.[65]

Levi as Writer

Levi's first book, *A Succinct Account of the Rites and Ceremonies of the Jews* (1783), mediates between Jewish knowledge and, according to the preface, both Gentile and Jewish ignorance. The 'rites and ceremonies of the Jews' was an established genre in Christian histories of the Jews. In Jacques Basnage's history, for example, all of Book 5 is devoted to 'Rites and Ceremonies'.[66] Levi targets for criticism some of the descriptions of Jewish belief in Humphrey Prideaux's immensely popular history of the Jews from the first temple to the time of Jesus.[67] Prideaux (1648–1724), Dean of Norwich, had many editions of his *The Old and New Testaments Connected in the History of the Jews and Neighbouring Nations* in print; I counted thirty-six separate editions from the first in 1716–18 to 1871. Levi is using the 1779 edition. Levi, who disputes specifically Prideaux's account of the Jewish doctrines of resurrection, predestination and free will,[68] refutes Prideaux rather than some other commentator because by 1783 Prideaux's text was the standard. Levi might not have known Basnage's history at that time for there are no references to it; he seems to have depended on his friend Henry Lemoine to get research materials but the Huguenot Lemoine probably would have known about his fellow Huguenot Basnage's very famous book and it was not until 1787 that Levi is citing Basnage.[69] Neither does Levi seem to know the apostate Abraham Mears's Jewish 'rites and ceremonies' that was published in English for an English audience forty-five years earlier.[70] According to one scholar, Levi's account must have been successful because there was no other 'rites and ceremonies' by a Jewish writer to appear for another fifty years.[71] Notable in Levi's text is an absence of defensiveness. Although he refutes Prideaux's misrepresentations, he otherwise provides straightforward, unapologetic descriptions of Jewish religious culture, including long sections on the history of the Mishna and the rabbinic sages. He does not defer in any manner to Christian and deist anti-Talmudic prejudices.

If his target audience were Jews who were ignorant of their religion or who had been misinformed by conversionist Christians, why use English? Levi states in the preface that many Jews did not know Hebrew and were fluent instead in English. He never mentions Yiddish but at that time many British Jews were

Sephardim who would not have known Yiddish. Indeed, the wealthiest Jews were Sephardim, so that the low prestige of Yiddish would have been even lower in London at that time. The synagogues in the early nineteenth century tried to banish Yiddish altogether but too many working-class Ashkenazim knew only Yiddish, so the battle against Yiddish had to be restrained.[72] Nevertheless, Yiddish was hardly an unproblematic option for Levi.

We do not know if Levi was tempted to write in Hebrew like Eliakim but Levi wrote a capable English prose. Indeed, he was chosen by London's Great Synagogue to translate into English several Hebrew texts in 1790.[73] As an artisan and tradesman with much contact with English-speaking customers, and as a London-born Jew, Levi used a prose that reflects the model of the Puritan plain style – Defoe – rather than the Augustan influence of Johnson. Levi's translations of the liturgy – his writing which undoubtedly had the greatest influence, reproduced many times in nineteenth-century daily and holiday prayer books – are either dependent on the King James Version when passages are biblical, or elsewhere cautiously literal, retaining somewhat the dignity of the original if at times being also a little stilted. Levi's first line of the *mahnishtinah* of the Haggadah (Passover Seder service), for example, reads: 'Wherefore is this night distinguished from all other nights?' Perhaps Levi got this from an earlier translation, but if he is the first to have phrased it thus, he would have been pleased to know that the North American 'Maxwell House Haggadah' used by millions of Jews retains that exact same phrasing in its translation.[74] If he did not originate the translation, his choice to retain the earlier translation rather than change it to a less stilted form of English he was fully capable of writing indicates the stylistic claims to dignity that scripture possessed for Levi. According to one of the few scholars who have studied English translations of the Jewish liturgy, Levi's translations became 'part of the religious outfit of almost every Anglo-Jewish family', Ashkenazi or Sephardic, throughout the nineteenth century.[75]

Levi's influence is not necessarily a sign of his skill at translation but is rather a sign of British Jewry's deference to British Protestant culture. Levi's 'translations' of the Torah are almost always identical with the King James Version. His commentary on the opposite page forthrightly quarrels with the King James translation on theological and grammatical grounds but he does not rework the English prose of the Pentateuch to reflect a specifically Jewish perspective. To take just one of many examples, he quarrels with the King James Version of Exodus 24:5 but offers his alternative translation only in the *commentary* not in the text proper: 'This I think, should be translated thus:–"And he sent the ministers of the children of Israel, and they offered burnt-offerings, &c." I must likewise, observe, that Scripture generally calleth upper servants lads, or young men, though they be aged.'[76] It is anachronistic but heuristically useful to compare the innovative way Martin Buber and Stefan Rosenzweig translate the Torah into

German; one sees how Buber and Rosenzweig succeed in producing a decidedly Hebraic German translation (1926–38).[77] Their work would be very much at one pole, reflecting a genuine Benjaminian dialogue between the two languages that marks the cultural specificity of the Jewish experience with the German language. Levi's translations would be very much at the other pole, mirroring the already existing dominant culture while at the same time acknowledging that the already existing 'translation' is not adequate. Levi's deference to the King James Version vies with his knowledge of its inadequacy but neither British Jewry nor Levi himself at this time desired to produce a uniquely different English to accommodate Jewish specificity. Although the English translations played no role in the synagogue service – even the Reform services were mostly in Hebrew – they are significant in this context in reflecting cultural identity by betraying an ambivalence about English. The holy language is of course Hebrew, but the retention of an 'Old Testament' style of translation suggests a tension that has not been fully resolved between Judaism and British identity.

Levi as a Controversialist

Cultural identity, not just theology, governs the logic of Levi's replies to Priestley and other Christian critics of Judaism. In David S. Katz's summary of the Priestley–Levi controversy, he concludes that this 'storm of controversy' was so important that it generated texts even after Levi's own death.[78] Open questions were the degree of toleration and acceptance British Gentiles would grant Jews and the degree of acculturation and Britishness Jews wanted to claim. As already mentioned, Todd Endelman captures nicely the tone of the controversy when he cites a contemporary print linking Daniel Mendoza's boxing victory in 1788 with Levi's theological victory over Priestley.[79] Levi responded to Priestley in the first place against the received wisdom of the Jewish community, whose posture was cautious, especially after the vehement repudiation of Jewish rights during the 'Jew Bill' controversy of 1753. The Jewish community blamed Levi for risking persecution of Jews by debating publicly with a prominent Christian, but despite these expectations, Christians 'of all denominations' approved of Levi's initial answer to Priestley's challenge.[80] Only one of the published counter-responses to Levi was abusively hostile. 'Anti-Socinus', the alias of Anselm Bayly, threatened to 'tear' Levi to 'pieces' if he mentioned Jesus Christ again in any of his subsequent writings. Levi was so confident of his public position that he was able to mock Bayly and sarcastically display a feigned dread at what Bayly might do to him.[81] (The pugilistic parallels seem to be obvious.) More indicative of public opinion than Bayly's coarse rant was James Bicheno's polite and respectful address, to which Levi responded with amicable disagreement in the spirit of enlightened debate.[82] Bicheno, a Baptist and millenarian, is interesting in his own right; he was rare among millenarians to declare that Jews could return to Zion without converting to Christianity first.[83] Even one of the latest responses to Levi written a decade after Levi's death by the theologically reactionary William Cunninghame who rehearses the charge of Jewish deicide for which Jews have properly suffered for centuries did not pose any threat to the Jewish community.[84] Rather than intimidating Jews, this commonplace rebuttal of Levi was followed seven years later by Jonathan 'Jew' King republishing Levi's *Dissertations on the Prophecies of the Old Testament*.[85] King, on the margins of the Jewish community, was a political radical and moneylender.[86] That Levi was usable by someone like King at a time of great political turmoil without fear of anti-Semitic scapegoating suggests that Jews enjoyed a surprisingly high degree of security and freedom of expression, exceeding their technically legal 'rights'. According to Endelman, King used the republication of Levi's book as an opportunity to announce publicly his return to Judaism.[87]

The controversy suggests that the public sphere, well ahead of the political institutions and law, acknowledged the equality of Jews to Christians. The harsh exchanges between Bayly and Levi, which might appear upon first glance to be almost violent, are in fact just the opposite. As Ruderman explains, 'Christians and Jews felt free to verbally assault each other and their faith'. A one-time friend of Levi's, Bayly is no bigot but a passionate partisan of his religious perspective.[88] Yet another indication of the quality of the public sphere is that Levi, despite his long and bitter conflict with Priestley, was the printer of Priestley's *Inquiry into the Knowledge of the Antient Hebrews Concerning a Future State* (1801). As Ruderman comments: 'Levi, the proud and unrepentant Jew' finds nevertheless 'common ground with his former antagonist'.[89] Enlightenment norms like the authority of the strongest argument, the impersonality of rational debate and reliance on evidence and logic supported the public sphere within which Levi influenced British culture and British culture influenced him.

Levi's theological polemics are moderately conservative but they project a vigorously assertive posture in terms of cultural politics. Levi never comes close to making the elegant connections between Judaism and natural religion that Mendelssohn made so famous but Mendelssohn never deployed the combative rhetoric Levi uses as a matter of course, such as this from the reply to Thomas Paine: 'Surely Sir, you must have considered your readers as no better than *heads* of onions ...'[90] The Berlin *Aufklärer* who deferred to his opponents never employed Yiddish-like phrases about the heads of onions. On the issue that mattered most in the public debates between Jews and Christians – the prospects of Jews converting to Christianity – Levi is provocatively bold: 'I am free to assert, that there is scarcely an instance of a Jew ever having embraced Christianity on the pure principles of religion'.[91] He illustrates this point by recalling someone who had converted five separate times and 'got a pretty sum of money'.[92] The locution 'pretty sum of money' is a colloquial turn of phrase one would not find in Mendelssohn either; such diction signals comfort with an urban commercial English, not just scholarship whose style does not betray the awkward bookishness of some autodidacts. Returning to the content of his statement, one takes note of its uncompromising indictment of Christian coercion. Mendelssohn had no choice in being more cautious in his public statements.

One notices something quite new in Levi's 1796 book on prophecy and his 1797 answer to Paine's *Age of Reason*. Levi displays a knowledge of writers – Morgan, Tindal, Bolingbroke, Hume, Voltaire, Spinoza, Lowth, Basnage, Kennicott and Newton – far broader than he had available in his responses to Priestley. As a consequence he can contest Christian writing on prophecy with more authority and show where Paine gets his deistic ideas to identify what is new with Paine. There is also a breadth of overall knowledge, as if he took Priestley's gibe about being ignorant of secular knowledge to heart.

Levi began his *Dissertations on the Prophecies of the Old Testament* in 1793 at a time of tumultuous political conflict in London. As Jon Mee has illustrated, during the 1790s secular Enlightenment and revolutionary writing mingled often harmoniously with religiously inspired millenarian writing.[93] Perhaps thinking of the revolutionary emancipation of French Jewry, Levi in the preface recapitulates British Jewish history highlighting many of the atrocities and injustices the English had inflicted on Jewry.[94] These eight pages of historical narrative are a rare reminder by Jew or Gentile of how badly the English had treated the Jews in the medieval period. Although couched in an ambiguous context – the atrocities are both historical and religiously semiotic, signs of divine displeasure – the short history assigns historical guilt. When Levi discusses the resurrection of the dead, he insists that all Jews, even the ones who have fallen from the faith, pretended to be Christian or converted to Christianity will enjoy a new birth because Christian coercion was so harsh for centuries that Jews were not wholly responsible for apostasy.[95] Apropos of a passage in Isaiah, Levi says that 'Christianity cannot be the Peaceable kingdom of the Messiah'; all one has to do is look at the history of Christian mistreatment of Jews.[96] However undeveloped, the use of history and the appeal to history point toward a secular politics of minority rights.

The logic Levi uses in his critique of Paine is even more insistently secular. Levi defends the Old Testament not just as the word of God, as divine revelation, but as literature and history. Citing Bishop Lowth's discussion of biblical literature, Levi praises the different literary genres in the Bible.[97] Echoing to some extent the *Haskalah*, Levi also defends the basic precepts of Judaism in terms of its influence on social morality, from loving the stranger to generous treatment of the poor and powerless.[98] Moreover, Jewish law embodies enduring insights into socio-economic justice, as the laws of land distribution, including the Jubilee, prevent concentrations of wealth and mitigate against poverty by institutionalizing God's morality over private property rights.[99] Levi's defence of a favourite deistic target, the conquest of Canaan, relies largely on a secular logic: the Mosaic sexual morality was superior and extermination of the residents came only after the resident tribes were offered a peaceful settlement.[100] Revelation, even if authentic and definitive in the eyes of an observant Jew, has to be consistent with universal morality. There are times when Levi's interpretive logic is like that of Alexander Geddes, the *Analytical*'s religious writer, but Levi's historical arguments lack the systematic consistency of Geddes's.

Another area that Levi develops in his reply to Paine is philological. Paine makes the mistake in *The Age of Reason* of discussing Ibn Ezra and the meaning of some Hebrew words, something about which Paine knew almost nothing but Levi a great deal, and he shows no mercy in illustrating Paine's ignorance.[101] He had, in three volumes of *Lingua Sacra*, produced a capable Hebrew grammar, dictionary and miscellaneous commentary; his level of Hebrew knowledge was far higher than any of his non-Jewish opponents and whenever he could make the debate one of philological analysis he was at a great advantage.

Levi: Conclusion

Mendelssohn's friendship with Lessing, which symbolized the unity between Jewish *maskil* and Gentile *Aufklärer*, promised a more tolerant Europe in the future. Levi's debates with Priestley and others also promised a more tolerant world – not because of elegant arguments, but because, in their sometimes coarse and vehement polemic, they demonstrate the vigour of the public sphere, suggesting that important issues can be debated non-violently between Jews and Gentiles. In Europe where the public sphere was more fragile, an apparent politeness concealed Jewish vulnerability. The Mendelssohn–Lessing circle maintained an amicable subculture because the idea of natural religion provided discursive openings for Jew, Christian and deist; Mendelssohn and his fellow Jews really needed the assistance of philo-Semitic Gentiles like Lessing to act as a buffer between them and the hostile Christian culture. Levi and the Jews in Britain were not in desperate straits at all. It is not that Britain lacked raw anti-Semitism but that Jews only infrequently had to experience it. As Endelman suggests, one contributing factor is that Britain had other scapegoats such as the colonial natives including the Irish Catholics who took the pressure off Jews.[102]

If we insert Levi into this frame of analysis, we find a mixed situation characteristic of deep ambivalence. Debating Christian critics of Judaism was boldly asserting Jewish difference, but the deference in Levi's translations to the King James Version moves toward an accommodating Britishness that is, in turn, subverted by the combative commentary. One way to look at the Jewish embrace

of the King James Version is to see it as a strategic move: the English translation is Protestant but the text behind it is Jewish, thus linking together Jew and
Briton. The edition of the Torah with Levi's translations and notes published by
Levy Alexander exemplifies acculturation with a vengeance. Instead of Torah or
Chumash it is entitled 'The Holy Bible'. Especially telling are the numerous coloured plates that illustrate the narrative; all of them, without exception, make no
attempt to represent the actual Middle Eastern environment in which the events
took place. Instead, Jerusalem and Beersheva look like London and Windsor.
The plate illustrating the birth of Esau and Jacob shows a huge, lush, regal interior, something like the inside of Windsor Castle. The plate illustrating Abraham
entertaining the three angels looks more like something from the set for a BBC
production of an Austen novel; more like Abraham the dapper squire getting
ready for tea than a desert nomad taking care of visitors. These plates reflect a
defensiveness about Jewish identity that is rarely present in Levi's writings.

Levi himself, who had nothing to do with these plates, is best represented
perhaps by *Lingua Sacra*, which was published initially in weekly numbers. The
early work, which was subsidized to some extent, required sixteen-hour days six
days a week. After he lost his subsidy he was relieved finally by a fund already
mentioned. Levi does not identify Eliakim or any other benefactor by name but
we know it was prosperous Jews who granted him the eighteen shillings a week.
He complains of a lack of fellow scholars with whom to consult. The picture
one gets from Levi's address 'To the Public' (vol. 3) is of a somewhat isolated
scholar who knows nevertheless that he is appreciated by the most knowledgeable Jews and who realizes he is performing a useful task by making Hebrew
lessons available to the uninstructed and by making Hebrew more accessible to
those Jews who need help. Levi says that most of the Jews he knows are not fluent in Hebrew. The Hebrew-to-English dictionary includes not just meanings
of words but long notes about rabbinic commentary and biblical scholarship
(some of which is Christian), including biographies of the most prominent rabbinical writers. For one man – without yeshiva training – to have written such
a work is truly remarkable. One can acquire much unsystematic learning by
reading around in the dictionary. The commentator to whom Levi turns more
than any other is Abravanel (1437–1508), a favourite as well with Eliakim. For
example, Levi takes Abravanel's side in the dispute with the more rationalistic
Maimonides over the Book of Daniel. For Maimonides it is a lesser text within
the Tanakh – the Hebrew Bible – because Daniel was not a prophet. The more
messianic Abravanel, with whom Levi agrees, makes Daniel a prophet and takes
seriously the prophetic content of the book in a way that traditional Judaism
ordinarily does not. The Book of Daniel, of course, was a favourite Christian text
for millenarian prophecy, including Priestley. In this one instance Levi is slightly
heterodox but the overall commentary is not theologically adventurous. Per-

haps we see here in the example of interpreting the Book of Daniel the influence of Protestant millennialism that was so strong during the French Revolution. In Levi's voluminous notes there is no equivalent to Mendelssohn's critique of the rabbinic *cherem* (excommunication) or the Haskalah's neo-Karaite tendencies (the authority of the Hebrew Bible over the Talmud). Several aspects of his revered Abravanel were recuperable as somewhat modernizing, Abravanel's historical understanding of scripture and his willingness to comment on and use Christian scholars, especially the humanists.[103] Despite the centrality of Abravanel, the dictionary has much on and by Maimonides, so it is not a narrowly focused study.

Lingua Sacra is a textbook with a strong personality. The hand of the autodidact is everywhere but Levi's passion for learning compensates many times over for the lack of philosophical polish. That someone like Levi was sponsored by the Jewish community to do the work of *Lingua Sacra* tells us that the community would support traditional learning, at least at sixteen shillings a week. Several things are noteworthy about the subscription list for *Lingua Sacra*. The 'Learned Society' in Berlin and Königsberg ordered fifty copies, more than any single British patron. An important goal of the Haskalah was to make Hebrew an object of scholarly study and literary use. The fifty copies suggest that Levi's level of Jewish learning was deemed fairly serious. Another thing stands out: although the overwhelming majority of the subscribers have names that seem Jewish, some subscribers are obviously Christian, such the Reverend W. B. A. Grant of Walworth and John McNair, printer of Edinburgh. Somehow Levi had tapped into a community of scholars, however small, that was interested in serious study of Hebrew and Judaism. Unlike the anachronistic prints in the Levy Alexander 'Holy Bible', *Lingua Sacra* has integrity intellectually and culturally. Gentiles and Jews who were reading that text experienced something quite other than Anglicized and Protestant versions of Judaism.

Levi's cosmopolitan role was twofold, teaching Jews a British way to be Jewish and teaching the British an authentic version of Judaism. He had the patience and skill to mediate between the two worlds with enough effectiveness that the liberals of the *Analytical Review* read him with attention and respect. Just as the Enlightenment had only a mixed record of achievement in opposing racism against Africans, it contributed to anti-Semitism almost as much as it contested it, especially with the notoriously hostile views of the most famous *philosophe* of all, Voltaire. Even the philo-Semites invariably accepted Jews into the European community only on condition they gave up most of their religion and culture. Levi, like Mendelssohn before him, insists that Jewish traditions are compatible with modernity and writes from a position that invites the Gentile audience to learn something from a different culture. The preponderant rhetorical situation of Jew and Gentile was condescending and paternalistic, with Gentiles informing Jews how they should best behave and Gentiles liberally forgiving Jews their unfortunate characteristics in need of improvement. Levi's brash persona in his writing imitates the toughness of the fighter Mendoza and presents to the well-meaning British an unapologetic defender of the faith who was eager to 'mix it up' with the Gentiles on theological and religious matters of controversy. His work demonstrates both a combativeness and an openness to intellectual exchanges, commerce des lumières.

Following the Muse: The Poetry of Emma Lyon, Anglo-Jewish Poet[104]

The public sphere within which David Levi conducted his theological disputes was masculine but another sphere allowed feminine writing within certain genres, one of which was poetry. By examining closely the neglected work of Emma Lyon one discovers how her efforts as an author were shaped by both her gender and her Jewish minority status. Her first and only volume of poetry was published in 1812 when she was twenty-three years old, as she enjoyed a brief moment of public attention. Her *Miscellaneous Poems*[105] was reviewed favourably but condescendingly in the *Monthly* and *Critical*, and Isaac Nathan (1792–1864), a former pupil at her father's boarding school, composed music for one of her songs, 'The Soldier's Farewell', which was sung by the famous Jewish tenor John Braham (1774–1856). (Nathan and Braham were involved with Lord Byron's *Hebrew Melodies* of 1815).[106] Also in April 1812, a poem of hers was sung at the annual meeting of a prominent charity, the Society of Friends of Foreigners in Distress, an appropriate organization for studying the cosmopolitan ideal. Lyon's literary career was beginning with some modest success but her public career seems to have ended after she got married to Abraham Henry (1789–1840) in 1816 and gave birth to ten children between 1817 and 1830.[107] Some of her poetry after her marriage was recited at the Jews' Hospital and the Jews' Free School and we know that she continued to write poetry but '*en amatrice*', as an amateur.[108] Her manuscript poems still might show up eventually but as for now they are not known to have survived.

Lyon's book was presented to the public as a charity case, not an unusual mode of publication for women in the eighteenth and nineteenth centuries. Lyon's apologetic preface declares that 'necessity', not 'choice', compelled her to publish her poetry as a way to raise money for her large family that was financially distressed because of the blindness of her father Solomon Lyon (1754–1820). The book was published by subscription, with most of the subscribers from Oxford, Cambridge and Eton where Lyon had taught Hebrew. At ten shillings six pence a copy with over 350 subscribers, the book would have raised a considerable sum of money – over £151 – for Emma Lyon and her fourteen siblings. One narrative to account for her short literary career is simply that because her father recovered his sight after his cataract operation in 1815 and because she married, the 'necessity' that compelled her to publish no longer held sway. Moreover, she had children of her own to care for and from 1840, when her husband died, sole responsibility as parent. The repressive norm of female modesty that discouraged women's literary ambition would be powerful enough to account for Lyon's literary silence after 1812. Nevertheless, the puzzling thing about her literary silence after 1812 is that a prominent theme in Lyon's poetry is her strong poetic ambition, her well delineated relationship to the Muse and sources of cultural authority. Uncomfortably aware of the norms under which she wrote, she did not simply internalize those norms. Also, women with large families did indeed publish – Charlotte Smith (1749–1806), an obvious influence on Lyon's poetry, also had ten children – and women found numerous ways to work around the modesty norm, notably writers like Grace Aguilar (1816–47) who defended Judaism within the parameters of the separate-spheres ideology.[109] As a first book by a young woman, *Miscellaneous Poems* is such a promising and ambitious effort that it is disconcerting that she published no more. Even as an only book, Lyon's work is valuable: one of the first Anglo-Jewish women to publish poetry – the daughters Sophia and Charlotte of Jonathan 'Jew' King seem to have been the first[110]– Lyon produced writing that raises issues of gender, religion and cultural identity by means of exploring the implications of poetic inspiration. In my conclusion I will speculate on why Lyon – both a promising romantic-era and a silenced Victorian-era writer – did not publish any more of her poetry during her long lifetime.

Observers of women's eighteenth- and nineteenth-century poetry will remark on several things: women were not supposed to write poetry but large numbers of women wrote anyway – and even larger numbers of women wrote in other genres as well, especially the romance and the novel. Prior to the full articulation of the 'Angel in the House' norm that Virginia Woolf deconstructed in her 'Professions for Women' (1942), separate-spheres ideology was powerful enough to force from almost every woman writer some gesture of visible obedience to its authority. The most inventive women writers also ironize this gesture and thereby call into question the entire ideology. Sandra Gilbert and Susan Gubar developed the concept of a 'poetics of duplicity' to describe women's writing and that concept pertains to certain aspects of Lyon's poetry.[111] Gilbert and Gubar write of 'submerged meanings' – 'meanings hidden within or behind the more accessible, "public" content of [women's] works, so that their literature could be read and appreciated even when its vital concern with female dispossession and disease was ignored'.[112] These 'palimpsestic' texts 'simultaneously' conform to and subvert 'patriarchal literary standards'.[113] I will set aside here the question of whether it is only women's writing that operates under a poetics of duplicity and suggest that part of Lyon's work seems to be palimpsestic in the way described by Gilbert and Gubar. Lyon appears to obey the rules of female modesty but contrary meanings frequently undermine the modest persona. She writes of both her 'blushing Muse' afraid of public notice and an insistently ambitious desire for fame and authority that is realized most boldly in her assuming the role of an inspired prophet.[114] She sometimes employs allegory or other forms of literary indirection to undermine modesty and she also simply contradicts the modesty norm as though she were not doing anything transgressive. Her strategy is reminiscent of the method of concealment in Poe's story, 'The Purloined Letter', where the best hiding place is in open view. I maintain that she can so boldly violate the norms she elsewhere upholds because of the process of framing: her poetry is carefully framed as culturally deferential, so that the actual poetry has much expressive latitude. As we have seen in Chapter 4, Equiano meticulously framed the way in which he, an African and former slave, would be read and interpreted. Deferential framing is so omnipresent in women's writing that we notice usually only when it is absent, as in Mary Wollstonecraft, not when it is routinely present, as in Charlotte Smith's preface to the sixth edition of *Elegiac Sonnets* (1792) where she self-deprecatingly devalues her literary accomplishments by pointing to the sphere that really counts for women: 'The post of honour is a private station'.[115]

As a woman and a Jew, Lyon wrote at two removes from the cultural norm. As an observant Jew, she wrote poetry that does not seem to have offended her largely Christian readership; only about 7 per cent of her subscribers appear to be Jewish. At a time when there were intensive efforts in London to convert Jews to Christianity, when an emerging model for the woman writer was the pious Christian,[116] Lyon deployed a sentimental idiom of personifications to explore the issues of poetic identity in one part of the book and in another she used poetic versions of nine psalms to affirm Jewish not Christian values. When her final poem expresses an urgent messianic hope, the palimpsestic text both refers to a Jehovah with whom Christian readers of the King James Bible would have been familiar, and echoes for Jewish readers liturgical invocations of the Messiah. One strategy is a rhetorical Judeo-Christian approach, avoiding those points of irreconcilable difference between Christianity and Judaism.

Before the reader gets to the poetry as such, the reader's perception gets shaped by a strenuous framing process just as Equiano's *Interesting Narrative* insistently framed its readability. The structure of the poetry's public meaning was fashioned by the subscription mode of publication, the dedication to Princess Charlotte, and the apologetic preface. Lyon performs a 'respectful deference' to the cultural authorities in order for her work to be published in the subscription format.[117] Deference is inscribed in the title page: 'Miscellaneous Poems, / by / Miss Emma Lyon, / Daughter of the Rev. S. Lyon, / Hebrew Teacher'. The title page highlights her status as daughter and omits any mention of her being a teacher of Hebrew. The adjective 'miscellaneous' suggests a lack of structure and pattern in the volume of poems, although in fact the book has been shaped very deliberately into a discernible form. As one proceeds from the title page there are further layers of deferential gesturing. The whole second page is a dedication to Princess Charlotte, who is the occasion for the volume's very first poem. Lyon has placed the royal most favoured by the Whigs and liberals in the position of patroness. Lyon then assumes a self-deprecating tone appropriate for the obligatory apologetic preface: her writing is 'simple', her imagination 'uncultivated', necessity' not 'choice' brings her unworthy productions before the public. Then follows the list of subscribers, 'respectable' to say the least: six royals, innumerable Oxford, Cambridge and Eton worthies, concluding with a list of names from the Society of Friends of Foreigners in Distress, a prominent charity supported by the political elite. If the academic, religious, political and social leaders have attached their names and money to a publication, then one can only assume that the poetry is ideologically inoffensive.

Thus is the way the reviews treat Lyon's volume, as the two reviews accept the book's appeal for charity, and exempt her poetry from the ordinary aesthetic strictures. In the *Critical Review,* the actual poetry of the 'authoress' is not taken seriously, as only one ode ['Stanzas to the Moon'] is mentioned, and almost all the attention in the brief review is to the preface and the dedication to Princess Charlotte.[118] Neither review mentions Emma Lyon's religion or preoccupation with poetic identity, nor does either review comment on the ambitious nine metrical psalm paraphrases. The *Monthly Review* refers to Lyon's 'pretty little poems'.[119] The reviewers are correctly reading according to the public script dictated by the deferential framing. However, there is a subtext of discontent, ambition and protest that undermines the overall appearance of cultural harmony that appears in almost all the poems, not just the psalms.

The 152 pages of *Miscellaneous Poems* consist of fifty-seven separate poems of several different kinds: most are short odes using personifications and a sentimental idiom; there are three sonnets, six ballads or songs, one blank-verse meditation and nine 'Paraphrases upon Psalms'. Lyon relies on rhymed quatrains, usually pentameter or tetrameter, for thirty of her fifty-seven poems and more than a third of the poems are in couplets. One prominent theme in the poetry is her relationship to her muse and to poetry in general. Poetry gives extraordinary pleasure but her gender, her social situation and especially her lack of a classical education seem to disqualify her from becoming a complete poet. Nevertheless, she speaks of her vocation as a poet, even a prophetic calling. When she tells us that 'necessity' alone compels her to publish her poetry, we know also that she expresses herself with such enthusiasm about the pleasures of poetry even from 'earliest infancy'.[120]

Many of the poems explicitly explore 'inspiration' as it affects and is affected by cultural authority. The poetry is ambivalent about 'fame' and its attendant processes, like competition, envy and masculine power but the nine psalms and final poems that conclude the volume resolve the ambivalence by incorporating the earlier figures of inspiration into a model of prophecy and by transforming poetic ambition into eagerness to spread the wisdom of God. Just as Levi and the *Analytical's* Geddes explored the onto-theological aspects of inspiration, Lyon treats inspiration in terms of her vocation as a poet.

The book's first poem positions Lyon in relation to the dominant masculine culture in 'Address to the University of Oxford'. Her 'weak' feminine Muse hesitantly and tremblingly appears among 'contemplation's studious sons' (l. 2). While ostensibly describing her situation as a timid, unlearned young woman, these lines also record a note of protest:

> Had it been mine in learning's path to tread,
> The Muse, perchance, had smil'd as fancy led:
> But fortune's cloud gloom'd o'er my earliest hour,
> And cares domestic drove me from her bow'r;
> Or I had haply trac'd each mystic page,
> And reap'd, like you, the fruits of ev'ry age. (ll. 13–18).

It is hardly just gender that kept her from learning at Oxford; Jews, of course, could not enroll at either Cambridge or Oxford where her father could teach Hebrew but not with the full privileges of a professing Christian. She also declares throughout the book a muse that is hobbled by a lack of learning, a lack about which she is not quiet, so that while she appears to be modest, making no excessive claims for her writing, she is also calling attention to an injustice.

The second piece, 'Lines to D. F*****, Esq. Barrister', is another poem of positioning, in this case in relation to a Gentile friend, Daniel French, the husband of one of her good friends, to whom she also writes a poem. Providing encouraging advice and a sympathetic reading of her work, Daniel French was one of Emma Lyon's Hebrew students and he intervened on her behalf shortly after the publication of the book when she was assaulted by a William Simmons, who lived in the same London building as Emma Lyon.[121] (I will discuss this incident in the conclusion to this chapter.) A 'patron', a sympathetic mediator between herself and the public before which her 'blushing Muse still shrinks' (l. 10), French validates the poet's sincerity, honesty and modesty – her 'moral' status, in short. It is almost as if he is co-signing a loan she is taking out, in this case, a purchase on the reading public's attention. As a Gentile barrister, he can play the role of authorizing presence to permit Lyon's imagination to explore her relationship with her muse, who is called here 'Goddess' and addressed in the second person. The classical idiom of the Muses and their shrine describes her relationship to her own poetry in many of the other forty-seven poems that precede the nine psalm paraphrases; in these poems there is a proliferation of female deities and female-gendered personifications that provide the basis for Lyon's poetics. The self-reflexiveness of her poetry is also a cosmopolitan quality of her writing that she does not accept naturalistically but as an effect of cultural history.

The tribute to French is an important poem because the patterns it establishes recur throughout the book. The five-part structure begins with a prologue (ll. 1–14) that pays tribute to French's generosity and encouragement while echoing the Preface in renouncing poetic ambition: 'No thought of fame, or yet ambitious pride / Bade me all fearful to the world confide' (ll. 7–8). Before these forbidden masculine values of competition her Muse blushes and shrinks but the speaker's first encounter with the Muse (ll. 15–36) seems to come from the world of Romance. After 'heaven's sweet zephyrs play'd around my head' and first breathing in for the first time '[t]hy sweets, fair fancy', she vows and prays to the Muse, her goddess, who then speaks to her:

> Sure some rude thorn
> Impels to seek me in life's early morn;
> They seldom wander near my mystic cell,
> Whom pleasure has not bid a long farewell.
> But if thou com'st a lonely hour to cheer,
> Remember! 'tis not happiness dwells here:
> The pow'r I boast is but to soothe the mind,
> When cares perplex, and fortune low'rs unkind. (ll. 25–32)

The Muse sternly directs the poet to stay within the bounds (and bonds) of female modesty but the Muse also speaks of the powerful creativity of imagination, as well as a 'mystic' (l. 58) power to which only the few, the elect and the spiritual elite ever have access. Although only those who are unhappy seek the Muse for solace, the pleasures of poetry seem more than just compensatory and therapeutic. The Muse's words are described thus: 'so gently flow'd / Each accent sweet, that still my bosom glow'd; / Still long'd to trace the varying shades of rhyme, / And catch the glimm'rings of a thought sublime' (ll. 33–6). Like someone who has just fallen in love, she realizes that her body, her feelings, and her intellect long for the presence of her Muse.

Precisely at this moment of her greatest pleasure – acquainting herself with her desire and identity as a poet – and her greatest embarrassment when she is aware of her poetic inadequacies in relation to the source of her inspiration, she returns to the figure of French for reassurance and guidance (ll. 37–54). As a Gentile man supposedly educated in the most prestigious kinds of secular poetry, he is Lyon's projection of cultural authority, whether he was really knowledgeable or not. By thanking French so profusely, she distracts herself and us from the more powerful and decisive encounter with her Muse who reappears in the next section side by side with French (ll. 55–72). French's presence both authorizes the Muse, 'the fair Queen' (l. 62), and her 'Sisters' (l. 58), and acts like a restraint on the Muse. Lyon steels herself against harsh criticism with the following logic: if French approves of the poetry, then so will the critics (ll. 65–6). Reassured and strengthened, she turns again to her Muse, referring to the necessity of *reining* her 'erring fancy' with 'wisdom' because of all that she lacks: an education in Milton, Homer and Virgil (ll. 67–71). For effect she seems to be exaggerating her ignorance and unfamiliarity with Milton and classical culture. Through several allusions it is evident she has read Milton, at least *Paradise Lost*, and it would have been quite unremarkable for her to have had access to Homer and Virgil through the numerous translations. Her son remarks that his mother Emma Lyon was 'well educated' and received at Cambridge University 'exceptional educational opportunities' – 'an astounding thing in her days'.[122] Nevertheless, here and elsewhere the poem's speaker abases herself before the icon of a masculine, Gentile, classical culture whose authority she seems to accept but whose figures of the Muses and model of inspiration she makes her own. 'Milton' seems to signify a forbidding cultural authority throughout the volume but this same 'Milton' also authorizes poetic inspiration and the figures of the muses. (Milton too could be invested emotionally as a projection of her blind father). The effect the poem is seeking is a continuation of the deferential framing process: by accepting her inferiority, even by exaggerating her lack of knowledge, she pacifies the censorious authority that otherwise would question the poetry's ideological soundness. The very Muse that will ultimately rule over an alternative poetic world developed throughout the volume of poetry receives a symbolic imprimatur in the first two poems through Lyon's strategic representation of French, Oxford and classical culture.

The allegory that concludes the poem (ll. 73–88) depicts 'Nature's' Muse in whose garden she is a lowly, orphaned 'weed' (l. 74) afflicted by a 'tempest' (l. 76); she finds shelter and comfort with 'thee, poor Muse' (l. 80) who oversees the trembling, unchecked, unguided strivings of the novice poet who looks toward the 'rich wand'rings' (l. 87) of the Muse's genius. A classical education seems too remote to acquire but to develop from a 'weed' to something more attractive in the garden of her Muse does not seem impossible. Allegorically her 'poor' Muse is the same one that inspires the 'wisdom' and 'genius' of 'classic' culture which she only 'in vain' tries to imitate but the Muse provides her with 'a sheltering home' (ll. 80, 86–8). The concluding section produces two effects, a secure sense of belonging to and being accepted by the feminine Muse and an extreme if not theatrical sense of inferiority to the 'bright effusions of a tow'ring mind' (l. 82) identified with the masculine classical culture. The book as a whole depicts a conflict between these two centres of value, the poet's own validating and supportive feminine Muse and a disapproving masculine culture. The conflict is also between a culture of sensibility and a neoclassical culture.

A cluster of eight other poems develops the figures, images, symbols and logic of the inspirational model Lyon is adopting ('Ode to Genius', 'An Ode on Solitude', 'An Ode to Sleep', 'Lines to the Muse', 'An Ode on Death', 'An Ode on Sympathy', 'An Ode on the Fear of Criticism' and 'Lines to Melancholy'). Inspired poetry, which is distinct from classically educated poetry, is aligned with the values of sensibility, like solitude, melancholy, suffering, authentic feeling, and existential truth. Using 'An Ode to Genius', I will illustrate the way a single poem works through aspects of poetic inspiration. First, I will quote the poem in full:

> All glorious power! Of keen celestial eye,
>   Genius! tumultuous ruler of the breast,
> By nature wing'd with wond'rous speed to fly,
>   Yet seldom visiting an earthly guest!
>
> Descend for once with all thy glowing fire,
>   And make my soul thy transitory shrine:
> Or oh! Forgive me if I deck my lyre
>   With gems or ornaments that are not thine!
>
> Come, guide my fancy when it seeks the Muse
>   That still to thee directs her daring flight!
> Through my chill veins one gentle beam infuse
>   Of splendor, visible to mortal sight!
>
> Lead to the bow'rs where haunt thy heavenly train,
>   And I will distant watch their mystic tread;
> From their rich harvest glean the scatter'd grain,
>   To weave a band fantastic for my head.
>
> By me unenvied, flattering crowds may throng,
>   Where Poets trace the never-varying round;
> If thou, bright genius! animate my song,
>   My name shall live, with endless glory crown'd.

'An Ode to Genius' suggests a compensation for the lack of a classical education: 'genius' descends to inspire the poet with unexpected, indeterminate creativity whose sources are once again the Muse and her 'mystic' and 'fantastic' powers. The last two lines of this five-stanza poem affirm competition for fame in a way the tribute to French seemed to make impossible: 'If thou, bright genius! animate my song, / My name shall live, with endless glory crown'd' (ll. 19–20). Nowhere in the poem can one find expressions of female modesty and the apologetic 'necessity' that compels the reluctant poet to make her verse public. Inspiration, introduced in the French poem, provides Lyon with a poetic model that is both classical (deriving from Plato's *Ion* and other classical sources) and anti-classical in its sensibility-based values. The most authentic kind of poetry, according to Lyon, is poetry that is unwilled, spontaneous, 'descending' from somewhere outside the self and momentarily dwelling within the soul. One can hear anticipations of Keats's preference for poetry coming as naturally as the leaves on a tree – or not at all – or Shelley's descriptions of inspiration in his *Defence of Poetry*. The moment of inspiration is intense but momentary – 'transitory' (l. 6). The fourth stanza suggests Ruth gleaning the barley, as Lyon imagines herself in the Muse's bowers, looking on from a distance and coming later to pick up the remnants of the most glorious moments of inspiration (when composition begins, as Shelley said, inspiration is already waning). Despite the modesty of the gesture, she also imagines making for herself a 'band fantastic' (l. 16) for her head. The final stanza contrasts Lyon with the poets whose creativity is diminished by uniformity but who nevertheless enjoy the attention of the 'flattering crowds' (l. 17); if Lyon's prayers for inspiration are granted, she will not envy the popular poets. The poem's stanzaic form appropriates Gray's 'Church-Yard' elegy for the obscure, the mute inglorious Milton's, the socially and culturally marginal without a voice.

Other poems develop different aspects of the sensibility repertoire of themes. The compensation for alienated solitude is a sense of power from 'wisdom' and 'the purest joy' from 'melancholy' ('Ode on Solitude'). Melancholy is also a 'goddess' and '[s]orceress' with the powers of 'magic' ('Lines to Melancholy', ll. 1, 9). As described by Jacques Khalip, melancholy is woman's 'alternative form of knowledge' to the knowledge of enlightened, masculine culture.[123] The enchanted ground of poetry is not exclusively feminine, for Lyon also writes of solitude's 'sequester'd grove, / Where sons of contemplation rove!' ('Ode on Solitude', ll. 5–6). The moon is the symbol of creativity that shines upon the insomniacs who are estranged from the sun-drenched world where the wicked prosper and the innocent suffer ('An Ode to Sleep' and 'An Ode on the Fear of Criticism'). The poet experiences common ties with the criminal, another victim of 'fate' and 'fortune' ('Lines to the Muse'). Assisted by the Moon and the Muse, the poet's feminine mentors and protectors, she combats the masculine cultural powers and produces a 'wild' song:

> Me hope inspires, with whisp'ring breath,
>   To tempt the air sublime,
> To triumph o'er the shades of death
>   And injuries of time.
>
> But lo! The Critics' grizly band!
>   That dash the fairest crown,
> Already lift the wasteful hand
>   To hurl me trembling down.

> Yet still in fields where fame is sought,
>   For fame shall Emma sigh,
> And shudder at the dismal thought,
>   To close th' inglorious eye.
>
> Still wildly singing all night long,
>   While Cynthia wond'ring views,
> With rude simplicity of song
>   Call down th' inspiring Muse.
>   ('An Ode on the Fear of Criticism')

Although the published reviews of her book were not harshly critical, even if they were condescending, the imagined critics are severe, forbidding, and violent, as they 'dash' the crown from the head and 'hurl' her down. The imaginary conflict with masculine critics perhaps reflects the treatment of Anna Barbauld's ambitious poem, *Eighteen Hundred and Eleven* (1812); the harsh criticism arguably ended the poetic career of one of the most prominent women poets at the time.[124] The 'fame' that Lyon and women are not supposed to want inspires the poem's speaker to attempt the arduous 'sublime' represented effectively in the poem's last stanza where her alienation, solitude, insomnia and persistence are turned into a striking image of almost maenad-like abandon and fierceness. Although called here by its classical name, Cynthia, Lyon also may have had in mind the significance of the Moon in Judaism, as the Jewish calendar is lunar, not solar, and special women's observances sometimes commemorated the new moon (*Rosh Hodesh*). The last six lines of 'Lines to Melancholy', however, strike another note of depression and abjection that is also a part of this cluster of poems.

> But not to me, with kind relief,
> Thy [Melancholy's] soft approach e'er tempers grief;
> Thou doom'st me all the sighs to know,
> That lay thy destin'd victim low;
> And these worn eyes with tears to steep,
> Till time brings on eternal sleep!

Echoing perhaps Charlotte Smith, the great poet of abjection and gloom, Lyon imagines her poet-figure being felled not by the masculine cultural powers but by the feminine power of melancholy, one of the goddesses. Fresh creativity emerges from the pain and isolation of the suffering woman poet but that same condition for creativity is also fatal to the well-being of the poet as a human being. The poet thrives on the misery of the person, a terrible paradox developed with frightening rigour much later by Sylvia Plath in her final poems.[125]

There is a similar dialectic of hope and despair in the four poems on the seasons. It is not until the final poem on winter that Lyon is able to balance the awareness of time, mortality and the ephemeral nature of existence – the *tempus fugit* theme that is prominent in works like *Kohelet* (Ecclesiastes) in the Hebrew Bible – with a sense of inner power and poetic strength, a confidence in the effectiveness of the 'visionary light' (l. 28) from the Muse to dispel the dreariness of cyclical temporality. Poetry, the imagination, the creative mind can overcome nature, but nature too overcomes poetry: 'Sweet Hope, thy fair anchor my motto shall be, / My soul shall repose, tho' deluded, in thee' ('Sonnet on Hope', ll. 13–14).

One image Lyon provides for the wages of hope is the lovelorn woman who is desperate or even mad. In 'Stanzas to the Moon' a lonely, unhappy 'Ellen' wanders alone in the moonlight, praying to the moon for mental relief. Those who have what they want are peacefully asleep, while those who yearn for what they cannot have disturb the night with their entreaties. The effectively anapaestic song, 'The Maniac', is another representation of the lovelorn woman, this time 'Anna' who becomes another instance of Lyon's transcendence. Still a third poem, 'Willow', represents another woman character – Agnes – who has lost her lover and is distraught and sleepless. Although conventional, these moony women with disyllabic names (like Emma) symbolize a desire that cannot be satisfied in the sunny world where the powerful rule over the weak and suffering.

The companion piece to the opening poem on Oxford is the 'Lines Addressed to the University of Cambridge', Lyon's second poetic encounter with the established culture. As in the first, there are moments of humiliation and weakness, as she calls herself 'unletter'd' with 'my rural verse' (l. 9) but there is also here a stronger sense of inspiration and its power as she affirms her 'wild' song with its 'ethereal fire' and as she attempts to 'catch Divinity's inspiring breeze' (ll. 23–5, 37). Indeed, here is a rare instance when the lack of a classical education becomes a virtue: 'No learning checks me as I wildly sing' (l. 23). The tribute to Cambridge's Bacon, Newton and Milton acquires some ironic edge as the poem enacts a performative contradiction: she makes a poetic homage to the great minds of the past but she is not supposed to have the authority to make such a tribute. There is also an intriguing contrast between the blind Milton and his daughters and the blind Solomon Lyon and his poetic daughter, as Solomon's blindness is the condition which enables the daughter to become a public poet, whereas Milton's daughters were merely used to record the father's verse. The 'Sonnet to my Father' expresses strong affection for the man who most likely taught Lyon Hebrew well enough to be able to teach it herself; indeed, her teaching Hebrew like her father indicates a degree of identification with the father one sees with some other women writers like Maria Edgeworth.[126] There is also the tradition of the rabbi's exceptional daughter whose intellectual brilliance was recognized, if begrudgingly. The most famous example of the type was Beruriah, wife of R. Meir, daughter of R. Hanina ben Teradion. Of Beruriah it was said that she could 'master three hundred *Halakhot* [religious laws or practices] a day'.[127] Rather than be overwhelmed by the priority of Milton – or the authority of her father – she finds a way to use an aspect of his poetry – and her father's learning – for her own purposes.

From Milton she makes use of his model of inspiration, which she then thoroughly feminizes. Lyon adds to her feminine pantheon in 'An Ode to Sorrow' by installing in it Minerva, goddess of wisdom, and Cecilia, saint of music. Perhaps the latter was influenced by Pope's 'Ode for Musick, on St. Cecilia's Day', a poem that includes other elements which recur in Lyon's book, including melancholy, the muses, sleep, envy and inspiration. Even the form of the short, Horatian ode that Lyon uses frequently (twenty-three times) could have been modelled after Pope's five-stanza, twenty-line 'Ode to Solitude'.[128]

A minor but not insignificant theme in Lyon's book is political, especially protesting against war, a cosmopolitan interest. In 'Beggar-Boy', before the happy ending resolves the action, a press-gang, still quite active in 1812, has separated a father from his family. The existence of the unpopular war is also registered in a poem like the 'Soldier's Farewel', while 'Wild Roses' is an effective song about begging, an activity of which there was no shortage in the famine year of 1812, the year also of massive Luddite riots. Her most Shelleyan poem, 'An Ode on Hope', of course precedes Shelley's mature work by a number of years, so there is no question of influence – unless Shelley was influenced by her, a real possibility. Shelley was in Oxford in 1810–11; in 1812 he was in Ireland and Wales promoting political reform. As a recent Oxonian he surely would have heard about Lyon, his blindness and his daughter's volume of poetry; whether he also read a copy is another matter. In this particular Lyon poem there is an apocalyptic hope – 'Celestial bliss may yet be nigh' – (l. 8) attached to volcanic imagery that works just as Shelley's symbolism of revolution does: pent up, repressed energies are bursting from confinement with violent heat and explosive light, as the emergence of the new entails destruction as well as birth. The 'ensanguin'd field' (l. 82) of the last stanza alludes to the war, a symptom of the historical disturbance that seems to portend mighty changes. This Shelleyan current in her work is safely ensconced in the middle parts of the book, the radicalism of which is disguised somewhat by the same kind of abstractions that Shelley also used.

However artful and expressive are the poems of sensibility that describe her emergent and conflicted poetic identity, the nine psalm paraphrases are surprising for their confident voice, as though the poet had finally discovered the kind of poetry she could write without self-division. Also, hardly any of the other poems even allude to God or religious themes, so the turn to explicitly biblical material is unanticipated; the dominant theme of the other poems is inspiration with rarely even hints at a religious motif. The psalms are not necessarily 'pretty little poems', as the *Monthly Review* called her poetry, but could be read as ambitiously competitive and culturally central, especially if her psalm paraphrases suggested an engagement with theology rather than merely pious sentiment. Duncan Wu, distilling the literary criticism of Francis Jeffrey and other male romantic-era critics who enforced the gendered aesthetic rules women were supposed to follow, identifies 'paraphrases of the Scriptures' as one of the genres allotted to women because they did not challenge 'conventional notions of femininity', but any writing that engaged theology, an exclusively male province, was strictly forbidden to women.[129] Lyon's prestigious precedents include the metrical paraphrases by Isaac Watts, Thomas Sternhold and John Hopkins; moreover, as liturgy in the Christian churches the psalms were hardly peripheral. Lyon achieves continuity with the rest of the poetry in her book, however, by turning inspiration away from a sentimental idiom and toward a biblical, prophetic discourse, and she does so in a provocatively bold manner, presenting herself as a prophetic voice inspired by God. Her turn from a sentimental to a biblical idiom mediated by the figure of inspiration suggests the validity of Jon Mee's contention that the discourse of 'enthusiasm' was broad enough to encompass different styles and ideological commitments.[130]

Beginning in the sixteenth century and influentially justified in Sir Philip Sidney's *Apologie for Poetrie* (1595), translated, metrical psalms were seen not just as devotional texts but as poetry. Sidney illustrates one category of imitation (of the 'horrible' made 'delightful' by mimesis) with 'that heavenly Psalm of Mercy'. Sidney also refers to 'Holy Scripture' as having 'whole parts in it poetical'.[131] Ramie Targoff has recently pointed to the centrality of Sidney's *Apologie* for literary reflections on the psalms.[132] Thomas Wyatt's 'highly introspective and complex translations' of the Penitential Psalms, which were well outside the parameters of devotional literature,[133] were published in 1550,[134] preceding the ambitious metrical versions of the psalms by Sidney himself and his sister.[135] By the late sixteenth century, according to Rivkah Zim, psalm paraphrases were a secure literary kind that required no special pleading.[136] The writing of psalm paraphrases was a type of imitation that was not 'an inferior, non-creative activity'.[137] The poet-translator was 'not obliged to preserve the author's meaning in the author's words' but the expectation was that the paraphrase would be 'respectful' of the 'original author's meaning'. Readers were so familiar with the psalms that a paraphrase's proximity or distance from the original was an aesthetic variable, so that the paraphrase generated a kind of palimpsest effect, with the poet's own version imposed on the already existing version – which for Emma Lyon's audience would have been the King James translation.[138] Two other versions of the psalms were so well known as to constitute yet another layer of context, the Sternhold-Hopkins metrical psalms (1562) – the most popular volume of verse published in the early modern period[139] – and especially Isaac Watts's version, of which there were numerous editions in the eighteenth and nineteenth centuries. Between 1801 and 1815, there were eighty-two separate editions of English Psalters, four of which were the metrical version authored by Isaac Watts (1674–1748). There were no editions of Sternhold and Hopkins that were advertised as such but it is likely that their translations were within some of the eighty-two editions published then.[140]

Lyon's choice of nine psalms reflects her preoccupation with inspiration and social justice, as she makes two emphases: validating the poet as God's prophet inspired by God's wisdom and vindicating God's justice in a world where the wicked seem to prosper while the righteous seem only to suffer. Her paraphrases also accentuate language, orality and consciousness, bringing into prominence a linguistic stress and an inwardness present in the original but heightened by Lyon. Three of the psalms she chooses are didactic, coming out of the 'wisdom' tradition (19, 49, 73); two are prophetic exhortations (50, 58); others are a liturgy (15), a royal psalm (72), a Zion hymn (76) and a psalm of individual confidence (91). She notably ignores all the Penitential Psalms, general hymns and laments (more than half of all the psalms are within these three sub-genres).[141] To illustrate the overall quality of the psalm paraphrases, I will discuss two.

The psalm first presented is Psalm 19, which is striking for its last stanza that is only tangentially related to the original. She turns the Authorized Version's verse 14, the last verse, 'Let the words of my mouth, and the meditation of my heart, be acceptable in thy sight, O Lord, my strength, and my redeemer', into the following:

> O Thou, who erst on David's holiest lyre,
> Didst dart thy sacred vehemence of fire,
>   Come, teach me to reveal thy ways,
>   And scatter round a dazzling blaze;
> Unfolding bright, inspir'd with silent awe,
> The' unclouded prospect of thy heavenly law! (ll. 55–60)

The actual Hebrew of verse 14 is '*y'hu l'ratzon imrei fi v'higion libi lifanecha Adonai tsuri v'goali*', a very familiar sentence spoken in the prayers after the *Amidah*;[142] it is something with which Lyon would have been entirely familiar. Lyon transforms a cluster of words that deals with the proper state of mind for praying into a statement about prophetic inspiration. The grammar shifts from a petitionary 'may' to an invocatory 'come' and 'scatter'. The stanza here is not unlike the last stanza of Shelley's 'Ode to the West Wind', where the imperative verbs call for prophetic power. From God to David to Emma Lyon, the divine authority passes as the stanza invokes God's power in a way that is at once modest – she is after all *praying* for inspiration – and bold – she is claiming the mantle of a prophet. She is deferring to traditional authority but transgressing the gender code, vowing obedience to God's law but claiming for herself a role, one that was not permitted at the time by religious institutions, in transmitting the law.

Although Psalm 19 is one of David's psalms in almost everyone's canon, the final stanza explicitly distinguishes between a first-person speaker and David. The only way to read Lyon's paraphrase is to read the first-person in the eighth stanza as referring to Lyon, not David, or better, Lyon impersonating David, appropriating his role, his status, prestige and authority:

> O give me, Lord! Thy glorious tracks to see,
> To find my solace and delight in thee;
>   To feel that holy fear within,
>   That makes it agony to sin;
> Thy laws are amiable and sweet indeed,
> As virgin honey from the flowery mead! (ll. 42–8)

In one sense, what could be more pious and socially inoffensive than psalm paraphrases, one of the genres deemed feminine enough for women writers? In another sense, what could be more daring for a twenty-three year old Jewish woman in the early nineteenth century than assuming the Davidic role? As the first paraphrase, as the only psalm appearing out of order, its importance has to be ascribed to the role of prophet Lyon is here assuming. Here is an example of Benjaminian translation where something new comes out of the interaction between the received psalm in its Hebrew and English versions and the bold desire of the translator.

Other psalm paraphrases also develop the theme of prophetic election. In Psalm 15, the fourth stanza focuses on the idea of prophetic poetry: 'Who dares to give free utterance to truth, / Beneath the frowns of a tyrannic foe' (ll. 15–16). First, the idea of speaking truth to power is nowhere to be found in the original Psalm 15, and second, speaking truth to power reinforces the theme of prophetic vocation that she introduced in Psalm 19. The person worthy of God's favour is a fearless prophet who also – in the last stanza – protests against and sheds tears over the 'undeserv'd' sufferings of the 'good'. The idea of undeserved suffering, which is also lacking in the original Psalm 15, is another important theme in Lyon's psalms. She turns Psalm 49 into a poem about inspiration and vindicating the morally worthy who are not socially powerful. Psalm 50, originally about divorcing ritual sacrifice from truly moral behaviour, Lyon makes into a prophetic address to the 'priests' about the false and true 'music' for God. The next paraphrase, of Psalm 58, another prophetic exhortation, continues to distinguish between corrupt and innocent speech by contrasting 'words of innocence' with 'guilt', 'falsehood', flattery, seduction, 'slander' and 'deceit'. Lyon's paraphrase of Psalm 72 mixes contemporary and historically remote references, plays with the equivalence of poet and king (both David and Solomon were poets) and supplies a subtext of political exhortation advocating justice for the poor, 'the sons of toil' (l. 16) and 'the orphan' (l. 34).

I want to examine closely Lyon's version of Psalm 49 for the way it brings together inspiration and prophetic statement that vindicates the morally right-eous who are not socially powerful. The original is a wisdom psalm about the 'transitory nature of wealth and pleasure' and the paradise with God that awaits the just man,[143] but Lyon makes her psalm relate to prophetic truth, as it lays claim to the allegiance of the 'nations' (l. 1), the obedience of 'royalty' (l. 3) and as it takes possession of the prophet herself:

> Heaven's holy Spirit breathes upon my lyre,
>   And cheers the fainting courage of my soul;
> The truths I sing no mortal tongues inspire,
>   From heaven's high fount the sacred numbers roll. (ll. 5–8)

The second line makes the reader think inevitably of the poet's self-doubt that has been developed throughout the volume. Whereas Psalm 19 invoked holy inspiration, in this paraphrase she can announce confidently that the 'Spirit breathes upon my lyre'. In the original Psalm 49 there is nothing whatsoever about inspiration, so that the innovation is wholly Lyon's. She also turns the psalm's message of the transience of wealth and pleasure into a mode of political protest as her paraphrase notes with satisfaction that the most powerful members of society cannot avoid death, the sublime equalizer. Lyon imagines the humiliation of the rich and powerful in their existential moment of facing their ultimate destiny: they either repress awareness or face a death they cannot comprehend.

> Slaves to the pride and emptiness of life,
>   Alone reflection is your deadly foe;
> But when she comes, with momentary strife,
>   Ye veil the gulph that ever yawns below. (ll. 41–4)

It is noteworthy that 'reflection' is a she, joining Lyon's vast feminine pantheon of exalted virtues and powers. As the activity associated with reason and intellect, not feelings and sentiment, reflection is marked as feminine, counter to the gen-dered norms of the cultural code. The socially powerful, labelled here 'the sons of crime' (l. 52), cannot avoid death or God's judgment, as even their immoral 'fame' (l. 46) will not endure – anticipating Shelley's 'Ozymandias' sonnet. Ech-oing traditional Jewish doctrine, the paraphrase affirms the immortality of the righteous. The Authorized Version's psalm lacks the edge of class conflict that is prominent in Lyon as well as in many of the metrical psalms in Isaac Watts's collection. The King James translation warns and advises the rich man but Lyon's version gloats over his ruin and celebrates the triumph of the powerless. All three of the paraphrases of Psalm 49 in Watts's collection emphasize strongly the wickedness of the rich and the dire fate that awaits them; typical is the following quatrain in the conventional fourteener with alternating rhymes: 'Why doth he [the man of riches] treat the poor with scorn, / Made of the self-same clay, / And boast as though his flesh was born / Of better dust than they?'[144] It appears that the poverty of the Lyon family, the widespread social suffering in 1812 and the specific disabilities and prejudices with which Jews were afflicted assisted Lyon's identification with other poor people and permitted her to draw upon the egalitarian themes in the Watts psalms. She turns the psalm unexpectedly into a cosmopolitan genre.

If Lyon's paraphrases share the edge of class resentment in the Isaac Watts Psalter, they differ from Watts fundamentally in their Jewishness. The Watts psalms invoke, despite the anachronism, the name of Jesus Christ in numerous metrical paraphrases. The psalms were a secure part of the Christian liturgy and devotional service, both Catholic and Protestant. Her choice of psalms, the omissions and *midrashic* inventions in her paraphrases and the subtle shadings have a this-worldly, ethical focus on social justice. She uses the psalms to establish her status as an inspired poet with prophetic authority, thus linking the earlier poems with the psalms.

The two poems that conclude her book, 'Stanzas Sung with great applause at the Anniversary Meeting of the Society of Friends of Foreigners in Distress, Held at the New London Tavern, April 27, 1812' and 'Conclusion' use nationalism and messianic hope to punctuate her complex treatment of poetic inspiration. She exploits her connection with the Society to emphasize her acceptance as a poet and as a moral agent by the most powerful members of society. Established in 1807, the Society of Friends of Foreigners in Distress granted 'pecuniary relief and other assistance to FOREIGNERS of any nation in this country, who, from misfortune, may fall into distress' and who do not qualify for parish assistance. Of the over 4,000 people the Society had helped between 1807 and 1816, only a small number – forty – received 'pensions' to stay in Britain, while the others were assisted in returning to their country of origin.[145] Two of the three trustees of the Society in 1816 were subscribers to Lyon's poetry, Sir William Paxton and William Vaughan. The only other prominent Society figure who was a subscriber is D. H. Rucker – four of the Ruckers subscribed to Lyon's poetry. The Society was not designed to assist only or principally Jews but Nathan Rothschild was one of the directors and one of the fourteen 'cases' represented in the 1816 report seems to be Jewish, although no one is identified by religion, only country.[146] A large proportion of those receiving assistance in 1816 were from the German-speaking parts of Europe, precisely where most of the Ashkenazi Jews – like Solomon Lyon from Bohemia who in his blindness could not as a foreigner seek parish assistance – came from who settled in Britain at that time. The Society provided a vehicle for helping foreign Jews in distress but in an ecumenical way that was not politically controversial. Indeed, the Society had the support of the royal family as well as the Russian and Prussian leaders.

Lyon also uses her own identity as a needy outsider requiring assistance as a point of departure to establish Britain as a multicultural haven for exiles and victims of tyranny. The third stanza, which was censored at the Meeting, is restored in her book:

> When flying from a tyrant's sway
> In quest of freedom's glorious ray,
> The famish'd exiles wander here,
> Safe shelter'd from the murd'ring spear;
> They bless the hospitable Isle,
> And through the clouds of sorrow smile,
> Reposing in the hallow'd rest
> Of *Friends to Foreigners distrest!*

Probably because both the Russian and Prussian governments supported the Society and would not have appreciated these allusions to murderous tyranny, especially from a Jewish woman, the authorities in charge suppressed the stanza. Lyon's intention is quite apparent: by flattering the generosity of the British, she hopes to generate a cosmopolitan myth of national identity quite unlike what was actually normative in 1812. In fact, most of the recipients of aid from the Society were sent back to their country of origin; only the exceptional cases were permitted to receive aid and remain in Britain. Lyon's song does not go as far as Emma Lazarus's 'The New Colossus' (1883), for the fourth stanza refers approvingly of the distressed foreigner returning to his native home, but the principle of assisting everyone who has a need, regardless of religion or national origin, in conjunction with the rhetoric of foreign tyrannies from which people are justifiably fleeing, prepares the way for the myth of a multicultural haven – something a later Anglo-Jewish writer, Grace Aguilar, will develop further.

The final poem in her volume affirms and underlines Lyon's role as an inspired prophet, as she invokes the source of poetic inspiration: 'Descend, O Muse, with more than wonted fire, / Ere deadly silence steals upon my lyre' (ll. 1–2). The self-fashioned image of modest young woman fearful of public exposure is displaced with expressions of 'soaring pride' in her spreading the name of Jehovah 'far and wide' (l. 7). She echoes the sentiment of the *Aleinu* prayer[147] and assumes the messianic tones of the prophet Isaiah in her hope that all the nations will hearken to the divine message of social justice:

> A language that all nations hear
> Alike with one harmonious ear:
> No clime so dark, no ignorance so blind,
> But reads the splendor of th' Almighty mind (ll. 17–20).

The appeal here is universal and cosmopolitan, not unlike the previous poem and its multicultural nationalism. Lyon has skilfully placed her Jewish themes in contexts designed to win favour with British, Christian readers. The pedagogy of her poetry implies a progressive revelation from multicultural nationalism to a higher universal emancipation. The final stanza affirms that God works an ethical effect through history by means of the exemplary 'good man' whose 'upright heart' and 'pure unsullied hand' enjoy the protection of a militant God, who 'fights' for the morally virtuous.

The anxiety about public poetry and transgressing her gender role is resolved by her writing cosmopolitan poetry that is also nationalist and religious and which displaces the guilt of poetic representation and competitive struggle onto political and moral conflict. The inadequacies of her education become less debilitating when the poetic subject is biblical and political. On the Hebrew Bible and the experiences of the outsider she is much more expert than the gentlemen from Oxbridge. Her ability to shift the terms of cultural debate in a way favourable to her suggests a sure grasp of the possibilities available to her within the kind of book she was permitted to write. These poems seem anything but 'miscellaneous'; rather, the volume is a well-crafted whole with a very particular design. There is a progression from the earlier poems with their sentimental idiom, feminine pantheon of goddesses, nearly ecstatic celebrations of the inspired pleasures of poetry and gloomy excursions into the melancholic world of madness and sleepless nights to the self-assured psalms and final poems. There are numerous points of continuity between the secular-sentimental and religious-prophetic poems, including the themes of social justice and political protest, not just the inspirational model for creating poetry. With such strong command over her poetry, with such confidence, it is difficult to understand why she ceased publication after 1812. Perhaps the reason was not the modesty norm and the separate-spheres ideology but an episode of violence with which she would always associate her ambition and moment of fame.

I return to the incident alluded to earlier when she was assaulted by William Simmons. According to the London *Times*, there were conflicting versions of what had happened in Emma Lyon's apartment building on the weekend of 13–14 June 1812. The version that was accepted by the jury is as follows: on Saturday Simmons engaged in 'violent conduct' against Emma Lyon so that when Daniel French and his wife visited her on Sunday, she was 'confined to her room, by the very severe indisposition occasioned, as she informed Mrs. French, by the violent conduct of Mr. Simmons towards her'. Mrs. French urged her husband to speak with William Simmons who lived in Emma Lyon's building. When Simmons heard the name of Emma Lyon, he called French 'a damned Jew' and accused French of trying to murder him. A fight ensued between French, Simmons and a friend of Simmons who was a 'peace officer'. French, who was beaten up, was dragged to a watch-house and kept in jail until ten o'clock at night when he was finally released by a magistrate. The version of events presented by Simmons and his friend Squires was that Daniel French attacked Simmons without any provocation; they made no mention apparently of the assault of Emma Lyon.[148]

What can we make of this story? Let me offer a narrative that mixes fact and speculation: Emma Lyon is living alone in a flat shortly after the publication of her poetry book and the public meeting where her poem – minus one crucial stanza – was read before royalty and dignitaries. She is teaching Hebrew and has just experienced the satisfaction of having assisted her large family. Her younger sisters take care of her father and the youngest siblings, so that her living alone is framed as one less mouth to feed. On Saturday, most likely she would have spent the Sabbath with her family and would have gone back to her apartment after sundown. Presumably it was while she was returning on Saturday night that a possibly drunk Simmons confronted her. Was his violent conduct only verbal? If it were just verbal, would she have taken to her bed and confided first to Mrs. French? She was assaulted – at least verbally, perhaps physically – by a drunken, anti-Semitic Simmons. After confiding to Mrs. French, Emma Lyon then witnesses her friend Daniel French beaten up, arrested and tried for assaulting her attacker. Although French is acquitted and Simmons and his accomplice are convicted and sentenced to six months in the House of Correction, she now associates her literary ambition with violent anti-Semitism and public notoriety, if not shame, possibly rape. She had to testify in court on behalf of Daniel French and we know she was accompanied by two of her brothers.

This incident might have decisively persuaded her to avoid further publication. The mainstream Jewish community of which she was a part did not prohibit women from publishing secular books, as the examples of the Moss sisters (Celia and Marion) and Grace Aguilar testify.[149] If, however, she associated efforts to promote her poetic fame with violence and public notoriety, she might have chosen to keep the rest of her poetry private. One cannot, however, underestimate the power of the separate-spheres ideology, with which Lyon struggled mightily in her single volume of poetry, to coerce women writers into silence and self-repression. Even a writer like Lyon – living on her own, teaching Hebrew at a time when the issue of women even learning Hebrew was controversial within the Jewish community (and one can imagine how someone hostile to Jews and women might construe Emma Lyon's giving Hebrew lessons to men), earning money for her family and appropriating a prophetic role in her poetry – even she might not have been strong enough to overcome the cultural norm.

In the literary public sphere that was allotted to women Emma Lyon skilfully manipulated the literary and cultural conventions to express a strongly cosmopolitan perspective. Deferentially framed like Equiano's *Interesting Narrative*, *Miscellaneous Poems* palimpsestically and quietly undermines the gender code.

Because Levi's pugnacious style was not an available option, Lyon assumed the role of deferential and polite daughter to pursue what her poetic desire impelled her to write. 'Inspiration' was a convenient topos for both the sentimental and biblical poems because the topos gave her access to cultural authority and the power of expression.

Maria Edgeworth and Her Jewish Problem

The complex and conflicted instance of Maria Edgeworth counterpoises the two examples of Jewish writing. Lyon's project as a writer precludes a critical examination of an anti-Semitism which victimized her, and Levi's public role as defender of the faith addresses prejudice only as it arises in religion and theology. One of the most surprising, unexpected and insightful treatments of anti-Semitism came not from a Jewish writer but an Anglo-Irish writer whose previous fiction had been uniformly anti-Jewish until the remarkable *Harrington*. How Edgeworth managed to write the novel that she did write is truly puzzling.

Because Edgeworth's novel powerfully challenges racism and its underlying assumptions, I want to isolate the central assumptions of the biological determinism of early race theory of which she and her father, Enlightenment intellectuals, would have been fully aware. Firstly, just as plants and the lower animals were known scientifically as objects within a system of classification, so too were human beings, as the three-part classification of peoples in the Noah story became replaced by scientific procedures of measurement and comparison. Secondly, race, however defined, was seen as a constraint on human development that could not be transcended. Thirdly, even before Charles Darwin, races were understood in a hierarchy that was Eurocentric. Finally, ineffaceable signs of race were believed to be ubiquitous, from physical appearance to moral behaviour.

The late eighteenth and early nineteenth century was a period when theories of race – 'the biological transmission of innate qualities'[150] – originated and when some of the most toxic ideas were being developed. Although there was a spectrum of views on race from the polygenists to the monogenists, from the defenders of slavery to the abolitionists, scientific racialism was able to find a home within Enlightenment thought for two principal reasons: firstly, if the natural world was scientifically knowable by means of an objectifying, taxonomic system, the human world could also be objectified in a similar way; secondly, a fundamental premise of modernity was that the material world determined to some extent the world of the mind and the emotions. These two assumptions could not be dismissed without at the same time repudiating the project of Enlightenment. It was by no means clear in this period that scientific racialism, as opposed to the customary prejudices people had about 'foreigners', would lead to things like eugenics and exterminationist anti-Semitism. However, both eugenics and exterminationist anti-Semitism made use of the earlier ideas and assumptions that were refined, revised and rhetorically heightened. Robert Young also suggests plausibly that political events made the European public more receptive to the most poisonous strains of race science: the revolutions of 1848, the Indian Mutiny of 1857 and the Jamaica rebellion of 1865.[151] These events, in addition to the European competition for empires, provided a political atmosphere where scientific justifications for white, Christian, European supremacy were received with great respect. The earlier period was somewhat more benign because of the popular efforts to abolish the slave trade and slavery itself but one has to remember that abolitionists were not necessarily wise on the issue of race. Dr William Lawrence, a radical physician who opposed slavery, had no doubts that black Africans were innately inferior to white Europeans.[152] Lawrence's views were by no means idiosyncratic, as white supremacists sometimes assumed the perspective of racial noblesse oblige, paternalistically inclined to assist the inferior dark peoples. Jewish emancipation in France and Germany was always conditioned by a project of educational, cultural and religious improvement

As one turns to romantic-era literature in this context of emergent race science, there is a pattern of ambivalence whereby two cultural logics coexist uneasily, the emergent philo-Semitic discourse following Lessing, Mendelssohn and the French Revolution's emancipation of French Jewry and the emergent race science developed in physiognomy, phrenology and ethnology. Writing could be and frequently was both philo-Semitic and complicit with biological determinism and racial essentialism. I will illustrate this ambivalence in the writing of Maria Edgeworth.

The example of Edgeworth is especially intriguing because prior to the remarkably anti-anti-Semitic novel *Harrington*, Edgeworth's writing negatively represented Jews. The plot of 'The Prussian Vase' hinges on a Jew's attempt to get revenge on the Gentiles who laugh at Jews who are training to be soldiers – one of whom is his son; in this story Jews are either evil or comically contemptible in a physical way. An anti-Semitic assumption was that Jews were unfit to become soldiers because their loyalty and physical courage were questioned. The Jewish character Solomon lies, cheats and plans revenge that is thwarted by a wise English lawyer.[153] The only Jewish character in 'The Good Aunt' is a dishonest receiver of stolen goods whose public exposure, like that in 'The Prussian Vase', echoes to some extent Shylock's treatment at the end of Shakespeare's play.[154] 'The Limerick Glove' ridicules the English prejudice against and stereotyping of the Irish but only at the expense of the gypsies and Jews who are negatively stereotyped as dishonest crooks.[155] In the oriental tale 'Murad the Unlucky' the evil Jewish character sells a parcel of clothes that are infected with plague to an unsuspecting Gentile who then inadvertently spreads the disease to the entire city. A wiser, more sceptical character says of the Jewish merchant that he does not like his 'countenance', nor his eye nor his voice, as the Jew's very physical being expresses his evil disposition.[156] This, one of Edgeworth's *Popular Tales*, fuses biological determinism with older anti-Semitic libels of poisoning. In *The Absentee* (1812) it is not simply that Mordecai the coach-maker is a dishonest, greedy businessman in the Shylock tradition but that his appearance itself is meaningfully evil: he does not seem to have a fully human face.[157] Nevertheless, even in these and other pre-*Harrington* fictions one finds a counter-movement to racial stereotyping. Lady Clonbrony's grotesque attempts in *The Absentee* to conceal her Irishness and to pass as an English woman comically illustrate the way status hierarchies become internalized even to the point of affecting speech, as she tries to efface Irishness from her pronunciation only to produce a sound that calls attention to her Irish identity anyway; she is a poor mimic. The Jewish villain in 'The Prussian Vase' forges the signature of Count Laniska, thus suggesting that even signatures cannot be assumed always to belong to the person signified. Here is a form of the deconstructive scepticism that will be developed further in *Harrington*. In 'Madamoiselle Panache' there is an interpretive problem of fixing the meaning of a woman's blush.[158] The difficulty of determining the meaning of the physical sign suggests other epistemological problems with trying to affix meaning to bodily signs. Such an emphasis obviously undermines the whole project of racial semiotics. The pasteboard dog that is taken for a real dog in 'The Good French Governess' is an allegory, if we needed one, for the duplicity of fiction itself.[159] Edgeworth's scepticism about signs, however, coexists with a full-fledged stereotyping of Jews, Welsh, Creoles, mulattos and Irish. These 'Others' are fixed to specific forms of speech, physical appearance as well as moral behaviour. These forms of representation are readily compatible with a biological determinism that is challenged in her 1817 novel, *Harrington*.

As is well known by now, a young American Jewish woman, Rachel Mordecai, politely protested to the famous author (whose liberal and Enlightenment credentials were strong) that in Edgeworth's fiction Jewish characters were uniformly despicable. Edgeworth was shocked by the allegation of anti-Jewish prejudice and she vowed to correct her errors with the self-reflexive *Harrington*, a novel about not just anti-Semitism but about how it is learned and overcome. It seems that Étienne Dumont, Mirabeau's speechwriter and the French translator of Bentham, had earlier exposed Edgeworth to the discourse about Jewish oppression and emancipation. The superb readings of the novel by Michael Ragussis, Judith Page, Susan Manly and Sheila Spector have made it an intriguing text to interpret.[160] Whether one emphasizes the novel's achievement (Ragussis and Manly) or its limitations in overcoming traditions of anti-Semitic representations (Page and Spector) depends to some extent on which aspects of the novel one chooses to highlight. One sees the good intentions of Edgeworth in the uniform saintliness of all the Jewish characters but one finds also real insight in her making Jewish representation itself a central feature of the novel, from Macklin's *Merchant of Venice* to the medieval painting of the tortured Jew that Montenero purchases and then destroys. The novel's ending is notoriously equivocal, as Harrington's object of desire, his *belle juive* (beautiful Jewess) turns out to be Protestant rather than Jewish but that his Protestant wife has a Jewish father and their children a Jewish grandfather. There is mixing, just not exactly what had seemed to be promised, and the resolution seems evasive. With Edgeworth's anti-anti-Semitic novel there is enough blindness and insight to make for richly various readings.

First, a brief summary of the novel. The main character, Harrington, who grows up terrified of Jews because of a servant's cruel tale of Jews killing children, and whose Judeophobia is reinforced by his father and friends during the 'Jew Bill' controversy of 1753, falls in love with Berenice Montenero, a beautiful Jewess. Harrington's childhood friend Lord Mowbray, the aristocratic and anti-Semitic villain and rival for the attentions of Berenice, manipulates the servant Fowler who first terrified Harrington with child-murder stories about Simon the Jew. Harrington, who becomes progressively disillusioned with the anti-Semitism of his childhood and of his companion Mowbray, works through his prejudice as he befriends Simon the Jew's son and the father of beautiful Berenice. After the protagonist learns the treachery of Mowbray, whose paid agents tried to frighten him into mental illness by means of his Judeophobia, Harrington has a clear path to proposing marriage to Berenice but his father opposes the match. The novel comically resolves the conflicts when Harrington's parents overcome their anti-Jewish prejudice and Montenero reveals finally that Berenice is Christian just as her mother was. Harrington has passed the test set by Berenice's father, namely, he was willing to marry a Jewess but cared enough about his own religion to decline converting.

As an Enlightenment moral tale *Harrington* shows how anti-Semitism is a psychological effect with numerous material and textual causes. If hatred of Jews can be learned, then it can be unlearned too by means of a properly rational education. The propaganda against Jews during the 'Jew Bill' controversy and the enormously popular version of Shakespeare's *Merchant of Venice* by Charles Macklin, who played Shylock not as a comic buffoon but a dangerous villain, are shown to be several of the sources of anti-Semitism. Not race but politics and culture constructed the negative stereotypes of the Jew. Moral development and education provide the antidote to the sickness of Jew-hatred cynically exploited by aristocrats eager to consolidate their power against the enlightened regime of reason and mutual understanding. In addition to the straightforward exposure of prejudice as contrived and unjust, the novel operates at another level to explore the power of imagination to cause social harm and benefit. Harrington the character is feminized by anti-Semitism, in the sense that his fear renders him physically and emotionally ill, unable to function in the social world. This in itself is a peculiar angle on the prejudice which ordinarily makes those who are performing the scapegoating feel powerful and in control. Oddly Harrington's experience of anti-Semitism makes him 'Jewish' in the sense that he experiences helplessness, thus laying the psychological groundwork for his being able to identify with the real victims of anti-Semitism. The novel's over-all critique of prejudice, while successful, leads to a forceful scepticism about the stable meanings of all signs. The morbid romanticism to which Harrington falls victim expresses itself not simply in anti-Semitism but in hypochondria and emotionally inflated reactions to conflict. The novel discriminates between the undisciplined emotionalism of the romantic imagination and the moral benefits of the sympathetic imagination. When Harrington learns to experience anti-Semitic representations – plays and paintings – through the point of view of Jews, he begins to overcome his feminizing hysteria about supposedly murder-ous Jews. Frightened by his nurse's story of child-killing Jews, Harrington the child falls ill and helpless, weakly and passive, dreamy and inactive. The adult Harrington is vulnerable to psychological regression and nervous disorder when Mowbray stages scenes of Gothic terror starring the Jew as the villain. As an Enlightenment fable against prejudice *Harrington* coheres at several levels but it also develops a scepticism about signs that is more than is really needed to undermine anti-Semitism.

In chapter fifteen there is a staging of the Gordon riots of 1780. Edgeworth arranges for the Monteneros and their friends to be in peril and attacked by the rioters but they are saved by the efforts of an enigmatic character, the widow Levy who is also called the orange woman and who is identified as an Irish Catholic. What is this character doing in the middle of an anti-Catholic English riot? She has connections with the rioters, whom she calls affectionately 'the boys', and she is able to pass from one community to the other and back again effortlessly. This character and episode might very well represent in some way Edgeworth's own recollection of the 1798 events in Ireland when her family's estate was spared while the other Protestant great houses were attacked; in 1798 the Edgeworths were threatened more directly by their fellow Protestants than the Catholics who protected them. Edgeworth palimpsestically stages the 1780 political violence in London over the 1798 political violence in Longford, Ireland. Also, however, the widow Levy illustrates the anarchic signifier, the instability of signs and the subversion of stereotypes. The excessive meaning of the signifier is reinforced with the absurd chant of the rioters, 'No Jews, No wooden shoes', as the accident of the rhyme creates a political position. In this instance, the signifier's instability leads to violence and hatred but the widow Levy illustrates the opposite. As an 'orange' woman – a woman who sells oranges in the street as many Jewish Lon-doners did at the time – she is associated with Irish Protestants and unionists.

As the widow Levy – although she never identifies her dead husband as Jewish and he could have had the name Levy without being Jewish – she is known as the wife of a Jew. As an Irish Catholic in an anti-Catholic riot, she becomes, despite her religion, a member of the rebellious crowd – class perhaps here trumping religion and nationality. In addition to all this, she wants to protect Montenero not because he is Jewish but because he is, in her experience, a good man who should not be harmed. In its exuberant unpredictability and defiance of stereotype the character of the widow Levy disrupts the logic of racial/religious/national determinism perhaps as effectively as the laborious deconstructions of anti-Semitism and the idealizing of all the Jewish characters. Identity is not fixed and loyalties are multiple and not contradictory; one can pass between communities without loss of one's own identity; names are as misleading as they are meaningful. The logic of biological determinism is that one's social and moral being is determined by inherited, innate structures over which one has no control. The way in which the widow Levy functions in the novel subverts any kind of determinist logic, including the wordplay in her defence of Montenero, calling him a 'jewel of a Jew', using the accidental meanings of the signifier to reverse a stereotype.

Chapter fifteen is not a deconstructive moment that pulls the rug out from under the feet of stable Enlightenment reason. Rather, the chapter deepens and complicates the meaning of the Enlightenment critique and pushes it further into cosmopolitan directions. As argued persuasively by Robert Young, one of the strongest forces against racial essentialism and ethnic prejudice is hybridity and openness to dialogue, a form of irony within what Bakhtin calls double-voicedness.[161] Habermas's discourse ethics have the same kind of critical power to expose and overcome illegitimate claims of authority that cannot stand up to argument. Chapter fifteen provides a fine example of the deconstructive power of the figure of 'mixing' and impurity.

When one reads in the correspondence between Edgeworth and her Jewish friend Rachel Mordecai that the author of *Harrington* was disappointed that the Jewish community did not thank her for the novel, the limitations of Edgeworth's philo-Semitism are annoyingly apparent.[162] Having penned more odious fictional Jews than most writers of her time, Edgeworth expects that when finally a text of hers does not promote Jew-hatred it should win her the warm gratitude of a whole community. The uneven record of Maria Edgeworth suggests that insights achieved by the cosmopolitan imagination are often only momentary – intense and valuable but ephemeral.

Conclusion

When an article in the *Analytical Review* quotes the 'hath not a Jew' speech from *The Merchant of Venice* but substitutes 'negro' for 'Jew' in order to argue against slavery, it not only links the common oppression of Jew and black but makes the cosmopolitan argument that scapegoating is possible only if there is prior dehumanization.[163] The stereotypes of blacks and Jews are not identical, for the social anxieties associated with each group are different, but the ultimate effect is similar. The Enlightenment sponsored slavery abolition and Jewish emancipation but it also created race science, a tradition of writings and ideas fatal to millions. One finds the discourse of blood purity about blacks in eighteenth-century West Indies and nineteenth-century America and about Jews in fifteenth-century Spain and in nineteenth-century Europe. Although race science did not invent the notion of blood purity, it lent this appalling idea the authority of a science that was monological and impervious to argument. The examples of Levi, Lyon and Edgeworth illustrate the ideological rewards of making use of the literary public sphere, despite its gender- and genre-specific limitations. Levi's courage to argue with the Gentiles tested and expanded the limits of the public sphere, while Lyon's cautious probing of what it was possible to say employed a 'duplicity' taken by many other minority writers. Lessing's plays and Edgeworth's novel both discover a deconstructive energy by which to undermine the cultural forces of racial essentialism. Edgeworth's novel represents a dialogical process that is impressive to behold, for (while her Jewish characters were not particularly believable), she understood that hatred of Jews was a socially constructed process that could be reformed and she began the process with the re-experiencing of *The Merchant of Venice*, the key text in English for reproducing anti-Semitic attitudes in the eighteenth and nineteenth century.

CONCLUSION: POSTNATIONAL COSMOPOLITANISM?

Dominant social groups with political power now and always find it irresistible to sponsor and validate the most flattering representations of their exercise of authority. Aesthetic representations of all kinds have invariably upheld the legitimacy and ideals of the ruling class – no matter the composition and actions of that class. Exceptions to this sociological truism are rare and notable prior to the Enlightenment and slightly more common after the eighteenth century. When Britain found itself after 1815 the most powerful nation in the world, on the verge of an unprecedented economic take-off fuelled by the Industrial Revolution, with an empire that spanned the globe, it was not eager to embrace cosmopolitan political ideas that would weaken state sovereignty and promote international cooperation. If the new race science discovered that Caucasians (and the Anglo-Saxon subgroup) were the first, the primary, the most physically attractive and intellectually endowed race, who were the British to dispute the findings of the most up-to-date research? The dark-skinned people of the empire, it turned out, were fated by biological necessity to occupy the lowest rungs of the world hierarchy; if the British Empire happened to benefit economically from the subordination of the 'inferior' races, then it was no fault of the dominant race which was doing its best to 'lift up' the biologically disadvantaged masses with Christian and civilized values.

World peace and international cooperation had always been good ideas but in the eighteenth century, for the first time in history, cosmopolitanism started to be taken seriously – not because people were suddenly more morally sagacious but because modern warfare had become so appallingly destructive and politically disruptive. Similarly, religious toleration became developed conceptually and seriously considered only after the massive devastation and political disorder of the religious wars in sixteenth- and seventeenth-century Europe.[1] The Thirty Years' War (1618–48) produced an audience receptive to ideas of toleration, ideas which became compelling and even necessary for practical reasons. Even when the rational case for religious toleration was irrefutable on pragmatic grounds alone, it took centuries before toleration was fully in place in Europe. The history of the world citizenship idea has been similar. The immediate and indirect effects of eighteenth-century war were disturbing enough to produce genuine interest in cosmopolitan political schemes. The contrast between spectacular war-profiteering (the Duke of Marlborough and Walpole) and labouring-class sea impressment and war casualties was so morally obscene that it threatened to erode political legitimacy and weaken national social cohesion. The banking system that grew out of the national debt incurred by war disturbed traditionalists and introduced an instability into the economic structure that announced itself with periodic crashes. Cosmopolitanism attracted only a minority of liberals, republicans and socialists because most of the British learned to live with empire and war as the benefits seemed to outweigh the liabilities. In the nineteenth century Metternichian balance of power and British imperial domination crowded out Kantian notions of world peace and cooperation. After the unprecedented catastrophe of World War I – just as now after the end of the Cold War – cosmopolitanism suddenly acquired appeal.

Even when the historical conditions are not completely favourable, untimely ideas get developed and cultivated. Kant's 'Perpetual Peace' essay was translated and circulated in Britain almost immediately because the French Revolution had already internationalized Europe and because long-existing Enlightenment structures of intellectual exchange still operated. Because Enlightenment and scientific inquiry did not respect national boundaries it was inevitable that enlightened political ideas about the relations between political states would follow suit. What was rational in one realm would seem rational in another. Nothing assisted the cosmopolitan ideal more than the three revolutions of the eighteenth century – the American, the French and the Haitian – and nothing retarded and undermined that ideal more than the cultural and political reaction against the Enlightenment and the revolutions. The revolutions, which expanded the public sphere and de-legitimated slavery and the subordination of women, Africans and Jews, introduced the cosmopolitan rhetoric of human solidarity and the principle of rational persuasion as the alternative to political violence. In Wollstonecraft's *Wrongs of Woman* the exchange of the three stories between Maria, Jemima and Darnford is not wholly without its problems, but it represents the fundamental cosmopolitan structure of communicative reciprocity that replaces the older structures of authoritarian deference.

One final glance at the romantic-era cosmopolitans will suggest areas for further inquiry and remind us how important were the literary – not just the political and philosophical – treatments of cosmopolitanism. The romantic-era cosmopolitanism of the Godwin-Wollstonecraft-Shelley circle acquires interest in relation to the contemporary renaissance of political cosmopolitanism. Habermas's revival of Kantian 'perpetual peace' makes what might have seemed earlier only a kind of bohemian rebelliousness a serious project of intellectual reconstruction – which of course was what it always was.

The Shelley Circle's Cosmopolitanism

As the French Revolution and the political reaction against the Revolution strengthened nationalism and weakened cosmopolitanism, a group of English writers promoted cosmopolitanism, not as the writers of the 1790s did by engaging France and its political culture (a 'core' country in Immanuel Wallerstein's taxonomy of economic powers), but instead by identifying with and learning from the Mediterranean, especially Italy but also Greece and Spain (semi-peripheral if not peripheral countries in the Wallerstein model).[2] The so-called second generation of English romantics worked through an ascendant Counter-Enlightenment that coloured their overall approach to the Enlightenment. These writers, inspired more by the Enlightenment cosmopolitan ideal than by liberal nationalism, championed countries as weak as Spain, Italy and Greece for a new internationalism. They approached the French Revolution not as Wordsworth had experienced it – 'Bliss was it in that dawn to be alive!'– but as something morally complicated, temporally differentiated, a mixed inheritance that had to be interpreted, in which achievement had to be separated from failure and ideal from historical contingency. Avoiding the path of British nationalism described so vividly by Linda Colley, they cultivated cosmopolitan engagements even at the level of literary form, through Hunt's and Keats's use of Boccaccio, Byron's of ottava rima, Shelley's of Dante and terza rima, and Mary Shelley's of Italian history. Byron, Percy, and Mary Shelley, who all wrote and spoke Italian fluently, were not mere tourists but in some sense Anglo-Italians or Italo-English, as they made themselves available to the other culture, which in fact shaped their thinking.[3] That their cosmopolitanism was more than just love of Italy is indicated by their engagement with Greece as well. Percy Shelley's work as translator suggests the range of his openness to other cultures: Calderon's plays, Goethe's *Faust*, Plato's *Symposium*, Spinoza's *Tractatus* and Dante's poetry. Mary Shelley's *Valperga* (1823), a historical novel of thirteenth-century Tuscany, reflects not only her intensive historical research and historiographical reflection but her exploration of feminist and republican ideas within a historically specific context, much like her mother had in texts like the *Short Residence in Sweden, Norway and Denmark* (1796), an important text that prefigures the cosmopolitanism of the second-generation writers.[4] The entirely cosmopolitan journal, *The Liberal* (1822–3), a joint production of Shelley, Byron and Hunt, flagged its location in the South where it mocked the narrow nationalism and puritanical morality of the Evangelicals and the 'Lakers'. Shelley's most ambitious poem *Prometheus Unbound* (1820) is readable as a kind of poetic 'Perpetual Peace', part of the Enlightenment project of imagining pacific structures that would fend off war and nationalistic hatred. Saint-Pierre, Rousseau and Bentham also partake in this cosmopolitan enterprise which Shelley carries to uniquely complex expression, revising and deconstructing myths from a variety of cultural sources. Byron's irony, Mary Shelley's historicism and Percy Shelley's mythographic revisionism counter the nationalism that fuels war and disguises injustice; their work anarchistically erodes and undermines essentialist constructions of national identity.

The second-generation English romantics nevertheless appreciated the lessons of Herder and Staël that, while communities and nations have organically evolving identities, they exist internationally – as Percy Shelley describes in his *Philosophical View of Reform* (1820?), one of the strongest expressions of political cosmopolitanism. Shelley's descriptive survey of the political condition of the modern world depicts a universal process of Enlightenment and republican insurgence, not the rise of nationalism.[5] Within the counter-revolutionary settlement of Europe from 1815 to 1848 progressive nationalism was a vehicle for expressing thwarted democratic aspirations, but reactionary nationalism thrived as well in events like the anti-Semitic Hep-Hep riots of 1819 in Germany.

When one reads the following passage in Mary and Percy Shelley's neglected cosmopolitan work, *History of a Six Weeks' Tour Through A Part of France, Switzerland, Germany, and Holland* (1817), it is impossible to ignore the lines of continuity between the generations: 'The wind was violently against us, but the stream, aided by a slight exertion from the rowers, carried us on; the sun shone pleasantly, S— read aloud to us Mary Wollstonecraft's *Letters from Norway*, and we passed our time delightfully'.[6] Shortly after the defeat of Napoleon and the beginning of the counter-revolutionary era, the cash-poor travellers – Percy, Mary and Claire Clairmont –while headed toward Holland on a Rhine boat in the summer of 1814 amused themselves by listening to the words of Mary's mother. One of her great cosmopolitan writings, *A Short Residence in Sweden, Norway and Denmark* (1796) was evidently a model of some kind for the Shelleys' *History of a Six Weeks' Tour*.

When Richard Holmes emphasizes the romantic, inward and confessional qualities of Wollstonecraft's *A Short Residence*, he thereby slights the cosmopolitan features of a text that is wholly within the assumptions of the radical Enlightenment.[7] In a sequence of twenty-five letters addressed to an unnamed masculine correspondent who was in fact Gilbert Imlay, the father of her child Fanny and the lover who had recently rejected her, the Wollstonecraft persona creates Rousseauvian reveries of solitary reflection within beautiful and sublime Scandinavian landscapes and reads the social and political text of the societies she encounters. Only by privileging the former can one identify *A Short Residence* as inwardly romantic. The reveries are in fact understandable as enlightened culture because solitary walks and meditations enlarge the mind and open the heart just like conversation, social observation, reading and urban culture.[8] Although the persona moves in and out of melancholy, she protests several times against the rarity of true 'affection' between men and women, as affection requires more than just sexual attraction.[9] As indebted to Rousseau as the text is for the reveries and the spontaneously unrevised style that captures the temporality of writing, Wollstonecraft will have nothing to do with Rousseau's primitivist ideas, dismissed curtly with the phrase 'Rousseau's golden age of stupidity'.[10] Her interest in inwardness and disclosing the process of thinking and feeling is continuous with the overall project of understanding the world progressively better. Self-knowledge is not instantaneous but something that is difficult to attain and that requires time and painful, patient reflection.[11] Knowing oneself does not preclude knowing other people and the external world because the two are always in a dialectical interplay. Defending the cosmopolitan effects of urban culture, she writes that '[m]ixing with mankind we are obliged to examine our prejudices, and often imperceptibly lose, as we analyse them'.[12] Travel, for example, is not an occasion for displaying feelings and offering personal opinions; travel rather is a civilizing activity. Travel too erodes prejudice and travel narratives 'promote inquiry and discussion'. Wollstonecraft's interest is not inwardness as such but overall attentiveness to both the inner and outer worlds. 'The spirit of inquiry ... and ... its diffusion will in a great measure destroy the factitious national characters which have been supposed permanent, though only rendered so by the permanency of ignorance.'[13] Inquiry, discussion, diffusion and nationalistic bias: these all belong to public culture where her writing is focused and situated.

The persona of *A Short Residence* makes shrewd sociological observations that rest upon enlightened assumptions about reason and society. Even trivial events are subject to her sociological imagination: the difficulty of finding a Swedish boat, for example, is ascribed to the policy of royal monopoly and low wages for boatmen.[14] Appalled by the indolence of the poorest Swedish peasants, she recalls the people of Paris whose love of novelty and 'curiosity appeared to me a proof of the progress they had made in refinement'.[15] Although the preponderance of her comments praise urban at the expense of rural culture, she finds the peasantry and labourers more admirable in their generosity and genuine feeling than the imitative, prejudiced middle class.[16] Wollstonecraft makes not just precise descriptions of nature, as Richard Holmes correctly notes,[17] but equally precise observations of social phenomena like the specific wages of wet nurses. Their shockingly low compensation is part of the general oppression of labouring-class women.[18]

Her comparative interpretive method is at its best in the nineteenth letter where the sequence of reflections and observations illustrates a penetrating and rapidly-working critical mind. The letter begins with a disgusted reaction to the public execution of an arsonist in Copenhagen where she was staying; she briefly argues against all capital punishment and explains the brutalizing effects of public executions. Because some blamed the devastating fire on agents of the British government, she briefly touches on the power of conspiratorial thinking. Several people obtained the blood of the hanged man because drinking the blood of an executed criminal was a popular way to cure some diseases. Wollstonecraft's persona is not just repulsed but analytical, as she describes the difficulty of public education, which she strongly supports, in overcoming superstition. The huge fire produced also a rash of fraudulent property claims, which provokes her to launch a polemic against the 'adoration of property', something that is 'the root of all evil'.[19]

Protesting the reifying and alienating effects of property-worship, she returns to a figure of great interest, Queen Matilda, who outraged the nation's puritans not just because of her sexual behaviour (real or alleged) but because she introduced 'elegance' in public life, an aesthetic and pleasurable dimension separate from mere property and wealth. Sister of George III, Matilda, whose story occupies letter eighteen, was married to a mentally ill monarch when she and her advisor – also her lover, apparently – initiated some modernizing reforms that disturbed traditionalists. Her lover was eventually beheaded as a traitor and Matilda, forced to flee the country, died at the age of twenty-four. Wollstonecraft's narrative strongly sympathizes with and defends Matilda as though she were a character in *Wrongs of Woman*. One of Matilda's reforms, building a hospital for foundlings, illustrates her compassion for unmarried mothers.[20] In the context of the anti-property polemic, Matilda is morally superior to those who care only about money; enlightened values are ultimately on her side, not the side of the puritanical Lutherans. The hypocritical sexual practices of the Danes include middle-class men having sex with women servants, as each group pursues its own self-interest. Wollstonecraft's description of the Danish sexual customs is not moralistic but coldly analytical: the women are ambitious and the men petty tyrants. The persona anticipates the objection from a reader that Wollstonecraft once again is protesting against injustice to women. She reassures her reader that she is hardly against sexuality that arises from 'an exuberance of life' but asserts that the Danish customs do not derive from that source. The harshness of her criticism of Danish culture makes her regret the severity of her criticism against the French in her recent book on the French Revolution. The letter's penultimate paragraph focuses on the nature of 'piety', which she defines as 'a blind faith in things contrary to the principles of reason'. Lutheran piety in Denmark has not produced a more ethically responsive political culture. The last paragraph reflects on travel itself and its function in relation to a 'liberal education'. The northern countries rather than the more polished nations of the Grand Tour are more educationally useful for instructing the understanding; France and Italy cater too readily to the pleasure of travellers.[21]

The level of interpretive analysis and the quality of the writing are unfailingly high. She responds to social phenomena from the 'situated body', as phrased by Toril Moi after Simone de Beauvoir.[22] Justifying her frequent attention to women's plight, she explains: 'How can I avoid it, when most of the struggles of an eventful life have been occasioned by the oppressed state of my sex: we reason deeply, when we forcibly feel'.[23] Reason and feeling, the outer and the inner, the objective and the subjective, the abstract and the concrete all go together and mutually inform one another. Applying the category of romantic inwardness to Wollstonecraft's text distorts the dialectical and situated quality of her writing. *A Short Residence* reminds the reader on numerous occasions that the first-person narrator has a sexed body: the possibility of being raped comes to mind at one point;[24] she calls attention to some of the times she is nursing her baby and she makes note of her distress when she is weaning her child;[25] by calling attention so frequently to the most attractive young women in the social gatherings, she depicts the sexual dynamics of the social interactions.[26] In the different societies she visits, the sexual customs, treatment of unmarried mothers, premarital and extramarital sex, the divorce laws and courtship traditions provide occasion for her engaged and comparative reflections, eventually taking her to Britain and its sexual practices.

The situated body from which she is writing also defends a Christiana food riot and then moves on to a polemic against the commercial logic that caused the riot in the first place; from that analysis she arrives at a more abstract conceptual location from where she draws parallels between colonially subjugated Norway and colonially subjugated Ireland.[27] Travel is an opportunity to exercise the critical intelligence, to compare and contrast different cultures but not from some kind of neutral, value-free perspective. The French Revolution, established Enlightenment precepts, recent and older history and the situated body of the writer all provide meaningful contexts for observing and reflecting on cultures unlike one's own. 'Travellers who require that every nation should resemble their native country, had better stay at home.'[28] Few writers demonstrated the cosmopolitan effects of travel narratives as effectively as Wollstonecraft.

The *History of a Six Weeks' Tour*, which has not attracted much critical attention,[29] is readable as a strongly political protest against the counter-revolutionary settlement of Europe after the defeats of Napoleon – first in 1814 and then, of course, at Waterloo in 1815. The palimpsestic layering of time frames begins with the elopement trip in the summer of 1814 through France to Switzerland, returning home by way of the Rhine River to Holland. Percy, Mary and Claire all wrote journal accounts of the events at the time they transpired. The trio returned to Switzerland in 1816 where they joined Byron, briefly Claire's lover, and stayed on Lake Geneva visiting the various sites where Rousseau placed his characters from the novel *Julie* (1761). Percy and Mary again wrote journal accounts and recorded in letters their response to the people and landscape. The final layer is the 1817 composition of the travel narrative itself, splicing the 1814 and 1816 trips and structuring the whole as a polemic against reactionary political and literary culture.

The Preface acknowledges that the sites described in the *History of a Six Weeks' Tour* are familiar with their readers through actual visits or Grand Tour descriptions.[30] Unlike Wollstonecraft's book, which provided discussion of places about which British readers knew very little, the Shelleys' volume has no similar depictions of exotic places. The justification they give in the Preface is that their writing is animated by youthful enthusiasm but the real novelty is its political nature. The first part of the book describes the three young people making their way toward Switzerland as they pass one war-devastated town after another. France is not a nation 'liberated' from the evils of the French Revolution and the oppression of Napoleon; it is a desert and wasteland destroyed by the Cossacks.[31] The second part that describes their return to France in 1816 characterizes the Bourbon restoration in terms of 'a detested dynasty on the throne'.[32] As they enter Geneva, Switzerland, the text remarks that the magistrates, successors of those who exiled Rousseau, had been recently 'shot by the populace', an act of political violence recorded in a factual not a moralistic manner.[33] Rousseau is the dominant presence in the book, both in terms of commentary on his life and works and in terms of his role as allegorical figure for the Enlightenment and French Revolution. These seem but are not completely defeated by the temporary restoration of the Bourbons. Letter 3, an extended homage to Rousseau and especially *Julie*, records the visits of the Shelleys to the places alluded to in the fiction. That Empress Maria Louisa slept at Meillerie to honour St. Preux, main character of the novel, illustrates according to the Shelleys the superiority of 'Genius' to 'Power' and 'how unfit and how impossible it is for the ancient system of opinions, or for any power built upon a conspiracy to revive them, permanently to subsist among mankind'.[34] Despite the restoration of 'Power' it is the even greater of authority of 'Genius' that determines the course of history. Political figures like the Empress are mere effects of historical causes that original writers like Rousseau sustain. The maxim that the Shelleys want to register is the one animating the sonnet 'Ozymandias': tyrannical political power is ephemeral but the power of great art is more enduring. When they come to Lausanne and the house from which Gibbon put the finishing touches on his *Decline and Fall of the Roman Empire* (1766–88), the Shelleys use the occasion to praise Rousseau at the expense of Gibbon.[35] British readers were troubled by Gibbon's depiction of Christianity but Rousseau was widely believed to have been a major author of the French Revolution itself.

Letter 4 is a magnificent prose description of Mont Blanc and the surrounding area, something like a prose version of the poem 'Mont Blanc' that concludes the book. The philosophical scepticism embodied in these two texts is reinforced in the Journal section that follows Letter 4. One part of the Journal discloses four tales of the supernatural told by 'Monk' Lewis to the Shelleys and Byron. These stories would seem to be mere narrative padding for a thin book until one notices the comment that 'none could believe in ghosts without believing in God'.[36] The Mont Blanc material and the ghost stories go hand in hand because the governing assumption of the latter is that the supernatural in the stories is as fictional as it is in religion. The last part of the Journal seems at first a merely factual description of passing through Versailles and Paris as the Shelleys return from Geneva on their way to London but the prose is too strongly republican to sustain that kind of reading. Rather, the Shelleys highlight the extravagant wealth of Versailles as a symbol of the *ancien régime* that caused the French Revolution. Versailles, like Ozymandias's empire, will be swept away and the destruction of Versailles and all that it symbolizes will be effected by 'Rousseau' – not the historical person or even author but all the historical forces that become attached to what his name has come to mean. The Bourbons are back in power, like ghosts returning from the grave, but the revival of the discredited political ideas is partial and temporary. 'Rousseau' is the ghost who should be scaring the defenders of social and political privilege; 'Rousseau' is the one who will be meting out justice.

Compared with Wollstonecraft's, the Shelleys' travel book is harder-edged, not nearly as carefully written (except for the extraordinary passages on Mont Blanc) but perhaps entirely appropriate for a post-revolutionary era. Wollstonecraft wanted people to visit Scandanavia; the Shelleys want people to read Rousseau in the revolutionary manner they are sketching out. The encounter with otherness in Wollstonecraft was cultural and social – in the Shelleys, political and textual. Even Mont Blanc as such was hardly a novelty. What was new was Percy Shelley's writing and thinking about this icon of the Grand Tour.

The Shelleys' good friend, Lord Byron, wrote about both familiar and exotic places in his poetry and prose. One hardly needs to read the inscription for *Childe Harold* from Louis Charles Fougeret de Monbron's *Le Cosmopolite, ou le Citoyen du Monde* (1752) to recognize that Byron was one of the most cosmopolitan writers of the romantic era. One states only the obvious that the worldliness in his life, the internationalism in his politics and in his writing make him one of the most cosmopolitan figures of the time. The most popular writer of the Shelley circle, Byron performed his role of world citizen as effectively as anyone both in his life and in his writing. It was Byron who used terza rima for a poem in English (*The Prophecy of Dante* (1819)) even before Shelley and he was politically active in nationalist struggles in both Italy and Greece. *Childe Harold* and other poems contributed decisively to the phil-Hellenistic myth that would attract European volunteers to fight with the Greeks against the Turks.

As William St Clair illustrates, the actual Greek war for independence, which was extraordinarily brutal, was nothing like the myth.[37] Byron also demythologized war, depicting its savagery and irrationality in the seventh canto of the great romantic-era epic *Don Juan* (1819–24). Starting with *Beppo* (1818) and continuing with *Don Juan*, Byron made the Italian poetic form of ottava rima his own, a much better form for his particular style of writing than terza rima, which was to suit Shelley so well. Transforming the poetic aristocratic Grand Tour in both *Childe Harold* and *Don Juan* into something entirely new, Byron represented both the tormented soul of inward-looking romanticism and the engaged observer of the external world fascinated with human and geographical variety and difference. The satire of Counter-Enlightenment romanticism in the writing of the 'Lakers' – Wordsworth, Coleridge and Southey – appears in numerous poems and prose comments to form a consistent and coherent position: the Lake School is too narrowly focused, too inward, too nationalistic and sacrifices a broader knowledge of other cultures and literary traditions for the false ideal of self-expression. Long before Jerome McGann developed his essays on the 'romantic ideology' – and long before Heine's incisive critique of reactionary romanticism – Byron had developed a cosmopolitan criticism of a nationalistic romanticism.[38] Although McGann in his influential study gives full credit to both Byron and Heine, it is nevertheless often forgotten how devastating and on-target are Byron's satirical attacks on a particular kind of romanticism.

Byron's rival and friend, Percy Shelley was at least as cosmopolitan in outlook even if the cosmopolitanism did not become translated into fighting with the Carbonari and the Greek nationalists. From *Queen Mab* (1813) to *The Revolt of Islam* (1817) to *Prometheus Unbound* (1820) and *Hellas* (1821), Shelley engages the Enlightenment and fosters a critical view of the American and French revolutions in search of an adequate ideological synthesis to embody poetically the process of human emancipation. He tries to achieve and assumes as normative a universalism we now might call Eurocentric but only at the price of being historically anachronistic. In *The Philosophical View of Reform* he attends to nations outside Europe and in *Prometheus Unbound*, the great mythographic drama, he syncretically brings together non-European – especially Persian – legends with European myths. The Prometheus–Jupiter conflict he conceives as 'the Champion' and 'the Oppressor of mankind'.[39] When Mercury acting as Jupiter's agent offers Prometheus a 'deal' in act one of the lyrical drama to give up the 'secret' in exchange for liberation and access to pleasure, Prometheus turns down the proposed treaty in this way: 'Let others flatter Crime where it sits throned / In brief Omnipotence' because he is waiting for 'Justice' (I.401–5). Characteristically Shelleyan is the depersonalization of political conflict as Jupiter becomes an 'it' and 'Crime', impersonal qualities that are only accidentally connected with something as specific as a named character. Jupiter plays a role but that role could be played by some otherwise named figure. The wonderful paradox of 'brief Omnipotence' is a way to signify the illusion of tyrannical power's permanence. Rather than make a deal, Prometheus waits for the moment of justice when the throne itself, not just a particular occupant, will be completely displaced. The poem is of the Enlightenment rather than the Counter-Enlightenment because the imagined process is one in which tyranny itself is fully worked through, toward a site of emancipation. Shelley uncompromisingly pushes the dissolution of local and national meanings to produce something abstract enough to accommodate universal human history:

> The loathsome mask has fallen, the man remains
> Sceptreless, free, uncircumscribed – but man:
> Equal, unclassed, tribeless and nationless,
> Exempt from awe, worship, degree, – the King
> Over himself ... (III.iv.193–7)

The poem cannot say of what exactly freedom, tribelessness, classlessness and nationlessness consists, other than to point to the empty space after the series of negations. To supply anything more specific would be to re-inscribe another tyranny, class system and nationalism.

Shelley's wife Mary does not have the cosmopolitan reputation of her husband Percy and her friend Byron, but her writing has a strongly cosmopolitan perspective. In the eleventh chapter of *Mathilda* (1820) there is an important response by the character Woodville to Mathilda's invitation to a joint suicide, an aesthetically beautiful and painless exit from the sufferings that both of them had experienced. Woodville has lost his young wife to an illness, while Mathilda herself is not even able to tell Woodville her secret trauma, that her father had returned to her after sixteen years' absence following the death of his wife – Mathilda's mother – only to ruin their happy reunion by declaring his incestuous passion for his daughter. The only way Mathilda can tell her shameful story is by writing to Woodville while knowing that she herself will be dead by the time he reads it – so great is her embarrassment, so difficult it is for her to disclose her secrets. Woodville counters Mathilda's passionate invitation by offering her an alternative: to live for others rather than die to satisfy one's own wishes. It is one's 'duty' to 'smooth the way for our posterity', to be 'virtuous now' for the sake of 'future inhabitants of this fair world'. He depicts his 'labours' as forming 'a link in the chain of gold with which we ought all to strive to drag Happiness from where she sits enthroned above the clouds, now far beyond our reach, to inhabit the earth with us'. If Socrates, Shakespeare, or Rousseau had allowed despair to end their productive lives prematurely, then the 'improvement' lost to humanity would have been 'incalculable'.[40]

Shelley's contrast of Woodville's cosmopolitan identity with Mathilda's romantic identity effectively clarifies what is at stake. Woodville's identity is intersubjective, formed in relation to a past and a future, oriented to a social project of enlightened modernity, informed by attention to the suffering of other people ('The inhabitants of this world suffer so much pain').[41] Mathilda's identity is tragically constrained within romantic parameters because her extraordinary suffering has so traumatized her to the point that, while she recognizes the cogency of the cosmopolitan ideal, she herself cannot regulate her own life by its logic. Mathilda rather repeats the pattern established by her father, whose aristocratic privilege allowed him to indulge every whim until he experienced the necessity and compulsion of love for the exemplary Diana, who unfortunately died giving birth to Mathilda before she had time to undo his aristocratic mis-education. Mary W. Shelley's text treats romanticism as a symptom rather than a solution: Mathilda's solitude is the pathological effect of an irresponsible father who victimizes her with his self-indulgent abandonments and revelations; her love of nature, which begins in childhood and is continued throughout her short life, is depicted as a traumatic 'internal witness' to provide an affective centre to her motherless and fatherless emotional world. When Mathilda looks forward to joining her father in death at the end of the novella, the triumph of myth – Pluto kidnapping Proserpina for the underworld – is hardly a critique of Woodville's cosmopolitan idealism, as some critics have suggested. The critique rather is levelled against aristocratic privilege, irresponsible parenting that can masquerade as tragic romantic suffering, antisocial isolation and retreat from community that can appear as the effects of genius. The Dantean allusion to Mathilda gathering flowers, a passage in the *Purgatorio* dear to both Percy and Mary Shelley, is ironic in that Dante's Mathilda evokes both an earthly paradise and the progression of the active life to the *via contemplativa* associated with Beatrice and the higher Christian paradise. Shelley's Mathilda has no active life and she is eager to pass into a realm that mirrors rather than transcends the false paradise with her father.

The novella illustrates vividly several premises of enlightened modernity: people have to tell their stories because the stories that cannot be told mark the limits of community, outside of which there is unrelieved suffering and death. If incest was the untellable story of Shelley's day, later periods would have their own tales of horror unbearable to tell and unbearable to hear. Shelley's text is not sceptically postmodernist in suggesting the inadequacy of Woodville's narrative of intersubjectivity and history. Mathilda submits to myth in the end but she performs what is a demythologizing action by writing her story to a man she knows will understand her and feel compassion for her pain. Mathilda's narrative critiques certain kinds of Counter-Enlightenment romanticism. However beautiful the Scottish landscape with which the young Mathilda affectively related, this romantic nature worship is conditioned by actual motherlessness, a cold caretaker and an absent father. The beauty of Mathilda's death, consumptive and solitary, is diminished by her disturbingly strong desire to reunite with her father, a desire that only calls attention to the body she so desperately wants to transcend.

In this context *Frankenstein* (1818) is an interesting work because it has one of the most effective challenges to biological determinism in romantic-era writing: the narrative of the Frankenstein creature. The premise of biological determinism and race science is that physical being determines moral status, but the creature's physical being in *Frankenstein* does not determine his moral being, as Shelley makes him benevolent and generous until he is victimized and rejected so often that he finally retaliates. Also, his conventionally ugly appearance does not signify his membership in a race that is unchangeably evil. Something one could learn from the *Vindication of the Rights of Woman* is that beauty is not a reliable category for judging moral value, an important point in a context where the moral and intellectual superiority of Caucasians was supposedly proven by the superior Caucasian beauty. If the creature had been treated humanely, the novel suggests, he would not have been a murderer. The reader experiences the creature's language and can only imagine his appearance, so at the level of experiencing the novel, the reader finds the creature primarily as someone belonging to discourse and speech, only secondarily as weirdly other. Shelley ingeniously undermines the logic of biological determinism, especially when the creature outperforms both Victor Frankenstein and Walton in terms of moral self-awareness. The creature experiences guilt, remorse and repentance at the novel's end, whereas Victor still has hope that someone may succeed in his project of creating life and Walton ceases his polar quest not because sailors have died but only because he fears a mutiny.

Shelley's cosmopolitanism acquires more substance when one includes *Valperga* (1823) which, according to Stuart Curran, is the feminist, liberal-democratic alternative to Walter Scott's nationalistic historical novels.[42] The early-modern republicanism championed by the heroine Euthanasia is historically specific but also abstract enough to warrant Tilottama Rajan's description of it as Leibnizian 'counter-factuality'.[43] As a counterpoint to Castruccio's education that led to competition and zealous ambition, Euthanasia's education supervised by her blind father is cosmopolitan: her reading is designed to teach her some distance from her own society because the present moment and its norms are the consequence of historical process. She is encouraged to cultivate an idealistic 'hope of freedom for Italy, of revived learning and the reign of peace for all the world'.[44] Euthanasia achieves distance from her own actions defending her castle and community when she doubts that even defensive war is morally justifiable; these doubts are not idle because the military resistance is ultimately futile and produces many casualties that seem unnecessary.[45]

If Percy Shelley had not drowned in 1822 it is possible that the collaborative effort of *The Liberal* would have continued beyond a few years and would have made a stronger cosmopolitan effect than it did. Recent scholarly work on the 'Cockney School' of Leigh Hunt and Keats brings out cosmopolitan qualities in its work as well, especially the energetic reading and appropriation of Italian literature and culture.[46]

Habermas's Cosmopolitanism

Habermas's most recent reflections on postnational cosmopolitanism continue to uphold a revised Kantian approach to international relations. To protect human rights and prevent war Habermas proposes a strengthened United Nations with a reformed Security Council, a fully functioning International Criminal Court and especially a global public sphere that works at a high level of openness free from coercion, manipulation and propaganda.[47] The path sketched out by Habermas is the 'constitutionalization of international law', a process that entails nations giving up sovereignty to cosmopolitan structures. For global democracy to achieve legitimacy 'civic solidarity' has to be established 'across former national borders within the enlarged communities'.[48] A daunting obstacle to achieving any kind of trans-national solidarity is the massive 'systemic inequality' where 1.2 billion people 'live on less than a dollar a day' and a fifth of the world's people consume 'more than 80 percent of global income'. Despite the self-congratulatory and self-deceiving rhetoric of the neoliberals, free trade, the economic doctrine and practice of the ruling elites everywhere, will do nothing to diminish global inequality.[49] Yet another obstacle to moving toward cosmopolitan political structures is what Habermas calls the 'reversal' in American policy from internationalism to unilateralism under the leadership of George Bush, who is described as having 'contempt for one of the greatest achievements of human civilization' – namely, cosmopolitan structures of international relations.[50] The problem of terrorism can be addressed not by military action but by, firstly, more effective international cooperation among the intelligence and criminal justice institutions and by, secondly, more self-critical dialogue between cultures undergoing social modernization.[51] In many respects we have already entered a 'postnational constellation' as the globalized economy, disease pandemics, terrorism and ecological catastrophe do not respect national borders; however, neither the political institutions nor the cultural structures that provide social cohesion have adequately recognized the new cosmopolitan realities. As we make our way within this new postnational constellation, the writing of the late-Enlightenment and romantic-era cosmopolitans suggests ways of orienting ourselves as citizens of the world.

NOTES

Introduction

1. S. Benhabib, 'Toward a Deliberative Model of Democratic Legitimacy', in S. Benhabib (ed.), *Democracy and Difference: Contesting the Boundaries of the Political* (Princeton: Princeton University Press, 1996), pp. 67–94; p. 80.
2. M. Scrivener, *Seditious Allegories. John Thelwall and Jacobin Writing* (University Park: Pennsylvania State University Press, 2001).

1 Cosmopolitanism Then and Now

1. I. Kant, 'Idea for a Universal History with a Cosmopolitan Purpose' [1784], in H. Reiss (ed.), *Kant: Political Writings*, trans. H. B. Nisbet, 3rd edn (Cambridge: Cambridge University Press, 1991), pp. 41–53; p. 51.
2. J. Habermas, *The Inclusion of the Other: Studies in Political Theory*, ed. C. Cronin and P. De Greiff, trans. C. Cronin (Cambridge, MA, and London: The MIT Press, [1996] 1998), p. 183. The chapter is entitled 'Kant's Idea of Perpetual Peace: At Two Hundred Years' Remove'.
3. D. M. McMahon, *Enemies of the Enlightenment: The French Counter-Enlightenment and the Making of Modernity* (Oxford: Oxford University Press, 2001), p. viii.
4. E. Cassirer, *The Philosophy of the Enlightenment*, trans. F. C. A. Koellin and J. P. Pettegrove (Princeton: Princeton University Press, [1932] 1951); P. Gay, *The Enlightenment: An Interpretation*, 2 vols (New York: Knopf, 1966).
5. I. Berlin, *Three Critics of the Enlightenment: Vico, Hamaan, Herder*, ed. H. Hardy (Princeton: Princeton University Press, 2000).
6. T. W. Adorno and M. Horkheimer, *The Dialectic of Enlightenment*, trans. J. Cumming (New York: Continuum, [1947] 1972).
7. J. Habermas, *Autonomy and Solidarity: Interviews with Jürgen Habermas*, ed. J. P. Dews (London: Verso, 1986), p. 158.
8. T. J. Schlereth, *The Cosmopolitan Ideal in Enlightenment Thought: Its Form and Function in the Ideas of Franklin, Hume, and Voltaire, 1694–1790* (Notre Dame and London: University of Notre Dame Press, 1977).
9. Ibid., p. 134.
10. Ibid., p. 10.
11. Ibid., pp. 14, 36.
12. On the Enlightenment and racism, see E. C. Eze (ed.), *Race and Enlightenment: A Reader* (London: Blackwell, 1997).

13. Schlereth, *Cosmopolitan Ideal in Enlightenment Thought*, p. 97.
14. T. Frank, *What's the Matter with Kansas? How Conservatives Won the Heart of America* (New York: Metropolitan Books, 2004).
15. Kant, 'Idea for a Universal History', p. 42. *Kants gesammelte Schriften*, ed. Koenigliche Preußische Akademie der Wissenschaften, 24 vols (Berlin: Vruck und Verlag von Georg Reimer, 1902–), vol. 8, p. 18.
16. Kant, 'Idea for a Universal History', p. 43.
17. Ibid., p. 46. *Kants gesammelte Schriften*, vol. 8, p. 23.
18. J. G. Herder, *On Social and Political Culture*, ed. and trans. F. M. Barnard (Cambridge: Cambridge University Press, 1969), p. 323.
19. C. Gilligan, *In a Different Voice: Psychological Theory and Women's Development* (Cambridge, MA, and London: Harvard University Press, 1993), and J. Habermas, *Moral Consciousness and Communicative Action*, trans. C. Lenhardt and S. W. Nicholsen (Cambridge, MA, and London: The MIT Press, [1983] 1990), pp. 116–94.
20. Herder, *On Social and Political Culture*, p. 324.
21. Kant, 'Idea for a Universal History', pp. 49, 51. *Kants gesammelte Schriften*, vol. 8, p. 25.
22. Kant, 'Idea for a Universal History', pp. 51–2.
23. I. Kant, 'On the Common Saying: "This May be True in Theory, but it does not Apply in Practice"' [1793] in *Kant: Political Writings*, pp. 61–92; p. 90.
24. T. W. Adorno, *Kant's Critique of Reason*, ed. R. Tiedemann, trans. R. Livingstone (Stanford: Stanford University Press, [1995] 2001), p. 4.
25. Ibid., p. 18. For a study that connects Kantian enlightenment with Kantian critique, see W. Goetschel, *Constituting Critique: Kant's Writing as Critical Praxis*, trans. E. Schwab (Durham and London: Duke University Press, 1994).
26. I. Kant, *The Critique of Pure Reason*, ed. and trans. P. Guyer and A. W. Wood (Cambridge: Cambridge University Press, [1781, 1787] 1998), pp. 484–9.
27. K-O Apel, 'Kant's "Toward Perpetual Peace" as Historical Prognosis from the Point of View of Moral Duty', in J. Bohman and M. Lutz-Bachman (eds), *Perpetual Peace: Essays on Kant's Cosmopolitan Ideal* (Cambridge, MA, and London: The MIT Press, 1997), pp. 79–110.
28. Kant, 'Perpetual Peace: A Philosophical Sketch' [1795] in *Kant: Political Writings*, pp. 93–130; p. 93; *Kants gesammelte Schriften*, vol. 8, p. 343.
29. Kant, 'Perpetual Peace', pp. 99–105; *Kants gesammelte Schriften*, vol. 8, pp. 349–57.
30. J. Derrida, 'Hostipitality', trans. B. Stocker and F. Morlock, in L. Thomassen (ed.), *The Derrida-Habermas Reader* (Edinburgh and Chicago: University of Chicago Press, 2006), pp. 208–30.
31. Kant, 'Perpetual Peace', pp. 102–5; *Kants gesammelte Schriften*, vol. 8, p. 357.
32. Kant, 'Perpetual Peace', p. 105; *Kants gesammelte Schriften*, vol. 8, p. 358.
33. Kant, 'Perpetual Peace', p. 106; *Kants gesammelte Schriften*, vol. 8, p. 358.
34. Kant, 'Perpetual Peace', p. 106; *Kants gesammelte Schriften*, vol. 8, p. 358.
35. Kant, 'Perpetual Peace', p. 107; *Kants gesammelte Schriften*, vol. 8, p. 359.
36. Kant, 'Perpetual Peace', p. 107; *Kants gesammelte Schriften*, vol. 8, p. 359.
37. Kant, 'Perpetual Peace', pp. 107–8; *Kants gesammelte Schriften*, vol. 8, p. 360.
38. Kant, 'Perpetual Peace', pp. 112–3.
39. Ibid., p. 109.
40. T. Serequeberhan, 'Eurocentrism in Philosophy: The Case of Immanuel Kant', *Philosophical Forum*, 27 (1996), p. 337, quoted in R. B. Louden, *Kant's Impure Ethics: From*

Rational Beings to Human Beings (New York and Oxford: Oxford University Press, 2000), p. 210, n. 80.

41. R. Bernasconi, 'Who Invented the Concept of Race? Kant's Role in the Enlightenment Construction of Race', in R. Bernasconi, (ed.), *Race* (Oxford and Malden, MA: Blackwell, 2001), pp. 11–36.

42. T. McCarthy, 'On the Way to a World Republic? Kant on Race and Development', in L. R. Waas (ed.), *Politik, Moral und Religion – Gegensätze und Ergänzungen ... Festschrift zum 65. Geburtstag von Karl Graf Ballestrem* (Berlin: Duncker and Humblot, 2004), pp. 223–42. See also the treatment of race and Kant in F. Moten, 'Knowledge of Freedom', *CR: The New Centennial Review*, 4:2 (2004), pp. 269–310.

43. Louden, *Kant's Impure Ethics*, p. 15.

44. Ibid., p. 105.

45. Habermas, *The Inclusion of the Other*, p. 166.

46. J. Habermas, *Postnational Constellation: Political Essays*, trans. M. Pensky (Cambridge, MA, and London: The MIT Press, [1998] 2001), p. 67.

47. Ibid., p. 78.

48. Ibid., p. 81.

49. J. Habermas, *Theory of Communicative Action: Reason and the Rationalization of Society*, trans. T. McCarthy, 2 vols (Boston: Beacon Press, [1981] 1984), vol. 1, p. 287.

50. J. Habermas, *Religion and Rationality: Essays on Reason, God, and Modernity*, ed. E. Mendieta, trans. M. Pensky (Cambridge, MA: The MIT Press, 2002), p. 158.

51. Habermas, *Postnational Constellation*, p. 121.

52. Ibid., p. 125.

53. T. McCarthy, "On the Idea of a Reasonable Law of Peoples', in J. Bohman and M. Lutz-Bachman, (eds), *Perpetual Peace: Essays on Kant's Cosmopolitan Ideal* (Cambridge, MA, and London: The MIT Press, 1997), pp. 201–7; p. 215.

54. Habermas, *Postnational Constellation*, p. 128.

55. Ibid., p. 133.

56. J. Habermas, 'Coping with Contingencies – The Return of Historicism', in J. Niznik and J. T. Sanders (eds), *Debating the State of Philosophy: Habermas, Rorty, and Kolakowski* (Westport, CT and London: Praeger, 1996), pp. 1–24.

57. J. Habermas, *Postmetaphysical Thinking: Philosophical Essays*, trans. W. M. Hohengarten (London and Cambridge, MA: The MIT Press, [1988] 1992), p. 17.

58. Habermas, *The Inclusion of the Other*, p. 37.

59. Habermas, *Postmetaphysical Thinking*, p. 18.

60. Habermas, *Moral Consciousness and Communicative Action*, p. 19.

61. Habermas, *The Inclusion of the Other*, p. 14.

62. Ibid., p. 86.

63. Ibid., p. 138.

64. Ibid., pp. 132, 146.

65. J. Habermas and J. Derrida, 'February 15, or What Binds Europeans Together: A Plea for a Common Foreign Policy, Beginning in the Core of Europe', trans. M. Pensky, in L. Thomassen (ed.), *The Derrida-Habermas Reader* (Chicago and Edinburgh: University of Chicago Press, 2006), pp. 270–7.

66. J. Habermas, 'The Kantian Project of Cosmopolitan Law', lecture at Purdue University, West Lafayette, Indiana, 15 October 2004; http://www.cla.purdue.edu/phil-lit/events/habermas.cfm.

67. Habermas, *The Inclusion of the Other*, p. 201.

68. J. Habermas, *Between Facts and Norms: Contributions to a Discourse Theory of Law and Democracy*, trans. W. Rehg (Cambridge, MA, and London: The MIT Press, [1992] 1996), p. 371.

69. Habermas, *The Inclusion of the Other*, p. xxxvi.

70. Ibid., p. 142.

71. Ibid., p. 149. See Charles Taylor's 'The Politics of Recognition' and the various responses to his essay by Appiah, Habermas and others in A. Gutmann (ed.), *Multiculturalism and 'The Politics of Recognition'* (Princeton: Princeton University Press, 1994).

72. A. Appiah, *Cosmopolitanism: Ethics in a World of Strangers* (New York: W. W. Norton, 2006), p. 126.

73. Ibid., p. 71.

74. Ibid., pp. 72–85.

75. Ibid., p. 163.

76. M. Mandelbaum, *The Case for Goliath: How America Acts as the World's Government in the Twenty-First Century* (New York: Public Affairs, 2005).

77. S. Pollock, 'Cosmopolitan and Vernacular in History', *Public Culture*, 12:3 (2000), pp. 591–625.

78. O. Nnaemeka and J. N. Ezeile (eds), *Engendering Human Rights: Cultural and Socioeconomic Realities in Africa* (New York: Palgrave Macmillan, 2005). See especially the essays by Nawal El Saadawi (pp. 27–36), Sekai Nzena Shad (pp. 61–79), and Corinne Packer (pp. 223–47).

79. W. D. Mignolo, 'The Many Faces of Cosmo-polis: Border Thinking and Critical Cosmopolitanism', *Public Culture*, 12:3 (2000), pp. 721–48.

80. M. Hardt and A. Negri, *Empire* (London and Cambridge: MA, Harvard University Press, 2000), pp. 396–407.

81. M. Hardt and A. Negri, *Multitude: War and Democracy in the Age of Empire* (New York: Penguin Press, 2004), p. 32.

82. T. L. Dumm and M. Hardt, 'The *Theory & Event* Interview: Sovereignty, Multitudes, Absolute Democracy: A Discussion between Michael Hardt and Thomas L. Dumm about Hardt's and Negri's *Empire*', in P. A. Passavant and J. Dean (eds), *Empire's New Clothes: Reading Hardt and Negri* (New York and London: Routledge, 2004), pp. 136–74; p. 166.

83. Hardt and Negri, *Multitude*, p. 276.

84. Ibid., p. 261.

85. Ibid., pp. 330–1.

86. E. Laclau, 'Can Immanence Explain Social Struggles?', in Passavant and Dean (eds) *Empire's New Clothes* , pp. 21–30; pp. 25–8.

87. S. Žižek, 'The Ideology of the Empire and Its Traps', in Passavant and Dean (eds), *Empire's New Clothes*, pp. 253–64; p. 264.

88. Hardt and Negri, *Multitude*, pp. 330–1.

89. C. Schmitt, *Political Theology: Four Chapters on the Concept of Sovereignty*, trans. George Schwab (Cambridge, MA, and London: The MIT Press, [1922, 1934] 1985), p. 5.

90. Ibid., p. 33.

91. Ibid., pp. 53–66.

92. C. Schmitt, *Political Romanticism*, trans. G. Oakes (London and Cambridge, MA: The MIT Press [1919, 1925] 1986), p. 61.

93. Ibid., pp. 61–3.

94. Ibid., p. 109.

95. C. Schmitt, *The Crisis of Parliamentary Democracy*, trans. Ellen Kennedy (Cambridge, MA, and London: The MIT Press, [1923, 1926] 1985), p. 28.
96. Ibid., pp. 36–8.
97. Ibid., pp. 66–71.
98. Ibid., p. 16.
99. Habermas, *The Inclusion of the Other*, p. 138.
100. Ibid., pp. 134–8, 192–201.
101. E. Kennedy, 'Carl Schmitt and the Frankfurt School', *Telos*, 71 (1987), pp. 37–66; M. Jay, 'Reconciling the Irreconcilable? Rejoinder to Kennedy', *Telos*, 71 (1987), pp. 67–80.
102. Berlin, *Three Critics of the Enlightenment*, pp. 304–7.
103. Ibid., p. 296.
104. Ibid., p. 254.
105. Ibid., p. 187.
106. H. Heine, *The Romantic School and Other Essays*, ed., J. Hermand and R. C. Holub, trans. H. Mustard (New York: Continuum, 1985), p. 14.
107. Ibid., p. 21; H. Heine, *Sämtliche Werke*, ed. J. Perfahl, 4 vols (Munich: Winkler-Verlag, 1972), vol. 3, p. 280.
108. I. Berlin 'The Counter-Enlightenment', in *Dictionary of the History of Ideas*, ed. P. P. Wiener, 4 vols (New York: Scribner's Sons, 1973), vol. 2, p. 112.
109. Habermas, *Postmetaphysical Thinking*, p. 17.

2 Expanding the Public Sphere

1. J. Habermas, *The Structural Transformation of the Public Sphere: An Inquiry into a Category of Bourgeois Society*, trans. T. Burger and F. Lawrence (Cambridge, MA: The MIT Press [1962] 1989), p. 25.
2. M. McKeon, 'Parsing Habermas's "Bourgeois Public Sphere"', *Criticism*, 46:2 (2004), pp. 273–7; p. 276.
3. A. E. B. Coldiron, 'Public Sphere/Contact Zone: Habermas, Early Print, and Verse Translation', *Criticism*, 46:2 (2004), pp. 207–22, shows the centrality of cosmopolitan translations in the earliest manifestations of print culture. K. Pask, 'The Bourgeois Public Sphere and the Concept of Literature', *Criticism*, 46:2 (2004), pp. 241–56, illustrates how seventeenth-century letter-writing undergirds the representation of the intimate sphere in the bourgeois novel.
4. Habermas, *Structural Transformation*, pp. 117–40; quoted in p. 126. K. Marx, *The Eighteenth Brumaire of Louis Bonaparte* (New York: International Publishers, 1963), p. 66.
5. Habermas, *Structural Transformation*, p. 98; J.-J. Rousseau, *Du Contrat Social*, in B. Gagnegin and M. Raymond (eds), *Jean-Jacques Rousseau: Oeuvres Complètes*, 5 vols (Paris: Gallimard, 1964), vol. 3, pp. 371–2 (book 2, chapter 3).
6. I. Kant, *The Conflict of the Faculties* (*Der Streit der Fakultäten*), trans. and intro. M. J. Gregor (Lincoln and London: University of Nebraska Press, 1979), pp. 34–5.
7. Ibid., pp. 48–51.
8. Ibid., pp. 160–1.
9. Ibid., pp. 46–7.
10. I. Kant, *The Metaphysics of Morals*, trans. M. Gregor (Cambridge: Cambridge University Press, 1991), p. 36.
11. Quoted in H. Arendt, *Lectures on Kant's Political Philosophy*, ed. R. Beemer (Chicago: University of Chicago Press, 1982), p. 39.

12. I. Kant, *Critique of Judgment*, trans. W. S. Pluhar (Indianapolis and Cambridge: Hackett, 1987), p. 159.
13. Ibid., p. 160.
14. Ibid., pp. 160–1.
15. Ibid., p. 160.
16. Ibid., p. 161.
17. Ibid., p. 162.
18. Ibid., p. 162.
19. S. M. Shell, *The Rights of Reason: A Study of Kant's Philosophy and Politics* (Toronto, Buffalo and London: University of Toronto Press, 1980), p. 171.
20. I. Kant, *Groundwork for the Metaphysics of Morals*, ed. L. Denis, trans. T. K. Abbott (Toronto: Broadview Press, 2005), pp. 80–1.
21. O. O'Neill, *Constructions of Reason: Explorations of Kant's Practical Philosophy* (Cambridge: Cambridge University Press, 1989), p. 52.
22. Arendt, *Lectures on Kant's Political Philosophy*, p. 39.
23. Louden, *Kant's Impure Ethics*, p. 160.
24. Ibid., p. 169.
25. I. Kant, *Religion Within the Limits of Reason Alone*, trans. and ed. T. M. Greene and H. H. Hudson (New York: Harper Torchbooks, 1960), pp. 187–8.
26. Kant, *The Conflict of the Faculties*, pp. 10–11.
27. Ibid., p. xi.
28. P. B. Nicholson, 'Kant, Revolutions and History', in H. Williams (ed.), *Essays on Kant's Political Philosophy* (Cardiff: University of Wales Press, 1992), pp. 249–68.
29. S. Lestition, 'Kant and the End of the Enlightenment in Prussia', *Journal of Modern History*, 65:1 (1993), pp. 53–112; pp. 92–8.
30. Kant, 'On the Common Saying', p. 88.
31. Kant, *Conflict of the Faculties*, pp. 148–51.
32. Ibid., pp. 152–3.
33. J. Schmidt, 'What Enlightenment Was: How Moses Mendelssohn and Immanuel Kant Answered the *Berlinische Monatsschrift*', *Journal of the History of Philosophy*, 30:1 (1992), pp. 77–101; p. 98.
34. C. Cronin, 'Kant's Politics of Enlightenment', *Journal of the History of Philosophy*, 41:1 (2003), pp. 53–80; p. 73.
35. Schmidt, 'What Enlightenment Was', p. 95.
36. Kant, *Critique of Judgement*, pp. 196–8.
37. Cronin, 'Kant's Politics of Enlightenment', p. 80. S. Splichal, 'Bentham, Kant, and the Right to Communicate', *Critical Review*, 15 (2003), pp. 285–305; p. 297.
38. Cronin, 'Kant's Politics of Enlightenment', p. 52, n. 7.
39. An earlier version of this section on Habermas and the public sphere appeared as 'Habermas, Romanticism, and Literary Theory', *Literature Compass*, 1 RO 127 (2004), pp. 1–18.
40. For perceptive comments on the anglophonic reception of Habermas's concept of the public sphere, see K. Hirschkop, 'Justice and Drama: On Bakhtin as a Complement to Habermas', in N. Crossley and J. M. Roberts (eds), *After Habermas: New Perspectives on the Public Sphere* (Oxford: Blackwell, 2004), pp. 49–66; pp. 49–51.
41. G. Lottes, *Politische Aufklärung und plebejisches Publikum: Zur Theorie und Praxis des englischen Radikalismus im späten 18: Jahrhundert* (München: R. Oldenbourg Verlag, 1979).

42. J. Habermas, 'Further Reflections on the Public Sphere', trans. T. Burger, in *Habermas and the Public Sphere*, ed. C. Calhoun (Cambridge, MA, and London: The MIT Press, 1992), pp. 421–61; pp. 425–7.

43. Ibid., pp. 427–8.

44. That Habermas has been receptive to feminist ideas is illustrated by his favourable citing of one of his harshest feminist critics, Nancy Fraser, some of whose central ideas he fully endorses. See J. Habermas, 'Struggles for Recognition in the Democratic Constitutional State', trans. S. W. Nicholsen, in Gutmaan (ed.), *Multiculturalism*, pp. 107–48; pp. 114–16.

45. P. Hohendahl, *The Institution of Criticism* (Ithaca and London: Cornell University Press, 1982), p. 41.

46. Ibid., pp. 37, 255–9. See also N. Luhmann, *The Differentiation of Society*, trans. S. Holmes and C. Larmore (New York: Columbia University Press, 1982).

47. M. Hansen, "Foreword," O. Negt, and A. Kluge, *Public Sphere and Experience: Toward an Analysis of the Bourgeois and Proletarian Public Sphere*, trans. P. Labanyi, J. O. Daniel & A. Oksiloff (Minneapolis and London: University of Minnesota Press, 1993), pp. ix–xlii; p. xxxv.

48. O. Wang, 'Romancing the Counter-Public Sphere', *Studies in Romanticism*, 33:4 (Winter 1994), pp. 579–88.

49. K. Gilmartin, *Print Politics: The Press and Radical Opposition in Early Nineteenth-Century England* (Cambridge: Cambridge University Press, 1996); A. Janowitz, *Lyric and Labour in the Romantic Tradition* (Cambridge and New York: Cambridge University Press, 1998); P. Magnuson, *Reading Public Romanticism* (Princeton: Princeton University Press, 1998); J. Cox, *Poetry and Politics in the Cockney School: Keats, Shelley, Hunt, and Their Circle* (Cambridge and New York: Cambridge University Press, 1998); P. Keen, *The Crisis of Literature in the 1790s: Print Culture and the Public Sphere* (Cambridge: Cambridge University Press, 1999); A. McCann, *Cultural Politics in the 1790s: Literature, Radicalism and the Public Sphere* (London and New York: Macmillan Press and St. Martin's Press, 1999); M. Scrivener, *Seditious Allegories*; A. K. Mellor, *Mothers of the Nation: Women's Political Writing in England, 1780–1830* (Bloomington and Indianapolis: Indiana University Press, 2000); J. Mee, *Romanticism, Enthusiasm and Regulation: Poetics and the Policing of Culture in the Romantic Period* (Oxford: Oxford University Press, 2003); S. Makdisi, *William Blake and the Impossible History of the 1790s* (Chicago and London: University of Chicago Press, 2003); K. Binfield, *Writings of the Luddites* (Baltimore and London: Johns Hopkins University Press, 2004);, *Women, Writing and the Public Sphere* (Cambridge: Cambridge University Press, 2001); G. Russell and C. Tuite (eds), *Romantic Sociability: Social Networks and Literary Culture in Britain, 1770–1840* (Cambridge: Cambridge University Press, 2002).

50. M. Ellis, 'Coffee-Women, *The Spectator* and the Public Sphere in the Early Eighteenth Century', in Eger, Grant, O'Gallchoir, and Warburton (eds), *Women, Writing and the Public Sphere*, pp. 27–52; pp. 44–5.

51. B. Cowan, 'What Was Masculine about the Public Sphere? Gender and the Coffeehouse Milieu in Post-Restoration England', *History Workshop Journal*, 51 (2001), pp. 127–58.

52. A. Clark, *The Struggle for the Breeches: Gender and the Making of the British Working Class* (Berkeley: University of California Press, 1995), p. 35.

53. Ibid., pp. 29, 36.

54. Ibid., pp. 92–118.

55. Keen, *The Crisis of Literature in the 1790s*, p. 73.

56. W. St Clair, *The Reading Nation in the Romantic Period* (Cambridge: Cambridge University Press, 2004), pp. 13, 47, 53.
57. J. Klancher, *The Making of English Reading Audiences, 1780–1832* (Madison and London: University of Wisconsin Press, 1987), p. 23.
58. G. Claeys (ed.), *Utopias of the British Enlightenment* (Cambridge: Cambridge University Press, 1994), p. xxviii.
59. Kant, 'Idea for a Universal History', p. 51.
60. G. Claeys (ed.), *The Politics of English Jacobinism: The Writings of John Thelwall* (University Park: Pennsylvania State University Press, 1995), p. 401. An extensive discussion of Thelwall and the public sphere – but one that does not develop the centrality of cosmopolitanism – appears in Scrivener, *Seditious Allegories*.
61. I am using interchangeably 'radical', 'democratic', 'Jacobin' and 'reformist' to describe the political activities of Thelwall and the London Corresponding Society; in *Seditious Allegories* I delineate carefully the nuances of these words, especially 'Jacobin', pp. 21–42.
62. J. Thelwall, 'Introductory Narrative', *Political Lectures. Volume the First – Part the First: Containing The lecture on Spies and Informers, and The First Lecture on Prosecutions for Political* ... (London: J. Thelwall, 1795), pp. v–xviii.
63. Claeys (ed.), *The Politics of English Jacobinism*, p. 57.
64. E. P. Thompson, 'Hunting the Jacobin Fox', *Past and Present*, 142 (1994), pp. 94–140; pp. 103–4. See also Thelwall's own account in *An Appeal to Popular Opinion, Against Kidnapping and Murder; Including A Narrative of the Late Atrocious Proceedings, at Yarmouth. 2nd ed. With a Postscript; Containing A Particular Account of the Outrages, At Lynn and Wisbeach.* (London: J. S. Jordan, 1796).
65. A more extensive summary of Thelwall's career, from which this is taken, is in Scrivener, *Seditious Allegories*, pp. 3–13.
66. Scrivener, *Seditious Allegories*, pp. 115–19, and M. Scrivener, 'John Thelwall and Popular Jacobin Allegory, 1793–5', *ELH*, 67:4 (2000), pp. 951–71.
67. M. T. Davis, 'Introduction', *London Corresponding Society, 1792–1799*, ed. M. T. Davis, 6 vols (London: Pickering & Chatto, 2002), vol. 1, p. xxv.
68. For an extensive treatment of *Democracy Vindicated*, see my essay, 'John Thelwall and the Revolution of 1649', in T. Morton and N. Smith (eds), *Radicalism in British Literary Culture, 1650–1830: From Revolution to Revolution* (Cambridge: Cambridge University Press, 2002), pp. 119–32.
69. St Clair, *The Reading Nation*, pp. 66–72.
70. Claeys (ed.), *The Politics of English Jacobinism*, p. 265.
71. Godwin's qualms about the plebeian public sphere were expressed strongly in his dispute with Thelwall in 1795 (*Considerations on Lord Grenville's and Mr. Pitt's Bills* (London: Joseph Johnson, 1795). For ambivalence over popularisation among the British romantics, see A. W. Cafarelli, 'The Common Reader: Social Class in Romantic Poetics', *Journal of English and Germanic Philology*, 96 (1997), pp. 222–46.
72. Thelwall, *Political Lectures. Volume the First – Part the First*, p. 69.
73. Claeys (ed.), *The Politics of English Jacobinism*, p. 219.
74. M. Scrivener, 'Literature and Politics', in T. Keymer and J. Mee (eds), *The Cambridge Companion to English Literature 1740–1830* (Cambridge: Cambridge University Press, 2004), pp. 43–60; p. 51.
75. Claeys (ed.), *The Politics of Jacobinism*, p. 221.
76. *Analytical Review*, 25 (January 1797), p. 1.
77. Davis (ed.), *London Corresponding Society*, vol. 4, pp. 65–6.

78. Claeys (ed.), *The Politics of English Jacobinism*, p. 376.
79. Ibid., p. 400.
80. Ibid., p. 318.
81. Ibid., p. 125.
82. Ibid., p. 199.
83. J. Thelwall, *Political Lectures. Volume the First – Part the First*, pp. 8–9.
84. Claeys (ed.), *The Politics of English Jacobinism*, p. 92.
85. J. Mee, *Dangerous Enthusiasm: William Blake and the Culture of Radicalism in the 1790s* (Oxford: Clarendon Press, 1992), and *Romanticism, Enthusiasm, and Regulation*.
86. Claeys (ed.), *The Politics of English Jacobinism*, pp. 104–5.
87. Ibid., p. 107.
88. I. McCalman, 'Preface', in P. A. Pickering and A. Tyrrell (eds), *Contested Sites: Commemoration, Memorial and Popular Politics in Nineteenth-Century Britain* (Aldershot: Ashgate, 2004), p. xv. See also P. A. Pickering and A. Tyrrell, 'The Public Memorial of Reform: Commemoration and Contestation', pp. 1–24, A. Tyrrell with M. T. Davis, 'Bearding the Tories: The Commemoration of the Scottish Political Martyrs of 1793–4', pp. 25–56, and P. A. Pickering, 'A "Grand Ossification": William Cobbett and the Commemoration of Tom Paine', pp. 57–80, in the same collection.
89. St Clair, *The Reading Nation*, pp. 312–38.
90. Davis, 'Introduction', *London Corresponding Society*, vol. 1, p. xxxvii.
91. St Clair, *The Reading Nation*, p. 333.
92. H. T. Dickinson, *Liberty and Property: Political Ideology in Eighteenth-Century Britain* (New York: Holmes & Meier, 1977), p. 239.
93. L. Colley, *Britons: Forging a Nation 1707–1837* (New Haven and London: Yale University Press, 1992).
94. D. Simpson, *Romanticism, Nationalism, and the Revolt Against Theory* (Chicago and London: University of Chicago Press, 1993).
95. J. R. Dinwiddy, *Radicalism and Reform in Britain, 1780–1850* (London: Hambledon Press, 1992), pp. 169–94.
96. William St Clair disputes the much higher figures for Paine's pamphlet given in R. D. Altick's *The English Common Reader: A Social History of the Mass Reading Public, 1800–1900* (Chicago and London: University of Chicago Press, 1957), pp. 72–3. St Clair, *The Reading Nation*, pp. 623–4.
97. D. Roper, *Reviewing Before the 'Edinburgh'* (Newark: University of Delaware Press, 1978), pp. 36–47.
98. Klancher, *The Making of the English Reading Audiences*, pp. 59–73.
99. Roper, *Reviewing Before the 'Edinburgh'*, p. 37.
100. Keen, *The Crisis of Literature in the 1790s*, pp. 108–19.
101. Roper, *Reviewing Before the 'Edinburgh'*, p. 38.
102. *Analytical Review*, 22 (December 1795), pp. 586–9.
103. *Analytical Review*, 14 (October 1792), pp. 204–7.
104. *Analytical Review*, 26 (August 1797), pp. 196–202.
105. H. Braithwaite, *Romanticism, Publishing and Dissent: Joseph Johnson and the Cause of Liberty* (Basingstoke and New York: Palgrave Macmillan, 2003), pp. 86–9.
106. *Analytical Review*, 16 (June 1793), pp. 222–230; *Analytical Review*, 22 (December 1795), p. 589.
107. *Analytical Review*, 1 (May 1788), p. iii.
108. *British Critic*, 1 (May 1793), p. 2.

109. *Analytical Review*, 1 (May 1788), p. iv.

110. Roper, *Reviewing Before the 'Edinburgh'*, pp. 42–3.

111. *Analytical Review*, 27 (March 1798), pp. 327–30.

112. *Analytical Review*, 27 (January 1798), p. 1.

113. The motto for the *Analytical* is a quotation in Latin from Francis Bacon's *Advancement of Learning*, the main point of which is to contrast factual narration with private judgment.

114. *Analytical Review*, 15 (May 1793), pp. 19–23.

115. *Analytical Review*, 14 (December 1792), pp. 519–21.

116. *Analytical Review*, 26 (July 1797), pp. 85–6.

117. G. Micheli, 'The Early Reception of Kant's Thought in England 1785–1805', in G. M. Ross and T. McWalter (eds), *Kant and His Influence* (Bristol: Thoemmes, 1990), pp. 273–80.

118. *Analytical Review*, 22 (December 1795), pp. 605–8.

119. M. Butler (ed.), *Burke, Paine, Godwin, and the Revolution Controversy* (Cambridge: Cambridge University Press, 1984), p. 220.

120. Braithwaite, *Romanticism, Publishing and Dissent*, pp. 155–81.

121. S. M. Colclough, 'Procuring Books and Consuming Texts: The Reading Experience of a Sheffield Apprentice, 1798', *Book History*, 3 (2000), pp. 21–44; p. 33.

122. *Analytical Review*, 12 (March 1792), pp. 287–304.

123. *Analytical Review*, 14 (November 1792), pp. 319–24.

124. *Analytical Review*, 15 (February 1793), pp. 185–9.

125. On the counter-discourses and radical theatricality of the political trials of the 1790s, see M. T. Davis, 'Prosecution and Radical Discourse during the 1790s: The Case of the Scottish Sedition Trials', *International Journal of the Sociology of Law*, 98 (2005), pp. 1–11. On the John Frost trial, see J. Barrell, 'Coffee-House Politicians', *Journal of British Studies*, 43 (2004), pp. 206–32.

126. *Analytical Review*, 13 (June 1792), pp. 193–7.

127. *Analytical Review*, 22 (December 1795), pp. 650–2.

128. *Analytical Review*, 25 (January 1797), pp. 86–7.

129. *Analytical Review*, 26 (August 1797), pp. 177–8.

130. Keen, *The Crisis of Literature in the 1790s*, pp. 238–45.

3 Women and Justice

1. S. H. Myers, *The Bluestocking Circle: Women, Friendship, and the Life the Mind in Eighteenth-Century England* (Oxford: Clarendon Press, 1990), p. 121.

2. H. Guest, *Small Change: Women, Learning, Patriotism, 1750–1810* (Chicago and London: University of Chicago Press, 2000), p. 155.

3. B. Taylor, *Eve and the New Jerusalem: Socialism and Feminism in the Nineteenth Century* (New York: Pantheon Books, 1983).

4. A. K. Mellor, 'Mary Wollstonecraft's *A Vindication of the Rights of Woman* and the Women Writers of Her Day', in C. L. Johnson (ed.), *The Cambridge Companion to Mary Wollstonecraft* (Cambridge: Cambridge University Press, 2002), pp. 141–59; p. 145.

5. V. Sapiro, *A Vindication of Political Virtue: The Political Theory of Mary Wollstonecraft* (Chicago and London: Univeristy of Chicago Press, 1992), pp. 278–9.

6. An earlier version of this section on the scene of justice appeared as 'Trials in Romantic-Era Writing: Modernity, Guilt, and the Scene of Justice', *Wordsworth Circle*, 35:3 (2004), pp. 128–33.

7. J. H. Wiener, *Radicalism and Freethought in Nineteenth-Century Britain: The Life of Richard Carlile* (Westport, CT: Greenwood Press, 1983); Scrivener, *Seditious Allegories*, pp. 146–66.

8. J. Epstein, *Radical Expression: Political Language, Ritual, and Symbol in England, 1790–1850* (Oxford and New York: Oxford University Press, 1994).

9. M. Foucault, *Discipline and Punish: The Birth of the Prison*, trans. A. Sheridan (New York: Pantheon Books, [1975] 1977), pp. 3–7.

10. E. Halevy, *The Growth of Philosophic Radicalism*, trans. M. Morris (Boston: Beacon Press, 1955), pp. 35–74.

11. Habermas, *Between Facts and Norms*; S. Critchley, *The Ethics of Deconstruction: Derrida and Levinas*, 2nd edn (East Lafayette: Purdue University Press, 1999).

12. Habermas, *The Theory of Communicative Action*; Habermas, *Between Facts and Norms*; Habermas, 'Modernity: An Unfinished Project', trans. N. Walker, in *Habermas and the Unfinished Project of Modernity: Critical Essays on 'The Philosophical Discourse of Modernity'*, ed. M. P. d'Entrèves and S. Benhabib (Cambridge, MA, and London: The MIT Press, 1997), pp. 38–55.

13. W. Blackstone, *Commentaries on the Laws of England*, 3rd edn, ed. T. M. Cooley, 2 vols (Chicago: Callaghan, 1884), vol. 2, p. 379

14. J. Langbein, 'The English Criminal Trial Jury in the Eve of the French Revolution', in *The Trial Jury in England, France, Germany 1700–1900*, ed. A. P. Schioppa (Berlin: Duncker and Humblot, 1987), pp. 13–39; P. J. R. King, '"Illiterate Plebeians, Easily Misled": Jury Composition, Experience, and Behavior in Essex, 1735–1815', in *Twelve Good Men and True: The Criminal Trial Jury in England, 1200–1800*, ed. J. S. Cockburn and T. A. Green (Princeton: Princeton University Press, 1988), pp. 254–304; D. Hay, 'The Class Composition of the Palladium of Liberty: Trial Jurors in the Eighteenth Century', in *Twelve Good Men and True*, pp. 305–57.

15. *Shelley's Poetry and Prose*, ed. D. H. Reiman and N. Fraistat (New York: W. W. Norton, 2002), p. 516.

16. M. C. Nussbaum, *Poetic Justice: The Literary Imagination and Public Life* (Boston: Beacon Press, 1995), p. 72.

17. W. Godwin, *Enquiry Concerning Political Justice*, ed. F. E. L. Priestley, 3 vols (Toronto: University of Toronto Press, 1946), vol. 2, pp. 210–12.

18. *The Complete Works of Percy Bysshe Shelley*, ed. R. Ingpen and W. E. Peck, 10 vols (New York: Gordian Press, 1965), vol. 6, p. 291.

19. Scrivener, *Seditious Allegories*, pp. 188–9.

20. T. Vargish, *The Providential Aesthetic in Victorian Fiction* (Charlottesville: University Press of Virginia, 1985), pp. 163–243.

21. B. Beiderwell, *Power and Punishment in Scott's Novels* (Athens: University of Georgia Press, 1992), p. 77.

22. W. Scott, *The Heart of Midlothian*, ed. John Henry Raleigh (Boston: Houghton Mifflin, [1818] 1966), pp. 356–67.

23. Beiderwell, *Power and Punishment in Scott's Novels*, p. 80.

24. Scott, *The Heart of Midlothian*, p. 340.

25. W. Scott, *Ivanhoe*, ed. A. N. Wilson (Harmondsworth: Penguin Books, [1819] 1982), p. 506.

26. Scott, *Ivanhoe*, p. 445.
27. Keen, *Crisis of Literature in the 1790s*, p. 29. Halevy, *The Growth of Philosophic Radicalism*, pp. 15, 97.
28. W. Godwin, *Caleb Williams*, ed. G. Handwerk and A. A. Markley (Peterborough, ON: Broadview Press, [1794] 2000), p. 207.
29. Godwin, *Caleb Williams*, p. 427.
30. V. Myers, 'William Godwin and the *Ars Rhetorica*', *Studies in Romanticism*, 41 (2002), p. 416.
31. P. Brooks, *Troubling Confessions* (Chicago and London: University of Chicago Press, 2000).
32. J. Rieger, 'Shelley's Paterin Beatrice', *Studies in Romanticism*, 4 (1965), pp. 169–84.
33. S. Curran, *Shelley's Cenci: Scorpions Ringed with Fire* (Princeton: Princeton University Press, 1970), pp. 129–31.
34. *The Letters of Percy Bysshe Shelley*, ed. F. L. Jones, 2 vols (Oxford: Clarendon Press, 1964), vol. 2, p. 167; *Shelley's Poetry and Prose*, p. 166.
35. A. Moore, *The Annals of Gallantry; or, The Conjugal Monitor*, 3 vols (London: M. Jones, 1814), vol. 1, pp. 139–51.
36. M. Wollstonecraft, *The Wrongs of Woman; or, Maria. A Fragment*, in *The Works of Mary Wollstonecraft*, ed. J. Todd and M. Butler, 7 vols (London: Pickering & Chatto, 1989), vol. 1, pp. 180–1.
37. *Collected Letters of Mary Wollstonecraft*, ed. R. Wardle (Ithaca and London: Cornell University Press, 1979), pp. 391–2.
38. Wollstonecraft, *The Wrongs of Woman*, p. 157.
39. Ibid., p. 152.
40. R. Phillips, *Putting Asunder: A History of Divorce in Western Society* (Cambridge: Cambridge University Press, 1988), pp. 175–90.
41. M. Wollstonecraft, *The Vindications: The Rights of Men. The Rights of Woman*, ed. D. L. Macdonald and K. Scherf (Peterborough, ON: Broadview Press, 1997), p. 341.
42. Godwin, *Enquiry Concerning Political Justice*, vol. 3, p. 221.
43. Ibid., vol. 2, pp. 506–11.
44. Wollstonecraft, *The Wrongs of Woman*, p. 184.
45. M. Wollstonecraft, *On Poetry; Contributions to the 'Analytical Review', 1788–1797*, in *The Works of Mary Wollstonecraft*, ed. Todd and Butler, vol. 7, p. 314.
46. J-J. Rousseau, *Émile*, trans. B. Foxley (London and Vermont: J. M. Dent and C. E. Tuttle, 1993), p. 385;, *Rousseau: Oeuvres Completes*, ed. B. Gagnebin and M. Raymond, 5 vols (Paris: Gallimard, 1980), vol. 4, pp. 693–4.
47. Rousseau, *Émile*, p. 386; *Rousseau: Oeuvres Completes*, vol. 4, p. 695.
48. Rousseau, *Émile*, p. 388; *Rousseau: Oeuvres Completes*, vol. 4, p. 697.
49. Rousseau, *Émile*, p. 399; *Rousseau: Oeuvres Completes*, vol. 4, pp. 710–11.
50. Rousseau, *Émile*, pp. 400–1; *Rousseau: Oeuvres Completes*, vol. 4, p. 711.
51. E. Cassirer, *Kant's Life and Thought*, trans. J. Haden (New Haven and London: Yale University Press, [1918] 1981), pp. 86–7.
52. Rousseau, *Émile*, p. 287; *Rousseau: Oeuvres Completes*, vol. 4, p. 581.
53. Rousseau, *Émile*, p. 301; *Rousseau: Oeuvres Completes*, vol. 4, p. 598.
54. Rousseau, *Émile*, p. 324; *Rousseau: Oeuvres Completes*, vol. 4, p. 625.
55. Rousseau, *Émile*, p. 11; *Rousseau: Oeuvres Completes*, vol. 4, p. 253.
56. Rousseau, *Émile*, pp. 36–43; *Rousseau: Oeuvres Completes*, vol. 4, pp. 284–93.
57. Rousseau, *Émile*, p. 262; *Rousseau: Oeuvres Completes*, vol. 4, p. 552.

58. Rousseau, *Émile*, p. 12; *Rousseau: Oeuvres Completes*, vol. 4, p. 255.
59. Rousseau, *Émile*, p. 64; *Rousseau: Oeuvres Completes*, vol. 4, p. 319.
60. Rousseau, *Émile*, p. 66; *Rousseau: Oeuvres Completes*, vol. 4, p. 321.
61. Rousseau, *Émile*, p. 87; *Rousseau: Oeuvres Completes*, vol. 4, p. 348.
62. Rousseau, *Émile*, p. 197; *Rousseau: Oeuvres Completes*, vol. 4, p. 480.
63. Rousseau, *Émile*, pp. 218–23; *Rousseau: Oeuvres Completes*, vol. 4, pp. 503–9.
64. Rousseau, *Émile*, p. 267; *Rousseau: Oeuvres Completes*, vol. 4, p. 558.
65. Rousseau, *Émile*, p. 407; *Rousseau: Oeuvres Completes*, vol. 4, p. 721.
66. *Analytical Review*, 2 (October 1788), p. 225.
67. *Analytical Review*, 4 (June 1789), p. 360.
68. Wollstonecraft, *The Vindications*, pp. 49, 59.
69. Ibid., pp. 127, 133, 151.
70. E. Burke, *A Letter to John Farr and John Harris, Esquires, Sheriffs of the City of Bristol, On the Affairs of America* (1777) in *The Works of the Right Honorable Edmund Burke*, 3rd edn, 12 vols (Boston: Little Brown, 1869), vol. 2, pp. 188–245.
71. R. Price, *Two Tracts* (1778), in *Richard Price: Political Writings*, ed. D. O. Thomas (Cambridge: Cambridge University Press, 1991), pp. 14–100.
72. R. Price, *A Discourse on the Love of Our Country* (1789), in *Richard Price: Political Writings*, p. 180.
73. Ibid., p. 178.
74. Ibid., p. 181.
75. Ibid., p. 178.
76. Ibid., p. 179.
77. Ibid., p. 178.
78. Wollstonecraft, *The Vindications*, p. 33.
79. Ibid. pp. 80–3.
80. Ibid., p. 79.
81. T. Moi, *What Is A Woman? And Other Essays* (Oxford: Oxford University Press, 1999), p. 46.
82. Wollstonecraft, *The Vindications*, p. 42.
83. Ibid., p. 43.
84. Ibid., p. 78.
85. Ibid., p. 38, 66, 92–4.
86. Ibid., pp. 88–9.
87. P. N. Miller (ed.), *Joseph Priestley: Political Writings* (Cambridge: Cambridge University Press, 1993), p. 6; *Richard Price: Political Writings*, pp. 77, 111, 152–75.
88. Wollstonecraft, *The Vindications*, p. 92.
89. Ibid., pp. 42–7 (game laws), 53 (primogeniture), 94 (land reform).
90. Ibid., pp. 42, 44.
91. Ibid., p. 47.
92. M. Ferguson, 'Mary Wollstonecraft and the Problematic of Slavery', in M. J. Falco (ed.), *Feminist Interpretations of Mary Wollstonecraft* (University Park, PA: Pennsylvania State University Press, 1996), pp. 125–49.
93. Wollstonecraft, *The Vindications*, p. 330.
94. Ibid., p. 333.
95. Ibid., p. 163.
96. Ibid., p. 158.
97. Ibid., pp. 101–5.

98. D. V. Erdman, *Commerce des Lumières: John Oswald and the British in Paris, 1790–1793* (Columbia, MO: University of Missouri Press, 1986).

99. Mellor, 'Mary Wollstonecraft's *A Vindication of the Rights of Woman* and the Women Writers of Her Day', p. 147.

100. A. K. Mellor, *Mothers of the Nation: Women's Political Writing in England, 1780–1830* (Bloomington and Indianapolis: Indiana University Press, 2000), pp. 13–38.

101. M. Myers, '"Reform or Ruin": A Revolution in Female Manners', *Studies in Eighteenth-Century Culture*, 11 (1982), pp. 199–216; Guest, *Small Change*, pp. 271–89.

102. Wollstonecraft, *The Vindications*, p. 275.

103. S. J. Wolfson, 'Mary Wollstonecraft and the Poets', in C. L. Johnson (ed.), *The Cambridge Companion to Mary Wollstonecraft* (Cambridge: Cambridge University Press, 2002), p. 160.

104. Wolfson, 'Mary Wollstonecraft and the Poets', pp. 170–1.

105. Wollstonecraft, *The Vindications*, p. 200.

106. Ibid., p. 135.

107. M. Hays, *Appeal to the Men of Great Britain in Behalf of Women*, ed. G. Luria (New York and London: Garland, 1974), pp. 4–5.

108. Wollstonecraft, *The Vindications*, pp. 131–2.

109. Ibid., pp. 173–4.

110. M. Robinson, *Letter to the Women of England on the Injustice of Mental Subordination* (Oxford: Woodstock Books, [1799] 1998), pp. 17–18, 74.

111. Wollstonecraft, *The Vindications*, p. 144.

112. Ibid., p. 175.

113. Ibid., pp. 190–1.

114. M. Hays, *The Victim of Prejudice*, ed. E. Ty (Peterborough, ON: Broadview Press, 1994).

115. Wollstonecraft, *The Vindications*, p. 267.

116. Ibid., p. 223.

117. J. Austen, *Northanger Abbey*, ed. S. Fraiman (New York and London: W. W. Norton, 2004), p. 76.

118. Wollstonecraft, *The Vindications*, p. 147.

119. Ibid., p. 174.

120. Ibid., p. 242.

121. Ibid., p. 157.

122. C. Kaplan, 'Wild Nights: pleasure/sexuality/feminism', in N. Armstrong and L. Tennenhouse (eds), *The Ideology of Conduct: Essays in Literature and the History of Sexuality* (London: Methuen, 1987), pp. 160–84.

123. Wollstonecraft, *The Vindications*, p. 172.

124. Ibid., pp. 137–8.

125. Ibid., pp. 149, 153, 155, 179, 208, 306.

4 Writing Against Slavery, Race and Empire

1. P. J. Kitson, 'Introduction', P. J. Kitson and D. Lee (gen. eds), *Slavery, Abolition and Emancipation: Writings in the British Romantic Period*, 8 vols (London: Pickering & Chatto, 1999), vol. 2: 'Debate on the Abolition of the Slave Trade', ed. P. J. Kitson, p. xi.

2. E. Williams, *Capitalism & Slavery* (Chapel Hill, NC: University of North Carolina Press, 1944); W. Rodney, *How Europe Underdeveloped Africa* (Washington, D. C.: Howard University Press, 1981).

3. R. W. Fogel and S. L. Engerman, *Time on the Cross: The Economics of American Negro Slavery* (Boston: Little, Brown, 1974).

4. D. B. Davis, *Slavery and Human Progress* (New York and Oxford: Oxford University Press, 1984), pp. xv–xvi.

5. Davis, *Slavery and Human Progress*, p. 107.

6. Kitson, 'Introduction', *Slavery, Abolition and Emancipation*, vol. 2, p. xiii; Davis, *Slavery and Human Progress*, p. 108.

7. Davis, *Slavery and Human Progress*, p. 131.

8. Ibid., pp. 178, 200.

9. Kitson, 'Introduction', *Slavery, Abolition and Emancipation*, vol. 2, pp. xxiv–xxv.

10. J. Walvin, 'Abolishing the Slave Trade: Anti-Slavery and Popular Radicalism, 1776–1807', in C. Emsley and J. Walvin (eds), *Artisans, Peasants and Proletarians, 1760–1860* (London: Croom Helm, 1985), pp. 32–56; p. 50; Kitson, 'Introduction', *Slavery, Abolition and Emancipation*, vol. 2, p. xix; Davis, *Slavery and Human Progress*, p. 169.

11. Kitson, 'Introduction', *Slavery, Abolition and Emancipation*, vol. 2, p. x.

12. W. D. Jordan, *White Over Black: American Attitudes Toward the Negro, 1550–1812* (Chapel Hill, NC: University of North Carolina Press, 1968).

13. Davis, *Slavery and Human Progress*, p. 148.

14. Walvin, 'Abolishing the Slave Trade', pp. 32–56.

15. Colley, *Britons: Forging the Nation*, pp. 101–5.

16. *Analytical Review*, 1 (June 1788), p. 145.

17. Davis, *Slavery and Human Progress*, pp. xvi–xvii.

18. S. R. Wells, *How To Read Character: A New Illustrated Hand-Book of Phrenology and Physiognomy, For Students and Examiners; With a Descriptive Chart* (New York: Samuel R. Wells, 1872).

19. P. J. Kitson, 'Introduction', *Slavery, Abolition and Emancipation*, vol. 8: 'Theories of Race', ed. P. J. Kitson, p. xvii

20. J. F. Blumenbach, *On the Natural Varieties of Mankind* [*De Generis Humani Varietate Nativa*], trans. and ed. T. Bendyshe (New York: Bergman Publishers, [1865] 1969), pp. 264–9.

21. Blumenbach, *On the Natural Varieties of Mankind*, pp. 305–12.

22. Ibid., p. 307.

23. S. J. Gould, *The Mismeasure of Man*, rev. edn (New York and London: W. W. Norton, 1996), pp. 401–12.

24. Ibid., p. 412.

25. R. T. Gray, *About Face: German Physiognomic Thought from Lavater to Auschwitz* (Detroit: Wayne State University Press, 2004), p. 109.

26. *Analytical Review*, 24 (July 1796), pp. 1–5.

27. L. F. Chard, III, 'Joseph Johnson in the 1790s', *Wordsworth Circle* 33:3 (2002), pp. 95–100; p. 100, n.7; Braithwaite, *Romanticism, Publishing and Dissent*, p. 94.

28. E. Shookman, 'Pseudo-Science, Social Fad, Literary Wonder: Johann Caspar Lavater and the Art of Physiognomy', in E. Shookman (ed.), *The Faces of Physiognomy: Interdisciplinary Approaches to Johann Caspar Lavater* (Columbia, SC: Camden House, 1993), pp. 1–24; p. 4.

29. *Analytical Review*, 5 (October 1789), pp. 454–63.

30. Gould, *The Mismeasure of Man*, p. 54.
31. *Analytical Review*, 11 (December 1791), p. 375.
32. Gray, *About Face*, p. xlviii.
33. Ibid., p. 30.
34. Eze (ed.), *Race and the Enlightenment*, p. 105.
35. *Analytical Review*, 1 (July 1788), p. 286.
36. Kitson and Lee (gen. eds), *Slavery, Abolition and Emancipation*, vol. 8, p. 41.
37. *Analytical Review*, 2 (December 1788), p. 432.
38. Kitson and Lee (gen. eds), *Slavery, Abolition and Emancipation*, vol. 8, p. 67.
39. Ibid., vol. 8, p. 68.
40. *Analytical Review*, 2 (December 1788), p. 431.
41. *Analytical Review*, 4 (June 1789), p. 139.
42. *Analytical Review*, 25 (May 1797), pp. 464–75.
43. Ibid., p. 474.
44. *Analytical Review*, 24 (September 1796), pp. 225–37.
45. *Analytical Review*, 25 (March 1797), pp. 266–9.
46. *Analytical Review*, 1 (June 1788), p. 221.
47. *Analytical Review*, 4 (July 1789), pp. 77–81.
48. *Analytical Review*, 28 (September 1798), p. 230.
49. *Analytical Review*, 28 (July 1798), pp. 1–5.
50. *Analytical Review*, 2 (November 1788), pp. 376–7.
51. *Analytical Review*, 3 (February 1789), pp. 176–83.
52. *Analytical Review*, 10 (August 1791), p. 491.
53. For the German translations, see A. Esterhammer, 'Continental Literature, Translation, and the Johnson Circle', *Wordsworth Circle*, 33:3 (2002), pp. 101–4; for the French translations, see Braithwaite, *Romanticism, Publishing and Dissent*, pp. 93–4.
54. *Analytical Review*, 15 (January 1793), pp. 1–16.
55. W. Benjamin, 'The Task of the Translator', trans. H. Zohn, in M. Bullock and M. N. Jennings (eds), *Walter Benjamin: Selected Writings*, 4 vols (Cambridge, MA, and London: Belknap Press of Harvard University Press, 1996), vol. 1, pp. 253–63; p. 256.
56. Benjamin, 'The Task of the Translator', p. 254.
57. Ibid., p. 255.
58. H. G. Gadamer, *Truth and Method*, trans. G. Barden and J. Cumming (New York: Crossroad, [1965] 1982), p. 346.
59. Benjamin, 'The Task of the Translator', p. 261.
60. Ibid., p. 260.
61. *Analytical Review*, 26 (July 1797), pp. 26–8.
62. *Analytical Review*, 7 (August 1790), pp. 271–6.
63. *Analytical Review*, 4 (May 1789), pp. 23–7.
64. Ibid., p. 27.
65. Ibid., p. 28.
66. *Monthly Review*, 80 (June 1789), p. 551.
67. H. L. Gates, Jr, *The Signifying Monkey: A Theory of African-American Literary Criticism* (Oxford and New York: Oxford University Press, 1988), pp.127–69.
68. S. Aravamudan, *Tropicopolitans: Colonialism and Agency, 1688–1804* (Durham, NC and London: Duke University Press, 1999), pp. 233–88.
69. O. Equiano, *The Interesting Narrative of the Life of Olaudah Equiano*, ed. A. Costanzo (Peterborough, ON: Broadview Press, 2001), pp. 264–5.

70. O. Equiano, *Olaudah Equiano: The Interesting Narrative and Other Writings*, ed. V. Carretta (Harmondsworth: Penguin Books, 1995), p. 347; Equiano, *The Interesting Narrative*, ed. Costanzo, pp. 255–6.

71. J. Bugg, 'The Other Interesting Narrative: Olaudah Equiano's Public Book Tour', *PMLA*, 121:5 (October 2006), pp. 1424–42; p. 1426; Walvin, 'Abolishing the Slave Trade', p. 46.

72. Equiano, *Olaudah Equiano*, ed. Carretta, p. 346; Walvin, 'Abolishing the Slave Trade', p. 50. Cf. S. Aravamudan who characterizes Equiano's connection with the London Corresponding Society as a 'flirtation': *Tropicopolitans*, p. 268.

73. Equiano, *Olaudah Equiano*, ed. Carretta, p. 347.

74. Ibid., p. xxix; Bugg, 'The Other Interesting Narrative', p. 1438.

75. V. Carretta, 'Olaudah Equiano or Gustavus Vassa?: New Light on an Eighteenth-Century Question of Identity', *Slavery and Abolition. A Journal of Slave and Post-Slave Societies*, 20:3 (1999), pp. 96–105.

76. R. Pudaloff, 'No Change Without Purchase: Olaudah Equiano and the Economies of Self and Market', *Early American Literature*, 40:3 (2005), pp. 499–527; p. 503.

77. P. Youngquist, 'The Afro-Futurism of DJ Vassa', *European Romantic Review*, 16:2 (2005), pp. 181–92.

78. S. Marren, 'Between Slavery and Freedom: The Transgressive Self in Olaudah Equiano's Autobiography', *PMLA*, 108:1 (1993), pp. 94–105.

79. Pudaloff, 'No Change Without Purchase', p. 501.

80. Ibid., pp. 517–18.

81. H. Baker, Jr., *Blues, Ideology, and Afro-American Literature: A Vernacular Theory* (Chicago: University of Chicago Press, 1987), p. 36.

82. Bugg, 'The Other Interesting Narrative', p. 1425.

83. Monod's analysis is in a long footnote in Pudaloff, 'No Change Without Purchase', p. 522, n. 11.

84. Pudaloff, 'No Change Without Purchase', p. 504.

85. Equiano, *The Interesting Narrative*, ed. Costanzo, pp. 39–40. For a reading of the frontispiece similar to mine, see V. Carretta (ed.), *Unchained Voices: An Anthology of Black Authors in the English-Speaking World of the 18th Century* (Lexington: University Press of Kentucky, 1996), pp. 9–10. Some readers have found Equiano's Christianity to be form of colonial self-hatred or 'complete assimilation': S. Aravamudan, *Tropicopolitans*, p. 236.

86. Equiano, *The Interesting Narrative*, ed. Costanzo, pp. 41–2.

87. Kitson, 'Introduction', *Slavery, Abolition and Emancipation*, vol. 2, p. xvii.

88. Equiano, *Olaudah Equiano*, ed. Carretta, pp. 5–14.

89. Equiano, *The Interesting Narrative*, ed, Costanzo, pp. 45–60.

90. Ibid., p. 71.

91. Ibid., p. 73.

92. Ibid., pp. 75–6.

93. Baker, Jr., *Blues, Ideology, and Afro-American Literature*, p. 37.

94. Equiano, *The Interesting Narrative*, ed. Costanzo, pp. 165–6.

95. Ibid., pp. 168–75.

96. Ibid., p. 169.

97. Cf. Aravamudan, *Tropicopolitans*, p. 250, for Equiano and *Robinson Crusoe*. My reading of Equiano finds more ironic treatment of Defoe than does Aravamudan.

98. Equiano, *The Interesting Narrative*, ed. Costanzo, p. 92.

99. Ibid., p. 107.

100. Ibid., p. 109.

101. Ibid., pp. 114–15.

102. Ibid., p. 144–5.

103. Ibid., p. 137.

104. Ibid., p. 197.

105. Ibid., p. 220.

106. Ibid., p. 228.

107. For the texts of both plays along with introductory material and commentary, see J. Thelwall, *Incle and Yarico and The Incas: Two Plays by John Thelwall*, ed. F. Felsenstein and M. Scrivener (Madison and Teaneck, NJ: Fairleigh Dickinson University Press, 2006). For additional commentary on *The Incas*, see M. Scrivener, *Seditious Allegories*, pp. 235–40.

108. For a reading of Raynal in relation to colonialism and revolutionary politics, see S. Aravamudan, *Tropicopolitans*, pp. 289–325.

109. F. Felsenstein (ed.), *English Trader, Indian Maid: Representing Gender, Race, and Slaver in the New World: A Inkle and Yarico Reader* (Baltimore and London: Johns Hopkins University Press, 1999), pp. 82–8.

110. Felsenstein (ed.), *English Trader, Indian Maid*, p. 88.

111. M. Wollstonecraft, *The Female Reader*, in *The Works of Mary Wollstonecraft*, ed. Todd and Butler, vol. 4, pp. 97–9.

112. Felsenstein (ed.), *English Trader, Indian Maid*, p. 7.

113. Thelwall, *Incle and Yarico and The Incas*, p. 70.

114. Ibid., p. 52.

115. Ibid., p. 34.

116. Felsenstein notes the centrality of cannibalism in representations of the Amerindians, *English Trader, Indian Maid*, pp. 4–5.

117. Ibid., p. 15.

118. Thelwall, *Incle and Yarico and The Incas*, p. 63.

119. Ibid., p. 60.

120. Ibid., p. 55.

121. Ibid., p. 64.

122. A recent (May 2005) issue of the online journal *Praxis*, 'Opera and Romanticism', edited by Gillen D'Arcy Wood (www.rc.umd.edu/praxis/opera/index.html) points to a new interest in romantic-era opera. These five excellent essays contain up-to-date source material.

123. On the rebellion of the natives from the south Andes in 1780–1, see O. Cornblitt, *Power and Violence in the Colonial City: Oruro from the Mining Renaissance to the Rebellion of Tupac Amaru (1740–1782)*, trans. E. L. Glick (Cambridge: Cambridge University Press, 1975).

124. Felsenstein (ed.), *English Trader, Indian Maid*, pp. 167–233.

125. Thelwall, *Incle and Yarico and The Incas*, pp. 107–8.

126. Ibid., p. 97.

127. Ibid., p. 134.

128. Ibid., p. 106.

129. Ibid., p. 124.

130. Ibid., pp. 140–1.

131. R. Cole Heinowitz of Bard College asked me this very question at the NASSR convention in August, 2006, Purdue University, after I delivered a paper on Thelwall's two plays.

132. Godwin, *Enquiry Concerning Political Justice*, vol. 1, pp. 126–7.

133. There are at least two different 1801 editions, the four-volume London edition published by the radical publisher Richard Phillips and the two-volume Dublin edition. I quoted from the London edition in *Seditious Allegories*, pp. 240–4, but I am quoting here from the Dublin edition. I have not been able to study the two editions for textual variants but according to Jasmine Solomonescu (Cambridge University; personal communication) the Dublin edition is probably pirated. The extraordinary difficulty of getting access to any copy of the novel necessitates my using a text that is not ideal. It goes without saying that a modern edition with thorough research of the textual variants is necessary. Meanwhile, the edition cited in this book is the following: *The Daughter of Adoption; A Tale of Modern Times*, 2 vols (Dublin: N. Kelly, 1801).

134. G. Kelly, *The English Jacobin Novel 1780–1805* (Oxford and New York: Clarendon Press, 1976).

135. J. Thelwall, *Poems, Chiefly Written in Retirement*, 2nd edn (Hereford: W. H. Parker, 1801, rpt. Oxford: Woodstock Books, 1989,), pp. xlv–xlvi. Wollstonecraft complained to William Roscoe that *Vindication of the Rights of Woman*, which was rushed, could have been a better book if she had had more time (*Collected Letters of Mary Wollstonecraft*, p. 205). Charlotte Smith's prolific literary production, especially of novels, was notoriously dictated by her economic necessity as a single mother of twelve children. See her complaints about her material circumstances in the prefaces to her poetry, *Elegiac Sonnets and Other Poems* (London: Jones & Company, 1827).

136. *Analytical Review*, 26 (August 1797), pp. 112–5.

137. C. L. R. James, *The Black Jacobins: Toussaint L'Ouverture and the San Domingo Revolution*, 2nd edn (New York: Vintage, [1938] 1963), ch. 9.

138. James, *The Black Jacobins*, ch. 11.

139. Davis, 'Introduction', *London Corresponding Society*, vol. 1, p. xxxiii.

140. The name of Morton's son, 'Moroon', is close to the name for a runaway slave who has free status: 'Maroon'. Because of the Trelawney Maroon rebellion (1795–6) in the British Colony of Jamaica, the name 'Moroon' would be especially evocative of danger and anti-British hostility.

141. *Analytical Review*, 25 (March 1797), p. 268.

142. Thelwall, *Daughter of Adoption*, vol. 1, p. 16.

143. Ibid., vol. 1, pp. 8–9.

144. Ibid., vol. 2, pp. 70–1.

145. Ibid., vol. 1, pp. 56–7.

146. Ibid., vol. 1, pp. 58–9.

147. Ibid., vol. 1, p. 312.

148. Ibid., vol. 1, p. 312.

149. Ibid., vol. 1, p. 335–7.

150. Ibid., vol. 1, p. 337.

151. Ibid., vol. 1, p. 376.

152. Ibid., vol. 1, p. 377.

153. Ibid., vol. 1, p. 377.

154. Ibid., vol. 1, pp. 380–1.

155. *Collected Letters of Mary Wollstonecraft*, p. 318.

156. Thelwall, *Daughter of Adoption*, vol. 1, p. 280; Wollstonecraft, *The Vindications*, pp. 221–5.

157. Hays, *The Victim of Prejudice*.

158. Thelwall, *Daughter of Adoption*, vol. 2, p. 250.

159. Ibid., vol. 1, p. 38, 41.

160. Ibid., vol. 1, p. 155.

161. T. Holcroft, *Anna St. Ives*, in *The Novels and Selected Plays of Thomas Holcroft*, gen. ed. W. Verhoeven (London: Pickering & Chatto, 2007), vol. 2.

162. Thelwall, *Daughter of Adoption*, vol. 1, p. 73.

163. Ibid., vol. 1, pp. 165–72.

164. Ibid., vol. 1, p. 158.

165. Ibid., vol. 1, pp. 178–9.

166. H. N. Coleridge (ed.), *Specimens of the Table Talk of Samuel Taylor Coleridge* (Oxford: Oxford University Press, 1917), p. 122. See also P. Kitson, 'Coleridge's Anecdote of John Thelwall', *Notes and Queries*, n. s. 32:3 (September 1985), p. 345.

167. Thelwall, *Daughter of Adoption*, vol. 1, p. 179.

168. Ibid., vol. 1, p. 181.

169. Bryan Edwards, *The History, Civil and Commercial, of the British West Indies. With A Continuation to the Present Time*, 5th edn, 5 vols (London: G. and W. B. Whitaker, [1798] 1819), vol. 1, pp. 530–79, vol. 3, pp. 1–180.

170. Scrivener, *Seditious Allegories*, pp. 59–60.

171. Thelwall, *Daughter of Adoption*, vol. 1, pp. 212–15.

172. Ibid., vol. 1, p. 216.

173. Ibid., vol. 1, p. 217.

174. Ibid., vol. 1, p. 218.

175. Ibid., vol. 1, pp. 220–1.

176. Ibid., vol. 1, pp. 228–9.

177. Ibid., vol. 1, p. 287.

178. Ibid., vol. 1, p. 211.

179. Ibid., vol. 1, p. 232.

180. Ibid., vol. 1, p. 232.

181. *Analytical Review*, 25 (March 1797), pp. 266–9.

182. For an account of the Jamaica rebellions, see M. Craton, *Testing the Chains: Resistance to Slavery in the British West Indies* (Ithaca and London: Cornell University Press, 1982), pp. 125–39, 211–22.

183. Thelwall, *Daughter of Adoption*, vol. 1, pp. 226–7.

184. Edwards, *History, Civil and Commercial, of the British West Indies*, vol. 3, p. xvii.

185. Scrivener, *Seditious Allegories*, pp. 49–50.

186. Edwards, *History, Civil and Commercial, of the British West Indies*, vol. 3, pp. 17–18.

187. Ibid., vol. 3, p. 11.

188. Ibid., vol. 3, p. 62.

189. Ibid., vol. 3, p. 44.

190. Ibid., vol. 3, p. 64.

191. Ibid., vol. 3, p. 65.

192. Ibid., vol. 3, pp. 72–3.

193. Ibid., vol. 3, p. 75.

194. Ibid., vol. 3, p. 74.

195. Ibid., vol. 3, p. 99.

196. Ibid. vol. 3, pp. 79–80.

197. Ibid., vol. 3, p. 74.

198. Ibid., vol. 3, pp. 80–1.

199. Ibid., vol. 3, pp. 83–4.

200. *Analytical Review*, 24 (December 1796), pp. 616–17; *Analytical Review*, 25 (March 1797), pp. 266–9.

201. Edwards, *History, Civil and Commercial, of the British West Indies*, vol. 3, pp. 88–93.

202. M. Edgeworth, 'The Grateful Negro' [1803], in *Popular Tales. Tales and Novels*, 10 vols (New York: AMS Press, [1893] 1967), vol. 2, pp. 399–419.

203. Thelwall, *Daughter of Adoption*, vol. 1, p. 209.

204. Ibid., vol. 2, p. 252.

205. Ibid., vol. 2, p. 244.

206. Ibid., vol. 2, p. 245.

207. Ibid., vol. 2, p. 375.

5 Jewish Questions

1. A. Hertzberg, *The French Enlightenment and the Jews: The Origins of Modern Anti-Semitism* (New York: Columbia University Press, 1990), p. 360.

2. C. W. von Dohm, *Concerning the Amelioration of Civil Status of the Jews (Über die bürgerliche Verbesserung der Juden)*, trans. H. Lederer (Cincinnati, OH: Hebrew Union College, [1781] 1975).

3. F. Felsenstein, *Anti-Semitic Stereotypes: A Paradigm of Otherness in English Popular Culture, 1660–1830* (Baltimore and London: Johns Hopkins University Press, 1995), pp. 187–214.

4. T. M. Endelman, 'The Englishness of Jewish Modernity in England', in J. Katz (ed.), *Toward Modernity: The European Jewish Model* (New Brunswick, NJ and Oxford: Transaction Books, 1987), pp. 225–46; pp. 238–9.

5. B. Willey, *The Eighteenth-Century Background: Studies on the Idea of Nature in the Thought of the Period* (Boston: Beacon Press, [1940] 1961), pp. 168–204; J. Fruchtman, Jr, *The Apocalyptic Politics of Richard Price and Joseph Priestley: A Study on Late Eighteenth-Century English Republican Millennialism* (Philadelphia: American Philosophical Society, 1983); R. Porter, *The Creation of the Modern World: The Untold Story of the British Enlightenment* (New York and London: W. W. Norton, 2000), pp. 406–15.

6. On Geddes see J. McGann, 'The Idea of an Intermediate Text: Blake's Bible of Hell and Dr. Alexander Geddes', *Studies in Romanticism*, 25 (1986), pp. 303–25.

7. D. Ruderman, *Jewish Enlightenment in an English Key: Anglo-Jewry's Construction of Modern Jewish Thought* (Princeton and Oxford: Princeton University Press, 2000), p. 6.

8. G. E. Lessing, *Die Juden*, in *Gotthold Ephraim Lessing Werke 1743–1750*, 12 vols (Frankfurt am Main: Deutscher Klassiker, 1993), vol. 1, ed. J. Stenzel, p. 449. English translations here are mine.

9. Lessing, *Die Juden*, pp. 450–1.

10. Ibid., p. 452.

11. Ibid., pp. 474–5.

12. Ibid., p. 487.

13. M. A. Meyer, *The Origins of the Modern Jew: Jewish Identity and European Culture in Germany, 1749–1824* (Detroit: Wayne State University Press, 1967), pp. 17–18.

14. G. E. Lessing, *Nathan der Weise* in *Gotthold Ephraim Lessing Werke*, vol. 9, ed. K. Bohnen and A. Schilson, pp. 483–627.

15. Lessing, *Nathan der Weise*, pp. 532–3.

16. Ibid., p. 619.

17. R. S. Simon, 'Commerce, Concern, and Christianity: Britain and Middle-Eastern Jewry in the Mid-Nineteenth Century', in S. A. Spector (ed.), *The Jews and British Romanticism: Politics, Religion, Culture* (New York and Basingstoke: Palgrave Macmillan, 2005), pp. 181–94; p. 186.

18. Endelman, 'The Englishness of Jewish Modernity in England', p. 237.

19. Ibid., p. 242.

20. Davis (ed.), *London Corresponding Society*, vol. 5, pp. 198, 211–12, 225–6.

21. *Analytical Review*, 24 (July 1796), p. 2.

22. Ibid., p. 2.

23. For the Jewish nose and Jewish essence as social constructions, see S. Gilman, *The Jew's Body* (New York and London: Routledge, 1991), chs 7–8.

24. *Analytical Review*, 24 (July 1796), pp. 93–5.

25. *Analytical Review*, 19 (November 1794), pp. 436–45.

26. *Analytical Review*, 1 (May 1788), pp. 107–10.

27. Hertzberg, *The French Enlightenment and the Jews*, p. 298.

28. *Analytical Review*, 10 (June 1791), pp. 239–40.

29. *Analytical Review*, 5 (December 1789), pp. 602–4.

30. *Analytical Review*, 8 (October 1790), pp. 212–14.

31. *Analytical Review*, 11 (August 1791), pp. 26–32.

32. *Analytical Review*, 26 (December 1797), p. 563.

33. Ibid., p. 565.

34. Ibid., p. 564.

35. Ibid., p. 569.

36. S. T. Coleridge, *Confessions of an Inquiring* Spirit, in *Shorter Works and Fragments: Collected Works of Samuel Taylor Coleridge*, ed. T. H. J. Jackson and J. R. de Jackson, 16 vols (London and Princeton: Routledge and Princeton University Press, 1995), vol. 11, part 2, pp. 1111–71.

37. *Analytical Review*, 2 (September 1788), pp. 84–5.

38. *Analytical Review*, 3 (April 1789), pp. 569–76.

39. *Analytical Review*, 6 (April 1790), pp. 564–6.

40. *Analytical Review*, 18 (January 1794), pp. 47–51.

41. *Analytical Review*, 25 (April 1797), pp. 415–19.

42. An earlier version of the essay on David Levi appeared as 'British-Jewish Writing of the Romantic Era and the Problem of Modernity: The Example of David Levi', in Sheila A. Spector (ed.), *British Romanticism and the Jews: History, Culture, Literature* (New York: Palgrave Macmillan, 2002), pp. 159–77.

43. T. M. Endelman, *The Jews of Georgian England 1714–1830: Tradition and Change in a Liberal Society* (Ann Arbor: University of Michigan Press: 1999), D. S. Katz, *The Jews in the History of England 1485–1850* (Oxford: Clarendon Press, 1994), Ruderman, *Jewish Enlightenment*.

44. See T. M. Endelman '"A Hebrew to the end": the Emergence of Disraeli's Jewishness', in C. Richmond and P. Smith (eds), *The Self-Fashioning of Disraeli 1818–1851* (Cambridge: Cambridge University Press, 1998), pp. 106–30.

45. Ruderman, *Jewish Enlightenment*, p. 6.

46. P. Magriel (ed.), *The Memoirs of the Life of Daniel Mendoza* (London: B. T. Batsford, [1816] 1951), pp. 16, 23–4. The prints included are in the Magriel edition of Mendoza's *Memoirs*.

47. A. Barnett, 'Eliakim ben Abraham (Jacob Hart). An Anglo-Jewish Scholar of the Eighteenth Century', *Transactions of the Jewish Historical Society of England*, 14 (1935–9), pp. 207–20.

48. C. Roth, 'The Haskalah in England', in H. J. Zimmels, J. Rabinowitz, and I. Finestein (eds), *Essays Presented to the Chief Rabbi Israel Brodie on the Occasion of his Seventieth Birthday*, 2 vols (London: Soncino Press, 1967), vol. 1, pp. 365–76; pp. 372–3.

49. Barnett, 'Eliakim ben Abraham (Jacob Hart)', pp. 207–20.

50. Roth, 'The Haskalah in England', pp. 372–3.

51. Ruderman, *Jewish Enlightenment*, pp. 196–9.

52. Meyer, *The Origins of the Modern Jew*, pp. 115–18.

53. The front cover of Ruderman's *Jewish Enlightenment* reproduces the 1789 print.

54. For the discussions of Levi's critiques, see Ruderman, *Jewish Enlightenment*, ch. 2 and ch. 4; also, R. H. Popkin, 'David Levi, Anglo-Jewish Theologian', *Jewish Quarterly Review*, 87 (1996), pp. 79–101.

55. For Mendelssohn's statement on Judaism and modernity, see his *Jerusalem, or On Religious Power and Judaism*, trans. A. Arkush (Hanover and London: University of New England Press, 1983). For the Lavater affair, see A. Altmann, *Moses Mendelssohn: A Biographical Study* (Tuscaloosa: University of Alabama Press, 1973), ch. 3.

56. J. Priestley, *Letters and Addresses to the Jews* [1787–99], in *The Theological and Miscellaneous Works of Joseph Priestley*, ed. J. T. Rutt, 25 vols (New York: Kraus Reprint, [1817–32] 1972), vol. 20, pp. 227–300.

57. Popkin, 'David Levi', pp. 79–101.

58. Meyer, *The Origins of the Modern Jew*, p. 8.

59. Endelman, 'The Englishness of Jewish Modernity in England', p. 229. See also T. M. Endelman, *Radical Assimilation in English Jewish History, 1656–1945* (Bloomington: University of Indiana Press, 1990).

60. For the self-taught tradition of artisan writers see J. Rancière, 'The Myth of the Artisan. Critical Reflections on a Category of Social History', *International Labour and Working Class History*, 24 (1983), pp. 1–12; pp. 1–2, 11; B. Maidment (ed.), *The Poorhouse Fugitives: Self Taught Poets and Poetry in Victorian Britain* (Manchester, Carcanet, 1987); Janowitz, *Lyric and Labour*.

61. D. Levi, *Defence of the Old Testament, In a Series of Letters, Addressed to Thomas Paine* (London: J. Johnson, 1797).

62. See the *DNB* entry for Henry Lemoine and George Lackington. Also, see Lemoine's 'Elegiac Verses, To the Memory of the late learned David Levi, Author of *Lingua Sacra*, &c', *Gentleman's Magazine*, 71 (October 1801), pp. 934–5. In his memoirs, he writes of his origins in the labouring classes and spectacular business success with 'cheap' literature that appeals to the poor. J. Lackington, *Memoirs of the First Forty-Five Years of the life of James Lackington*, rev. edn (London: Lackington, 1792), pp. 381–9.

63. See the *DNB* entry for Lemoine.

64. Endelman, *Jews of Georgian England*, p. 264.

65. For Heine and Börne, see S. L. Gilman, *Jewish Self-Hatred: Anti-Semitism and the Hidden Language of the Jews* (Baltimore and London: The Johns Hopkins University Press, 1986), pp. 148–88.

66. J. de B. Basnage, *The History of the Jews*, trans. T. Taylor (London: T. Bever and B. Lintot, 1708).

67. H. Prideaux, *The Old and New Testaments Connected in the History of the Jews and Neighbouring Nations*, 4 vols (Charlestown: Middlesex, 1815).

68. D. Levi, *A Succinct Account of the Rites and Ceremonies of the Jews* (London: J. Parsons, 1783), pp. 261–7.

69. Endelman, *The Jews of Georgian England*, p. 263; Levi cites Basnage in his writings beginning with the reply to Priestley in 1787.

70. A. Mears [Gamaliel ben Pedahzur], *The Book of Religion, Ceremonies, and Prayers of the Jews, as Practiced in their Synagogues and Families* (London: J. Wilcox, 1738). See the brief discussion of Mears in Endelman, *The Jews of Georgian England*, p. 250.

71. S. Singer, 'Early Translations and Translators of the Jewish Liturgy in England', *Transactions of the Jewish Historical Society of England*, 3 (1896–8), pp. 36–71; p. 59.

72. Endelman, *The Jews of Georgian England*, p. 124.

73. C. Duschinsky, *The Rabbinate of the Great Synagogue, London, From 1756 to 1842* (Westmead: Gregg International, [1921] 1971), pp. 98–9.

74. One of the few who have studied comparatively and historically the various translations of the Jewish liturgy into English is Singer in his 'Early Translations and Translators of the Jewish Liturgy in England', pp. 36–71.

75. Ibid., pp. 66–7.

76. *The Holy Bible, In Hebrew ... English Translation [and] Notes of the Late David Levi. Revised by Levy Alexander*, 5 vols (London: L. Alexander, 5582 [1822]).

77. See their reflections on their biblical translation (*Schrift*) in M. Buber and S. Rosenzweig, *Scripture and Translation*, trans. L. Rosenwald and E. Fox (Bloomington and Indianapolis: Indiana University Press, [1936], 1994).

78. Katz, *The Jews in the History of England 1485–1850*, pp. 296–300. Katz also provides a useful bibliography on Priestley.

79. Endelman, *The Jews of Georgian England*, p. 220.

80. D. Levi, *Letters to Dr. Priestley, In Answer to His Letters to the Jews, Part II* (London: D. Levi, 1789), pp. 3, 5.

81. Ibid., p. 155.

82. Ibid., pp. 127–34.

83. M. Vreté, 'The Restoration of the Jews in English Protestant Thought 1790–1840', *Middle Eastern Studies*, 8 (1972), pp. 3–50; pp. 7–9.

84. W. Cunninghame, *Remarks Upon David Levi's Dissertations on the Prophecies Relative to The Messiah* (London: Black, Parry, and Kingsbury, 1810).

85. A. Rubens, 'Portrait of Anglo-Jewry 1656–1836', *Transactions of the Jewish Historical Society of England*, 19 (1955–9), pp. 13–52; pp. 36–9.

86. See T. M. Endelman, 'The Chequered Career of "Jew" King: a Study in Anglo-Jewish Social History', in F. Malino and D. Sorkin, (eds), *From East and West: Jews in a Changing Europe, 1750–1870* (Oxford: Basil Blackwell, 1990), pp. 151–81.

87. Ibid., pp. 179–80.

88. Ruderman, *Jewish Enlightenment*, p. 40.

89. Ibid., p. 177.

90. Levi, *Defence of the Old Testament*, p. 201.

91. D. Levi, *Dissertations on the Prophecies of the Old Testament*, 2 vols (London, D. Levi, 1796), vol. 2, p. 117.

92. Ibid., vol. 2, p. 117n.

93. J. Mee, 'Apocalypse and Ambivalence: The Politics of Millenarianism in the 1790s', *South Atlantic Quarterly*, 95 (1996), pp. 671–97; Mee, *Dangerous Enthusiasm*.

94. Levi, *Dissertations on the Prophecies*, vol. 1, pp. xxvi–xxxiii.

95. Ibid., vol. 1, p. 40.

96. Ibid., vol. 1, p. 117.

97. Levi, *Defence of the Old Testament*, p. 56.

98. Ibid., pp. 59–77.

99. Ibid., pp. 99–106.

100. Ibid., pp. 116–26.

101. Ibid., pp. 154–95.

102. Endelman, 'The Englishness of Jewish Modernity', p. 238.

103. Levi's essay on Abravanel is remarkably similar to what one will find in standard Jewish encyclopaedias such as the *Encyclopaedia Judaica*, 16 vols (Jerusalem, Judah Magnes, 1972) and the *Jewish Encyclopaedia*, 12 vols (New York and London: Funk and Wagnalls, 1901).

104. An earlier version of the essay on Emma Lyon appeared as 'Following the Muse: Inspiration, Prophecy, and Deference in the Poetry of Emma Lyon (1788–1870), Anglo-Jewish Poet', in Sheila A. Spector (ed.), *The Jews and British Romanticism: Politics, Religion, Culture* (New York: Palgrave Macmillan, 2005), pp. 105–26.

105. E. Lyon, *Miscellaneous Poems* (Oxford: J. Bartlett, 1812). The text is now available online through the University of California at Davis 'British Women Romantic Poets' project, http://www.lib.ucdavis.edu/BWRP/Works/#L.

106. I. Nathan, *A Selection of Hebrew Melodies, Ancient and Modern, and [text by] Lord Byron*, ed. F. Burwick and P. Douglass (Tuscaloosa: University of Alabama Press, 1988).

107. A surprisingly large amount of information about Emma Lyon, her father Solomon, and the Lyon family has been published by one of the descendants of the family, Naomi Cream, in two publications, 'Isaac Leo Lyon: The First Free Jewish Migrant to Australia?' *Journal of Australian Jewish Historical Society*, 12:1 (1993), pp. 3–16, and 'Revd Solomon Lyon of Cambridge, 1755–1820', *Jewish Historical Studies*, 36 (1999–2001), pp. 31–69.

108. The Jews Free School Governors Committee Minutes 1818–1831 of March 23, 1824 reports that at the anniversary dinner of February 11, one of the events was that 'Amelia Adolphus ... repeated an English Ode written by Mrs. Henry' (p. 159). I thank Naomi Cream for this information. A letter (12 June 1874) from her youngest son, Michael Henry (1830–75), to historian James Picciotto (1830–97), states that '[a]fter her marriage to my father, she ceased to write except *en amatrice*; she wrote poems which were recited at public Institutions, such as Jews' Hospital, Jews' Free School & Society of friends for foreigners in distress. I have a printed poem of hers recited at the Free School 50 years ago'. The letter (MS 116/59) is quoted by permission of the University of Southampton Library, Archives and Manuscripts.

109. On Aguilar, see E. Fay, 'Grace Aguilar: Rewriting Scott Rewriting History', in *British Romanticism and the Jews: History, Culture, Literature*, ed. S. A. Spector (New York: Palgrave Macmillan, 2002), pp. 215–34. In this same volume, see J. W. Page's 'Anglo-Jewish Identity and the Politics of Cultivation in Hazlitt, Aguilar, and Disraeli', pp. 197–214.

110. For the fascinating King sisters and their father, see D. Wu (ed.), *Romantic Women Poets* (Oxford: Blackwell, 1997), pp. 358–63, and Endelman, 'The Chequered Career of "Jew" King', pp. 151–81.

111. S. Gilbert and S. Gubar, *The Madwoman in the Attic: The Woman Writer and the Nine-teenth-Century Literary Imagination* (New Haven: Yale University Press, 1979), p. 82.

112. Ibid., p. 72.

113. Ibid., p. 82.

114. Lyon, *Miscellaneous Poems*, p. 3.

115. C. Smith, *Elegiac Sonnets, and Other Poems* (London: Jones and Company, 1827), p. ix.

116. For the importance of converting Jews, see M. Ragussis, *Figures of Conversion: The Jewish Question and English National Identity* (Durham: Duke University Press, 1995); for the religious identity of the woman writer, see C. Scheinberg, *Women's Poetry and Religion in Victorian England: Jewish Identity and Christian Culture* (Cambridge: Cambridge University Press, 2002).

117. Lyon, *Miscellaneous Poems*, pp. ix–x.

118. *Critical Review*, 2 n.s. (August 1812), p. 216.

119. *Monthly Review* 70, (February 1813), p. 214.

120. Lyon, *Miscellaneous Poems*, p. vii.

121. *The Times* (16 September 1812).

122. Letter of Michael Henry to James Picciotto (12 June 1874), University of Southampton Library, MS 116/59.

123. J. Khalip, 'A Disappearance in the World: Wollstonecraft and Melancholy Skepticism', *Criticism*, 47:1 (2005), pp. 85–106; p. 90.

124. For the poem and the description of the negative reviews, see Wu (ed.), *Romantic Women Poets*, pp. 8–18.

125. Irving Massey discusses the tension between survival and art in 'Yiddish Poetry of the Holocaust', in *Find You the Virtue: Ethics, Image, and Desire in Literature* (Fairfax, VA: George Mason University Press, 1987), pp. 79–112.

126. Professor Steven Newman, English Department, Temple University, pointed out to me the parallel between Lyon and Milton; for father-identified women writers, see E. Kowaleski-Wallace, *Their Fathers' Daughters: Hannah More, Maria Edgeworth, and Patriarchal Complicity* (New York: Oxford University Press, 1991).

127. H. N. Bialik and Y. H. Ravnitsky (eds), *The Book of Legends: Sefer Ha-Aggadah. Legends from the Talmud and Midrash*, trans. W. G. Braude (New York: Schocken Books, 1992), p. 446.

128. For Pope's influence on women writers, see D. Landry, *The Muses of Resistance: Labour-ing-Class Women's Poetry in Britain, 1739–1796* (Cambridge: Cambridge University Press, 1990), pp. 12, 43–55.

129. Wu, *Romantic Women Poets*, p. xxi.

130. Mee, *Dangerous Enthusiasm*.

131. Sir P. Sidney, *An Apology for Poetry*, in H. Adams, (ed.), *Critical Theory Since Plato*, rev. edn (New York: Harcourt Brace Jovanovich, 1992), pp. 151–3.

132. R. Targoff, *Common Prayer: The Language of Public Devotion in Early Modern England* (Chicago and London: University of Chicago Press, 2001), p. 73.

133. Targoff, *Common Prayer*, p. 78.

134. *Collected Poems of Sir Thomas Wyatt*, ed. K. Muir and P. Thomson, (Liverpool: Liverpool University Press, 1969), p. xviii.

135. J. C. A. Rathmell (ed.), *The Psalms of Sir Philip Sidney and The Countess of Pembroke* (New York: New York University Press, 1963). The Sidney Psalms circulated as manuscript poems among an influential elite readership but were not published until 1823 in a small edition (p. xxvii).

136. R. Zim, *English Metrical Psalms: Poetry as Praise and Prayer 1535–1601* (Cambridge: Cambridge University Press, 1987), p. 40.

137. Ibid., p. 3.

138. Ibid., pp. 12–15.

139. J. N. King, 'Religious Writing', in *The Cambridge Companion to English Literature 1500–1600*, ed. A. F. Kinney (Cambridge: Cambridge University Press, 2000), pp. 104–31; p. 126.

140. *Nineteenth-Century Short Title Catalogue, Series 1, 1801–1815, Volume 6* (Newcastle upon Tyne: Avero, 1984).

141. I am using the categories developed by S. E. Gillingham, *The Poems and Psalms of the Hebrew Bible* (Oxford: Oxford University Press, 1994), p. 231.

142. The *Amidah*, also known as *Shemonneh-Esreh* ('Eighteen', referring to the eighteen benedictions which it originally comprised), is the core element of the daily prayers.

143. M. J. Dahood (ed.), *The Anchor Bible. Psalms I. 1–50* (Garden City: Doubleday, 1966), p. 296.

144. I. Watts, *The Psalms, Hymns and Spiritual Songs of the Rev. Isaac Watts, D. D.* (Boston: Samuel T. Armstrong, Crocker, and Brewster, 1823), p. 124.

145. *Report and State of the Society of Friends of Foreigners in Distress* (London: W. Marchant, 1816), p. 23.

146. Ibid., pp. 13–21.

147. *Aleinu le-shabbe'ah* ('It is out duty to praise [the Lord of all things]'), prayer about the kingdom of God, originally part of the New Year's service, though now recited at the conclusion of statutory services.

148. *The Times* (16 September 1812).

149. M. Galchinsky, *The Origins of the Modern Jewish Woman Writer: Romance and Reform in Victorian England* (Detroit: Wayne State University Press, 1996).

150. I. Hannaford, *Race: The History of an Idea in the West* (Baltimore, London and Washington, DC: Johns Hopkins University Press and Woodrow Wilson Center Press, 1996), p. 3.

151. R. J. C. Young, *Colonial Desire: Hybridity in Theory, Culture and Race* (London and New York: Routledge, 1995).

152. Kitson, 'Introduction', *Slavery, Abolition and Emancipation*, vol. 8, p. xix.

153. M. Edgeworth, *Moral Tales* [1801] in *Tales and Novels*, 10 vols (New York: AMS Press, [1893] 1967), vol. 1, pp. 11–43.

154. Ibid., pp. 144–220.

155. M. Edgeworth, *Popular Tales* [1804] in *Tales and Novels*, 10 vols (New York: AMS Press, [1893] 1967), vol. 2, pp. 101–28.

156. Ibid., pp. 245–79.

157. M. Edgeworth, *The Absentee*, ed. W. J. McCormack and K. Walker (New York and Oxford: Oxford University Press, 1988), p. 7.

158. Edgeworth, *Moral Tales*, pp. 361–410.

159. Ibid., pp. 283–360.

160. Ragussis, *Figures of Conversion*, pp. 65–76; J. W. Page, *Imperfect Sympathies: Jews and Judaism in British Romantic Literature and Culture* (New York and Basingstoke: Palgrave Macmillan, 2004), pp. 133–58; S. Manly (ed.), 'Introduction' to M. Edgeworth, *Harrington*, ed. S. Manly (Peterborough, ON: Broadview Press, 2004), pp. 7–57; S. Spector, 'The Other's Other: The Function of the Jew in Maria Edgeworth's Fiction', *European Romantic Review*, 10:3 (1999), pp. 326–33.

161. Young, *Colonial Desire*, p. 27.
162. E. E. MacDonald (ed.), *The Education of the Heart: The Correspondence of Rachel Mordecai Lazarus and Maria Edgeworth* (Chapel Hill, NC: University of North Carolina Press, 1977), p. 23.
163. *Analytical Review* 6 (February 1790), p. 173.

Conclusion

1. P. Zagorin, *How the Idea of Religious Toleration Came to the West* (Princeton and Oxford: Princeton University Press, 2003).
2. I. Wallerstein, *The Modern World-System II: Mercantilism and the Consolidation of the European World-Economy, 1600–1750* (New York: Academic Press, 1980), and *The Modern World-System III: The Second Era of Great Expansion of the Capitalist World-Economy, 1730–1840s* (San Diego: Academic Press, 1989).
3. See R. Cavaliero, *Italia Romantica: English Romantics and Italian Freedom* (London and New York: I. B. Tauris, 2005).
4. See B. Colbert, *Shelley's Eye: Travel Writing and Aesthetic Vision* (Aldershot and Burlington: Ashgate Press, 2005), pp. 53–63.
5. P. B. Shelley, *A Philosophical View of Reform*, in *The Complete Works of Percy Bysshe Shelley*, vol. 7, pp. 13–19.
6. M. W Shelley and P. B. Shelley, *History of a Six Weeks' Tour Through a Part of France, Switzerland, Germany, and Holland: With Letters Descriptive of a Sail Round the Lake of Geneva, and of the Glaciers of Chamouni* (1817), in *The Complete Works of Percy Bysshe Shelley*, vol. 6, pp. 87–152; p. 107.
7. R. Holmes, 'Introduction', Mary Wollstonecraft, *A Short Residence in Sweden, Norway and Denmark* and William Godwin, *Memoirs of the Author of 'The Rights of Woman'* (Harmondsworth: Penguin 1987), pp. 16, 20, 26.
8. Wollstonecraft, *A Short Residence*, pp. 79–80.
9. Ibid., p. 136.
10. Ibid., p. 122.
11. Ibid., p. 122.
12. Ibid., p. 79.
13. Ibid., p. 93.
14. Ibid., p. 63.
15. Ibid., p. 65.
16. Ibid., p. 66, 83–4.
17. Holmes, 'Introduction', Wollstonecraft, *A Short Residence*, pp. 26–7.
18. Wollstonecraft, *A Short Residence*, p. 114.
19. Ibid., pp. 168–70.
20. Ibid., pp. 166–7.
21. Ibid., pp. 170–3.
22. E. A. Bohls, *Women Travel Writers and the Language of Aesthetics, 1716–1818* (Cambridge: Cambridge University Press, 1995), attends to the role of the body in Wollstonecraft's *A Short Residence*, pp. 141–2.
23. Wollstonecraft, *A Short Residence*, p. 171.
24. Ibid., p. 66.
25. Ibid., pp. 111, 127.
26. Ibid., pp. 88, 90–1.

27. Ibid., pp. 143–4.
28. Ibid., p. 93.
29. B. Colbert's *Shelley's Eye: Travel Writing and Aesthetic Vision* is one of the few treatments of the *History of a Six Weeks' Tour*; Colbert's approach is more aesthetic than political.
30. Shelley and Shelley, *History of a Six Weeks' Tour*, p. 87.
31. Ibid., pp. 95–7.
32. Ibid., p. 117.
33. Ibid., p. 122.
34. Ibid., p. 127.
35. Ibid., pp. 132–3.
36. Ibid., p. 147.
37. W. St Clair, *That Greece Might Still Be Free* (London: Oxford University Press, 1972).
38. J. McGann, *The Romantic Ideology: A Critical Investigation* (Chicago and London: University of Chicago Press, 1983). H. Heine, 'The Romantic School', in J. Hermand and R. Holub (eds), *The Romantic School and Other Essays* (New York: Continuum, 1985), pp. 127.
39. P. B. Shelley, *Prometheus Unbound*, in *Shelley's Poetry and Prose*, p. 206.
40. M. W. Shelley, *Mathilda*, in B. T. Bennett and C. E. Robinson (eds), *The Mary Shelley Reader* (New York and Oxford: Oxford University Press, 1990), pp. 236–7.
41. Ibid., p. 238.
42. S. Curran, 'Introduction', *Valperga or, The Life and Adventures of Castruccio, Prince of Lucca* (Oxford and New York: Oxford University Press, 1997), pp. xix–xxiii.
43. T. Rajan, 'Introduction', *Valperga: or, The Life and Adventures of Castruccio, Prince of Lucca*, ed. T. Rajan (Peterborough, ON: Broadview Press, 1998), p. 20.
44. M. W. Shelley, *Valperga*, p. 70.
45. Ibid., pp. 304–12.
46. J. Cox, *Poetry and Politics in the Cockney School: Keats, Shelley, Hunt and Their* Circle (Cambridge: Cambridge University Press, 1999).
47. J. Habermas, *The Divided West*, trans. C. Cronin (Cambridge and Malden: Polity Press, 2006), pp. 173–4.
48. Habermas, *The Divided West*, p. 177.
49. Ibid., p. 178.
50. Ibid., p. 182.
51. Ibid., p. 184.

WORKS CITED

Documents

The Jews Free School Governors Committee Minutes 1818–1831.

Letter (12 June 1874) from Michael Henry (1830–75) to James Picciotto (1830–97), MS 116/59, University of Southampton Library, Archives and Manuscripts.

Periodicals

Analytical Review (1788–99).

British Critic (1793).

Critical Review (1812).

Gentleman's Magazine (1801).

The Times (16 September 1812).

Monthly Review (1789, 1813).

Sources

Adorno, T. W., *Kant's Critique of Reason*, ed. R. Tiedemann, trans. R. Livingstone (Stanford: Stanford University Press, [1995] 2001)

—, and M. Horkheimer, *The Dialectic of Enlightenment*, trans. J. Cumming (New York: Continuum, [1947] 1972).

Alexander, L., *The Holy Bible, In Hebrew ... English Translation [and] Notes of the Late David Levi. Revised by Levy Alexander*, 5 vols (London: L. Alexander, [1822]).

Altick, R. D., *The English Common Reader: A Social History of the Mass Reading Public, 1800–1900* (Chicago and London: University of Chicago Press, 1957).

Altmann, A., *Moses Mendelssohn: A Biographical Study* (Tuscaloosa: University of Alabama Press, 1973).

Apel, K-O., 'Kant's "Toward Perpetual Peace" as Historical Prognosis from the Point of View of Moral Duty', in J. Bohman and M. Lutz-Bachman (eds), *Perpetual Peace. Essays on Kant's Cosmopolitan Ideal* (Cambridge, MA, and London: The MIT Press, 1997), pp. 79–110.

Appiah, A., *Cosmopolitanism: Ethics in a World of Strangers* (New York: W. W. Norton, 2006).

Aravamudan, S., *Tropicopolitans: Colonialism and Agency, 1688–1804* (Durham, NC and London: Duke University Press, 1999).

Arendt, H., *Lectures on Kant's Political Philosophy*, ed. R. Beemer (Chicago: University of Chicago Press, 1982).

Austen, J., *Northanger Abbey*, ed. S. Fraiman (New York and London: W. W. Norton, 2004).

Baker, Jr, H., *Blues, Ideology, and Afro-American Literature: A Vernacular Theory* (Chicago: University of Chicago Press, 1987).

Barnett, A., 'Eliakim ben Abraham (Jacob Hart). An Anglo-Jewish Scholar of the Eighteenth Century', *Transactions of the Jewish Historical Society of England*, 14 (1935–9), pp. 207–20.

Barrell, J., 'Coffee-House Politicians', *Journal of British Studies*, 43 (2004), pp. 206–32.

Basnage, J. de B., *The History of the Jews*, trans. T. Taylor (London: T. Bever and B. Lintot, 1708).

Beiderwell, B., *Power and Punishment in Scott's Novels* (Athens: University of Georgia Press, 1992).

Benhabib, S., 'Toward a Deliberative Model of Democratic Legitimacy', in S. Benhabib (ed.), *Democracy and Difference: Contesting the Boundaries of the Political* (Princeton: Princeton University Press, 1996), pp. 67–94.

Benjamin, W., 'The Task of the Translator' [1923], trans. H. Zohn, in M. Bullock and M. N. Jennings (eds), *Walter Benjamin: Selected Writings*, 4 vols. (Cambridge, MA, and London: Belknap Press of Harvard University Press, 1996), vol. 1, pp. 253–63.

Berlin, I., 'The Counter-Enlightenment', in *Dictionary of the History of Ideas*, ed. P. P. Wiener, 4 vols (New York: Scribner's Sons, 1973), vol. 2, pp. 100–12.

—, *Three Critics of the Enlightenment: Vico, Hamaan, Herder*, ed. H. Hardy (Princeton: Princeton University Press, 2000).

Bernasconi, R. (ed.), *Race* (Oxford and Malden: MA, Blackwell, 2001).

Bialik, H. N. and Y. H. Ravnitsky (eds), *The Book of Legends / Sefer Ha-Aggada: Legends from the Talmud and Midrash*, trans. W. G. Braude (New York: Schocken Books, 1992).

Binfield, K., *Writings of the Luddites* (Baltimore and London: Johns Hopkins University Press, 2004).

Blackstone, W., *Commentaries on the Laws of England*, ed. T. M. Cooley, 3rd edn, 2 vols (Chicago: Callaghan, 1884).

Blumenbach, J. F., *On the Natural Varieties of Mankind* [*De Generis Humani Varietate Nativa*], trans. and ed. T. Bendyshe (New York: Bergman Publishers, [1865] 1969).

Bohls, E. A., *Women Travel Writers and the Language of Aesthetics, 1716–1818* (Cambridge: Cambridge University Press, 1995).

Bohman. J. and M. Lutz-Bachman (eds), *Perpetual Peace: Essays on Kant's Cosmopolitan Ideal* (Cambridge, MA, and London: The MIT Press, 1997).

Braithwaite, H., *Romanticism, Publishing and Dissent: Joseph Johnson and the Cause of Liberty* (Basingstoke and New York: Palgrave Macmillan, 2003).

Brooks, P., *Troubling Confessions* (Chicago and London: University of Chicago Press, 2000).

Buber, M., and S. Rosenzweig, *Scripture and Translation*, trans. L. Rosenwald and E. Fox (Bloomington and Indianapolis: Indiana University Press, [1936], 1994).

Bugg, J., 'The Other Interesting Narrative: Olaudah Equiano's Public Book Tour', *PMLA*, 121:5 (2006), pp. 1424–42.

Burke, E., *The Works of the Right Honorable Edmund Burke*, 3rd edn, 12 vols (Boston: Little Brown, 1869).

Butler, M. (ed.), *Romantics, Rebels, and Reactionaries. English Literature and Its Background, 1760–1830* (New York: Oxford University Press, 1981).

—, *Burke, Paine, Godwin, and the Revolution Controversy* (Cambridge: Cambridge University Press, 1984).

Cafarelli, A. W., 'The Common Reader: Social Class in Romantic Poetics', *Journal of English and Germanic Philology*, 96 (1997), pp. 222–46.

Caretta, V. (ed.), *Unchained Voices. An Anthology of Black Authors in the English-Speaking World of the 18th Century* (Lexington: University Press of Kentucky, 1996).

—, 'Olaudah Equiano or Gustavus Vassa?: New Light on an Eighteenth-Century Question of Identity', *Slavery and Abolition. A Journal of Slave and Post-Slave Societies*, 20:3 (1999), pp. 96–105.

Cassirer, E., *Kant's Life and Thought*, trans. J. Haden (New Haven and London: Yale University Press, [1918] 1981).

—, *The Philosophy of the Enlightenment*, trans. F. C. A. Koellin and J. P. Pettegrove (Princeton: Princeton University Press, [1932] 1951).

Cavaliero, R., *Italia Romantica. English Romantics and Italian Freedom* (London and New York: I. B. Tauris, 2005).

Chandler, D. *England in 1819: The Politics of Literature, Culture and the Law of Romantic Histories* (Chicago: University of Chicago Press, 1998).

Chard, L. F., III, 'Joseph Johnson in the 1790s', *Wordsworth Circle*, 33:3 (2002), pp. 95–100.

Claeys, G. (ed.), *Utopias of the British Enlightenment* (Cambridge: Cambridge University Press, 1994).

—, (ed.), *The Politics of English Jacobinism: The Writings of John Thelwall* (University Park: Pennsylvania State University Press, 1995).

Clark, A., *The Struggle for the Breeches: Gender and the Making of the British Working Class* (Berkeley: University of California Press, 1995).

Cohen, J. L., 'Critical Social Theory and Feminist Critiques: The Debate with Jürgen Habermas', in J. Meehan (ed.), *Feminists Read Habermas: Gendering the Subject of Discourse* (New York; London: Routledge, 1995), pp. 57–90.

Colbert, B., *Shelley's Eye: Travel Writing and Aesthetic Vision* (Aldershot and Burlington: Ashgate Press, 2005).

Colclough, S. M., 'Procuring Books and Consuming Texts: The Reading Experience of a Sheffield Apprentice, 1798', *Book History*, 3 (2000), pp. 21–44.

Coldiron, A. E. B., 'Public Sphere/Contact Zone: Habermas, Early Print, and Verse Translation', *Criticism*, 46:2 (2004), pp. 207–22.

Coleridge, S. T., *Specimens of the Table Talk of Samuel Taylor Coleridge*, ed. H. N. Coleridge (Oxford: Oxford University Press, 1917).

—, *Confessions of an Inquiring Spirit*, in *Shorter Works and Fragments. Collected Works of Samuel Taylor Coleridge*, ed. T. H. J. Jackson and J. R. de Jackson, 16 vols (London and Princeton: Routledge and Princeton University Press, 1995), vol. 11, part 2, pp. 1111–71.

Colley, L., *Britons: Forging the Nation, 1707–1837* (New Haven and London: Yale University Press, 1992).

Cornblitt, O., *Power and Violence in the Colonial City: Oruro from the Mining Renaissance to the Rebellion of Tupac Amaru (1740–1782)*, trans. E. L. Glick (Cambridge: Cambridge University Press, 1975).

Cowan, B., 'What Was Masculine about the Public Sphere? Gender and the Coffeehouse Milieu in Post-Restoration England', *History Workshop Journal*, 51 (2001), pp. 127–58.

Cox, J., *Poetry and Politics in the Cockney School: Keats, Shelley, Hunt and Their Circle* (Cambridge: Cambridge University Press, 1998).

Craton, M., *Testing the Chains: Resistance to Slavery in the British West Indies* (Ithaca and London: Cornell University Press, 1982).

Cream, N., 'Isaac Leo Lyon: The First Free Jewish Migrant to Australia?', *Journal of Australian Jewish Historical Society*, 12:1 (1993), pp. 3–16.

—, 'Revd Solomon Lyon of Cambridge, 1755–1820', *Jewish Historical Studies*, 36 (1999–2001), pp. 31–69.

Critchley, S. *The Ethics of Deconstruction: Derrida and Levinas*, 2nd edn (East Lafayette: Purdue University Press, 1999).

Cronin, C., 'Kant's Politics of Enlightenment', *Journal of the History of Philosophy*, 41:1 (2003), pp. 51–80.

Cunninghame, W., *Remarks Upon David Levi's Dissertations on the Prophecies Relative to The Messiah* (London: Black, Parry, and Kingsbury, 1810).

Curran, S., *Shelley's Cenci: Scorpions Ringed with Fire* (Princeton: Princeton University Press, 1970).

—, 'Introduction', *Valperga or, The Life and Adventures of Castruccio, Prince of Lucca* (Oxford and New York: Oxford University Press, 1997), pp. xii–xxvi.

Dahood, M. J. (ed.), *The Anchor Bible: Psalms I. 1–50* (Garden City: Doubleday, 1966).

Davis, D. B., *Slavery and Human Progress* (New York and Oxford: Oxford University Press, 1984).

Davis, M. T., 'Introduction', in *London Corresponding Society, 1792–1799*, ed. M. T. Davis, 6 vols (London: Pickering & Chatto, 2002), vol. 1, pp. xxv–xlviii.

— (ed.), *London Corresponding Society, 1792–1799*, 6 vols (London: Pickering & Chatto, 2002).

—, 'Prosecution and Radical Discourse during the 1790s: The Case of the Scottish Sedition Trials', *International Journal of the Sociology of Law*, 98 (2005), pp. 1–11.

Derrida, J., 'Hostipitality', trans. B. Stocker and F. Morlock, in L. Thomassen (ed.), *The Derrida-Habermas Reader* (Edinburgh and Chicago: University of Chicago Press, 2006), pp. 208–30.

— and J. Habermas, 'February 15, or What Binds Europeans Together: A Plea for a Common Foreign Policy, Beginning in the Core of Europe', trans. M. Pensky, in L. Thomassen (ed.), *The Derrida-Habermas Reader* (Chicago and Edinburgh: University of Chicago Press, 2006), pp. 270–7.

Dickinson, H. T., *Liberty and Property: Political Ideology in Eighteenth-Century Britain* (New York: Holmes & Meier, 1977).

Dictionary of National Biography (Oxford, Oxford University Press, 1901–85).

Dinwiddy, J. R., *Radicalism and Reform in Britain, 1780–1850* (London: Hambledon Press, 1992).

Dohm, C. W. von, *Concerning the Amelioration of Civil Status of the Jews* (*Über die bürgerliche Verbesserung der Juden*), trans. H. Lederer (Cincinnati, OH: Hebrew Union College, [1781] 1975).

Dumm, T. L., and M. Hardt, 'The *Theory & Event* Interview: Sovereignty, Multitudes, Absolute Democracy: A Discussion between Michael Hardt and Thomas L. Dumm about Hardt's and Negri's *Empire*', in P. A. Passavant and J. Dean (eds), *Empire's New Clothes: Reading Hardt and Negri* (New York and London: Routledge, 2004), pp. 136–74

Duschinsky, C., *The Rabbinate of the Great Synagogue, London, from 1756 to 1842* (Westmead: Gregg International, [1921] 1971).

Eagleton, T., *The Function of Criticism: from the Spectator to Post-Structuralism* (London: Verso, 1984).

Edgeworth, M., *Moral Tales* [1801], in *Tales and Novels*, 10 vols (New York: AMS Press, [1893] 1967), vol. 1.

—, *Popular Tales* [1804], in *Tales and Novels*, 10 vols (New York: AMS Press, [1893] 1967), vol. 2.

—, *The Absentee*, ed. W. J. McCormack and K. Walker (New York and Oxford: Oxford University Press, 1988).

—, *Harrington*, ed. S. Manly (Peterborough, ON: Broadview Press, [1817] 2004).

Edwards, B., *The History, Civil and Commercial, of the British West Indies. With A Continuation to the Present Time*, 5th edn, 5 vols (London: G. and W. B. Whitaker, [1798] 1819).

Eger, E., C. Grant, C. O Gallchoir, and P. Warburton (eds), *Women, Writing and the Public Sphere* (Cambridge, Cambridge University Press, 2001).

Ellis, M. 'Coffee-Women, *The Spectator* and the Public Sphere in the Early Eighteenth Century', in *Women, Writing and the Public Sphere*, ed. E. Eger, C. Grant, C. O Gallchoir, and P. Warburton (Cambridge, Cambridge University Press, 2001), pp. 27–52.

Encyclopedia Judaica, 16 vols (Jerusalem, Judah Magnes, 1972).

Endelman, T. M., 'The Englishness of Jewish Modernity in England', in J. Katz (ed.), *Toward Modernity: The European Jewish Model* (New Brunswick, NJ and Oxford: Transaction Books, 1987), pp. 225–46.

—, 'The Chequered Career of "Jew" King: a Study in Anglo-Jewish Social History', in F. Malino and D. Sorkin, (eds), *From East and West: Jews in a Changing Europe, 1750–1870* (Oxford, Basil Blackwell, 1990), pp. 151–81.

—, *Radical Assimilation in English Jewish History, 1656–1945* (Bloomington: University of Indiana Press, 1990).

—, '"A Hebrew to the end": the Emergence of Disraeli's Jewishness', in C. Richmond and P. Smith (eds), *The Self-Fashioning of Disraeli 1818–1851* (Cambridge, Cambridge University Press, 1998), pp. 106–30.

—, *The Jews of Georgian England, 1714–1830: Tradition and Change in a Liberal Society* (Ann Arbor, University of Michigan Press, 1999).

Epstein, J., *Radical Expression: Political Language, Ritual, and Symbol in England, 1790–1850* (Oxford and New York: Oxford University Press, 1994).

Equiano, O., *The Interesting Narrative of the Life of Olaudah Equiano*, ed. A. Costanzo. (Peterborough, ON, Broadview Press, 2001).

—, *Olaudah Equiano: The Interesting Narrative and Other Writings*, ed. V. Carretta (Harmondsworth: Penguin Books, 1995).

Erdman, D. V., *Commerce des Lumières: John Oswald and the British in Paris, 1790–1793* (Columbia, University of Missouri Press, 1986).

Esterhammer, A., 'Continental Literature, Translation, and the Johnson Circle', *Wordsworth Circle*, 33:3 (2002), pp. 101–4.

Eze, E. C. (ed.), *Race and Enlightenment: A Reader* (London: Blackwell, 1997).

Fay, E., 'Grace Aguilar: Rewriting Scott Rewriting History', in *British Romanticism and the Jews: History, Culture, Literature*, ed. S. A. Spector (New York: Palgrave Macmillan, 2002), pp. 215–34.

Felsenstein, F., *Anti-Semitic Stereotypes: A Paradigm of Otherness in English Popular Culture, 1660–1830* (Baltimore and London: Johns Hopkins University Press, 1995).

— (ed.), *English Trader, Indian Maid: Representing Gender, Race, and Slavery in the New World. An Inkle and Yarico Reader* (Baltimore and London: Johns Hopkins University Press, 1999).

Ferguson, M., 'Mary Wollstonecraft and the Problematic of Slavery', in M. J. Falco (ed.), *Feminist Interpretations of Mary Wollstonecraft* (University Park, PA: Pennsylvania State University Press, 1996), pp. 125–49.

Fogel, F. W. and S. L. Engerman, *Time on the Cross: The Economics of American Negro Slavery* (Boston: Little, Brown, 1974).

Foucault, M., *Discipline and Punish: The Birth of the Prison*, trans. A. Sheridan (New York: Pantheon Books, [1975] 1977).

Frank, T., *What's the Matter with Kansas? How Conservatives Won the Heart of America* (New York: Metropolitan Books, 2004).

Fraser, N., 'What's Critical about Critical Theory? The Case of Habermas and Gender', *New German Critique*, 35 (Spring/Summer 1985), pp. 97–131.

—, *Unruly Practices: Power, Discourse and Gender in Contemporary Social Theory* (Minneapolis: University of Minnesota Press and Polity Press, 1989).

Fruchtman, Jr, J., *The Apocalyptic Politics of Richard Price and Joseph Priestley: A Study on Late Eighteenth-Century English Republican Millennialism* (Philadelphia: American Philosophical Society, 1983).

Gadamer, H. G., *Truth and Method*, trans. G. Barden and J. Cumming (New York: Crossroad, [1965] 1982).

Galchinsky, M., *The Origins of the Modern Jewish Woman Writer: Romance and Reform in Victorian England* (Detroit: Wayne State University Press, 1996).

Gates, Jr, H. L., *The Signifying Monkey: A Theory of African-American Literary Criticism* (Oxford and New York: Oxford University Press, 1988).

Gay, P., *The Enlightenment: An Interpretation*, 2 vols (New York: Knopf, 1966).

Gilbert, S., and S. Gubar, *The Madwoman in the Attic: The Woman Writer and the Nineteenth-Century Literary Imagination* (New Haven: Yale University Press, 1979).

Gilligan, C., *In a Different Voice: Psychological Theory and Women's Development* (Cambridge, MA, and London: Harvard University Press, 1993).

Gillingham, S. E., *The Poems and Psalms of the Hebrew Bible* (Oxford: Oxford University Press, 1994).

Gilman, S. L., *Jewish Self-Hatred: Anti-Semitism and the Hidden Language of the Jews* (Baltimore and London: Johns Hopkins University Press, 1986).

—, *The Jew's Body* (New York and London: Routledge, 1991).

Gilmartin, K., *Print Politics: The Press and Radical Opposition in Early Nineteenth-Century England* (Cambridge: Cambridge University Press, 1996).

Godwin, W., *Enquiry Concerning Political Justice*, ed. F. E. L. Priestley, 3 vols (Toronto: University of Toronto Press, [1793] 1946).

—, *Caleb Williams*, ed. G. Handwerk and A. A. Markley (Peterborough, ON: Broadview Press, [1794] 2000).

—, *Considerations on Lord Grenville's and Mr. Pitt's Bills* (London: Joseph Johnson, [1796] 1795).

Goetschel, W., *Constituting Critique: Kant's Writing as Critical Praxis*, trans. E. Schwab (Durham and London: Duke University Press, 1994).

Gould, S. J., *The Mismeasure of Man*, rev. edn (New York and London: W. W. Norton, 1996).

Gray, R. T., *About Face: German Physiognomic Thought from Lavater to Auschwitz* (Detroit: Wayne State University Press, 2004).

Guest, H., *Small Change: Women, Learning, Patriotism, 1750–1810* (Chicago and London: University of Chicago Press, 2000).

Gutmann, A. (ed.), *Multiculturalism and 'The Politics of Recognition'* (Princeton: Princeton University Press, 1994).

Habermas, J., *The Structural Transformation of the Public Sphere: An Inquiry into a Category of Bourgeois Society*, trans. T. Berger and F. Lawrence (Cambridge, MA: The MIT Press, [1962] 1989).

—, *Theory of Communicative Action: Reason and the Rationalization of Society*, trans. T. McCarthy, 2 vols (Boston: Beacon Press, [1981] 1984).

—, *Moral Consciousness and Communicative Action*, trans. C. Lenhardt and S. W. Nicholsen (Cambridge, MA, and London: The MIT Press, [1983] 1990).

—, *Autonomy and Solidarity. Interviews with Jürgen Habermas*, ed. J. P. Dews (London: Verso, 1986).

—, *Postmetaphysical Thinking: Philosophical Essays*, trans. W. M. Hohengarten (London and Cambridge, MA: The MIT Press, [1988] 1992).

—, *Between Facts and Norms. Contributions to a Discourse Theory of Law and Democray*, trans. W. Rehg (Cambridge, MA, and London: The MIT Press, [1992] 1996).

—, 'Further Reflections on the Public Sphere', trans. T. Burger, in *Habermas and the Public Sphere*, ed. C. Calhoun (Cambridge, MA, and London: The MIT Press, 1992), pp. 421–61.

—, 'Struggles for Recognition in the Democratic Constitutional State', trans. S. W. Nicholsen, in *Multiculturalism*, ed. A. Gutmann (Princeton: Princeton University Press, 1994), pp. 107–48.

—, *The Inclusion of the Other: Studies in Political Theory*, ed. C. Cronin and P. De Greiff, trans. C. Cronin (Cambridge, MA, and London: The MIT Press, [1996] 1998).

—, 'Coping with Contingencies – The Return of Historicism', in J. Niznik and J. T. Sanders (eds), *Debating the State of Philosophy: Habermas, Rorty, and Kolakowski* (Westport, CT and London: Praeger, 1996), pp. 1–24.

—, 'Modernity: An Unfinished Project', trans. N. Walker, in *Habermas and the Unfinished Project of Modernity: Critical Essays on 'The Philosophical Discourse of Modernity*, ed. M. P. d'Entrèves and S. Benhabib (Cambridge, MA, and London: The MIT Press, 1997), pp. 38–55.

—, *Postnational Constellation: Political Essays*, trans. M. Pensky (Cambridge, MA, and London: The MIT Press, [1998] 2001).

—, *Religion and Rationality: Essays on Reason, God, and Modernity*, ed. E. Mendieta, trans. M. Pensky (Cambridge, MA: The MIT Press, 2002).

—, 'The Kantian Project of Cosmopolitan Law', Lecture at Purdue University, West Lafayette, Indiana, 15 October 2004; http://www.cla.purdue.edu/phil-lit/events/habermas.cfm

—, *The Divided West*, trans. C. Cronin (Cambridge and Malden: Polity Press, 2006).

—, and J. Derrida, 'February 15, or What Binds Europeans Together: A Plea for a Common Foreign Policy, Beginning in the Core of Europe', trans. M. Pensky, in L. Thomassen (ed.), *The Derrida-Habermas Reader* (Chicago and Edinburgh: University of Chicago Press, 2006), pp. 270–7.

Halevy, E., *The Growth of Philosophic Radicalism*, trans. M. Morris (Boston: Beacon Press, 1955).

Hannaford, I., *Race: The History of an Idea in the West* (Baltimore, London and Washington, D. C.: The Johns Hopkins University Press and Woodrow Wilson Center Press, 1996).

Hansen, M., 'Foreword', O. Negt, and A. Kluge, *Public Sphere and Experience: Toward an Analysis of the Bourgeois and Proletarian Public Sphere*, ed. M. Hansen, trans. P. Labanyi, J. O. Daniel & A. Oksiloff (Minneapolis and London: University of Minnesota Press, 1993).

Hardt, M., and A. Negri, *Empire* (London and Cambridge, MA: Harvard University Press, 2000).

—, *Multitude: War and Democracy in the Age of Empire* (New York: Penguin Press, 2004).

Hay, D., 'The Class Composition of the Palladium of Liberty: Trial Jurors in the Eighteenth Century', in J. S. Cockburn and T. A. Green (eds), *Twelve Good Men and True: The Criminal Trial Jury in England, 1200–1800* (Princeton: Princeton University Press, 1988), pp. 305–57.

Hays, M., *Appeal to the Men of Great Britain in Behalf of Women*, ed. G. Luria (New York and London: Garland, 1974).

—, *The Victim of Prejudice*, ed. E. Ty (Peterborough, ON: Broadview Press, 1994).

Heine, H., *Sämtliche Werke*, ed. J. Perfahl, 4 vols (München: Winkler-Verlag, 1969–72).

—, *The Romantic School and Other Essays*, ed. J. Hermand and R. C. Holub, trans. H. Mustard (New York: Continuum, 1985).

Herder, J. G., *On Social and Political Culture*, ed. and trans. F. M. Bernard (Cambridge: Cambridge University Press, 1969).

Hertzberg, A., *The French Enlightenment and the Jews: The Origins of Modern Anti-Semitism* (New York: Columbia University Press, 1990).

Hirschkop, K., 'Justice and Drama: On Bakhtin as a Complement to Habermas', in N. Crossley and J. M. Roberts (eds), *After Habermas: New Perspectives on the Public Sphere* (Oxford: Blackwell, 2004), pp. 49–66.

Hohendahl, P., *The Institution of Criticism* (Ithaca and London: Cornell University Press, 1982).

Holcroft, T., *Anna St. Ives*, in *The Novels and Selected Plays of Thomas Holcroft*, gen. ed. W. Verhoeven (London: Pickering & Chatto, 2007), vol. 2.

Holmes, R., 'Introduction', Mary Wollstonecraft, *A Short Residence in Sweden, Norway and Denmark* and William Godwin, *Memoirs of the Author of 'The Rights of Woman'*, ed. R. Holmes (Harmondsworth: Penguin 1987), pp. 9–55.

James, C. L. R., *The Black Jacobins: Toussaint L'Ourverture and the San Domingo Revolution*, 2nd edn (New York, Vintage, [1938] 1963).

Janowitz, A., *Lyric and Labour in the Romantic Tradition* (Cambridge and New York: Cambridge University Press, 1998).

Jay, M., 'Reconciling the Irreconcilable? Rejoinder to Kennedy', *Telos*, 71 (1987), pp. 67–80.

Jewish Encyclopedia, 12 vols (New York and London: Funk and Wagnalls, 1901).

Jordan, W. D., *White Over Black: American Attitudes Toward the Negro, 1550–1812* (Chapel Hill: University of North Carolina Press, 1968).

Kant, I., *The Critique of Pure Reason*, ed. and trans. P. Guyer and A. W. Wood (Cambridge: Cambridge University Press, [1781, 1787] 1998).

—, 'Idea for a Universal History with a Cosmopolitan Purpose' [1784], in H. Reiss (ed.), *Kant: Political Writings*, trans. H. B. Nisbet, 3rd edn (Cambridge: Cambridge University Press, 1991), pp. 41–53.

—, *Groundwork for the Metaphysics of Morals*, ed. L. Denis, trans. T. K. Abbott (Toronto: Broadview Press, [1785] 2005).

—, *Critique of Judgment*, ed. and trans. W. S. Pluhar (Indianapolis and Cambridge: Hackett, [1790] 1987).

—, *Religion within the Limits of Reason Alone*, ed and trans. T. M. Greene and H. H. Hudson (New York: Harper Torchbooks, [1793] 1960).

—, 'On the Common Saying: "This May be True in Theory, but it does not Apply in Practice"' [1793] in H. Reiss (ed.), *Kant: Political Writings*, trans. H. B. Nisbet, 3rd edn (Cambridge: Cambridge University Press, 1991), pp. 61–92.

—, 'Perpetual Peace. A Philosophical Sketch' [1795], in H. Reiss (ed.), *Kant: Political Writings*, pp. 93–130.

—, *The Metaphysics of Morals*, ed. and trans. M. Gregor (Cambridge: Cambridge University Press, [1797] 1991).

—, *The Conflict of the Faculties* [*Der Streit der Fakultäten*], ed. and trans. M. J. Gregor, (Lincoln and London: University of Nebraska Press, [1798] 1979).

—, *Kants gesammelte Schriften*, ed. Koenigliche Preußische Akademie der Wissenschaften, 24 vols (Berlin: Vruck und Verlag von Georg Reimer, 1902–)

—, *Kant: Political Writings*, ed. H. Reiss, trans. H. B. Nisbet, 3rd edn (Cambridge: Cambridge University Press, 1991).

Kaplan, C., 'Wild Nights: pleasure/sexuality/feminism', in N. Armstrong and L. Tennenhouse (eds), *The Ideology of Conduct: Essays in Literature and the History of Sexuality* (London: Methuen, 1987), pp. 160–84.

Katz, D. S., *The Jews in the History of England 1485–1850* (Oxford: Clarendon Press, 1994).

Keen, P., *The Crisis of Literature in the 1790s: Print Culture and the Public Sphere* (Cambridge: Cambridge University Press, 1999).

Kelly, G., *The English Jacobin Novel 1780–1805* (Oxford and New York: Clarendon Press, 1976).

Kennedy, E., 'Carl Schmitt and the Frankfurt School', *Telos*, 71 (1987), pp. 37–66.

Khalip, J., 'A Disappearance in the World: Wollstonecraft and Melancholy Skepticism', *Criticism*, 47:1 (2005), pp. 85–106.

King, J. N., 'Religious Writing', in *The Cambridge Companion to English Literature 1500–1600*, ed. A. F. Kinney (Cambridge: Cambridge University Press, 2000), pp. 104–31.

King, P. J. R. "'Illiterate Plebeians, Easily Misled": Jury Composition, Experience, and Behavior in Essex, 1735–1815', in *Twelve Good Men and True: The Criminal Trial Jury in England, 1200–1800*, ed. J. S. Cockburn and T. A. Green (Princeton: Princeton University Press, 1988), pp. 254–304.

Kitson, P. J., 'Coleridge's Anecdote of John Thelwall', *Notes and Queries*, n.s. 32:3 (September 1985), p. 345.

—, 'Introduction', P. J. Kitson and D. Lee (gen. eds), *Slavery, Abolition and Emancipation: Writings in the British Romantic Period*, 8 vols (London: Pickering & Chatto, 1999), vol. 2: 'Debate on the Abolition of the Slave Trade', ed. P. J. Kitson, pp. ix–xxxiii.

—, 'Introduction', P. J. Kitson and D. Lee (gen. eds), *Slavery, Abolition and Emancipation: Writings in the British Romantic Period*, 8 vols (London: Pickering & Chatto, 1999), vol. 8: 'Theories of Race', ed. P. J. Kitson, pp. vii–xxxii.

— and D. Lee (gen. eds), *Slavery, Abolition and Emancipation: Writings in the British Romantic Period*, 8 vols (London: Pickering & Chatto, 1999).

Klancher, J. P., *The Making of the English Reading Audiences, 1790–1832* (Madison: University of Wisconsin Press, 1987).

— (ed.), *Studies in Romanticism* [Special Issue on the Habermasian Public Sphere], 33:4 (Winter 1994).

Kowaleski-Wallace, E., *Their Fathers' Daughters: Hannah More, Maria Edgeworth, and Patriarchal Complicity* (New York: Oxford University Press, 1991).

Lackington, J., *Memoirs of the First Forty-Five Years of the life of James Lackington*, rev. edn (London: Lackington, 1792).

Laclau, E. 'Can Immanence Explain Social Struggles?', in P. A. Passavant and J. Dean (eds), *Empire's New Clothes: Reading Hardt and Negri* (New York and London: Routledge, 2004), pp. 21–30.

Landes, J., *Women and the Public Sphere in the Age of the French Revolution* (Ithaca, NY: Cornell University Press, 1988).

Landry, D., *The Muses of Resistance: Labouring-Class Women's Poetry in Britain, 1739–1796* (Cambridge: Cambridge University Press, 1990).

Langbein, J., 'The English Criminal Trial Jury in the Eve of the French Revolution', in *The Trial Jury in England, France, Germany 1700–1900*, ed. A. P. Schioppa (Berlin: Duncker and Humblot, 1987), pp. 13–39.

Lemoine, H., 'Elegiac Verses, To the Memory of the late learned David Levi, Author of *Lingua Sacra*, &c', *Gentleman's Magazine*, 71 (October 1801), pp. 934–5.

Lessing, G. E., *Die Juden*, in *Gotthold Ephraim Lessing Werke 1743–1750*, 12 vols (Frankfurt am Main: Deutscher Klassiker Verlag 1993), vol. 1, ed. J. Stenzel.

—, *Nathan der Weise* in *Gotthold Ephraim Lessing Werke 1778–1789*, 12 vols (Frankfurt am Main: Deutscher Klassiker Verlag, 1993), vol. 9, ed. K. Bohnen and A. Schilson.

Lestition, S., 'Kant and the End of the Enlightenment in Prussia', *Journal of Modern History*, 65:1 (1993), pp. 57–112.

Levi, D., *A Succinct Account of the Rites and Ceremonies of the Jews* (London: J. Parsons, 1783).

—, *Letters to Dr. Priestley, In Answer to His Letters to the Jews, Part II* (London, D. Levi, 1789).

—, *Dissertations on the Prophecies of the Old Testament*, 2 vols (London: D. Levi, 1796).

—, *Defence of the Old Testament, In a Series of Letters , Addressed to Thomas Paine.* (London: J. Johnson, 1797).

—, *The Holy Bible, In Hebrew ... English Translation [and] Notes of the Late David Levi. Revised by Levy Alexander*, 5 vols (London: L. Alexander, [1822]).

Lottes, G., *Politische Aufklärung und plebejisches Publikum. Zur Theorie und Praxis des englischen Radikalismus im späten 18. Jahrhundert* (München: R. Oldenbourg Verlag, 1979).

Louden, R. B., *Kant's Impure Ethics: From Rational Beings to Human Beings* (New York and Oxford: Oxford University Press, 2000).

Luhmann, N., *The Differentiation of Society*, trans. S. Holmes and C. Larmore (New York: Columbia University Press, 1982).

Lyon, E., *Miscellaneous Poems* (Oxford: J. Bartlett, 1812).

McCalman, I., *Radical Underworld: Prophets, Revolutionaries and Pornographers in London, 1795–1840* (Cambridge: Cambridge University Press, 1988).

—, 'Preface', in P. A. Pickering and A. Tyrrell (eds), *Contested Sites. Commemoration, Memorial and Popular Politics in Nineteenth-Century Britain* (Aldershot: Ashgate, 2004).

McCann, A., *Cultural Politics in the 1790s: Literature, Radicalism and the Public Sphere* (London and New York: Macmillan Press and St. Martin's Press, 1999).

McCarthy, T., 'On the Idea of a Reasonable Law of Peoples', in J. Bohman and M. Lutz-Bachman, (eds), *Perpetual Peace: Essays on Kant's Cosmopolitan Ideal* (Cambridge, MA, and London: The MIT Press, 1997), pp. 201–17.

—, 'On the Way to a World Republic? Kant on Race and Development', in L. R. Waas (ed.), *Politik, Moral und Religion – Gegensätze und Ergänzungen ... Festschrift zum 65. Geburtstag von Karl Graf Ballestrem* (Berlin: Duncker and Humblot, 2004), pp. 223–42.

MacDonald, E. E. (ed.), *The Education of the Heart: The Correspondence of Rachel Mordecai Lazarus and Maria Edgeworth* (Chapel Hill, NC: University of North Carolina Press, 1977).

McGann, J., *The Romantic Ideology: A Critical Investigation* (Chicago and London: University of Chicago Press, 1983).

—, *The Poetics of Sensibility: A Revolution in Literary Style* (Oxford: Clarendon Press, 1996).

McKeon, M., 'Parsing Habermas's "Bourgeois Public Sphere"', *Criticism*, 46:2 (2004), pp. 273–7.

McMahon, D. M., *Enemies of the Enlightenment: The French Counter-Enlightenment and the Making of Modernity* (Oxford: Oxford University Press, 2001).

Magnuson, P., *Reading Public Romanticism* (Princeton: Princeton University Press, 1998).

Maidment, B. (ed.), *The Poorhouse Fugitives. Self Taught Poets and Poetry in Victorian Britain* (Manchester: Carcanet, 1987).

Makdisi, S., *William Blake and the Impossible History of the 1790s* (Chicago and London: University of Chicago Press, 2003).

Mandelbaum, M., *The Case for Goliath: How America Acts As the World's Government in the Twenty-First Century* (New York: Public Affairs, 2005).

Manly, S. (ed.), 'Introduction', Maria Edgeworth, *Harrington* (Peterborough, ON, Broadview Press, 2004), pp. 7–57.

Marren, S., 'Between Slavery and Freedom: The Transgressive Self in Olaudah Equiano's Autobiography', *PMLA*, 108:1 (1993), pp. 94–105.

Marx, K., *The Eighteenth Brumaire of Louis Bonaparte* (New York: International Publishers, 1963).

Massey, I., *Find You the Virtue: Ethics, Image, and Desire in Literature* (Fairfax, VA: George Mason University Press, 1987).

Mears, A. [Gamaliel ben Pedahzur], *The Book of Religion, Ceremonies, and Prayers of the Jews, as Practiced in their Synagogues and Families* (London: J. Wilcox, 1738).

Mee, J., *Dangerous Enthusiasm: William Blake and the Culture of Radicalism in the 1790s* (Oxford: Clarendon Press, 1992).

—, 'Apocalypse and Ambivalence: The Politics of Millenarianism in the 1790s', *South Atlantic Quarterly*, 95 (1996), pp. 671–97.

—, *Romanticism, Enthusiasm and Regulation: Poetics and the Policing of Culture in the Romantic Period* (Oxford: Oxford University Press, 2003).

Meehan, J. (ed.), *Feminists Read Habermas: Gendering the Subject of Discourse* (New York; London: Routledge, 1995).

Mellor, A. K., *Mothers of the Nation: Women's Political Writing in England, 1780–1830* (Bloomington and Indianapolis: Indiana University Press, 2000).

—, 'Mary Wollstonecraft's *A Vindication of the Rights of Woman* and the Women Writers of Her Day', in C. L. Johnson (ed.), *The Cambridge Companion to Mary Wollstonecraft* (Cambridge: Cambridge University Press, 2002), pp. 141–59.

Mendelssohn, M., *Jerusalem, or On Religious Power and Judaism*, trans. A. Arkush. (Hanover and London: University of New England Press, 1983).

Mendoza, D., *The Memoirs of the Life of Daniel Mendoza*, ed. P. Magriel (London: B. T. Batsford, [1816] 1951).

Meyer, M. A., *The Origins of the Modern Jew: Jewish Identity and European Culture in Germany, 1749–1824* (Detroit: Wayne State University Press, 1964).

Micheli, G., 'The Early Reception of Kant's Thought in England 1785–1805', in G. M. Ross and T. McWalter (eds), *Kant and His Influence* (Bristol: Thoemmes, 1990), pp. 273–80.

Mignolo, W. D., 'The Many Faces of Cosmo-polis: Border Thinking and Critical Cosmopolitanism', *Public Culture*, 12:3 (2000), pp. 721–48.

Moi, T., *What Is A Woman? And Other Essays* (Oxford: Oxford University Press, 1999).

Moore, A., *The Annals of Gallantry; or, The Conjugal Monitor*, 3 vols (London: M. Jones, 1814).

Moten, F., 'Knowledge of Freedom', *CR: The New Centennial Review*, 4:2 (2004), pp. 269–310.

Myers, M., '"Reform or Ruin": A Revolution in Female Manners', *Studies in Eighteenth-Century Culture*, 11 (1982), pp. 199–216.

Myers, S. H., *The Bluestocking Circle: Women, Friendship, and the Life the Mind in Eighteenth-Century England* (Oxford: Clarendon Press, 1990).

Myers, V., 'William Godwin and the *Ars Rhetorica*', *Studies in Romanticism*, 41 (2002), pp. 415–44.

Nathan, I., *A Selection of Hebrew Melodies, Ancient and Modern, and [text by] Lord Byron*, ed. F. Burwick and P. Douglass (Tuscaloosa: University of Alabama Press, 1988).

Negt, O., and A. Kluge, *Public Sphere and Experience: Toward an Analysis of the Bourgeois and Proletarian Public Sphere*, ed. M. Hansen, trans. P. Labanyi, J. O. Daniel and A. Oksiloff (Minneapolis and London: University of Minnesota Press, [1972] 1993).

Nicholson, P. B., 'Kant, Revolutions and History', in H. Williams (ed.), *Essays on Kant's Political Philosophy* (Cardiff: University of Wales Press, 1992), pp. 249–68.

Nineteenth-Century Short Title Catalogue, Series 1, 1801–1815, Volume 6 (Newcastle upon Tyne: Avero, 1984).

Nnaemeka, O. and J. N. Ezeile (eds), *Engendering Human Rights: Cultural and Socioeconomic Realities in Africa* (New York: Palgrave Macmillan, 2005).

Nussbaum, M. C., *Poetic Justice: The Literary Imagination and Public Life* (Boston: Beacon Press, 1995).

O'Neill, O., *Constructions of Reason: Explorations of Kant's Practical Philosophy* (Cambridge: Cambridge University Press, 1989).

Page, J. W., 'Anglo-Jewish Identity and the Politics of Cultivation in Hazlitt, Aguilar, and Disraeli', in *British Romanticism and the Jews: History, Culture, Literature*, ed. S. A. Spector (New York: Palgrave Macmillan, 2002), pp.197–214.

—, *Imperfect Sympathies: Jews and Judaism in British Romantic Literature and Culture* (New York and Basingstoke: Palgrave Macmillan, 2004).

Paley, M. D., *Apocalypse and Millennium in English Romantic Poetry* (Oxford: Clarendon Press, 1988).

Pask, K., 'The Bourgeois Public Sphere and the Concept of Literature', *Criticism*, 46:2 (2004), pp. 241–56.

Passavant, P. A., and J. Dean (eds), *Empire's New Clothes: Reading Hardt and Negri.* (New York and London: Routledge, 2004).

Phillips, R., *Putting Asunder: A History of Divorce in Western Society* (Cambridge: Cambridge University Press, 1988).

Pickering, P. A., 'A "Grand Ossification": William Cobbett and the Commemoration of Tom Paine', in P. A. Pickering and A. Tyrrell (eds), *Contested Sites: Commemoration, Memorial and Popular Politics in Nineteenth-Century Britain* (Aldershot: Ashgate, 2004), pp. 57–80

—, and A. Tyrrell, 'The Public Memorial of Reform: Commemoration and Contestation', in P. A. Pickering and A. Tyrrell (eds), *Contested Sites: Commemoration, Memorial and Popular Politics in Nineteenth-Century Britain* (Aldershot: Ashgate, 2004), pp. 1–24.

—, and A. Tyrrell (eds), *Contested Sites: Commemoration, Memorial and Popular Politics in Nineteenth-Century Britain* (Aldershot: Ashgate, 2004).

Pollock, S., 'Cosmopolitan and Vernacular in History', *Public Culture*, 12:3 (2000), pp. 591–625.

Popkin, R. H., 'David Levi, Anglo-Jewish Theologian', *Jewish Quarterly Review*, 87 (1996), pp. 79–101.

Porter, R., *The Creation of the Modern World: The Untold Story of the British Enlightenment* (New York and London: W. W. Norton, 2000).

Price, R., *Richard Price: Political Writings*, ed. D. O. Thomas (Cambridge: Cambridge University Press, 1991).

Prideaux, H., *The Old and New Testaments Connected in the History of the Jews and Neighbouring Nations*, 4 vols (Charlestown: Middlesex, 1815).

Priestley, J., *Letters and Addresses to the Jews* [1787–99], in *The Theological and Miscellaneous Works of Joseph Priestley*, ed. J. T. Rutt, 25 vols (New York: Kraus Reprint, [1817–32] 1972), vol. 20, pp. 227–300.

—, *Joseph Priestley: Political Writings*, ed. P. N. Miller (Cambridge: Cambridge University Press, 1993).

Pudaloff, R., 'No Change Without Purchase: Olaudah Equiano and the Economies of Self and Market', *Early American Literature*, 40:3 (2005), pp. 499–527.

Ragussis, M., *Figures of Conversion: The Jewish Question and English National Identity* (Durham and London: Duke University Press, 1995).

Rajan, T., 'Introduction', *Valperga: or, The Life and Adventures of Castruccio, Prince of Lucca*, ed. T. Rajan (Peterborough, ON: Broadview Press, 1998), pp. 7–42.

Rancière, J., 'The Myth of the Artisan. Critical Reflections on a Category of Social History', *International Labour and Working Class History*, 24 (1983), pp. 1–12.

Report and State of the Society of Friends of Foreigners in Distress (London: W. Marchant, 1816).

Richardson, A., *Literature, Education, and Romanticism: Reading as a Social Practice, 1780–1832* (Cambridge: Cambridge University Press, 1996).

Rieger, J., 'Shelley's Paterin Beatrice', *Studies in Romanticism*, 4 (1965), pp. 169–84.

Robbins, B. (ed.), *The Phantom Public Sphere* (Minneapolis; London: Minneapolis University Press, 1993).

Robinson, M., *Letter to the Women of England on the Injustice of Mental Subordination* (Oxford: Woodstock Books, [1799] 1998)

Rodney, W., *How Europe Underdeveloped Africa* (Washington, DC: Howard University Press, 1981).

Roe, N., *Wordsworth and Coleridge: The Radical Years* (Oxford: Clarendon Press, 1990).

Roper, D., *Reviewing Before the 'Edinburgh'* (Newark: University of Delaware Press, 1978).

Roth, C., 'The Haskalah in England', in H. J. Zimmels, J. Rabinowitz, and I. Finestein (eds), *Essays Presented to the Chief Rabbi Israel Brodie on the Occasion of his Seventieth Birthday*, 2 vols (London: Soncino Press, 1967), vol. 1, pp. 365–76.

Rousseau, J.-J., *Rousseau: Oeuvres Completes*, ed. B. Gagnebin and M. Raymond, 5 vols (Paris: Gallimard, 1980).

—, *Émile*, trans. B. Foxley (London and Vermont: J. M. Dent and C. E. Tuttle, 1993).

Rubens, A., 'Portrait of Anglo-Jewry 1656–1836', *Transactions of the Jewish Historical Society of England*, 19 (1955–9), pp. 13–52.

Ruderman, D. B., *Jewish Enlightenment in an English Key: Anglo-Jewry's Construction of Modern Jewish Thought* (Princeton and Oxford: Princeton University Press, 2000).

Russell, G., and C. Tuite (eds), *Romantic Sociability: Social Networks and Literary Culture in Britain, 1770–1840* (Cambridge: Cambridge University Press, 2002).

Ryan, M. P., *Women in Public: Between Banners and Ballots, 1825–1880* (Baltimore and London; John Hopkins University Press, 1990).

St Clair, W., *That Greece Might Still Be Free* (London: Oxford University Press, 1972).

—, *The Godwins and the Shelleys: The Biography of a Family* (New York and London: W. W. Norton, 1989).

—, *The Reading Nation in the Romantic Period* (Cambridge: Cambridge University Press, 2004).

Sapiro, V., *A Vindication of Political Virtue: The Political Theory of Mary Wollstonecraft* (Chicago and London: University of Chicago Press, 1992).

Scheinberg, C., *Women's Poetry and Religion in Victorian England: Jewish Identity and Christian Culture* (Cambridge: Cambridge University Press, 2002).

Schlereth, T. J., *The Cosmopolitan Ideal in Enlightenment Thought: Its Form and Function in the Ideas of Franklin, Hume, and Voltaire, 1694–1790* (Notre Dame and London: University of Notre Dame Press, 1977).

Schmidt, J., 'What Enlightenment Was: How Moses Mendelssohn and Immanuel Kant Answered the *Berlinische Monatsschrift*', *Journal of the History of Philosophy*, 30:1 (1992), pp. 77–101.

Schmitt, C., *Political Romanticism*, trans. G. Oakes (London and Cambridge: MA, The MIT Press, [1919, 1925] 1986).

—, *Political Theology: Four Chapters on the Concept of Sovereignty*, trans. G. Schwab. (Cambridge, MA, and London: The MIT Press, [1922, 1934] 1985).

—, *The Crisis of Parliamentary Democracy*, trans. E. Kennedy (Cambridge, MA, and London, The MIT Press, [1923, 1926] 1985).

Scott, W., *The Heart of Midlothian*, ed. John Henry Raleigh (Boston: Houghton Mifflin, [1818] 1966).

—, *Ivanhoe*, ed. A. N. Wilson (Harmondsworth: Penguin Books, [1819] 1982).

Scrivener, M., *Radical Shelley: The Philosophical Anarchism and Utopian Thought of Percy Bysshe Shelley* (Princeton: Princeton University Press, 1982).

— (ed.), *Poetry and Reform: Periodical Verse from the English Democratic Press 1792–1824* (Detroit: Wayne State University Press, 1992).

—, 'John Thelwall and Popular Jacobin Allegory, 1793–5', *ELH*, 67:4 (2000), pp. 951–71.

— (ed.), *Reading Shelley's Interventionist Poetry, 1819–20*, in *Romantic Circles Praxis Series* (May 2001), http://www.rc.umd.edu/praxis/interventionist.

—, *Seditious Allegories: John Thelwall and Jacobin Writing* (University Park, Pennsylvania State University Press, 2001).

—, 'British-Jewish Writing of the Romantic Era and the Problem of Modernity: The Example of David Levi', in S. A. Spector (ed.), *British Romanticism and the Jews: History, Culture, Literature* (New York: Palgrave Macmillan, 2002), pp. 159–77.

—, 'John Thelwall and the Revolution of 1649', in T. Morton and N. Smith (eds), *Radicalism in British Literary Culture, 1650–1830: From Revolution to Revolution* (Cambridge: Cambridge University Press, 2002), pp. 119–32.

—, 'Habermas, Romanticism, and Literary Theory', *Literature Compass*, 1 RO 127 (2004), pp. 1–18.

—, 'Literature and Politics', in T. Keymer and J. Mee (eds), *The Cambridge Companion to English Literature 1740–1830* (Cambridge: Cambridge University Press, 2004), pp. 43–60.

—, 'Trials in Romantic-Era Writing: Modernity, Guilt, and the Scene of Justice', *The Wordsworth Circle*, 35:3 (2004), pp. 128–33.

—, 'Following the Muse: Inspiration, Prophecy, and Deference in the Poetry of Emma Lyon (1788–1870), Anglo-Jewish Poet', in Sheila A. Spector (ed.), *The Jews and British Romanticism: Politics, Religion, Culture* (New York: Palgrave Macmillan, 2005), pp. 105–26.

—, and F. Felsenstein (eds), *Incle and Yarico and The Incas: Two Plays by John Thelwall* (Madison and Teaneck, NJ: Fairleigh Dickinson University Press, 2006).

Shell, S. M., *The Rights of Reason: A Study of Kant's Philosophy and Politics* (Toronto, Buffalo and London: University of Toronto Press, 1980).

Shelley, M. W., *Valperga: Or, The Life and Adventures of Castruccio, Prince of Lucca*, ed. S. Curran (Oxford and New York: Oxford University Press, 1997).

—, *Valperga: Or, The Life and Adventures of Castruccio, Prince of Lucca*, ed. T. Rajan, (Peterborough, ON: Broadview Press, 1998).

—, *Mathilda*, in B. T. Bennett and C. E. Robinson (eds), *The Mary Shelley Reader* (New York and Oxford: Oxford University Press, 1990), pp. 175–246.

—, and P. B. Shelley, *History of a Six Weeks' Tour Through a Part of France, Switzerland, Germany, and Holland: With Letters Descriptive of a Sail Round the Lake of Geneva, and of the Glaciers of Chamouni* (1817), in R. Ingpen and W. E. Peck (eds), *The Complete Works of Percy Bysshe Shelley*, 10 vols (New York: Gordian Press, 1965), vol. 6, pp. 87–152.

Shelley, P. B., *The Letters of Percy Bysshe Shelley*, ed. F. L. Jones, 2 vols (Oxford: Clarendon Press, 1964).

—, *A Philosophical View of Reform*, in R. Ingpen and R. Peck (eds), *The Complete Works of Percy Bysshe Shelley*, 10 vols (New York: Gordian Press, 1965), vol. 7, pp. 3–55.

—, *Shelley's Poetry and Prose*, ed. D. H. Reiman and N. Fraistat (New York: W. W. Norton, 2002).

Shookman, E., 'Pseudo-Science, Social Fad, Literary Wonder: Johann Caspar Lavater and the Art of Physiognomy', in E. Shookman (ed.), *The Faces of Physiognomy. Interdisciplinary Approaches to Johann Caspar Lavater* (Columbia, SC: Camden House, 1993), pp. 1–24.

Sidney, Sir P., *The Psalms of Sir Philip Sidney and The Countess of Pembroke*, ed. J. C. A. Rathmell (New York: New York University Press, 1963).

—, *An Apology for Poetry*, in H. Adams (ed.), *Critical Theory Since Plato*, rev. edn (New York: Harcourt Brace Jovanovich, 1992), pp. 142–62.

Simon, R. S, 'Commerce, Concern, and Christianity: Britain and Middle-Eastern Jewry in the Mid-Nineteenth Century', in S. A. Spector (ed.), *The Jews and British Romanticism: Politics, Religion, Culture* (New York and Basingstoke: Palgrave Macmillan, 2005), pp. 181–94.

Simpson, D., *Romanticism, Nationalism, and the Revolt against Theory* (Chicago: University of Chicago Press, 1993).

Singer, S., 'Early Translations and Translators of the Jewish Liturgy in England', *Transactions of the Jewish Historical Society of England*, 3 (1896–8), pp. 36–71.

Smith, C., *Elegiac Sonnets and Other Poems* (London: Jones & Company, 1827).

Spector, S., 'The Other's Other: The Function of the Jew in Maria Edgeworth's Fiction', *European Romantic Review*, 10.3 (1999), pp. 326–33.

Splichal, S., 'Bentham, Kant, and the Right to Communicate', *Critical Review*, 15 (2003), pp. 285–305.

Targoff, R., *Common Prayer: The Language of Public Devotion in Early Modern England* (Chicago and London: University of Chicago Press, 2001).

Taylor, B., *Eve and the New Jerusalem: Socialism and Feminism in the Nineteenth Century* (New York: Pantheon Books, 1983).

Taylor, C., 'The Politics of Recognition' in A. Gutmann (ed.), *Multiculturalism and 'The Politics of Recognition'* (Princeton: Princeton University Press, 1994), pp. 25–74.

Thelwall, J., *Political Lectures. Volume the First – Part the First: Containing The lecture on Spies and Informers, and The First Lecture on Prosecutions for Political Opinion ...* (London: J. Thelwall, 1795).

—, *An Appeal to Popular Opinion, Against Kidnapping and Murder; Including A Narrative of the Late Atrocious Proceedings, at Yarmouth. 2nd edn. With a Postscript; Containing A Particular Account of the Outrages, At Lynn and Wisbeach* (London: J. S. Jordan, 1796.

—, *The Daughter of Adoption; A Tale of Modern Times* 2 vols (Dublin: N. Kelly, 1801).

—, *Poems, Chiefly Written in Retirement*, 2nd edn (Hereford: W. H. Parker, 1801; repr. Oxford: Woodstock Books, 1989).

—, *Incle and Yarico and The Incas: Two Plays by John Thelwall*, ed. F. Felsenstein and M. Scrivener (Madison and Teaneck, NJ: Fairleigh Dickinson University Press, 2006).

Thomassen, L. (ed.), *The Derrida-Habermas Reader* (Edinburgh and Chicago: University of Chicago Press, 2006).

Thompson, E. P., *The Making of the English Working Class* (New York: Vintage, 1963).

—, 'The Moral Economy', in *Customs in Common* (London: Merlin Press, 1991), pp. 185–258.

—, 'Hunting the Jacobin Fox', *Past and Present*, 142 (1994), pp. 94–140.

—, *The Romantics: England in a Revolutionary Age* (New York: New Press, 1997).

Tompkins, J. M. S., *The Popular Novel in England, 1770–1800* (Westport, CT: Greenwood Press, [1961] 1976).

Tyrrell, A. with M. T. Davis, 'Bearding the Tories: The Commemoration of the Scottish Political Martyrs of 1793–4', in P. A. Pickering and A. Tyrrell (eds), *Contested Sites. Commemoration, Memorial and Popular Politics in Nineteenth-Century Britain.* (Aldershot: Ashgate, 2004), pp. 25–56.

Vargish, T., *The Providential Aesthetic in Victorian Fiction* (Charlottesville: University Press of Virginia, 1985).

Vreté, M., 'The Restoration of the Jews in English Protestant Thought 1790–1840', *Middle Eastern Studies*, 8 (1972), pp. 3–50.

Wallerstein, I., *The Modern World-System II. Mercantilism and the Consolidation of the European World-Economy, 1600–1750* (New York: Academic Press, 1980).

—, *The Modern World-System III. The Second Era of Great Expansion of the Capitalist World-Economy, 1730–1840s* (San Diego: Academic Press, 1989).

Walvin, J., 'Abolishing the Slave Trade: Anti-Slavery and Popular Radicalism, 1776–1807', in C. Emsley and J. Walvin (eds), *Artisans, Peasants and Proletarians, 1760–1860* (London: Croom Helm, 1985), pp. 32–56.

Wang, O., 'Romancing the Counter-Public Sphere', *Studies in Romanticism*, 33:4 (Winter 1994), pp. 579–88.

Watts, I., *The Psalms, Hymns and Spiritual Songs of the Rev. Isaac Watts, D. D.* (Boston: Samuel T. Armstrong, Crocker, and Brewster, 1823).

Wells, S., *Sweet Reason: Rhetoric and the Discourses of Modernity* (Chicago; London: University of Chicago Press, 1996).

Wells, S. R., *How To Read Character. A New Illustrated Hand-Book of Phrenology and Physiognomy, For Students and Examiners; With a Descriptive Chart* (New York: Samuel R. Wells, 1872).

Wiener, J. H., *Radicalism and Freethought in Nineteenth-Century Britain: The Life of Richard Carlile* (Westport, CT: Greenwood Press, 1983).

Willey, B., *The Eighteenth-Century Background: Studies on the Idea of Nature in the Thought of the Period* (Boston: Beacon Press, [1940] 1961).

Williams, E., *Capitalism & Slavery* (Chapel Hill: University of North Carolina Press, 1944).

Wolfson, S. J., 'Mary Wollstonecraft and the Poets', in C. L. Johnson (ed.), *The Cambridge Companion to Mary Wollstonecraft* (Cambridge: Cambridge University Press, 2002), pp. 160–88.

Wollstonecraft, M., *Collected Letters of Mary Wollstonecraft*, ed. R. Wardle (Ithaca and London: Cornell University Press, 1979).

—, *The Works of Mary Wollstonecraft*, ed. J. Todd and M. Butler, 7 vols (London: Pickering & Chatto, 1989).

—, *The Vindications: The Rights of Men and The Rights of Woman*, ed. D. L. Macdonald and K. Scherf (Peterborough, ON: Broadview Press, 1997).

—, *A Short Residence in Sweden, Norway and* Denmark and William Godwin, *Memoirs of the Author of 'The Rights of Woman'*, ed. R. Holmes (Harmondsworth: Penguin 1987).

Wolper, R. S. (ed.), *Pieces on the "Jew Bill" (1753)* (Los Angeles: Clark Memorial Library, 1983).

Wood, G. D., 'Opera and Romanticism', *Praxis* (May 2005), www.rc.umd.edu/praxis/opera/index.html.

Wood, M., 'William Cobbett, John Thelwall, Radicalism, Racism and Slavery. A Study in Burkean Parodics', *Romanticism on the Net*, 15 (1999), http://users.ox.ac.uk/~scat0385/guest6.html.

Wu, D. (ed.), *Romantic Women Poets. An Anthology* (Oxford: Blackwell, 1997).

Wyatt, T., *Collected Poems of Sir Thomas Wyatt*, ed. K. Muir and P. Thomson, (Liverpool: Liverpool University Press, 1969).

Young, R. J. C., *Colonial Desire: Hybridity in Theory, Culture and Race* (London and New York: Routledge, 1995).

Youngquist, P., 'The Afro-Futurism of DJ Vassa', *European Romantic Review*, 16:2 (2005), pp. 181–92.

Zagorin, P., *How the Idea of Religious Toleration Came to the West* (Princeton and Oxford: Princeton University Press, 2003).

Zim, R., *English Metrical Psalms: Poetry as Praise and Prayer 1535–1601* (Cambridge: Cambridge University Press, 1987).

Žižek, S., 'The Ideology of the Empire and Its Traps', in P. A. Passavant and J. Dean (eds), *Empire's New Clothes: Reading Hardt and Negri* (New York and London: Routledge, 2004), pp. 253–64.

INDEX

For Product Safety Concerns and Information please contact our EU
representative GPSR@taylorandfrancis.com
Taylor & Francis Verlag GmbH, Kaufingerstraße 24, 80331 München, Germany